PARADIGMS AND REVOLUTIONS

APPRAISALS AND APPLICATIONS OF THOMAS KUHN'S PHILOSOPHY OF SCIENCE

Edited by Gary Gutting

NOTRE DAME • LONDON
UNIVERSITY OF NORTE DAME PRESS

Library of Congress Cataloging in Publication Data

Main entry under title:
Paradigms and revolutions.

Includes index.
1. Science—Philosophy—Addresses, essays,
lectures. 2. Kuhn, Thomas S.—Addresses, essays,
lectures. I. Gutting, Gary.
Q175.3.P37   501   80-20745
ISBN 0-268-01542-2

CONTENTS

III. HUMANITIES

IV. HISTORY OF SCIENCE

PREFACE

Thomas Kuhn's *Structure of Scientific Revolutions* (SSR) has had a wider academic influence than any other single book of the last twenty years. This anthology aims to provide an overview of this influence by gathering a group of articles that represent most of the disciplines that have found Kuhn's work important and the main sorts of reactions there have been to it. My assumption is that most readers will have some acquaintance with the reception of Kuhn's work in one or two areas and will find it interesting and profitable to see how it has been received elsewhere. Accordingly, I have tried to select pieces that not only are of significance within their own disciplines but also have something important to offer readers with other dominant interests. Incompleteness and dissatisfaction inevitably accompany an enterprise of this sort. But, at the very least, this volume should provide a hitherto unavailable starting-point for those who want to trace and evaluate Kuhn's remarkably widespread impact.

My editor's introduction makes no attempt to summarize or systematize the multifarious content of the vast literature on Kuhn or even of the selections that follow. Rather, it offers brief interpretative and critical comments on what I see as some major issues that have not yet emerged clearly in discussions of Kuhn.

Thanks are due first of all to James Langford, Director of the University of Notre Dame Press, who first conceived the idea of this book and has supported its development throughout. I am also especially grateful to Ernan McMullin for his continuing advice and encouragement. Karl Ameriks and Thomas Kuhn gave me helpful comments on the first draft of the editor's introduction, and Richard Allen suggested numerous stylistic improvements. Janet Kourany, David Lewis, and Stephen Worland provided crucial advice regarding the selections. Most of all, I am grateful to my wife, Anastasia, for her constant support, both intellectual and domestic.

ACKNOWLEDGMENTS

Dudley Shapere, "The Structure of Scientific Revolutions," *Philosophical Review* 73 (1964), 383-394. Reprinted by permission of the author and the publisher.

Alan Musgrave, "Kuhn's Second Thoughts," *British Journal for the Philosophy of Science* 22 (1971), 287-297. Reprinted by permission of the author and the publisher.

Wolfgang Stegmüller, "Accidental ('Non-substantial') Theory Change and Theory Dislodgment," in R. Butts and J. Hintikka (eds.), *Historical and Philosophical Dimensions of Logic, Methodology, and Philosophy of Science*, Dordrecht and Boston: D. Reidel, 1977, pp. 269-268. Copyright © 1977 by D. Reidel Publishing Company. Reprinted by permission of D. Reidel Publishing Company.

Alasdair MacIntyre, "Epistemological Crises, Dramatic Narrative, and the Philosophy of Science," *The Monist* 60 (1977), 453-471. Reprinted by permission of the author and the publisher.

M. D. King, "Reason, Tradition, and the Progressiveness of Science," *History and Theory* 10 (1971), 3-15, 17-32. Copyright © 1971 by Wesleyan University. Reprinted by permission of Wesleyan University and M. D. King.

D. L. Eckberg and L. Hill, Jr., "The Paradigm Concept and Sociology: A Critical Review," *American Sociological Review* 44 (1979), 925-937. Reprinted by permission of the authors and the American Sociological Association.

Mark Blaug, "Kuhn versus Lakatos, or Paradigms versus Research Programmes in the History of Economics," *History of Political Economy* 7 (1975), 399-419. Reprinted by permission of the author.

Sheldon Wolin, "Paradigms and Political Theories," in P. King and B. C. Parekh (eds.), *Politics and Experience*, Cambridge: Cambridge University Press, 1968, pp. 125-152. Reprinted by permission of the author and publisher.

David Hollinger, "T. S. Kuhn's Theory of Science and Its Implications for History," *American Historical Review* 78 (1973), 370-393. Reprinted by permission of the author and the American Historical Association.

INTRODUCTION

1. KUHN ON THE RATIONAL AUTHORITY OF SCIENCE

The Structure of Scientific Revolutions is about the authority of science. This is a very important topic because science is the only generally recognized cognitive authority in the world today. Kuhn's treatment is important because he proposes a new interpretation of this authority that most readers have found either plausible or challenging. The proposal is that science's authority ultimately resides not in a rule-governed method of inquiry whereby scientific results are obtained but in the scientific community that obtains the results. Kuhn embedded this proposal in a general account, illustrated and supported by specific episodes in the history of science, of the way scientific results are developed and abandoned. The central concept of this account is that of a paradigm. Almost all commentators agree that Kuhn's use of this concept is extremely loose and variable. (Here a jocular reference is usually made to Masterman's[1] catalogue of the twenty-one — some say twenty-two or twenty-three — different meanings of 'paradigm' she finds in Kuhn's book.) In my reading, however, I have found Kuhn surprisingly consistent and precise in his use of this key term. In spite of some inevitable (but usually fruitful) ambiguities, it can generally be construed in terms of the definition by which Kuhn introduces it: ". . . universally recognized scientific achievements that for a time provide model problems and solutions to a community of practitioners" (SSR, x). The alleged vagueness and ambiguity of 'paradigm' derives from the fact, which Kuhn explicitly notes, that we can abstract from any such scientific achievement a variety of "rules" (empirical and theoretical laws, experimental techniques, methodological directives, and even metaphysical principles). In a given context, Kuhn's talk of a "paradigm" may refer to one or more of these items. But at the heart of his analysis is always the idea that all these rules are relevant to the practice of science only to the extent that they are embodied in some concrete scientific achievement and that this achievement is not reducible to the rules implicit in it.

Thus, the flexibility of 'paradigm' derives from the fact that it refers simultaneously to two aspects of a paradigmatic scientific achievement: first, to a body of *content* implicit in the achieve-

1

ment and second to a *function* of the achievement in the scientific community. The content is typically a diverse assemblage of law, method, and metaphysics that constitutes a "super-theory" — a very general scientific worldview — associated with the paradigm. The function of the paradigm is its role as a focal point for the consensus of the scientific community. This consensus need not involve an acceptance of any explicit formulation of the paradigm's content but is rather a general acknowledgement of the exemplary role of the approach taken by the paradigm.

Given the applicability of this notion of paradigm, Kuhn's thesis about scientific authority follows immediately for the case of *normal science*, which he defines as science that uses a past achievement as a model and guide for formulating and solving new problems about the world. Since the paradigm cannot be reduced to any set of explicit rules, neither can normal scientific work on new problems. But not all science can be normal science, since normal science always presupposes a prior paradigmatic achievement. How do such achievements themselves come about? This question is particularly important for Kuhn because he thinks history shows that there are changes of paradigm, revolutionary episodes in which one paradigm is replaced by another.[2] Many of his most famous and controversial claims about scientific revolutions derive from his attempt to show that the acceptance of a new paradigm is not simply a matter of applying rules.

This is particularly true of his thesis that competing paradigms are "incommensurable" with one another. Contrary to many critics, incommensurability does not mean that rival paradigms cannot be comparatively evaluated but just that the comparative evaluation cannot be effected by a neutral set of rules and facts. Kuhn first introduces the term "incommensurable" (SSR, 102) to express the fact that rival paradigms often select different problems as the most important to solve and employ different standards for success of solution. He later extends the term (SSR, 148-149) to refer to the fact that rival paradigms do not share a common body of observational data that provides a neutral standard for their comparison; their fundamentally different theoretical viewpoints lead to different perceptions of the "facts." In both cases, the reason for saying that rival paradigms are incommensurable is to point out that scientific judgments of their relative merits are not just a matter of applying rules that could *prove* one paradigm superior to another: "Just because it is a transition between incommensurables, the transition between paradigms cannot be made a step at a time, forced by logic and neutral experience" (SSR, 149).[3] This is not to say that the judgment in favor of a given paradigm is arbitrary and irrational: "...to say that...paradigm changes cannot be justified by proof, is not to say that no arguments are relevant...." (SSR, 151). Kuhn thinks, for example, that arguments for the superior puzzle-solving resources of a paradigm are particularly important. But the incommensurability of rival paradigms means that the ultimate issue of debates about them will depend on the scientific community's judgment as to the overall significance of the considerations urged by the various conflicting arguments. Given that scientists are specifically trained to make fair and informed judgments of this sort, Kuhn asks, "What better criterion than the decision of the scientific group could there be?" (SSR, 169). This emphasis on the scientific community's judgment as the ultimate locus of science's rational authority is the most fundamental feature of his account of science.

2. KUHN AND THE HISTORY OF SCIENCE

Some of Kuhn's early reviewers (e.g., Schegel and Buchdahl) suggested that *The Structure of Scientific Revolutions* would itself become a paradigm for future work by historians of science. This has not happened and, in fact, should not have been expected. As Kuhn himself made clear, his book was an attempt to sketch a general view of science that he saw emerging from a revolution in historiography of science — a revolution that had begun before he even conceived of his work and for which a paradigm had already been provided by the work of Alexandre Koyré (SSR, 3). Kuhn's book is not so much an instance of the new historiography as an interpretation of the results previously attained by it. It could have become a paradigm of such interpretation, but historians of science are not currently very interested in general interpretative schemata, which may have a Procrustean effect on their efforts to understand specific episodes. Here L. Pearce Williams' summary comment on the dispute between Kuhn and Popper is typical: "We simply do not know enough to permit a philosophical structure to be erected on a historical foundation....We need a lot more examples."[4] It would seem that, as a historian, Kuhn himself shares something of this attitude. He has said that current philosophy of science (including, presumably, his own) does not have much relevance for the historian of science; and most of his own historical work could not be readily identified as that of the author of *The Structure of Scientific Revolutions*. (For example, in a review of Kuhn's recent book on blackbody radiation, Trevor Pinch notes that Kuhn's discussion ignores all the central philosophical and sociological issues he raised in his earlier work.[5]) In any case, *The Structure of Scientific Revolutions*, though the work of one of the most prominent historians of science, has had far more impact on philosophical and sociological studies of science than it has on historiography. An unfortunate result of this is the surprising dearth of evaluations of Kuhn's main theses through detailed case-studies by professional historians. There is some compensation for this lack in the work of historically minded philosophers of science (e.g., Toulmin, Shapere, Feyerabend, Lakatos). But as Lakatos has noted "none of these critics applied a systematic *historiographical* criticism to [Kuhn's] work."[6]

3. KUHN AND THE PHILOSOPHY OF SCIENCE

While historians of science seem to have paid Kuhn's work less attention than they should because of its philosophical character, philosophers of science have overwhelmed it with their attentions. But, in so doing, they have often forgotten that, for all is philosophical content, it is the work of a historian with preconceptions and preoccupations other than their own and have read into it philosophical claims and arguments that seem far from the author's intentions. In this connection, Kuhn's comments — in a different context — on the way philosophers approach texts are very appropriate. Comparing the work of prospective philosophers and historians in his graduate seminars, he says:

> Subtle analytic distinctions that had entirely escaped the historians would often be central when the philosophers reported on their reading. The resulting confrontations were invariably educational for the historians, but the fault was not always theirs. Sometimes the distinctions dwelt upon by the philosophers were not to be found at all in the original text. They were products of the subsequent development of science or philosophy, and their introduction during the philosophers' processing of signs altered the argument.[7]

It seems to me that philosophers have generally treated the text of *The Structure of Scientific Revolutions* in much the way that

Kuhn's philosophical students treated historical texts. In reading it they have automatically formulated its philosophical claims in terms of the categories and distinctions characteristic of positivist philosophy of science, thereby misrepresenting Kuhn's actual meaning. As a result, Kuhn has been widely presented and criticized as defending extreme and implausible philosophical theses that in fact cannot be found in this book.[8]

Israel Scheffler's influential discussion in *Science and Subjectivity* (SS) provides a very clear example of philosophical misreading of Kuhn.[9] Unlike some philosophical critics of Kuhn, Scheffler does make many specific textual references. Nonetheless, the philosophical presuppositions and preoccupations with which he approaches the text lead him to major distortions of its meaning. Consider, for example, his statement of Kuhn's view of the nature of paradigm changes: "Evaluative arguments over the merits of alternative paradigms are vastly minimized, such arguments being circular, and the essential factor consisting anyway not in deliberation or interpretation but rather in the gestalt switch" (SS, 78).

Here Scheffler attributes two main theses to Kuhn: that the arguments put forward by scientists in disputes about paradigms are of little importance because they are circular and that "the essential factor" in a paradigm change is not any sort of rational deliberative process but rather a gestalt switch. (A bit later, Scheffler implies that on Kuhn's view, debates about paradigm choice are "mere persuasive displays without deliberative substance.") In fact, Kuhn does not assert either of these theses. Regarding the first thesis, Kuhn's one statement (cited by Scheffler) about the circularity of arguments in paradigm debates is this:

> To the extent, as significant as it is incomplete, that two scientific schools disagree about what is a problem and what a solution, they will inevitably talk through each other when debating the merits of their respective paradigms. In the partially circular arguments that regularly result, each paradigm will be shown to satisfy more or less the criteria that it dictates for itself and to fall short of a few of those dictated by its opponent. (SSR, 108-9).

Kuhn's view here is clearly much less radical than the one Scheffler attributes to him. He is not saying that *all* arguments in paradigm disputes are circular, only that some of them are. Circularity will be a problem *to the extent* that there is disagreement among the disputants about "what is a problem and what a solution." Though Kuhn says that such disagreement will be significant he at the same time emphasizes that it is not complete. So the obvious interpretation of this passage is not that circularity excludes an important role for arguments but that it limits the extent to which they can be effective.

As to the second thesis, the text Scheffler cites in which Kuhn speaks of the irrelevance of deliberation and interpretation is the following:

> Paradigms are not corrigible by normal science at all. Instead
> ... normal science ultimately leads only to the recognition of
> anomalies and to crises. And these are terminated, not by deliberation and interpretation, but by a relatively sudden and
> unstructured event like the gestalt switch. (SSR, 121).

Here Kuhn does not say, as Scheffler thinks, that interpretation and deliberation have no essential role in paradigm switches. He says only that they do not *terminate* a crisis; i.e., they by themselves are not sufficient to effect the transition from one paradigm to another. But this is not to say that interpretation and deliberation are not necessary components of the process that leads to a paradigm change and that a gestalt switch is "the essential factor." Indeed, when Kuhn discusses the nature of the "extraordinary research" with which the scientist attempts to resolve a crisis, he cites a variety of deliberative and interpretative procedures (ranging from laboratory experiments to philosophical analysis) that characterize such research. (Cf. SSR, 86-88.)

Scheffler also misreads the arguments by which Kuhn supports his position. Here I will cite just one striking instance. After putting forward the idea that, even if there may be difficulties in comparing competing paradigms in their own terms, there will be "second-order" standards of comparison shared even by those committed to different paradigms, Scheffler presents Kuhn as replying in the following way:

> ... to accept a paradigm is to accept not only theory and
> methods, but also governing standards or criteria which serve
> to justify the paradigm as against its rivals, in the eyes of its
> proponents. Paradigm differences are thus inevitably reflected
> upward, in critical differences at the second level. It follows
> that each paradigm is, in effect, inevitably self-justifying and
> the paradigm debates must fail of objectivity; again we appear
> driven back to nonrational conversion as the final characterization of paradigm shifts. ... (SS, 84).

The passage from Kuhn which Scheffler cites as suggesting this argument is this:

> In learning a paradigm the scientist acquires theory, methods, and standards together, usually in an inextricable mix. Therefore when paradigms change, there are usually significant shifts in the criteria determining the legitimacy both of problems and of proposed solutions.
>
> That observation ... provides our first explicit indication of why the choice between competing paradigms regularly raises questions that cannot be resolved by the criteria of normal science. ... There are other reasons, too, for the incompleteness of logical contact that consistently characterizes paradigm debates. For example, since no paradigm ever solves all the problems it defines and since no two paradigms leave all the same problems unsolved, paradigm debates always involve the question: Which problems is it more significant to have solved? Like the issue of competing standards, that question of values can be answered only in terms of criteria that lie outside of normal science altogether, and it is that recourse to external criteria that most obviously makes paradigm debates revolutionary. (SSR, 108-9).

But not only does Kuhn not say here that paradigms are self-justifying and paradigm debates not objective, he also asserts that paradigm debates involve appeals to criteria external to the two competing paradigms. So in fact the passage from which Scheffler. extracts his "Kuhnian" argument explicitly denies the conclusion of that argument. (Oddly, Scheffler later [p. 85] refers to the final sentence of the above quotation in support of his own view and remarks that, having said this, it is gratuitous of Kuhn to claim that paradigms are self-justifying.)

Scheffler — like many of Kuhn's philosophical critics — misreads his text because he does not regard what Kuhn is in fact suggesting to be a real possibility. This is apparent from the characterization of objectivity he offers in the opening sentence of his first chapter: "A fundamental feature of science is its ideal of objectivity, an ideal that subjects all scientific statements to the test of independent and impartial criteria, recognizing no authority of persons in the realm of cognition" (SS, 1). This statement presupposes the following dichotomy concerning the authority of science: The authority by which scientific claims are evaluated is either that of impersonal criteria (i.e., methodological rules), in which case science is objective and rational; or that of persons (i.e., the subjective preferences of

7

individuals), in which case science is subjective and irrational. Scheffler sees that Kuhn rejects the former account of scientific authority and so concludes that he holds the latter. As a result, he inevitably reads Kuhn's text as a defense of a psychologistic irrationalism concerning science. Such a reading greatly distorts Kuhn's text; he hardly ever even employs the terms "rational" and "irrational" and never says that the scientific community's acceptance of paradigms is irrational. (The closest he comes to anything like this is one passage in which he says that *early* endorsements of a new paradigm by *individual* scientists *need not* be rational. Cf. SSR, 157.) But this reading is the only one available to someone who sees irrationalism as the only alternative to an account of scientific authority entirely in terms of explicit methodological rules. In fact, however, Kuhn is trying to express a third alternative: an account of scientific authority in terms of the informed *judgment* of the community of trained scientists. (Here, as Kuhn acknowledges [SSR, 44], his view is very similar to Polanyi's.) Such judgment is informed by logical arguments based on methodological rules including some shared by all scientists at all times (cf. SSR, 42). But it is not *determined* by these arguments. Nor, however, is it determined, as Kuhn's critics suggest, by personal idiosyncracies, prejudices, or whims. The judgment is ultimately determined by the carefully nurtured ability of members of the scientific community to assess rationally the overall significance of a wide variety of separately inconclusive lines of argument. Kuhn refers explicitly to the distinction I have in mind here in a comment on Popper's rejection of 'the psychology of knowledge':

> When he rejects 'the psychology of knowledge', Sir Karl's explicit concern is only to deny the methodological relevance of an *individual's* source of inspiration or of an individual's sense of certainty. With that much I cannot disagree. It is, however, a long step from the rejection of psychological idiosyncracies of an individual to the rejection of common elements induced by nurture and training in the psychological make-up of the licensed membership of a *scientific group*.[10]

Of course, it may be that the distinction on which Kuhn's view is based is not viable and that any retreat from rules to judgment as the ultimate locus of scientific authority does fall into subjectivism and irrationalism. But if so — and I think it very unlikely — then the proper approach to Kuhn's text is to point this out and to criticize him for trying to distinguish what cannot be distinguished, not simply to attribute to him the view his distinction is trying to avoid. Scheffler and many other philosophical critics have approached Kuhn's text with a view of the issues being discussed that excludes apriori the sort of possibility he is trying to articulate. As a result, they don't even see the position Kuhn is proposing.

4. KUHN AND THE SOCIOLOGY OF SCIENCE

Sociologists of science have responded far more positively and enthusiastically to Kuhn's work than have historians and philosophers. They often perceive Kuhn as revolutionizing the discipline's understanding of the questions it can treat and the way it should approach them. Thus, Peter Weingart has written: "Kuhn's influence on the sociology of science has proved to be so profound that he has all but attained the rank of Merton. It seems he is even replacing him, if one takes account of the change in the basic constellation of problems of the sociology of science which has emerged."[11] The transformation of sociology of science said to be effected by Kuhn is this: Traditional sociology of science (i.e., that primarily associated with the work of Robert Merton) is based on a sharp distinction between science as a cognitive system and science as a social system. The former refers to the laws and theories scientists develop and the rational processes whereby they evaluate them, the latter to the way in which scientists are organized into communities of researchers guided by characteristically scientific values and norms. The sociology of science is seen as having no relevance to an understanding of the cognitive aspect of science, since this operates on the basis of objective rules or rational methodology, the validity of which is entirely independent of contingent social facts. But though the cognitive validity of scientific methodology is trans-social, there is need for a sociological account of the conditions under which a community devoted to the application of this methodology can emerge and flourish. Such an account is provided by Mertonian sociology of science. By contrast, Kuhn's work has been seen as breaking down the distinction between science as a cognitive system and science as a social system and thus as opening up the possibility of sociological studies of the development and evaluation of specific ideas. Thus, Kuhnian, as opposed to Mertonian, sociology of science is seen as able to deal with the specific intellectual content and methods of science. (This line of

9

thought is developed by M. D. King in his paper reprinted below.)

To some extent the positive reception of Kuhn among sociologists of science has been unfortunately based on the distorted view that Kuhn has undermined the rationality of science. Thus, Richard Whitley says: "By allowing for a degree of epistemological irrationality among scientists, Kuhn opened the door for a sociological analysis of scientific development."[12] Barry Barnes has developed this interpretation and application of Kuhn in some detail.[13] Indeed, Barnes sees Kuhn's work as applicable to sociology as a whole. He invokes him as the inspiration and partial justification for the claim that, for sociologists who are investigating people's beliefs, distinctions between true and false or rational and irrational have no significance. *Any* belief is a proper object of sociological explanation, quite apart from its alleged cognitive status. Barnes' argument here is as follows: The idea that not all beliefs are open to sociological explanation derives from the claim that some beliefs are explainable simply by the fact that it is rational to have them. Further, science is regarded as the source of judgments of the rationality or irrationality of beliefs. But, Barnes claims, Kuhn has shown that science does not provide standards for separating beliefs into rational and irrational, true or false. Hence, there is no basis for excluding any belief from the scope of sociological explanation.

The first criticism of this sort of view is, of course, that it misinterprets Kuhn's claims. Like so many philosophers, sociologists of science are mistaking a new approach to scientific rationality for an attack on it. But even more important, this misinterpretation leads to an *underestimation* of Kuhn's significance for sociology. On the construal of Barnes and others, Kuhn permits a sociological study of all beliefs only on the condition that we reject any prescriptive sense to a distinction of rational and irrational beliefs. Such a rejection amounts to a very strong form of epistemological skepticism. Now, though sociologists sometimes show no qualms about being skeptics (cf. Barnes, 374, n.1), the fact is that skepticism has never been able to establish itself as an intellectually or socially significant worldview. Meant seriously, it represents a despairing withdrawal from human affairs. But most often it is not meant seriously. It is rather a verbal formula expressing a rejection of some specific intellectual pretensions that are viewed as particularly oppressive. This, I suspect, is the real significance of the "skepticism" for which Barnes and other sociologists feel an affinity: a rejection of the pretensions of philosophers to set apriori limits to sociological investigation.

However, a proper appreciation of Kuhn would both maintain the scope Barnes wants sociology to have and avoid the artificial extreme of skepticism. For, as I have been arguing, the real significance of Kuhn's work is that the ultimate locus of science's rational authority is the scientific community. The objectivity and rationality of scientific judgments is not simply a matter of following transcendent rules but depends essentially on the social origins and context of the judgments. If this is correct, then a proper understanding of scientific rationality requires a kind of sociological analysis. Thus, all beliefs are open to sociological analysis not because they are all irrational (or because there is no distinction of rational and irrational), but because even the rationality of a belief depends on social factors.[14]

More specifically, the social factors relevant to an analysis of scientific rationality will be closely related, if not identical, to various interests motivating and affecting concrete instances of scientific practice. From this viewpoint, the rejection of epistemological skepticism entails the recognition of certain interests as possessing a cognitive authority that others do not. Only when scientists act exclusively on the basis of these interests are they being entirely rational. In this regard, it is important to note that rejecting skepticism (the view that there is no significant distinction between rational and irrational beliefs) does not require rejecting relativism (the view that the rational/irrational distinction can be drawn in different but equally legitimate ways — e.g., in different cultures). *Prima facie*, at least, a rejection of skepticism is consistent with an acceptance of relativism. In Barry Barnes' more recent work,[15] he seems to take just this sort of position; on the one hand acknowledging (contrary to his earlier view in the article on Kuhn) a distinction between cognitively legitimate and cognitively illegitimate interests and, on the other hand, denying the universal validity of any body of knowledge.

An alternative approach is that of Jürgen Habermas, who holds that any knowledge worthy of the name must derive from universal human interests and competences and so be unrestrictedly valid.[16] He would argue against Barnes that an interest cannot be cognitively legitimate if it is not universal. If Barnes is right, then the sociological analysis of scientific rationality can treat cognitive interests as ordinary contingent social facts to be studied by the standard methods of empirical sociology (though there may be difficulties in using such methods to identify certain interests as legitimate). If Habermas is right, the study of scientific rationality requires an analysis of factors that are not simply empirical but have, as he terms it, a "quasi-transcendental" status as essential features of any human community and as conditions on the possibility of knowledge. Hence, for him scientific rationality must be studied by a new discipline that, being both grounded in specific empirical studies and oriented toward very general, in principle conclusions, could be plausibly regarded as the legitimate successor to parts of both sociology and philosophy. Habermas' work on cognitive interests and communicative competence provides some idea of what such a discipline might be like. In any case, sociology of science will not have properly appreciated its "Kuhnian revolution" until it ceases to view it as a vindication of irrationalism and sets itself the task of constructing a sociology of rationality.

5. KUHN AND THE SOCIAL SCIENCES

Kuhn's new approach to the question of the rationality of science derives in large part from his new account of the unit of scientific achievement. For the positivists, the unit of achievement (the primary product of successful science) is new empirical laws and explanations and predictions of facts on the basis of these laws. For Kuhn, the fundamental unit of achievement, the paradigm, is much richer, implicitly involving not only empirical laws but also models, methodological rules, values, metaphysical principles, and indeed a distinctive way of "seeing" all the phenomena of its domain. To accept a paradigm is to accept a comprehensive scientific, metaphysical, and methodological worldview — what I called above a "super-theory." Because of their comprehensiveness, there is no non-question-begging way of assessing super-theories or the paradigms that embody them on the basis of neutral observation reports or methodological rules. This, ultimately, is the reason why Kuhn needs to develop a new approach to the nature of scientific rationality.

It is primarily the association of paradigms with super-theories that has made Kuhn's account so attractive to social scientists. Given the positivist view that specific empirical laws and explanations are the fundamental units of scientific achievement and the obvious lack of such achievements in most areas of social science, the social scientist had either to concede that his discipline had not yet attained scientific status (and to keep working toward the positivist ideal), or admit that his discipline could not be scientific, at least not in the same sense as the natural sciences. Kuhn's account, however, suggests a much more congenial view: that the social sciences are and, in many cases, have long been sciences quite on a par with the natural sciences. For the social sciences surely have produced many influential super-theories. Freudian psychology, functionalist sociology, behavioralist political science, and Keynesian economics are just a few examples of comprehensive views that have served as the inspiration for numerous social scientific research projects. Accordingly, Kuhn's work stimulated many attempts by social scientists — especially economists and sociologists — to give "Kuhnian" accounts of the history and current status of their disciplines.[17]

Although such accounts have not been entirely fruitless, they are entirely misdirected as efforts to exhibit the scientific status of the social sciences or to discover how to put them on the "sure path of a science." Kuhn's account of the natural sciences emphasizes the fact that their scientific status depends essentially on the emergence of a consensus among the community of practitioners as to the authority of a given paradigm. Since this consensus is remarkably absent in the social sciences, there should be no question of Kuhn's account supporting the scientific status of these disciplines. (In fact, Kuhn remarks that he developed his account of the natural sciences in conscious contrast to what he saw in the social sciences [cf. SSR, ix-x].) This point becomes obscured if we think, as some have, of consensus as just a matter of widespread agreement. Various social scientific super-theories have, during certain periods, been in some sense widely accepted, at least among certain subgroups of researchers. But the sign of Kuhnian consensus is not just some sort of general endorsement of a super-theory but an acceptance that is so strong it eliminates the need for further discussion of foundational questions about the subject-matter and methodology of the disciplines and enables the discipline to devote most of its energy to puzzle-solving. A consensus that does not have this character will not be sufficient to sustain the practice of Kuhnian normal science; and it is this practice that is the mark of a mature science. The very existence of so many attempts by social scientists to use Kuhn's work to arrive at a basic understanding of what is going on in their disciplines shows that they have no consensus in Kuhn's sense. (And the lack of consensus is further indicated by the fact that there is no agreement among the various analysts as to what the paradigms of their disciplines are or have been.)

Even the hope that Kuhn can be a guide to the *development* of truly scientific social inquiry is based on a fundamental misunderstanding of his position. For, if it is clear that, from a Kuhnian viewpoint, social inquiry falls short of full scientific status because it lacks consensus, it is equally clear that Kuhn offers no directions for generating such consensus. Consensus for Kuhn emerges from nothing more or less than concrete instances of highly successful scientific practice. Given a consensus about the success of some such instances (and about the likelihood of further successes along the same lines), the scientific community (or informed philosophers of science) can formulate, by abstraction from the successful instances, rules for the practice of the science in question. (However, no set of rules can ever entirely express the guidance offered by the paradigm-instances.) But there are no specific rules for the successful practice of science prior to the emergence of a paradigmatic achievement. The positivists, of course, were quite ready to provide such rules, since they thought science was defined by a methodology independent of any particular scientific achievements. But to look to Kuhn for guidance of this sort is to ignore his fundamental disagreement with the positivists on this point. (In this regard, it is interesting to note Herminio Martins' comment that "Kuhnianism in social science is beginning to act as a functional equivalent and substitute for philosophical positivism.[18]) The methodological disputes that have so occupied social scientists will remain fruitless until their disciplines attain effective consensus about concrete achievements (Kuhnian paradigms) that can serve as touchstones in such disputes. So Kuhn's ultimate message to social scientists would seem to be along the same lines as the injunction, "Cultivate your own garden"; that is, forget about trying to figure out strategies for becoming mature sciences and get on with the job of doing good individual pieces of scientific work.

Many social scientists have sought in Kuhn not so much sanctions or advice as simply an overall understanding of the past or present state of their disciplines.[19] But even this less ambitious application of Kuhn is, I think, misdirected. For the paradigms of a discipline can be uniquely specified only on the basis of their function as foci of consensus. If, as in the case of the social sciences, we can identify paradigms only in terms of their super-theoretical content, there will be an unlimited variety of ways of dividing a discipline into paradigms. For any interrelated set of beliefs, values, and methods that have been held by a fairly substantial number of practitioners can be justly dubbed paradigms in this sense; and, depending on how general or specific our characterizations of the paradigmatic content is, we can find paradigms held by the members of just about any subset of a discipline's practitioners we please. This is illus-

14

trated by Eckberg and Hill's survey (reprinted below) of analyses of sociology in terms of paradigms. They catalogue twelve different analyses, each finding from one to eight paradigms, with over twenty different paradigms put forward by one or another of the analysts and no one paradigm on more than four lists. It is only a consideration of the function of a paradigm in generating consensus in a discipline that allows us to decide among the wide variety of ways of dividing the discipline. Since this function is seldom, if ever achieved by social science paradigms, attempts at Kuhnian analyses are bound to be unsatisfactory.

6. KUHN AND THE HUMANITIES

Although the social sciences themselves do not seem to contain counterparts to the paradigms Kuhn found in the natural sciences, it does not follow that there are not other contexts to which Kuhn's approach might be fruitfully extended. For there are non-scientific communities that embody a consensus strikingly similar to that found in the natural sciences. This suggests that social scientists would have been more successful if they looked for paradigms not among themselves but among the communities that they study. In, fact, however, this sort of application of Kuhn's work has usually been made not by social scientists but by scholars in humanistic disciplines such as history, art, and philosophy (although there has been much less use of Kuhn in these disciplines than in the sciences). For example, several historians and political theorists have suggested that it is profitable to talk of paradigms operative not in history or political theory but in the political groups (nations, ruling elites) that are studied by history and political theory.[20] Likewise, some critics and historians of art have proposed a role for paradigms in the analysis of artistic styles and schools.[21] And some philosophers of religion have offered accounts of the beliefs and actions of religious communities as paradigm-governed.[22]

Of course, the mere fact of consensus among the members of a group is not sufficient for the applicability of a Kuhnian account. The consensus must focus on specific achievements taken as paradigms by the group and must function as a basis for solving new problems along the lines suggested by the paradigmatic achievement. But these further conditions do seem to be met by at least some important non-scientific groups. It has, for example, been plausibly suggested[23] that Woodrow Wilson's international policies after World War I functioned as a paradigm for the conduct of American foreign

policy from the 1940s through the 1960s (the paradigm being rejected in the wake of the Vietnam crisis). Also, the paradigmatic role
of certain judicial decisions is built into the role of precedents in
legal deliberations. In the area of religion, the life of Christ seems
to have a paradigmatic status for Christian religious communities:
Christians are supposed to solve the problems of their lives on the
model provided by New Testament accounts of Christ. The existence
of universally recognized artistic achievements is obvious, and it is
clear that artists try to extend the achievement of a masterpiece to
new subject-matters and media.

Of course, it would take a great deal of work to turn these suggestions into results; but there does seem to be a good *prima facie*
case for the claim that Kuhn's account is extendible — though not
mechanically or even univocally — to non-scientific communities.
However, the prospect of such extensions raises the fundamental
question of whether Kuhn's approach allows for any significant distinction between science and non-science. It is worthwhile to pursue
this question a bit for the case of art. Kuhn has said that his book on
scientific revolutions derives from "my own discovery of the close
and persistent parallels" between art and science, and he has endorsed the remark that "the more carefully we try to distinguish
artist from scientist, the more difficult this becomes."[24] Nonetheless,
he rightly insists that there are deep differences between art and
science and suggests that "if *careful* analysis makes art and science
seem so implausibly alike, that may be due less to their intrinsic
similarity than to the failure of the tools we use for close scrutiny"
(341). But where is the failure that makes it so difficult to distinguish
art and science on a Kuhnian analysis? My suspicion is that it lies
in one of Kuhn's central assertions about science that we have not
yet discussed: his claim, put forward in the concluding chapter of
The Structure of Scientific Revolutions, that puzzle-solving rather
than truth is the primary aim of science.

Kuhn relies heavily on this feature of his account of science in his
efforts to make a start in distinguishing science from art. He suggests that most of the main apparent differences between the two
enterprises derive from the fact that "the artist's goal is the production of aesthetic objects; technical puzzles are what he must resolve
to produce such objects." By contrast, "for the scientist . . . the solved
technical puzzle is the goal, and the aesthetic object is a tool for its
attainment" (343).

Kuhn invokes the priority of puzzle-solving in science to explain
the fact that artists, but not scientists, pay serious attention to the

16

judgments of outsiders not trained in their craft and to past achievements of their enterprise. Puzzle-solving, unlike aesthetic judgment, is the unique province of specially trained practitioners; and the aesthetic qualities of an artistic achievement remain even after the puzzle-solutions (if any) that produced it have become irrelevant. Kuhn offers a similar explanation of differences in the way art and science develop through time; e.g., in art successful revolutions mean the acceptance of new traditions but generally not (as in science) the abandonment of older traditions; and as a result art but not science characteristically gives simultaneous support to incompatible traditions.

However, it is not at all clear that Kuhn's notion of puzzle-solving as opposed to truth-seeking is able to sustain these explanations. If the ultimate goal of science is just puzzle-solving, then it is not at all clear why past scientific achievements and traditions should not be maintained as presently relevant in much the same way that past artistic achievements and traditions are. After all, Galileo, Newton, and even Aristotle *do* solve many of the problems they set for science; and in some cases, theirs are the only solutions to these problems since (as Kuhn himself points out) the problems are not even formulable in the terms of later science. It is not that past science can no longer solve puzzles but that its solutions are based on what we now have good reason to think are false accounts of the physical world. Indeed, when we are only interested in solving a puzzle (e.g., plotting a ship's course or calculating a satellite's orbit) we are perfectly willing to proceed on Newtonian or even Ptolemaic assumptions. It is when we are concerned about the way the world really is that we reject these assumptions. Kuhn himself seems to implicitly recognize this fact when he says: "Asked why his work is like that of, say, Einstein or Schrödinger rather than Galileo or Newton, the scientist replies that Galileo and Newton, whatever their genius, were wrong, made mistakes" (346). What can it mean to say that Galileo and Newton were wrong if not that their theories were false? But, then, surely we now prefer Einstein and Schrodinger because their theories are closer to the *truth*.

Kuhn is right to be wary of the "number of vexing problems" (SSR, 170) associated with the notion of truth. But his apparent belief that these problems cannot be overcome and that truth must be simply omitted from our account of science seems to be based on the view that talk of truth (at least in any correspondence sense) presupposes a naive objectivism that ignores the inevitable role of our own concepts in our accounts of reality. Thus he says: "There is,

I think, no theory-independent way to reconstruct phrases like 'really there'; the notion of a match between the ontology of a theory and its 'real' counterpart now seems to me illusive in principle."[25] But this view ignores the possibility — illustrated by the work of philosophers such as Sellars and Putnam — of an account of the truth (real reference) of scientific theories that avoids the pitfalls of a naive objectivism. In any case, it seems that unless we acknowledge the orientation of science toward truth, we will not be able to distinguish it properly from enterprises such as art.

By way of conclusion, let me state in a summary way what I see as the main desiderata for further discussions of Kuhn's work. (1) First, of course, there is need for much more scrutiny of Kuhn's central theses on the basis of historical case-studies in the natural sciences. Historians are rightly wary of the dangers of mechanical applications of Kuhn's (or any one else's) general categories. But this should not exclude a careful assessment and even refinement or revision of these categories on the basis of careful historical inquiry.

(2) Philosophers need to get beyond their caricatures of Kuhn as a proponent of science's irrationality and instead develop and evaluate the very promising positive theory of rationality sketched in his work. There is, for example, a need for detailed epistemological analysis of judgments that are informed but not determined by methodological rules and of the idea that there are intellectual equivalents of perceptual Gestalt-shifts. Further, as Kuhn himself has emphasized,[26] his account of the difficulties of scientific communication suggests that he shares concerns with the problems of translation so central for post-Quinean philosophy of language. Another valuable enterprise would be the comparison of Kuhn's approach to scientific rationality with other philosophical accounts of rationality — e.g., those offered by Wittgensteinians in discussions of skepticism, religious belief, and anthropological research and those developed by moral philosophers concerned with the rationality of ethical decisions. There is also need, as suggested by my comments just above, for a confrontation of Kuhn's relativism with recent philosophical discussions of truth and realistic interpretations of scientific theories.

(3) Philosophers and sociologists should both — it would be inviting disaster to say "together" — reflect on how, if at all, their two approaches can be integrated into a unified account of scientific communities and their rationality. Habermas' critical theory of society is an obvious focal point for such reflection, and the encounter between Habermas' work and a more fully articulated Kuhnian

social epistemology would surely be extremely fruitful. (Also relevant here would be a comparison of Kuhn's approach to history with that of Michel Foucault.[27])

(4) Finally, although it would almost surely be a good idea to declare a moratorium on applications of Kuhn to the methodology and history of the social sciences, there is need for a great deal of work on the extension of Kuhnian ideas to the analysis of non-scientific communities. It is here more than anywhere else that the power of Kuhn's thought still remains untapped.

NOTES

1. Margaret Masterman, "The Nature of a Paradigm," in Lakatos and Musgrave (eds.), *Criticism and the Growth of Knowledge*, Cambridge: Cambridge University Press, 1970, pp. 59-89.

2. Kuhn also thinks that the nature of normal science makes revolutions inevitable. Every paradigm is to some extent "arbitrary" in the sense that it contains elements not ultimately compatible with our scientific encounters with nature. Accordingly, "the very nature of normal science ensures that novelty shall not be suppressed for very long" (SSR, 5); and we should expect the developments guided by a given paradigm to encounter difficulties leading to its replacement by another paradigm. This is a point overlooked by many critics — e.g., Popper — who think that what Kuhn calls normal science is just an unfortunate tendency of some scientists to be uncritical and to resist innovation. As Kuhn presents it, normal science plays a central role in the production of scientific innovation.

3. Kuhn has also emphasized that the differences referred to by the term 'incommensurability' pose significant obstacles to communication between proponents of rival paradigms. This is plausible, since even our everyday experience shows that those who disagree over many points on a given topic often have difficulties understanding one another's statements about it. (This seems due to the fact, emphasized recently by philosophers of language, that successful understanding of another's claims is typically based on the assumption that most of what he says is true.) Kuhn's critics have often taken his comments here to mean that he is applying some dubious theory of meaning to conclude that communication between proponents of rival paradigms is simply impossible. (Cf., for example, Carl Kordig, *The Justification of Scientific Change*, Reidel, 1971, p. 59.) However, Kuhn never goes farther than emphasizing the difficulty and partialness of communication across paradigms: "The proponents of competing paradigms are always at least slightly at cross-purposes" (SSR, 147); "communication across the revolutionary divide is inevitably partial" (SSR, 148). Further, there is no reason to think that a failure to *completely* understand a viewpoint excludes the possibility

of a rational judgment about its validity. (How often can a philosopher claim to completely understand a position — say of Kant or Hegel — that he rejects?)

4. "Normal Science, Scientific Revolutions and the History of Science," in Lakatos and Musgrave (eds.), as cited in n.1, p. 50.

5. "Paradigm Lost? A Review Symposium," *Isis*, 70 (1979), 429-479.

6. "History of Science and Its Rational Reconstructions," in C. Howson, (ed.), *Method and Appraisal in the Physical Sciences*, Cambridge: Cambridge University Press, 1976, p. 29, n. 111).

7. *The Essential Tension*, Chicago: University of Chicago Press, 1977, p. 6.

8. No doubt Kuhn himself is (as he has acknowledged) to some extent responsible for being misunderstood. For example, he compares scientists' changes of paradigm to religious conversions, says that those working with different paradigms "live in different worlds," cites with approval Planck's dictum that new views triumph only by the deaths of their opponents, etc. Interpreted in their context, none of these passages in fact supports the irrationalism that has been attributed to him. But it is easy to see how philosophers — especially those imbued with positivism — would be likely to read them in this way, and Kuhn does very little (in the first edition of SSR) to prevent this sort of misunderstanding. On the other hand, his frequent insistence that he is merely sketching in a tentative and often halting way a new picture of science should have suggested the need for sympathetic attention to context and qualifications. Another way in which philosophers have distorted Kuhn's views has been by presenting him and a number of other critics of positivism (usually, Hanson, Feyerabend, and Toulmin) as sharing a common philosophy of science. Although there are some important similarities in the views of these men, our understanding and evaluation of their contributions has been hindered more than helped by the attempt to treat them as a school.

9. Israel Scheffler, *Science and Subjectivity*, Indianapolis: Bobbs-Merrill, 1967.

10. "Logic of Discovery or Psychology of Research?" in Lakatos and Musgrave (eds.), as cited in n.1, p. 22.

11. "On a Sociological Theory of Scientific Change" in R. Whitley (ed.), *Social Processes of Scientific Development*, London: Routledge and Kegan Paul, 1974.

12. "Introduction" to R. Whitley (ed.), as cited in n. 11.

13. "Sociological Explanation and Natural Science: A Kuhnian Reappraisal," *Archives européennes de sociologie* 13 (1972), 373-393.

14. Here it is interesting to note Kuhn's comment in *The Essential Tension* (n. 7 above): ". . . my work has been deeply sociological, but not in a way that permits that subject to be separated from epistemology" (p. xx).

15. Cf. *Interests and the Growth of Knowledge*, London: Routledge and Kegan Paul, 1977. My colleague, Ed Manier, called my attention to this development in Barnes' views.

16. Cf. Habermas' *Knowledge and Human Interests*, Trans. J. Shapiro, Boston: Beacon Press, 1971. Thomas McCarthy's *The Critical*

Theory of Jürgen Habermas, Amherst: M.I.T. Press, 1978, provides an invaluable guide to Habermas' work.

17. Cf. the references given in the papers in this volume by Eckberg and Hill and by Blaug.

18. "The Kuhnian 'Revolution' and Its Implications for Sociology," in T. J. Nossiter, A. H. Hanson, and S. Rokkan (eds.), *Imagination and Precision in the Social Sciences*, London: Faber and Faber, 1972.

19. Cf. for example, George Ritzer, *Sociology: A Multiple Paradigm Science*, New York: Allyn and Bacon, 1975.

20. Cf. for example, Sheldon Wolin's "Paradigms and Political Theories" (reprinted in this volume) and J. C. A. Pocock, *Politics, Language, and Time*, New York: Atheneum, 1971, pp. 13ff.

21. Cf. James S. Ackerman, "The Demise of the Avant Garde: Notes on the Sociology of Recent American Art," *Comparative Studies in Society and History*, 11 (1969), 371-384.

22. Cf. Basil Mitchell, *The Justification of Religious Belief*, London: Oxford University Press, 1974, and Ian Barbour, *Models, Myths, and Paradigms* (from which a selection is reprinted below).

23. Bruce Kuklick, "History as a Way of Learning," *American Quarterly* 22 (1970), 609-628.

24. "Comment on the Relations of Science and Art," in *The Essential Tension*, Chicago: University of Chicago Press, 1977, pp. 340-341. (This is a reprint of Kuhn's comments, originally appearing in *Comparative Studies in Society and History* 11 (1969), on papers by Ackerman, et al. [cf. n.21 above].) Further references to this article will be given in the text.

25. "Postscript" to the second edition of *The Structure of Scientific Revolutions*, Chicago: University of Chicago Press, 1970.

26. Cf. *The Essential Tension*, p. xxiix and "Reflections on My Critics" in Lakatos and Musgrave (as cited in n. 1), 266 ff.

27. For some points of such a comparison, see my "Continental Philosophy of Science" in P. Asquith and H. Kyberg (eds.), *Current Research in Philosophy of Science*, Philosophy of Science Association, 1979, 94-120.

NOTES ON THE SELECTIONS

I have divided the discussions of Kuhn collected here into four general categories: philosophical, social scientific, humanistic, and historical. In making selections of philosophical reactions to Kuhn, I have deliberately omitted some very important but widely known and readily available discussions, such as those by Scheffler, Toulmin, Popper, Lakatos, and Feyerabend. (The reader who is not familiar with these discussions will find them helpfully summarized in the first half of the selection from Ian Barbour on Kuhn and religion.) Instead, I have represented the mainline of philosophical criticisms of Kuhn by two reviews of *The Structure of Scientific Revolutions*: Dudley Shapere's of the first edition and Alan Musgrave's of the second. Shapere's review has been very influential and was one of the first statements of what have become standard philosophical difficulties about the vagueness of 'paradigm' and the apparent irrationality of science on Kuhn's account. Musgrave argues that the Kuhn of the second edition is sounder but less interesting than the Kuhn of the first. The papers by MacIntyre and by Stegmüller are two very different attempts to do what has been very rare among philosophers who have commented on Kuhn: to go beyond criticism to an integration of Kuhn's results with other philosophical approaches and views. MacIntyre connects Kuhn's work with his own approach to epistemology in terms of "dramatic narratives." Stegmüller takes the initially surprising line of trying to clarify and develop Kuhn's ideas by embedding them in a formal logical analysis of scientific theories. He suggests a very interesting approach to unifying Kuhn's "historicist" approach with recent technical work (especially by J. D. Sneed) on the logic of scientific theories.

Among the selections from social scientists, M. D. King's paper presents what many have perceived as the Kuhnian alternative to Mertonian sociology of science and raises the crucial issue of the significance of this alternative for the rationality of science. The piece by Eckberg and Hill provides a comprehensive survey and critique of the many attempts to apply Kuhn's account of science to sociology by finding a set of "paradigms" in terms of which the history or present state of sociology can be understood. Mark Blaug examines attempts to apply Kuhn's views to the history of economics — particularly to the Keynesian revolution — and argues that Lakatos' methodology of scientific research programmes provides a more adequate framework for the historian of economics. Sheldon Wolin reflects on Kuhn's significance for political science, developing both the idea that this discipline can be understood in terms of paradigms and that the political communities it studies embody paradigms.

In the section on the humanities, David Hollinger presents an assessment of the significance of Kuhn's work for history in general (apart from the history of science). He treats a wide variety of topics, particularly, the heuristic value of generalizing Kuhn's model of scientific change to studies of non-scientific communities, the significance of Kuhn's work for the historian's understanding of the validity of his results, and the importance for the historian in general of controversies about the nature of science. Ian Barbour's discussion begins with a useful survey of the philosophical debate about Kuhn and goes on to propose his own version of a Kuhnian account of rational theory choice; he then argues that this account can be extended to the case of choosing a set of religious beliefs and that, accordingly, religious belief can be rational in essentially the same sense that science is. Richard Vernon offers a comparison of Kuhn's account of scientific revolutions with Newman's account of theological development, emphasizing the use of an analogy with political communities in both accounts and suggesting that Newman provides a helpful perspective for criticizing and remedying some flaws in Kuhn's work.

Finally, there are three selections by historians of the natural sciences. Michael Heidelberger challenges Kuhn on his own home ground of the Copernican revolution, arguing that Kuhn's notions of crisis and paradigm-switch do not apply to this classic case of a scientific revolution. Rachel Laudan comments on the appropriateness of describing the recent acceptance of the continental drift hypothesis as a Kuhnian revolution in geology. John Greene offers a case-study of the Darwinian revolution in biology and argues that Kuhn's model of scientific change does not provide an adequate account of this development.

One final comment: Most of these selections begin with a summary of Kuhn's main ideas. This makes for some redundancy, but I have decided not to eliminate it, first because I think it better to let each piece stand as an autonomous discussion but more importantly because there are often particular features of the way a given author presents Kuhn's ideas that are important for an understanding of his subsequent discussion.

I. PHILOSOPHY

THE STRUCTURE OF SCIENTIFIC REVOLUTIONS

DUDLEY SHAPERE

This important book[1] is a sustained attack on the prevailing image of scientific change as a linear process of ever-increasing knowledge, and an attempt to make us see that process of change in a different and, Kuhn suggests, more enlightening way. In attacking the "concept of development-by-accumulation," Kuhn presents numerous penetrating criticisms not only of histories of science written from that point of view, but also of certain philosophical doctrines (mainly Baconian and positivistic philosophies of science, particularly verification, falsification, and probabilistic views of the acceptance or rejection of scientific theories) which he convincingly argues are associated with that view of history. In this review, I will not deal with those criticisms or with the details of the valuable case studies with which Kuhn tries to support his views; rather, I will concentrate on certain concepts and doctrines which are fundamental to his own interpretation of the development and structure of science. His view, while original and richly suggestive, has much in common with some recent antipositivistic reactions among philosophers of science — most notably, Feyerabend, Hanson, and Toulmin — and inasmuch as it makes explicit, according to Kuhn, "some of the new historiography's implications" (p. 3), it is bound to exert a very wide influence among philosophers and historians of science alike. It is therefore a view which merits close examination.

Basic to Kuhn's interpretation of the history of science is his notion of a paradigm. Paradigms are "universally recognized scientific achievements that for a time provide model problems and solutions to a community of practitioners" (p. x). Because a paradigm is "at the start largely a promise of success discoverable in selected and still incomplete examples" (pp. 23-24), it is "an object for further articulation and specification under new or more stringent conditions" (p. 23); hence from paradigms "spring particular coherent traditions of scientific research" (p. 10) which Kuhn calls "normal science." Normal science thus consists largely of "mopping-up operations" (p. 24) devoted to actualizing the initial promise of the paradigm "by extending the knowledge of those facts that the paradigm displays as particularly revealing, by increasing the extent of the match between those facts and the paradigm's predictions, and by further articulation of the paradigm itself" (p. 24). In this process of paradigm development lie both the strength and weakness of normal science: for though the paradigm provides "a criterion for choosing problems that, while the paradigm is taken for granted, can be assumed to have solutions" (p. 37), on the other hand those phenomena "that will not fit the box are often not seen at all" (p. 24). Normal science even "often suppresses fundamental novelties because they are necessarily subversive of its basic commitments. Nevertheless, so long as those commitments retain an element of the arbitrary, the very nature of normal research ensures that novelty shall not be suppressed for very long" (p. 5). Repeated failures of a normal-science tradition to solve a problem or other anomalies that develop in the course of paradigm articulation produce "the tradition-shattering complements to the tradition-bound activity of normal science" (p. 6).

The most pervasive of such tradition-shattering activities Kuhn calls "scientific revolutions."

Confronted with anomaly or with crisis, scientists take a different attitude toward existing paradigms, and the nature of their research changes accordingly. The proliferation of competing articulations, the willingness to try anything, the expression of explicit discontent, the recourse to philosophy and to debate over fundamentals, all these are symptoms of a transition from normal to extraordinary research [p. 90].
Scientific revolutions are inaugurated by a growing sense ... that an existing paradigm has ceased to function adequately in the exploration of an aspect of nature to which that paradigm itself had previously led the way [p. 91].

The upshot of such crises is often the acceptance of a new paradigm:

Scientific revolutions are here taken to be those non-cumulative developmental episodes in which an older paradigm is replaced in whole or in part by an incompatible new one [p. 91].

This interpretation of scientific development places a heavy burden indeed on the notion of a paradigm. Although in some passages we are led to believe that a community's paradigm is simply "a set of recurrent and quasi-standard illustrations of various theories," and that these are "revealed in its textbooks, lectures, and laboratory exercises" (p. 43), elsewhere we find that there is far more to the paradigm than is contained, at least explicitly, in such illustrations. These "accepted examples of actual scientific practice... include law, theory, application, and instrumentation together" (p. 10). A paradigm consists of a "strong network of commitments — conceptual, theoretical, instrumental, and methodological" (p. 42); among these commitments are "quasi-metaphysical" ones (p. 41). A paradigm is, or at least includes, "some implicit body of intertwined theoretical and methodological belief that permits selection, evaluation, and criticism" (pp. 16-17). If such a body of beliefs is not implied by the collection of facts (and, according to Kuhn, it never is), "it must be externally supplied, perhaps by a current metaphysic, by another science, or by personal and historical accident" (p. 17). Sometimes paradigms seem to be patterns (sometimes in the sense of archetypes and sometimes in the sense of criteria or standards) upon which we model our theories or other work ("from them as models spring particular coherent traditions"); at other times they seem to be themselves vague theories which are to be refined and articulated. Most fundamentally, though, Kuhn considers them as not being rules, theories, or the like, or a mere sum thereof, but something more "global" (p. 43), from which rules, theories, and so forth are abstracted, but to which no mere statement of rules or theories or the like can do justice. The term "paradigm" thus covers a range of factors in scientific development including or somehow involving laws and theories, models, standards, and methods (both theoretical and instrumental), vague intuitions, explicit or implicit metaphysical beliefs (or prejudices). In short, anything that allows science to accomplish anything can be a part of (or somehow involved in) a paradigm.

Now, historical study does bear out the existence of guiding factors which are held in more or less similar form, to greater or less extent, by a multitude of scientists working in an area over a number of years. What must be asked is whether anything is gained by referring to such common factors as "paradigms," and whether such gains, if any, are offset by confusions that ensue because of such a way of speaking. At the very outset, the explanatory value of the notion of a paradigm is suspect: for the truth of the thesis that shared paradigms are (or are behind) the common factors guiding scientific research appears to be guaranteed, not so much by a close examination of actual historical cases, however scholarly, as by the breadth of definition of the term "paradigm." The suspicion that this notion plays a determinative role in shaping Kuhn's interpretation of history is strengthened by his frequent remarks about what *must* be the case with regard to science and its development: for example, "No natural history can be interpreted in the absence of at least some ... belief" (pp. 16-17); "Once a first paradigm through which to view nature has been found, there is no such thing as research in the absence of any paradigm" (p. 79); "no experiment can be conceived without some sort of theory" (p. 87); "if, as I have already urged, there can be no scientifically or empirically neutral system of language or concepts, then the proposed construction of alternate tests and theories must proceed from within one or another paradigm-based tradition" (p. 145). Such views appear too strongly and confidently held to have been extracted from a mere investigation of how things *have* happened.

Still greater perplexities are generated by Kuhn's view that paradigms cannot, in general, be formulated adequately. According to him, when the historian tries to state the rules which scientists follow, he finds that "phrased in just that way, or in any other way he can imagine, they would almost certainly have been rejected by some members of the group he studies" (p. 44). Similarly, there may be many versions of the same theory. It would appear that, in Kuhn's eyes, the concepts, laws, theories, rules, and so forth that are common to a group are just not common enough to guarantee the coherence of the tradition; therefore he concludes that the paradigm, "the concrete scientific achievement" that is the source of that coherence, must not be identified with, but must be seen as "prior to the various concepts, laws, theories, and points of view that may be abstracted from it" (p. 11). (It is partly on the basis of this argument that Kuhn rejects the attempt by philosophers of science to formulate a "logic" of science in terms of precise rules.) Yet if it is true that all that can be said about paradigms and scientific development can and must be said only in terms of what are mere "abstractions" from paradigms, then it is difficult to see what is gained by appealing to the notion of a paradigm.

In Kuhn's view, however, the fact that paradigms cannot be described adequately in words does not hinder us from recognizing them: they are open to "direct inspection" (p. 44), and historians can "agree in their *identification* of a paradigm without agreeing on, or even attempting to produce, a full *interpretation* or *rationalization* of it" (p. 44). Yet the feasibility of a historical inquiry concerning paradigms is exactly what is brought into question by the scope of the term "paradigm" and the inaccessibility of particular paradigms to verbal formulation. For on the one hand, as we have seen, it is *too* easy to identify a paradigm; and on the other hand, it is not easy to determine, in particular cases treated by Kuhn, what the paradigm is supposed to have been in that case. In most of the cases he discusses, it is the theory that is doing the job of posing problems, providing criteria for selection of data, being articulated, and so forth. But of course the theory is not the paradigm, and we might assume that Kuhn discusses the theory because it is as near as he can get in words to the inexpressible paradigm. This, however, only creates difficulties. In the case of "what is perhaps our fullest example of a scientific revolution" (p. 132), for instance, what was "assimilated" when Dalton's theory (paradigm) became accepted? Not merely the laws of combining proportions, presumably, but something "prior to" them. Was it, then, the picture of matter as constituted of atoms? But contrary to the impression Kuhn gives, that picture was never even nearly universally accepted: from Davy to Ostwald and beyond there was always a very strong faction which "regarded it with mis-giving, or with positive dislike, or with a constant hope for an effec-tive substitute" (J. C. Gregory, *A Short History of Atomism* [London, 1931], p. 93), some viewing atoms as convenient fictions, others eschewing the vocabulary of atoms entirely, preferring to talk in terms of "proportions" or "equivalents." (It is noteworthy that Dalton was presented with a Royal Medal, not unequivocally for his devel-opment of the atomic theory, but rather "for his development of the Theory of Definite Proportions, usually called the Atomic Theory of Chemistry"; award citation, quoted in Gregory, p. 84.) No, it was certainly not atoms to which the most creative chemists of the century were "committed" — unless (contrary to his general mode of expression) Kuhn means that they were "committed" to the atomic theory because they — most of them — used it even though they did not believe in its truth. Further, what else was "intertwined" in this behind-the-scenes paradigm? Did it include, for instance, some in-expressible Principle of Uniformity of Nature or Law of Causality? Is this question so easy to answer — a matter of "direct inspection" — after all these years of philosophical dispute? One begins to doubt that paradigms are open to "direct inspection," or else to be amazed at Professor Kuhn's eyesight. (And why is it that such historical facts should be open to direct inspection, whereas scientific facts must always be seen "through" a paradigm?) But if there are such difficulties, how can historians know that they agree in their identi-fication of the paradigms present in historical episodes, and so deter-mine that "the same" paradigm persists through a long sequence of such episodes? They cannot, by hypothesis, compare their formula-

31

tions. Suppose they disagree: how is their dispute to be resolved?

On the other hand, where do we draw the line between different paradigms and different articulations of the same paradigm? It is natural and common to say that Newton, d'Alembert, Lagrange, Hertz, Hamilton, Mach, and others formulated different versions of classical mechanics; yet certainly some of these formulations involved different "commitments" — for example, some to forces, others to energy, some to vectorial, others to variational principles. The distinction between paradigms and different articulations of a paradigm, and between scientific revolutions and normal science, is at best a matter of degree, as is commitment to a paradigm: expression of explicit discontent, proliferation of competing articulations, debate over fundamentals are all more or less present throughout the development of science; and there are always guiding elements which are more or less common, even among what are classified as different "traditions." This is one reason why, in particular cases, identification of "the paradigm" is so difficult: not just because it is hard to see, but because looking for the guiding elements in scientific activity is not like looking for a unitary entity that either is there or is not.

But furthermore, the very reasons for supposing that paradigms (nevertheless) exist are unconvincing. No doubt some theories are very similar — so similar that they can be considered to be "versions" or "different articulations" of one another (or of "the same subject"). But does this imply that there must be a common "paradigm" of which the similar theories are incomplete expressions and from which they are abstracted? No doubt, too, many expressions of methodological rules are not as accurate portrayals of scientific method as they are claimed to be; and it is possible that Kuhn is right in claiming that no such portrayal can be given in terms of any one set of precise rules. But such observations, even if true, do not compel us to adopt a *mystique* regarding a single paradigm which guides procedures, any more than our inability to give a single, simple definition of "game" means that we must have a unitary but inexpressible idea from which all our diverse uses of "game" are abstracted. It may be true that "The coherence displayed by the research tradition ... may not imply even the existence of an underlying body of rules and assumptions" (p. 46); but neither does it imply the existence of an underlying "paradigm."

Finally, Kuhn's blanket use of the term "paradigm" to cover such a variety of activities and functions obscures important differences between those activities and functions. For example, Kuhn claims that "an apparently arbitrary element ... is always a formative in-gredient" (p. 4) of a paradigm; and, indeed, as we shall see shortly, this is a central aspect of his view of paradigms and scientific change. But is the acceptance or rejection of a scientific theory "arbitrary" in the same sense that acceptance or rejection of a stan-dard (to say nothing of a metaphysical belief) is? Again, Newtonian and Hertzian formulations of classical mechanics are similar to one another, as are the Einstein, Whitehead, Birkhoff, and Milne versions of relativity, and as are wave mechanics and matrix mechanics. But there are significant differences in the ways in and degrees to which these theories are "similar" — differences which are masked by viewing them all equally as different articulations of the same paradigm.

There are, however, deeper ways in which Kuhn's notion of a paradigm adversely affects his analysis of science; and it is in these ways that his view reflects widespread and important tendencies in both the history and philosophy of science today.

Because a paradigm is

the source of the methods, problem-field, and standards of solu-tion accepted by any mature scientific community at any given time, ... the reception of a new paradigm often necessitates a redefinition of the corresponding science. ... And as the prob-lems change, so, often, does the standard that distinguishes a real scientific solution from a mere metaphysical speculation, word game, or mathematical play. The normal-scientific tradi-tion that emerges from a scientific revolution is not only in-compatible but often actually incommensurable with that which has gone before [p. 102].

Thus the paradigm change entails "changes in the standards gov-erning permissible problems, concepts, and explanations" (p. 105). In connection with his view that concepts or meanings change from one theory (paradigm) to another despite the retention of the same terms, Kuhn offers an argument whose conclusion is both intrinsi-cally important and crucial to much of his book. This argument is directed against the "positivistic" view that scientific advance is cumulative, and that therefore earlier sciences are derivable from later; the case he considers is the supposed deducibility of New-tonian from Einsteinian dynamics, subject to limiting conditions. After summarizing the usual derivation, Kuhn objects that

the derivation is spurious, at least to this point. Though the [derived statements] are a special case of the laws of relativistic mechanics, they are not Newton's Laws. Or at least they are not unless those laws are reinterpreted in a way that would have been impossible until after Einstein's work. . . . The physical referents of these Einsteinian concepts are by no means identical with those of the Newtonian concepts that bear the same name. (Newtonian mass is conserved; Einsteinian is convertible with energy. Only at low relative velocities may the two be measured in the same way, and even then they must not be conceived to be the same.) . . . The argument has still not done what it purported to do. It has not, that is, shown Newton's Laws to be a limiting case of Einstein's. For in the passage to the limit it is not only the forms of the laws that have changed. Simultaneously we have had to alter the fundamental structural elements of which the universe to which they apply is composed [pp. 100-101].

But Kuhn's argument amounts simply to an assertion that despite the derivability of expressions which are in every formal respect identical with Newton's Laws, there remain differences of "meaning." What saves this from begging the question at issue? His only attempt to support his contention comes in the parenthetical example of mass; but this point is far from decisive. For one might equally well be tempted to say that the "concept" of mass (the "meaning" of "mass") has remained the same (thus accounting for the deducibility) even though the *application* has changed. Similarly, rather than agree with Kuhn that "the Copernicans who denied its traditional title 'planet' to the sun . . . were changing the meaning of 'planet'" (p. 127), one might prefer to say that they changed only the application of the term. The real trouble with such arguments arises with regard to the cash difference between saying, in such cases, that the "meaning" has changed, as opposed to saying that the "meaning" has remained the same though the "application" has changed. Kuhn has offered us no clear analysis of "meaning" or, more specifically, no criterion of change of meaning; consequently it is not clear why he classifies such changes as changes of meaning rather than, for example, as changes of application. This is not to say that no such criterion could be formulated, or that a distinction between change of meaning and change of application could not be made, or that it might not be very profitable to do so for certain purposes. One might, for example, note that there are statements that can be made, questions that can be raised, views that may be suggested as possibly correct, within the context of Einsteinian physics that would not even have made sense — would have been self-contradictory — in the context of Newtonian physics. And such differences might (for certain purposes) be referred to with profit as changes of meaning, indicating, among other things, that there are differences between Einsteinian and Newtonian terms that are not brought out by the deduction of Newtonian-like statements from Einsteinian ones. But attributing such differences to alterations of "meaning" must not blind one to any resemblances there might be between the two sets of terms. Thus it is not so much Kuhn's conclusion that is objectionable as, first, the fact that it is based, not on any solid argument, but on the feature of meaning dependence which Kuhn has built into the term "paradigm" (scientists see the world from different points of view, through different paradigms, and therefore see different things through different paradigms); and second, the fact that this feature leads him to a distorted portrayal of the relations between different scientific theories. For Kuhn's term "paradigm," incorporating as it does the view that statements of fact are (to use Hanson's expression) theory-laden, and as a consequence the notion of (in Feyerabend's words) meaning variance from one theory or paradigm to another, calls attention excessively to the differences between theories or paradigms, so that relations that evidently do exist between them are in fact passed over or denied.

The significance of this point emerges fully when we ask about the grounds for accepting one paradigm as better than another. For if "the differences between successive paradigms are both necessary and irreconcilable" (p. 102), and if those differences consist in the paradigms' being "incommensurable" — if they disagree as to what the facts are, and even as to the real problems to be faced and the standards which a successful theory must meet — then what are the two paradigms disagreeing about? And why does one win? There is little problem for Kuhn in analyzing the notion of progress within a paradigm tradition (and, indeed, he notes, such evolution is the source of the prevailing view of scientific advance as "linear"); but how can we say that "progress" is made when one paradigm replaces another? The logical tendency of Kuhn's position is clearly toward the conclusion that the replacement is not cumulative, but is mere change: being "incommensurable," two paradigms cannot be judged according to their ability to solve the same problems, or deal with the same facts, or meet the same standards. "If there were but one set of scientific problems, one world within which to work on them, and one set of standards for their solution, paradigm competition might be settled more or less routinely. . . . But . . . The propo-

35

nents of competing paradigms are always at least slightly at cross-purposes" (pp. 146-147). Hence "the competition between paradigms is not the sort of battle that can be resolved by proofs" (p. 147), but is more like a "conversion experience" (p. 150). In fact, in so far as one can compare the weights of evidence of two competing paradigms — and, on Kuhn's view that after a scientific revolution "the whole network of fact and theory . . . has shifted" (p. 140), one must wonder how this can be done at all — the weight of evidence is more often in favor of the older paradigm than the new (pp. 155-156). "What occurred was neither a decline nor a raising of standards, but simply a change demanded by the adoption of a new paradigm" (p. 107)." In these matters neither truth nor error is at issue" (p. 150); indeed, Kuhn's view of the history of science implies that "We may . . . have to relinquish the notion, explicit or implicit, that changes of paradigm carry scientists and those who learn from them closer and closer to the truth" (p. 169).

Kuhn is well aware of the relativism implied by his view, and his common sense and feeling for history make him struggle mightily to soften the dismal conclusion. It is, for instance, only "often" that the reception of a new paradigm necessitates a redefinition of the corresponding science. Proponents of different paradigms are only "at least partially" at cross-purposes. Though they "see different things when they look from the same point in the same direction," this is "not to say that they can see anything they please. Both are looking at the world" (p. 149). It is only "in some areas" that "they see different things" (p. 149). But these qualifications are more the statement of the problems readers will find with Kuhn's views than the solutions of those problems. And it is small comfort to be told, in the closing pages of the book, that "a sort of progress will inevitably characterize the scientific enterprise" (p. 169), especially if that "progress," whether or not it is aimed toward final truth, is not at least an advance over past error. Nor will careful readers feel reassured when they are asked, rhetorically, "What better criterion [of scientific progress] than the decision of the scientific group could there be" (p. 169)? For Kuhn has already told us that the decision of a scientific group to adopt a new paradigm is not based on good reasons; on the contrary, what counts as a good reason is determined by the decision.

A view such as Kuhn's had, after all, to be expected sooner or later from someone versed in the contemporary treatment of the history of science. For the great advances in that subject since Duhem have shown how much more there was to theories that were supposedly overthrown and superseded than had been thought. Historians now find that "the more carefully they study, say, Aristotelian dynamics, phlogistic chemistry, or caloric thermodynamics, the more certain they feel that those once current views of nature were, as a whole, neither less scientific nor more the product of human idiosyncrasy than those current today" (p. 2). Yet perhaps that deep impression has effected too great a reaction; for that there is more to those theories than was once thought does not mean that they are immune to criticism — that there are not *good* reasons for their abandonment and replacement by others. And while Kuhn's book calls attention to many mistakes that have been made regarding the (good) reasons for scientific change, it fails itself to illuminate those reasons, and even obscures the existence of such reasons. We must, as philosophers of science, shape our views of the development and structure of scientific thought in the light of what we learn from science and its history. But until historians of science achieve a more balanced approach to their subject — neither indulgently relativistic nor intransigently positivistic — philosophers must receive such presentations of evidence with extremely critical eyes.

Certainly there is a vast amount of positive value in Kuhn's book. Besides making many valid critical remarks, it does bring out, through a wealth of case studies, many common features of scientific thought and activities which make it possible and, for many purposes, revealing to speak of "traditions" in science; and it points out many significant differences between such traditions. But Kuhn, carried away by the logic of his notion of a paradigm, glosses over many important differences between scientific activities classified as being of the same tradition, as well as important continuities between successive traditions. He is thus led to deny, for example, that Einsteinian dynamics is an advance over Newtonian or Aristotelian dynamics in a sense more fundamental than can consistently be extracted from his conceptual apparatus. If one holds, without careful qualification, that the world is seen and interpreted "through" a paradigm, or that theories are "incommensurable," or that there is "meaning variance" between theories, or that all statements of fact are "theory-laden," then one may be led all too readily into relativism with regard to the development of science. Such a view is no more implied by historical facts than is the opposing view that scientific development consists solely of the removal of superstition, prejudice, and other obstacles to scientific progress in the form of purely incremental advances toward final truth. Rather, I have tried to show, such relativism, while it may seem to be suggested by a half-century of deeper study of discarded theories, is a *logical* outgrowth of conceptual confusions, in Kuhn's case owing primarily to the use of a blanket term. For his view is made to appear convincing only by inflating the definition of "paradigm" until that term becomes so vague and ambiguous that it cannot easily be withheld, so general that it cannot easily be applied, so mysterious that it cannot help explain, and so misleading that it is a positive hindrance to the understanding of some central aspects of science; and then, finally, these excesses must be counterbalanced by qualifications that simply contradict them. There are many other facets of Kuhn's book that deserve attention — especially his view that a paradigm "need not, and in fact never does, explain all the facts with which it can be confronted" (p. 18), and his suggestion that no paradigm ever could be found which would do so. But the difficulties that have been discussed here indicate clearly that the expanded version of this book which Kuhn contemplates will require not so much further historical evidence (p. xi) as — at the very least — more careful scrutiny of his tools of analysis.

NOTE

1. Thomas S. Kuhn, *The Structure of Scientific Revolutions* (Chicago: University of Chicago Press, 1962), pp. xiv, 172. All page references, unless otherwise noted, are to this work.

KUHN'S SECOND THOUGHTS

ALAN E. MUSGRAVE

Thomas Kuhn's *Structure of Scientific Revolutions* is a justly famous book, and one which has caused quite a stir among philosophers of science since its first publication in 1962. In this second edition[1] Kuhn happily makes only two changes in the original, already classic text. But he adds a 36-page *"Postscript — 1969,"* in which he responds to his many critics and indicates how his views have developed.[2] The discussion in this *Postscript* centres around Kuhn's two basic ideas — the idea of *paradigms* as the basis of scientific research, and the idea of *scientific communities* as the units responsible for paradigm-based research.

Let us consider "communities" first, since Kuhn himself begins with them. He is worried about the circularity involved in defining a paradigm as that which the members of a scientific group share, and then defining the group by its shared paradigm. Now most philosophers of science, if they paid any attention at all to the sociological dimension of science, would presumably have a ready solution to this Kuhnian puzzle. They would insist that the content of science is primary, so that if scientists do organise themselves into different groups this must be a sociological reflection of their different problems, theories and techniques. Such philosophers of science would, therefore, define the group by the common scientific content of its activities, and not *vice versa*.[3]

Kuhn flirts with a different solution to his puzzle: "Scientific communities," he says, "can and should be isolated without prior recourse to paradigms; the latter can then be discovered by scrutinising the behaviour of a given community's members" (p. 176; also his (1970*b*), p. 271). Does this mean that the membership of a scientific group is somehow to be determined independently of the scientific content of its activities? This would indeed be "an inversion of our normal view of the relation between scientific activity and the community that practices it" (p. 162). How could such a thing be done?

At this point Kuhn assures us that the isolation of scientific communities "has recently become a significant subject for sociological research" and refers us to this research (p. 176; also his (1970*b*), p.

252). Perusal of this literature will reveal that most sociologists solve the problem of isolating scientific communities by somehow taking the word of scientists themselves. Thus Price and Beaver investigate a group the members of which receive membership lists, preprints and other memos — what they call the "basic difficulty of study" is solved for them by the scientists who organised themselves into this group ((1966), p. 1011). Diana Crane locates the members of her group by taking all the names listed by the compiler of a bibliography ((1969) p. 338). Other "methods" do exist, however — they involve sorting scientists into groups by inspecting footnotes in scientific papers, and seeing who cites whom.[4]

The sociologists to whom Kuhn refers us take pride in what they call the "objectivity" of their methods. What they mean is that their methods can be applied without taking any notice of the scientific content of the activities investigated. Kessler emphasises that his method "Even when performed by a human being . . . is completely mechanical" ((1965), p. 224). The results achieved using the Scientific Citation Index (a list of who cites whom prepared by a computer) are "based on a purely objective method which does not require a personality appraisal or a reading of the works by these men."[5] Price and Beaver complain that there has never been "an objective analysis of an Invisible College structure" and proceed to provide one, making it clear that "we have been at pains to preserve our primitive ignorance of the scientific content of the work of this group and also our lack of any personal knowledge of the participants in it" ((1966), p. 1011).

These sociologists of science take pride, then, in their curious "objectivity," that is, in paying no attention to the scientific content of the activities of the scientists they study. So the question recurs: does Kuhn propose to isolate the members of his scientific groups without taking into account their scientific activities?

The answer, not unexpectedly, is "No." His own summary of the distinguishing marks of members of a group is as follows: having "undergone similar educations and professional initiations," having "absorbed the same technical literature" so that a community has "a subject-matter of its own," and finally having their "professional judgment relatively unanimous" (p. 177; also his (1970b), p. 253). But the sociological methods to which Kuhn himself had referred can hardly be relied upon to isolate groups in *this* sense. Clearly, for example, the fact that one scientist cites another hardly guarantees that they share a subject-matter (he might, after all, cite him in distinguishing their subject-matters), or that their "professional judgment" coincides (he might, after all, cite him in disagreement). Citations, not to mention the papers containing them, will have to be read and understood to see if they provide evidence of common group membership in Kuhn's sense. But Kuhn's sociologists, as we have seen, appear to have a methodological aversion to reading what they so assiduously count, and therefore cannot solve Kuhn's problem.[6] It seems that Kuhn's own sociological citations should be taken with a pinch of salt.

But let us proceed, granting that communities in *Kuhn's* sense have, somehow, been isolated. They exist, he says, at "numerous levels" (p. 177), from the community of all scientists, to those of physicists, chemists, etc., then to sub-communities (e.g. solid-state physicists), and finally to sub-sub-communities. It is these last communities that Kuhn wants to concentrate upon: "Communities of this sort are the units that this book has presented as the producers and validators of scientific knowledge" (p. 178). They are relatively small, typically containing "perhaps one hundred members, occasionally significantly fewer" (p. 178; also his (1970*b*), p. 253) — elsewhere "fewer than twenty-five people" is mentioned (p. 181).

Kuhn asserts that, with his new emphasis on the micro-community structure of science, "several difficulties which have been foci for critical attention are likely to vanish" (p. 180). Quite so. As we shall see, what vanishes is the conception of "normal science" which was originally attributed to Kuhn.

According to this conception, the scientific community engages in "normal research" for relatively long periods between short bouts of "extraordinary research." During normal periods there is consensus on the guiding principles of research (the "paradigm"), a consensus reinforced by the dogmatic style of scientific education. Rival paradigms are not taught, their invention is discouraged, and controversy over fundamentals ceases. Instead, the scientific community concentrates on "puzzle-solving," on forcing nature to fit the paradigm to which it is committed. If nature is stubborn and a scientist fails to solve his puzzle, then he is blamed, not the paradigm. Only in "extraordinary" periods, when rival paradigms compete, do unsolved puzzles or "anomalies" turn into critical arguments against paradigms. But such periods are short-lived — soon consensus emerges on a new paradigm, and the scientific community devotes itself once again to "normal science."

This, roughly, is the conception of "normal science" to which Kuhn's critics took exception. They could not quite agree, as Kuhn indicates ((1970*b*), p. 233), whether it is a bad thing which fortunately does not exist, or a bad thing which unfortunately does exist. What does emerge clearly from Kuhn's present writings is that it is a conception to which he does not now, and perhaps never did, subscribe.

Several people criticised Kuhn for exaggerating the degree of consensus normally prevailing in the scientific community. Now although Kuhn still makes it a defining condition for a community that its members are agreed on something (I shall discuss presently exactly what this something is), this consensus condition becomes innocuous when the scientific community dissolves into numbers of micro-communities. Whole sciences need no longer be given over, for long periods, to the articulation of a single, universally accepted paradigm. Kuhn could allow for all the disagreement his critics wanted, by having his micro-communities compete with each other. But does Kuhn allow active competition between different groups?

His general position is not unequivocal. On the one hand he says that "professional communication across group lines" is comparatively rare and "often arduous"; and he insists that "communities ... which approach the same subject from incompatible viewpoints ... are far rarer [in the sciences] than in other fields" (p. 177). On the other hand, he says that there are "such things as schools in science, communities which approach the same subject from very different points of view" ((1970b), p. 252); and he predicts that "Research would ... disclose the existence of rival schools" ((1970b), p. 253).[7]

Kuhn's response to a particular example adduced by several of his critics is more enlightening. His critics claimed that there has been a continuing controversy over theories of matter in the history of physics. Kuhn agrees, but thinks it "no counterexample" to his idea of normal science being governed by consensus (p. 180; also his (1970b), p. 255). He allows that different micro-communities quarrelled over theories of matter. And he even allows that members of the *same* community did so, citing the controversy over the existence of atoms in early nineteenth-century chemistry as example.

These are significant remarks. According to Kuhn's *Postscript* fundamental metaphysical controversy, either between communities or even within the same community, *can* accompany "normal research." This takes us far from one of his original central theses (e.g. pp. 11, 15) that in normal periods fundamental metaphysical controversy ceases. Kuhn still insists that the members of a community practising normal science "take the foundations of their field for granted" (p. 178; cp. p. 21). But now "foundations" need no longer include metaphysics — so what does it include? According to Kuhn's *Postscript*, all that early nineteenth-century chemists needed to agree upon to remain in the same community were "research-tools" like the laws of constant and multiple proportions and combining weights. They could, and did, "disagree, sometimes vehemently, about the existence of atoms" (p. 180). Now this means that chemists could, and did, disagree vehemently about the explanation or interpretation of their "research-tools." Atomists like Dalton and Berzelius insisted that these "tools" made no sense unless seen as manifestations of the existence of atoms. And Dalton, as is well-known, refused to accept Gay-Lussac's law because he could not fit it into his atomist metaphysic. As we shall see, Kuhn does not favour a return to the positivist view that such metaphysical disputes have no real influence on the practice of science proper. And this has important repercussions on his view of the nature and functions of "paradigms."

(One of Kuhn's changes in his original text tends in a similar direction. He originally suggested that Newton's *Principia* became the universally accepted paradigm in the eighteenth century. He now qualifiies this picture of Newtonian dominance, albeit guardedly, by saying (pp. 30-3) that on the Continent different "techniques" persisted for a long time in the analysis of terrestrial phenomena.)

A further "difficulty" seized upon by Kuhn's critics also vanishes with his present emphasis on the micro-community structure of science. Some critics took Kuhn to assert that critical debate over paradigms was a comparatively rare phenomenon. And they argued, against this, that even in periods between major scientific revolutions, much discussion and revision of theory takes place, albeit on a smaller scale. Kuhn agrees: a revolution "need not be a large change" (p. 181) — "micro-revolutions," as Kuhn calls them ((1970*b*), p. 249, note 3), "occur regularly" (p. 181) in the intervals between major revolutions. He adds (p. 181) that micro-revolutions need not be preceded by any "crisis" in the community — they may, for example, be produced by developments in other communities (in such cases, presumably, communication between groups is not so "arduous" that it does not take place).

In his second amendment to the original text,[8] Kuhn allows that a state of crisis need not end with the revolutionary overthrow of the existing paradigm: it may be brought to an end with the solution of the "crisis-provoking problem" on the basis of the existing paradigm, or by temporarily shelving the problem. This amendment is also significant. Any anomaly can, it appears, produce a "crisis" and be seen, by one, some or all members of the relevant community, as "the end of an existing paradigm" (p. 84; also his (1970*b*), p. 249). Kuhn's "normal periods" were, it now appears, misconstrued as dogmatic interludes *between* crises — actually they are full of crises of their own. And paradigms were, it now appears, misconstrued as the unquestioned basis of normal science — actually they are continually brought into question by anomalies. (I shall later consider how these revelations bear on Kuhn's description of normal research as "puzzle-solving.")

Kuhn's present view of "normal science" will, it seems to me, cause scarcely a flutter among those who reacted violently against what they saw, or thought they saw, in his first edition. Yet one essential feature of it remains: Kuhn still insists that normal research in each of his micro-communities is based upon consensus about paradigms. Now we have already seen that this consensus need not extend to metaphysics. So what are the paradigms, consensus upon which remains a pre-requisite for normal research? This brings me to the second major topic of Kuhn's recent writings.

Kuhn's critics pointed out that he used the term "paradigm" in several different ways. Kuhn agrees, and now distinguishes two fundamentally different senses of the term. In the first sense, paradigms are what we will find "by examining the behaviour of the members of a *previously determined* scientific community" (p. 175). Since for Kuhn the community will have been "previously determined" by sociological methods, he calls this the sociological sense of the term "paradigm." A paradigm in this sense is "the entire constellation of beliefs, values, techniques, and so on shared by the members of a given community" (p. 175). Kuhn now proposes to call it a "disciplinary matrix" instead of a paradigm.

But how seriously are we to take this specification of a disciplinary matrix as the *entire* constellation of shared beliefs, values, and techniques? What if sociological investigation yields a group whose members happen to share beliefs about the Trinity, values about drug-taking, and techniques of love-making? Such shared elements will not, clearly, figure in their "disciplinary matrix." The point is not entirely frivolous. Members of a sociologically-determined group may share many elements which are irrelevant to their scientific work. And conversely, they may fail to share elements which are scientifically relevant. Clearly, we shall have to employ a philosophical thesis to demarcate between what is relevant to scientific work and what not. Kuhn himself lists four typical components of a disciplinary matrix or paradigm in the sociological sense (the last component turns out, rather confusingly, to be paradigms in Kuhn's second major sense of the term).

44

First, there are "symbolic generalisations" like $f = ma$. Kuhn makes two excellent points about these. The first, not new, is that they can function partly as laws and partly as definitions of their symbols, that scientific practice depends greatly on which function they are performing, and that the balance between these functions often changes over time. The second point is that symbolic generalisations are often better regarded as law-sketches rather than laws, for they yield very different laws as they are applied to different types of situation.

The second component of Kuhn's disciplinary matrices are metaphysical beliefs like those in atoms, or in fields of force, or in heat as a substance, or in heat as a mode of motion. These were previously called metaphysical paradigms (e.g. p. 41). They play an important role in scientific work, for they "supply the group with preferred or permissible analogies and metaphors . . . help to determine what will be accepted as an explanation and as a puzzle-solution . . . [and] assist in the determination of the roster of unsolved puzzles and in the evaluation of the importance of each" (p. 184). And yet, as we already saw with atomism, Kuhn no longer insists that metaphysical beliefs be shared by all members of a given group. This means that the "normal scientific" work of a group can contain disagreement about the interpretation of their results, about whether a proposed explanation or "puzzle-solution" is adequate, and about whether an unsolved problem is a significant one or not. Previously, Kuhn suggested that such disagreements were eliminated from normal science by consensus over "metaphysical paradigms" (e.g. pp. 18, 48).

The third component of Kuhn's disciplinary matrices are values to be attached to theories, like consistency or the ability to yield precise predictions and to suggest fertile problems. He remarks that values are "more widely shared among different communities" than the other components of disciplinary matrices (p. 184). This is, of course, significant for the analysis of competition between communities, when scientists must "choose between incompatible ways of practising their discipline" (p. 185). But before turning to the problem of theory-choice, and to the famous "incommensurability thesis," I shall consider the fourth component of Kuhn's disciplinary matrices.

These are "concrete puzzle-solutions . . . employed as models or examples" (p. 175). They provide Kuhn's second major sense of the term "paradigm," which is philosophically "the deeper of the two" (p. 175). He now calls them "exemplars" instead of paradigms, and says that they are "the most novel and least understood aspect of this book" (p. 187). It is the common possession of different sets of exemplars which does most to determine the "community fine-structure of science" (p. 187).

Exemplars figure essentially, first of all, in scientific education. Textbooks confront the student with exemplary problem-solutions, and invite him to work out similar problems for himself. A typical group of problems will involve the application of the same symbolic generalisations to different types of situation. And in acquiring from exemplars the ability to solve problems, the student simultaneously learns about the content of physical theory and about the world to which it applies.

This is an excellent description of, and partial justification for, the practice of including problems in science textbooks. But for Kuhn its significance does not stop there. "Scientists," he says, "solve puzzles by modelling them on previous puzzle solutions" (p. 189). Kuhn's description of normal scientific research as "puzzle-solving" stems from an analogy with textbook education: what the working scientist does is basically the same as what the student does. But is the analogy entirely appropriate?

A crossword puzzle has an assured solution, and challenges the ingenuity of its solver. This is why Kuhn adopts the term: "I use the term 'puzzle' in order to emphasize that the difficulties which *ordinarily* confront even the very best scientists are, like crossword puzzles or chess puzzles, challenges only to his ingenuity. *He* is in difficulty, not current theory." ((1970a), p. 5, note 1). Now the textbook problems faced by students might with justice be called "puzzles": there is an assured solution known to their compiler (unsolved problems do not figure in textbooks); it is the student who is in difficulty, not current theory; hence, if he fails to solve a problem, he is blamed and not his theoretical tools. But is scientific research like this? Is it really the case that normally, when a working scientist fails to solve his problem, "the practitioner is blamed, not his tools" ((1970a), p. 7)? Kuhn can hardly continue to maintain this — for he now allows, as we have already seen, that any unsolved puzzle or anomaly can be seen as "the end of an existing paradigm." Moreover, Kuhn now thinks it desirable that some scientists do react in just this way, and blame anomalies on the "tools" and not on the practitioner — if they did not "there would be few or no revolutions" (p. 186). But such reactions are only possible, after all, because the mature scientist, unlike the science student, works on a problem which, unlike a puzzle, has no assured solution. It is always an open question whether the working scientist can model a satisfactory solution to his problem on previously obtained exemplary solutions to other problems. It seems to me, therefore, that "puzzle-solving" should disappear, and "problem-solving" resume its place, as the most adequate description of scientific research.

At all events, the focus of Kuhn's present interest in paradigms as exemplary problem-solutions is different. He is interested in the sort of knowledge one acquires from them, "the ability to recognise a given situation as like some but unlike others one has seen before" (p. 192), and in its repercussions on the problem of perception. The days of "sense-data" are long past. Nowadays we all agree that a great deal goes on (Kuhn calls it "neural programming") between the stimuli impinging upon us and our actual sensations. But Kuhn objects to describing this "programming" as a process, even an unconscious process, of interpreting stimuli in the light of rules or generalisations. For we cannot experiment with different ways of having a sensation, as we can with different ways of interpreting a sensation once we have had it (p. 194). Kuhn insists, therefore, that the ability, acquired from exemplars, to "programme" a stimulus in a certain way cannot be inculcated by learning explicit rules, and is "misconstrued" if reconstructed in terms of such rules (p. 192). It represents "tacit knowledge" in Polanyi's sense (p. 191). Kuhn answers the charge that such "knowing" is unanalysable and irrational by informing us that he is "currently experimenting with a computer program" which simulates it (pp. 191-2; also his (1971)).

Kuhn's point emerges more clearly with his example. The layman confronted with a cloud-chamber will *see* water droplets — he will need to *interpret* these as the track of a particle. The physicist, on the other hand, literally *sees* the track of a particle — he only needs to *interpret* this track as signifying, say, the presence of an electron. The difference in the initial perceptions should not be ascribed, says Kuhn, to differences in the amount of unconscious interpretation which is taking place. For "interpretation begins where perception ends. The two processes are not the same, and what perception leaves for interpretation to complete depends drastically on the nature and amount of prior experience and training" (p. 198).

What hinges on this rather subtle distinction? It enables Kuhn to mean it literally when he says that scientists imbued with different paradigms (now "exemplars") *see* the world differently. They do not, for Kuhn, see the same thing and merely interpret it differently. And this brings me to the problem of theory-choice and incommensurability.

Some of Kuhn's critics took him to be claiming that the victory of one theory over another in a scientific revolution is not brought about

47

by rational argument. Rational standards can play no role in theory-choice, since each theory itself sets different standards for science. The victory of the new theory is accomplished partly by irrational propaganda, which prods a few scientists into making the necessary "leap of faith," and partly by the demise through natural causes of the old-guard. Revolutionary change substitutes one way of viewing the world and of practising science in it for another one, incommensurable and not merely incompatible with the first. Hence science cannot be said to make progress through scientific revolutions — unless we define "progress" as what the scientific community decides.

Kuhn now makes it clear that he subscribes to none of these radical theses. On the problem of theory-choice his thesis is, he says, "a simple one, long familiar in philosophy of science" (p. 199). It is merely that scientists cannot *prove* that one theory is superior to another in such a way as to *compel assent* to it. Instead, they must employ rational persuasion, appealing in the process to those values "usually listed by philosophers of science: accuracy, simplicity, fruitfulness, and the like" (p. 199). Kuhn does emphasise one point which most philosophers of science ignore: that scientists, while agreeing in general on what is to be valued, can quite genuinely disagree about their verdict in concrete cases. He suggests that this "individual variability in the application of shared values may serve functions essential to science." For it helps to ensure that no promising line of research is neglected, and thereby serves as the "community's way of distributing risk" (p. 186).

For Kuhn, then, theory-choice is far from being an irrational affair — indeed, he finds Feyerabend's defence of irrationalism "vaguely obscene" ((1970b), p. 264). He does accept some responsibility for his critics' misunderstanding him on this: "I now think it a weakness of my original text that so little attention is given to such values as internal and external consistency in considering sources of crisis and factors in theory choice" (p. 185). Yet he insists, and here he convinces me at any rate, that it was a misunderstanding.

What, then, of progress through revolutionary change? Kuhn allows this also. He claims that the value most often appealed to in comparing rival theories is their "demonstrated ability to set up and solve puzzles presented by nature" (p. 205). And he says that Newton's theory progresses beyond Aristotle's, and Einstein's beyond Newton's, as "instruments for puzzle-solving" (p. 206). Thus Kuhn is far from relativism, for there are theory-independent standards in the light of which a new theory may constitute progress over the old.

What Kuhn still doubts is only whether progress in puzzle-solving, or rather problem-solving, ability constitutes "progress towards the truth," if we mean by this that Newton's ontology represents reality better than Aristotle's, or Einstein's better than Newton's. For in some respects, says Kuhn, Einstein's ontology marks a return to an Aristotelian ontology. Thus Kuhn sharply separates the empirical success of a theory from the verisimilitude or "truth-likeness" of its ontology. Here he differs from Popper. Notice, however, that they do not appear to differ on the criteria of empirical success: what Kuhn describes as a theory's "ability to set up and solve puzzles presented by nature," Popper describes as a theory's empirical content, its ability to provide analyses of a variety of physical situations (presented ideally by the theory itself, however, not "by nature"), and its corroboration, its predicting successfully what happens in those situations. Their difference is merely that Kuhn will not follow Popper in calling progress in content and corroboration an increase in verisimilitude.

The main point, however, is that Kuhn does not, and never did, subscribe to that radical form of the "incommensurability thesis" which implies relativism. Incommensurability for him means only that those nourished on differing exemplars will see the world differently and will consequently often use the same term in different senses. Kuhn insists that the resulting difficulties of communication "cannot be resolved simply by stipulating the definitions of troublesome terms": this is so because these terms have been learned from exemplars, and the ability to apply them cannot be made explicit in the form of a definition or rule or criterion (p. 201).

I must confess that I remain unconvinced by this, and especially by Kuhn's examples. One must admit, of course, that terms change their meanings with different theories, in the sense that, to use one of Kuhn's examples, a Copernican will class the earth as a planet while an Aristotelian will not. But I fail to see why, if this leads to a "communication problem," the Copernican cannot explain that on his theory the earth, since it revolves around the sun like the other planets, must be classed with them. I also fail to see why the Aristotelian cannot understand this, without of course necessarily accepting it — or why he cannot make the Copernican understand his own reasons for classing the earth differently.[9] The same applies to Kuhn's other examples ("element," "mixture," "unconstrained motion"). What are the "exemplary problem-solutions" which, according to Kuhn, give scientists their tacit knowledge of the meanings of such words? Is not their meaning given instead by perfectly articulable theories?

Not that too much hinges on all this. For Kuhn allows that when incommensurable concepts lead to "communication breakdown" there is a way out. The participants can "recognise each other as members of different language communities and then become translators" (p. 202). And having translated each other's theory, the participants can engage in rational persuasion.

Kuhn's apparatus of "language communities" and "translation" may seem a heavy-handed way to describe what goes on when adherents of rival theories use a term or two differently and try to understand each other — especially when Kuhn admits that they will share their everyday and most of their scientific language (p. 201). It is the linguistic parallel, however, which enables Kuhn to retain the last vestiges of one of his characteristic theses. In his first edition, Kuhn described the adoption of a new paradigm as a "conversion experience which cannot be forced" (p. 151) and which occurs "all at once" like the gestalt switch (p. 150). Critics took this to mean that theory-choice was an irrational leap-of-faith, an interpretation which Kuhn denies. But he does now say that we can be *persuaded* to adopt a theory without being *converted* to it: "The two experiences are not the same, an important distinction that I have only recently fully recognized" (p. 203).

Kuhn derives this new subtlety from his linguistic parallel. In being persuaded to adopt a new theory, a scientist will usually have to translate that theory into his own language. However: "To translate a theory or worldview into one's own language is not to make it one's own. For that one must go native, discover that one is thinking and working in, not simply translating out of, a language that was previously foreign" (p. 204). Since "going native" happens all at once, and one cannot choose to do it, it has the features of a "conversion experience." Kuhn suggests that these conversion experiences come more easily to the young (thus elaborating the adage "You can't teach an old dog new tricks"), and that without such an experience a scientist will be unable to do effective work even with a theory to which he might be fully persuaded. Therefore, he claims, such experiences remain "at the heart of the revolutionary process" (p. 204).

This is all that remains of the idea that the adoption of a new theory incommensurable with the old is accomplished by "community conversion." Incommensurability has ceased to be a logical affair, and conversion has become a purely psychological, as opposed even to a socio-psychological, matter. Again, this present view will hardly upset those who objected to what they saw, or thought they saw, in Kuhn's first edition.

In his recent writings, then, Kuhn disowns most of the challenging ideas ascribed to him by his critics. I suppose one should not complain of this, especially when Kuhn's "I never said it" ploy often convinces. His original text really does not contain some, at least, of the revolutionary views which so disturbed his critics (in particular the views that theory-choice is irrational and that progress through scientific revolutions is a myth). But I shall not substantiate this with textual analyses, since this review is already overly long.

Instead, I shall end by confessing that Kuhn's *Postscript* left me feeling a little disappointed. I find the new, more real Kuhn who emerges in it but a pale reflection of the old, revolutionary Kuhn. Perhaps this revolutionary Kuhn never really existed – but then it was necessary to invent him (since Feyerabend gives substance only to some of his parts). It is true that Kuhn continues to emphasise the importance of the social dimension of science. His *Postscript* ends as it began, by exhorting us to pay heed to the "community structure of science," and to compare it with the community structure of other disciplines. Such exhortations had to be taken seriously when they were accompanied by the claim that by following them we would overthrow many of our cherished ideas about the nature of science. But now, it seems, following them will merely acquaint us with rather humdrum sociological aspects of what many of us already thought takes place. Sociological puzzle-solving will not be subversive of our basic philosophical commitments. And with luck, philosophers of science can still decline the invitation to indulge in it without being "read out of the profession."

NOTES

1. Thomas S. Kuhn (1970), *The Structure of Scientific Revolutions* (International Encyclopedia of Unified Science, vol. II, no. 2), 2nd ed., enlarged, pp. xii+210. Chicago and London: The University of Chicago Press.
2. There are considerable overlaps between this *Postscript* and Kuhn's (1970 *b*) and (1971*a*) cited in the bibliography; I shall refer to all three.
3. Thus they would apply some 'internal-external' distinction and regard internal history as primary and external history as secondary. Cf. especially Lakatos (1971); and also Kuhn (1971*b*).
4. The "method of bibliographic coupling" (Kessler (1965)) is based on this technique. Kessler proposes it as a new method of compiling

subject-indexes to journals. But it is worth noting that he tests its efficacy by comparing its results with those achieved by "traditional" methods, which do involve reading the papers to be classified into groups.

5. Garfield (1970), p. 671. The result achieved was to produce a list of the fifty most cited authors for 1967, two of whom got the Nobel prize in 1969 (they were listed in positions 6 and 41). This result is described as "impressive" by its author.

6. I need hardly point out that their aversion is misguided, and that taking into account the content of citations, and of scientific activities in general, is a far from "subjective" method.

7. Current sociological research is not much help, however. Price and Beaver find that over half of those who helped produce the papers distributed in their "invisible college" were not themselves members of it ((1966, p. 1013). And Diana Crane finds that half the persons mentioned by members of her group as having "influenced" their work were not members of that group ((1969), p. 340). Such data might suggest that "professional communication across group lines" is not quite so arduous as Kuhn says it is. But data like this can tell us nothing about the presence or absence of critical debate between groups — to find out anything about this, the content of scientific papers would have to be studied.

8. It affects page 84, and brings it into line with what Kuhn wrote in his (1961), p. 179.

9. Perhaps it is worth noting that neither needs recourse to a theoretically neutral observation language — for at this stage of the discussion, adherents of incommensurability usually launch into a diatribe against that positivist daydream.

REFERENCES

CRANE, D. (1969) Social Structure in a Group of Scientists: A Test of the 'Invisible College' Hypothesis. *American Sociological Review*, 34, 335-52.

GARFIELD, E. (1970) Citation Indexing for Studying Science. *Nature*, 227, August 15, 669-71.

KESSLER, M. M. (1965) Comparison of the Results of Bibliographic Coupling and Analytic Subject Indexing. *American Documentation*, 16, 223-33.

KUHN, T. S. (1961) The Function of Measurement in Modern Physical Science. *Isis*, 52, 161-93.

KUHN, T. S. (1970a) Logic of Discovery or Psychology of Research. *Criticism and the Growth of Knowledge*. Eds. I. Lakatos and A. Musgrave. London and New York: Cambridge University Press.

KUHN, T. S. (1970b) Reflections on My Critics. *Ibid.*

KUHN, T. S. (1971a) Second Thoughts on Paradigms. *The Structure of Scientific Theories*. Ed. F. Suppe. Urbana: Illinois University Press.

KUHN, T. S. (1971b) Notes on Lakatos, *Boston Studies in the Philosophy of Science.* Eds. R. Buck and R. S. Cohen. Dordrecht: D. Reidel Publishing Company.

LAKATOS, I. (1971) History of Science and its Rational Reconstructions. *Boston Studies in the Philosophy of Science,* Vol. 8. Eds. R. Buck and R. S. Cohen. Dordrecht: D. Reidel Publishing Company.

PRICE, D. J. and BEAVER, D. de B. (1966) Collaboration in an Invisible College. *American Psychologist,* 21, 1011-18.

EPISTEMOLOGICAL CRISES, DRAMATIC NARRATIVE, AND THE PHILOSOPHY OF SCIENCE

ALASDAIR MACINTYRE

I

What is an epistemological crisis? Consider, first, the situation of ordinary agents who are thrown into such crises. Someone who has believed that he was highly valued by his employers and colleagues is suddenly fired; someone proposed for membership of a club whose members were all, so he believed, close friends is blackballed. Or someone falls in love and needs to know what the loved one *really* feels; someone falls out of love and needs to know how he or she can possibly have been so mistaken in the other. For all such persons the relationship of *seems* to *is* becomes crucial. It is in such situations that ordinary agents who have never learned anything about academic philosophy are apt to rediscover for themselves versions of the other-minds problem and the problem of the justification of induction. They discover, that is, that there is a problem about the rational justification of inferences from premises about the behaviour of other people to conclusions about their thoughts, feelings, and attitudes and of inferences from premises about how individuals have acted in the past to conclusions expressed as generalizations about their behaviour — generalizations which would enable us to make reasonably reliable predications about their future behaviour. What they took to be evidence pointing unambiguously in some one direction now turns out to have been equally susceptible of rival interpretations. Such a discovery is often paralysing, and were we all of us all of the time to have to reckon with the multiplicity of possible interpretations open to us, social life as we know it could scarcely continue. For social life is sustained by the assumption that we are, by and large, able to construe each others' behaviour — that error, deception, self-deception, irony, and ambiguity, although omnipresent in social life, are not so pervasive as to render reliable reasoning and reasonable action impossible. But can this assumption in any way be vindicated?

Consider what it is to share a culture. It is to share schemata

54

which are at one and the same time constitutive of and normative for intelligible action by myself and are also means for my interpretations of the actions of others. My ability to understand what you are doing and my ability to act intelligibly (both to myself and to others) are one and the same ability. It is true that I cannot master these schemata without also acquiring the means to deceive, to make more or less elaborate jokes, to exercise irony and utilize ambiguity, but it is also, and even more importantly, true that my ability to conduct any successful transactions depends on my presenting myself to most people most of the time in unambiguous, unironical, undeceiving, intelligible ways. It is these schemata which enable inferences to be made from premises about past behaviour to conclusions about future behaviour and present inner attitudes. They are not, of course, empirical generalisations; they are prescriptions for interpretation. But while it is they which normally preserve us from the pressure of the other-minds problem and the problem of induction, it is precisely they which can in certain circumstances thrust those very problems upon us.

For it is not only that an individual may rely on the schemata which have hitherto informed all his interpretations of social life and find that he or she has been led into radical error or deception, so that for the first time the schemata are put in question — perhaps for the first time they also in this moment become visible to the individual who employs them — but it is also the case that the individual may come to recognise the possibility of systematically different possibilities of interpretation, of the existence of alternative and rival schemata which yield mutually incompatible accounts of what is going on around him. Just this is the form of epistemological crisis encountered by ordinary agents and it is striking that there is not a single account of it anywhere in the literature of academic philosophy. Perhaps this is an important symptom of the condition of that discipline. But happily we do possess one classic study of such crises. It is Shakespeare's *Hamlet*.

Hamlet arrives back from Wittenberg with too many schemata available for interpreting the events at Elsinore of which already he is a part. There is the revenge schema of the Norse sagas; there is the renaissance courtier's schema; there is a Machiavellian schema about competition for power. But he not only has the problem of which schema to apply, he also has the other ordinary agents' problem: whom now to believe? His mother? Rosencrantz and Guildenstern? His father's ghost? Until he has adopted some schema he does not know what to treat as evidence; until he knows what to treat as evidence he cannot tell which schema to adopt. Trapped in this epistemological circularity the general form of his problem is: 'what is going on here?' Thus Hamlet's problem is close to that of the literary critics who have asked: "What is going on in *Hamlet?*" And it is close to that of directors who have asked: "What should be cut and what should be included in my production so that the audience may understand what is going on in *Hamlet?*"

The resemblance between Hamlet's problem and that of the critics and directors is worth noticing; for it suggests that both are asking a question which could equally well be formulated as: 'what is going on in *Hamlet?*' or 'how ought the narrative of these events to be constructed?' Hamlet's problems arise because the dramatic narrative of his family and of the kingdom of Denmark through which he identified his own place in society and his relationships to others has been disrupted by radical interpretative doubts. His task is to reconstitute, to rewrite that narrative, reversing his understanding of past events in the light of present responses to his probing. This probing is informed by two ideals, truth and intelligibility, and the pursuit of both is not always easily coherent. The discovery of an hitherto unsuspected truth is just what may disrupt an hitherto intelligible account. And of course while Hamlet tries to discover a true and intelligible narrative of the events involving his parents and Claudius, Gertrude and Claudius are trying to discover a true and intelligible narrative of Hamlet's investigation. To be unable to render oneself intelligible is to risk being taken to be mad, is, if carried far enough, to be mad. And madness or death may always be the outcomes which prevent the resolution of an epistemological crisis, for an epistemological crisis is always a crisis in human relationships.

When an epistemological crisis is resolved, it is by the construction of a new narrative which enables the agent to understand *both* how he or she could intelligibly have held his or her original beliefs *and* how he or she could have been so drastically misled by them. The narrative in terms of which he or she at first understood and ordered experiences is itself made into the subject of an enlarged narrative. The agent has come to understand how the criteria of truth and understanding must be reformulated. He has had to become epistemologically self-conscious and at a certain point he may have come to acknowledge two conclusions: the first is that his new forms of understanding may themselves in turn come to be put in question at any time; the second is that, because in such crises the criteria of truth, intelligibility, and rationality may always them-

56

selves be put in question — as they are in *Hamlet* — we are never in a position to claim that now we possess the truth or now we are fully rational. The most that we can claim is that this is the best account which anyone has been able to give so far, and that our beliefs about what the marks of 'a best account so far' are will themselves change in what are at present unpredictable ways.

Philosophers have often been prepared to acknowledge this historical character in respect of scientific theories; but they have usually wanted to exempt their own thinking from the same historicity. So, of course, have writers of dramatic narrative; *Hamlet* is unique among plays in its openness to reinterpretation. Consider, by contrast, Jane Austen's procedure in *Emma*. Emma insists on viewing her protegé, Harriet, as a character in an eighteenth-century romance. She endows her, deceiving both herself and Harriet, with the conventional qualities of the heroine of such a romance. Harriet's parentage is not known; Emma converts her into the foundling heroine of aristocratic birth so common in such romances. And she designs for Harriet precisely the happy ending of such a romance, marriage to a superior being. By the end of *Emma* Jane Austen has provided Emma with some understanding of what it was in herself that had led her not to perceive the untruthfulness of her interpretation of the world in terms of romance. *Emma* has become a narrative about narrative. But Emma, although she experiences moral reversal, has only a minor epistemological crisis, if only because the standpoint which she now, through the agency of Mr. Knightly, has come to adopt, is presented as though it were one from which *the* world as it is can be viewed. False interpretation has been replaced not by a more adequate interpretation, which itself in turn may one day be transcended, but simply by the truth. We of course can see that Jane Austen is merely replacing one interpretation by another, but Jane Austen herself fails to recognise this and so has to deprive Emma of this recognition too.

Philosophers have customarily been Emmas and not Hamlets, except that in one respect they have often been even less perceptive than Emma. For Emma it becomes clear that her movement towards the truth necessarily had a moral dimension. Neither Plato nor Kant would have demurred. But the history of epistemology, like the history of ethics itself, is usually written as though it were not a moral narrative, that is, in fact as though it were not a narrative. For narrative requires an evaluative framework in which good or bad character helps to produce unfortunate or happy outcomes.

One further aspect of narratives and their role in epistemological crises remains to be noticed. I have suggested that epistemological progress consists in the construction and reconstruction of more adequate narratives and forms of narrative and that epistemological crises are occasions for such reconstruction. But if this were really the case then two kinds of questions would need to be answered. The first would be of the form: how does this progress begin? What are the narratives from which we set out? The second would be of the form: how is it, then, that narrative is not only given so little place by thinkers from Descartes onwards, but has so often before and after been treated as a merely aesthetic form? The answers to these questions are not entirely unconnected.

We begin from myth, not only from the myths of primitive peoples, but from those myths or fairy stories which are essential to a well-ordered childhood. Bruno Bettelheim has written: "Before and well into the oedipal period (roughly, the ages between three and six or seven), the child's experience of the world is chaotic. . . . During and because of the oedipal struggles, the outside world comes to hold more meaning for the child and he begins to try to make some sense of it . . . As a child listens to a fairy tale, he gets ideas about how he may create order out of the chaos that is his inner life."[1] It is from fairy tales, so Bettelheim argues, that the child learns how to engage himself with and perceive an order in social reality; and the child who is deprived of the right kind of fairy tale at the right age later on is apt to have to adopt strategies to evade a reality he has not learned how to interpret or to handle.

"The child asks himself, 'Who am I? Where did I come from? How did the world come into being? Who created man and all the animals? What is the purpose of life?'. . . . He wonders who or what brings adversity upon him and what can protect him against it. Are there benevolent powers in addition to his parents? *Are* his parents benevolent powers? How should he form himself, and why? Is there hope for him, though he may have done wrong? Why did all this happen to him? What will it mean to his future?"[2] The child originally requires answers that are true to his own experience, but of course the child comes to learn the inadequacy of that experience. Bettelheim points out that the young child told by adults that the world is a globe suspended in space and spinning at incredible speeds may feel bound to repeat what they say, but would find it immensely more plausible to be told that the earth is held up by a giant. But in time the young child learns that what the adults told him is indeed true. And such a child may well become a Descartes, one who feels that all narratives are misleading fables when com-

58

pared with what he now takes to be the solid truth of physics.

Yet to raise the question of truth need not entail rejecting myth or story as the appropriate and perhaps the only appropriate form in which certain truths can be told. The child may become not a Descartes, but a Vico or a Hamann who writes a story about how he had to escape from the hold which the stories of his childhood and the stories of the childhood of the human race originally had upon him in order to discover how stories can be true stories. Such a narrative will be itself a history of epistemological transitions and this narrative may well be brought to a point at which questions are thrust upon the narrator which make it impossible for him to continue to use it as an instrument of interpretation. Just this, of course, happens to Descartes, who having abjured history as a means to truth, recounts to us his own history as the medium through which the search for truth is to be carried on. For Descartes and for others this moment is that at which an epistemological crisis occurs. And all those questions which the child has asked of the teller of fairy tales arise in a new adult form. Philosophy is now set the same task that had once been set for myth.

II

Descartes's description of his own epistemological crisis has, of course, been uniquely influential. Yet Descartes radically misdescribes his own crisis and thus has proved a highly misleading guide to the nature of epistemological crises in general. The agent who is plunged into an epistemological crisis knows something very important: that a schema of interpretation which he has trusted so far has broken down irremediably in certain highly specific ways. So it is with Hamlet. Descartes, however, starts from the assumption that he knows nothing whatsoever until he can discover a presupposition-less first principle on which all else can be founded. Hamlet's doubts are formulated against a background of what he takes to be — rightly — well-founded beliefs; Descartes's doubt is intended to lack any such background. It is to be contextless doubt. Hence also that tradition of philosophical teaching arises which presupposes that Cartesian doubts can be entertained by anyone at any place or time. But of course someone who really believed that he knew nothing would not even know how to begin on a course of radical doubt; for he would have no conception of what his task might be, of what it would be to settle his doubts and to acquire well-founded beliefs.

Conversely, anyone who knows enough to know *that* does indeed possess a set of extensive epistemological beliefs which he is not putting in doubt at all.

Descartes's failure is complex. First of all he does not recognise that among the features of the universe which he is not putting in doubt is his own capacity not only to use the French and the Latin languages, but even to express the same thought in both languages; and as a consequence he does not put in doubt what he has inherited in and with these languages, namely, a way of ordering both thought and the world expressed in a set of meanings. These meanings have a history; seventeenth-century Latin bears the marks of having been the language of scholasticism, just as scholasticism was itself marked by the influence of twelfth and thirteenth-century Latin. It was perhaps because the presence of his languages was invisible to the Descartes of the *Discours* and the *Meditationes* that he did not notice either what Gilson pointed out in detail, how much of what he took to be the spontaneous reflections of his own mind was in fact a repetition of sentences and phrases from his school textbooks. Even the *Cogito* is to be found in Saint Augustine.

What thus goes unrecognised by Descartes is the presence not only of languages, but of a tradition — a tradition that he took himself to have successfully disowned. It was from this tradition that he inherited his epistemological ideals. For at the core of this tradition was a conception of knowledge as analogous to vision: the mind's eye beholds its objects by the light of reason. At the same time this tradition wishes to contrast sharply knowledge and sense-experience, including visual experience. Hence there is metaphorical incoherence at the heart of every theory of knowledge in this Platonic and Augustinian tradition, an incoherence which Descartes unconsciously reproduces. Thus Descartes also cannot recognise that he is responding not only to the timeless demands of scepticism, but to a highly specific crisis in one particular social and intellectual tradition.

One of the signs that a tradition is in crisis is that its accustomed ways for relating *seems* and *is* begin to break down. Thus the pressures of scepticism become more urgent and attempts to do the impossible, to refute scepticism once and for all, become projects of central importance to the culture and not mere private academic enterprises. Just this happens in the late middle ages and the sixteenth century. Inherited modes of ordering experience reveal too many rival possibilities of interpretation. It is no accident that there are a multiplicity of rival interpretations of both the thought and the lives of such figures as Luther and Machiavelli in a way that there are not for such equally rich and complex figures as Abelard and Aquinas. Ambiguity, the possibility of alternative interpretations, becomes a central feature of human character and activity. *Hamlet* is Shakespeare's brilliant mirror to the age, and the difference between Shakespeare's account of epistemological crises and Descartes's is now clear. For Shakespeare invites us to reflect on the crisis of the self as a crisis in the tradition which has formed the self; Descartes by his attitude to history and to fable has cut himself off from the possibility of recognising himself; he has invented an unhistorical self-endorsed self-consciousness and tries to describe his epistemological crisis in terms of it. Small wonder that he misdescribes it.

Consider by contrast Galileo. When Galileo entered the scientific scene, he was confronted by much more than the conflict between the Ptolemaic and Copernican astronomies. The Ptolemaic system was itself inconsistent both with the widely accepted Platonic requirements for a true astronomy and with the perhaps even more widely accepted principles of Aristotelian physics. These latter were in turn inconsistent with the findings over two centuries of scholars at Oxford, Paris, and Padua about motion. Not surprisingly, instrumentalism flourished as a philosophy of science and Osiander's instrumentalist reading of Copernicus was no more than the counterpart to earlier instrumentalist interpretations of the Ptolemaic system. Instrumentalism, like attempts to refute scepticism, is characteristically a sign of a tradition in crisis.

Galileo resolves the crisis by a threefold strategy. He rejects instrumentalism; he reconciles astronomy and mechanics; and he redefines the place of experiment in natural science. The old mythological empiricist view of Galileo saw him as appealing to the facts against Ptolemy and Aristotle; what he actually did was to give a new account of what an appeal to the facts had to be. Wherein lies the superiority of Galileo to his predecessors? The answer is that he, for the first time, enables the work of all his predecessors to be evaluated by a common set of standards. The contributions of Plato, Aristotle, the scholars at Merton College, Oxford, and at Padua, the work of Copernicus himself at last all fall into place. Or, to put matters in another and equivalent way: the history of late medieval science can finally be cast into a coherent narrative. Galileo's work implies a rewriting of the narrative which constitutes the scientific tradition. For it now became retrospectively possible to identify those anomalies which had been genuine counterexamples to received theories from those anomalies which could justifiably be dealt with by ad hoc explanatory devices or even ignored. It also became retrospectively possible to see how the various elements of various theories had fared in their encounters with other theories and with observations and experiments, and to understand how the form in which they had survived bore the marks of those encounters. A theory always bears the marks of its passage through time and the theories with which Galileo had to deal were no exception.

Let me cast the point which I am trying to make about Galileo in a way which, at first sight, is perhaps paradoxical. We are apt to suppose that because Galileo was a peculiarly great scientist, therefore he has his own peculiar place in the history of science. I am suggesting instead that it is because of his peculiarly important place in the history of science that he is accounted a particularly great scientist. The criterion of a successful theory is that it enable us to understand its predecessors in a newly intelligible way. It, at one and the same time, enables us to understand precisely why its predecessors have to be rejected or modified and also why, without and before its illumination, past theory could have remained credible. It introduces new standards for evaluating the past. It recasts the narrative which constitutes the continuous reconstruction of the scientific tradition.

This connection between narrative and tradition has hitherto gone almost unnoticed, perhaps because tradition has usually been taken seriously only by conservative social theorists. Yet those features of tradition which emerge as important when the connection between tradition and narrative is understood are ones which conservative theorists are unlikely to attend to. For what constitutes a tradition is a conflict of interpretations of that tradition, a conflict which itself has a history susceptible of rival interpretations. If I am a Jew, I have to recognise that the tradition of Judaism is partly constituted by a continuous argument over what is means to be a Jew. Suppose I am an American: the tradition is one partly constituted by continuous argument over what it means to be an American and partly by continuous argument over what it means to have rejected tradition. If I am an historian, I must acknowledge that the tradition of historiography is partly, but centrally, constituted by arguments about what history is and ought to be, from Hume and Gibbon to Namier and Edward Thompson. Notice that all three kinds of tradition — religious, political, intellectual — involve epistemological debate as a necessary feature of their conflicts. For it is not merely that different participants in a tradition disagree; they also disagree as to how to characterize their disagreements and as to how to resolve them. They disagree as to what constitutes appropriate reasoning, decisive evidence, conclusive proof.

A tradition then not only embodies the narrative of an argument, but is only to be recovered by an argumentative retelling of that narrative which will itself be in conflict with other argumentative retellings. Every tradition therefore is always in danger of lapsing into incoherence, and when a tradition does so lapse it sometimes can only be recovered by a revolutionary reconstitution. Precisely such a reconstitution of a tradition which had lapsed into incoherence was the work of Galileo.

It will now be obvious why I introduced the notion of tradition by alluding negatively to the viewpoint of conservative theorists. For they, from Burke onwards, have wanted to counterpose tradition and reason and tradition and revolution. Not reason, but prejudice; not revolution, but inherited precedent; these are Burke's key oppositions. Yet if the present arguments are correct it is traditions which are the bearers of reason, and traditions at certain periods actually require and need revolutions for their continuance. Burke saw the French Revolution as merely the negative overthrow of all that France had been and many French conservatives have agreed with him, but later thinkers as different as Péguy and Hilaire Belloc were able retrospectively to see the great revolution as reconstituting a more ancient France, so that Jeanne D'Arc and Danton belong within the same single, if immensely complex, tradition.

Conflict arises, of course, not only within but between traditions, and such a conflict tests the resources of each contending tradition. It is yet another mark of a degenerate tradition that it has contrived a set of epistemological defences which enable it to avoid being put in question or at least to avoid recognising that it is being put in question by rival traditions. This is, for example, part of the degeneracy of modern astrology, of some types of psychoanalytic thought, and of liberal Protestantism. Although, therefore, any feature of any tradition, any theory, any practice, any belief can always under certain conditions be put in question, the practice of putting in question, whether within a tradition or between traditions, itself always requires the context of a tradition. Doubting is a more complex activity than some sceptics have realised. To say to oneself or to someone else "Doubt all your beliefs here and now" without reference to historical or autobiographical context is not meaningless; but it is an invitation not to philosophy, but to mental breakdown, or rather to philosophy as a means of mental breakdown. Descartes concealed from himself, as we have seen, an unacknowledged background of beliefs which rendered what he was doing intelligible and sane to himself and to others. But suppose that he had put that background in question too — what would have happened to him then?

We are not without clues, for we do have the record of the approach to breakdown in the life of one great philosopher. "For I have already shown," wrote Hume,

> that the understanding, when it acts alone, and according to its most general principles, entirely subverts itself, and leaves not the lowest degree of evidence in any proposition, either in philosophy or common life ... The *intense* view of these manifold contradictions and imperfections in human reason has so wrought upon me, and heated my brain, that I am ready to reject all belief and reasoning, and can look upon no opinion even as more probable or likely than another. Where am I, or what? From what causes do I derive my existence, and to what condition shall I return? Whose favour shall I court, and whose anger must I dread? What beings surround me? and on whom have I any influence? I am confronted with all these questions, and begin to fancy myself in the most deplorable condition imaginable, inviron'd with the deepest darkness and utterly depriv'd of the use of every member and faculty.[3]

[*Treatise*, ed. Selby-Bigge, Bk. I, iv, vii, pp. 267-69]

We may note three remarkable features of Hume's cry of pain. First, like Descartes, he has set a standard for the foundations of his beliefs which could not be met; hence all beliefs founder equally. He has not asked if he can find good reasons for preferring in respect of the best criteria of reason and truth available some among others of the limited range of possibilities of belief which actually confront him in his particular cultural situation. Secondly, he is in consequence thrust back without any answers or possibility of answers upon just that range of questions that, according to Bettelheim, underlie the whole narrative enterprise in early childhood. There is indeed the most surprising and illuminating correspondence between the questions which Bettelheim ascribes to the child and the questions framed by the adult, but desperate, Hume. For Hume by his radical scepticism has lost any means of making himself — or others — intelligible to himself, let alone, to others. His very scepticism itself becomes unintelligible.

There is perhaps a possible world in which 'empiricism' would have become the name of a mental illness, while 'paranoia' would be the name of a well-accredited theory of knowledge. For in this world empiricists would be consistent and unrelenting — unlike Hume —

and they would thus lack any means to order their experience of other people or of nature. Even a knowledge of formal logic would not help them; for until they knew how to order their experiences they would possess neither sentences to formalize nor reasons for choosing one way of formalizing them rather than another. Their world would indeed be reduced to that chaos which Bettelheim perceives in the child at the beginning of the oedipal phase. Empiricism would lead not to sophistication, but to regression. Paranoia by contrast would provide considerable resources for living in the world. The empiricist maxims 'Believe only what can be based upon sense-experience' or Occam's razor, would leave us bereft of all generalizations and therefore of all attitudes towards the future (or the past). They would isolate us in a contentless present. But the paranoid maxims 'Interpret everything which happens as an outcome of envious malice' and 'Everyone and everything will let you down' receive continuous confirmation for those who adopt them. Hume cannot answer the question: "What beings surround me?" But Kafka knew the answer to this very well: "In fact the clock has certain personal relationships to me, like many things in the room, save that now, particularly since I gave notice — or rather since I was given notice . . . — they seem to be beginning to turn their backs on me, above all the calendar. . . . Lately it is as if it had been metamorphosed. Either it is absolutely uncommunicative — for example, you want its advice, you go up to it, but the only thing it says is 'Feast of the Reformation' — which probably has a deeper significance, but who can discover it? — or, on the contrary, it is nastily ironic."[4]

So in this possible world they will speak of Hume's Disease and of Kafka's Theory of Knowledge. Yet is this possible world so different from that which we inhabit? What leads us to segregate at least some types of mental illness from ordinary, sane behaviour is that they presuppose and embody ways of interpreting the natural and social world which are radically discordant with our customary and, as we take it, justified modes of interpretation. That is, certain types of mental illness seem to presuppose rival theories of knowledge. Conversely every theory of knowledge offers us schemata for accepting some interpretations of the natural and social world rather than others. As Hamlet discovered earlier, the categories of psychiatry and of epistemology must be to some extent interdefinable.

III

What I have been trying to sketch are a number of conceptual connections which link such notions as those of an epistemological crisis, a narrative, a tradition, natural science, scepticism, and madness. There is one group of recent controversies in which the connections between these concepts has itself become a central issue. I refer, of course, to the debates which originated from the confrontation between Thomas Kuhn's philosophy of science and the views of those philosophers of science who in one way or another are the heirs of Sir Karl Popper. It is not surprising therefore that the positions which I have taken should imply conclusions about those controversies, conclusions which are not quite the same as those of any of the major participants. Yet it is perhaps because the concepts which I have examined — such as those on epistemological crisis and of the relationship of conflict to tradition — have provided the largely unexamined background to the recent debates that their classification may in fact help to resolve some of the issues. In particular I shall want to argue that the positions of some of the most heated antagonists — notably Thomas Kuhn and Imre Lakatos — can be seen to converge once they are emended in ways towards which the protagonists themselves have moved in their successive reformulations of their positions.

One very striking new conclusion will however also emerge. For I shall want to reinforce my thesis that dramatic narrative is the crucial form for the understanding of human action and I shall want to argue that natural science can be a rational form of enquiry if and only if the writing of a true dramatic narrative — that is, of history understood in a particular way — can be a rational activity. Scientific reason turns out to be subordinate to, and intelligible only in terms of, historical reason. And if this is true of the natural sciences, *a fortiori* it will be true also of the social sciences.

It is therefore sad that social scientists have all too often treated the work of writers such as Kuhn and Lakatos as it stood. Kuhn's writing in particular has been invoked time and again — for a period of ten years or so, a ritual obeisance towards Kuhn seems almost to have been required in presidential addresses to the American Political Science Association — to license the theoretical failures of social science. But while Kuhn's work uncriticised — or for that matter Popper or Lakatos uncriticised — represent a threat to our understanding, Kuhn's work criticised provides an illuminating application for the ideas which I have been defending.

My criticisms of Kuhn will fall into three parts. In the first I shall suggest that his earlier formulations of his position are much more radically flawed than he himself has acknowledged. I shall then argue that it is his failure to recognise the true character of the flaws in his earlier formulations which leads to the weakness of his later revisions. Finally I shall suggest a more adequate form of revision.

What Kuhn originally presented was an account of epistemological crises in natural science which is essentially the same as the Cartesian account of epistemological crises in philosophy. This account was superimposed on a view of natural science which seems largely indebted to the writings of Michael Polanyi (Kuhn nowhere acknowledges any such debt). What Polanyi had shown is that all justification takes place within a social tradition and that the pressures of such a tradition enforce often unrecognised rules by means of which discrepant pieces of evidence or difficult questions are often put on one side with the tacit assent of the scientific community. Polanyi is the Burke of the philosophy of science, and I mean this analogy with political and moral philosophy to be taken with great seriousness. For all my earlier criticisms of Burke now become relevant to the criticism of Polanyi. Polanyi, like Burke, understands tradition as essentially conservative and essentially unitary. (Paul Feyerabend — at first sight so different from Polanyi — agrees with Polanyi in his understanding of tradition. It is just because he so understands the scientific tradition that he rejects it and has turned himself into the Emerson of the philosophy of science; not "Every man his own Jesus," but "Every man his own Galileo.") He does not see the omnipresence of conflict — sometimes latent — within living traditions. It is because of this that anyone who took Polanyi's view would find it very difficult to explain how a transition might be made from one tradition to another or how a tradition which had lapsed into incoherence might be reconstructed. Since reason operates only *within* traditions and communities according to Polanyi, such a transition or a reconstruction could not be a work of reason. It would have to be a leap in the dark of some kind.

Polanyi never carried his argument to this point. But what is a major difficulty in Polanyi's position was presented by Kuhn as though it were a discovery. Kuhn did of course recognise very fully how a scientific tradition may lapse into incoherence. And he must have (with Feyerabend) the fullest credit for recognising in an original way the significance and character of incommensurability. But the conclusions which he draws, namely that "proponents of competing paradigms must fail to make complete contact with each other's viewpoints" and that the transition from one paradigm to another requires a "conversion experience" do not follow from his premises concerning incommensurability. These last are threefold: adherents of rival paradigms during a scientific revolution disagree about what set of problems provide the test for a successful paradigm in that particular scientific situation; their theories embody very different concepts; and they "see different things when they look from the same point in the same direction." Kuhn concludes that "just because it is a transition between incommensurables" the transition cannot be made step by step; and he uses the expression "gestalt switch" as well as "conversion experience." What is important is that Kuhn's account of the transition requires an additional premise. It is not just that the adherents of rival paradigms disagree, but that *every* relevant area of rationality is invaded by that disagreement. It is not just that threefold incommensurability is present, but rationality apparently cannot be present in any other form. Now this additional premise would indeed follow from Polanyi's position and if Kuhn's position is understood as presupposing something like Polanyi's, then Kuhn's earlier formulations of his positions become all too intelligible; and so do the accusations of irrationalism by his critics, accusations which Kuhn professes not to understand.

What follows from the position thus formulated? It is that scientific revolutions are epistemological crises understood in a Cartesian way. Everything is put in question simultaneously. There is no rational continuity between the situation at the time immediately preceding the crisis and any situation following it. To such a crisis the language of evangelical conversion would indeed be appropriate. We might indeed begin to speak with the voice of Pascal, lamenting that the highest achievement of reason is to learn what reason cannot achieve. But of course, as we have already seen, the Cartesian view of epistemological crises is false; it can never be the case that everything is put in question simultaneously. That would indeed lead to large and unintelligible lacunas not only in the history of practices, such as those of the natural sciences, but also in the personal biographies of scientists.

Moreover Kuhn does not distinguish between two kinds of transition experience. The experience which he is describing seems to be that of the person who having been thoroughly educated into practices defined and informed by one paradigm has to make the transition to a form of scientific practice defined and informed by some radically different paradigm. Of this kind of person what Kuhn asserts may well on occasion be true. But such a scientist is always being invited to make a transition that has already been made by others; the very characterization of his situation presupposes that the new paradigm is already operative while the old still retains some power. But what of the very different type of transition made by those scientists who first invented or discovered the new paradigm? Here Kuhn's divergences from Polanyi ought to have saved him from his original Polanyi-derived conclusion. For Kuhn does recognise very fully and insightfully how traditions lapse into incoherence. What some, at least, of those who are educated into such a tradition may come to recognise is the gap between its *own* epistemological ideals and its actual practices. Of those who recognise this some may tend towards scepticism and some towards instrumentalism. Just this, as we have already seen, characterised late medieval and sixteenth-century science. What the scientific genius, such as Galileo, achieves in his transition, then, is not only a new way of understanding nature, but also and inseparably a new way of understanding the old science's way of understanding nature. It is because only from the standpoint of the new science can the inadequacy of the old science be characterized that the new science is taken to be more adequate than the old. It is from the standpoint of the new science that the continuities of narrative history are reestablished.

Kuhn has of course continuously modified his earlier formulations and to some degree his position. He has in particular pointed out forcefully to certain of his critics that it is they who have imputed to him the thesis that scientific revolutions are nonrational or irrational events, a conclusion which he has never drawn himself. His own position is "that, if history or any other empirical discipline leads us to believe that the development of science depends essentially on behavior that we have previously thought to be irrational, then we should conclude not that science is irrational, but that our notion of rationality needs adjustment here and there."

Feyerabend however, beginning from the same premises as Kuhn, has drawn on his own behalf the very conclusion which Kuhn so abhors. And surely if scientific revolutions were as Kuhn describes them, if there were nothing more to them than such features as the threefold incommensurability, Feyerabend would be in the right. Thus if Kuhn is to, as he says, "adjust" the notion of rationality, he will have to find the signs of rationality in some feature of scientific revolutions to which he has not yet attended. Are there such features? Certainly, but they belong precisely to the history of these episodes. It is more rational to accept one theory or paradigm and to reject its predecessor when the later theory or paradigm provides a stand-point from which the acceptance, the life-story, and the rejection of the previous theory or paradigm can be recounted in more intelligible historical narrative than previously. An understanding of the concept of the superiority of one physical theory to another requires a prior understanding of the concept of the superiority of one historical narrative to another. The theory of scientific rationality has to be embedded in a philosophy of history.

What is carried over from one paradigm to another are epistemological ideals and a correlative understanding of what constitutes the progress of a single intellectual life. Just as Descartes's account of his own epistemological crisis was only possible by reason of Descartes's ability to recount his own history, indeed to live his life as a narrative about to be cast into a history — an ability which Descartes himself could not recognise without falsifying his own account of epistemological crises — so Kuhn and Feyerabend recount the history of epistemological crises as moments of almost total discontinuity without noticing the historical continuity which makes their own intelligible narratives possible. Something very like this position, which I have approached through a criticism of Kuhn, was reached by Lakatos in the final stages of his journey away from Popper's initial positions.

If Polanyi is the Burke of the philosophy of science and Feyerabend the Emerson, then Popper himself or at least his disciples inherit the role of J. S. Mill — as Feyerabend has already noticed. The truth is to be approached through the free clash of opinion. The logic of the moral sciences is to be replaced by *Logik der Forschung*. Where Burke sees reasoning only within the context of tradition and Feyerabend sees the tradition as merely repressive of the individual, Popper has rightly tried to make something of the notion of rational tradition. What hindered this attempt was the Popperian insistence on replacing the false methodology of induction by a new methodology. This history of Popper's own thought and of that of his most gifted followers was for quite a number of years the history of successive attempts to replace Popper's original falsificationism by some more adequate version, each of which in turn fell prey to counterexamples from the history of science. From one point of view the true heir of these attempts is Feyerabend; for it is he who has formulated the completely general thesis that all such attempts were doomed to failure. There is *no* set of rules as to how science *must* proceed and all attempts to discover such a set founder in their encounter with actual history of science. But when Lakatos had finally accepted this he moved on to new ground.

In 1968, while he was still a relatively conservative Popperian, Lakatos had written: "the appraisal is rather of a *series of theories* than of an isolated *theory.*" He went on to develop this notion into that of a research program. The notion of a research program is of course oriented to the future and there was therefore a tension between Lakatos's use of this notion and his recognition that it is only retrospectively that a series of theories can be appraised. In other words what is appraised is always a history; for it is not just a series of theories which is appraised, but a series which stand in various complex relationships to each other through time which is appraised. Indeed what we take to be a single theory is always "a growing developing entity, one which cannot be considered as a static structure."[5] Consider for example the kinetic theory of gases. If we read the scientific textbooks for any period we shall find presented an entirely ahistorical account of the theory. But if we read all the successive textbooks we shall learn not only that the kinetic theory of 1857 was not quite that of 1845 and that the kinetic theory of 1901 is neither that of 1857 nor that of 1965. Yet at each stage the theory bears the marks of its previous history, of a series of encounters with confirming or anomalous evidence, with other theories, with metaphysical points of view, and so on. The kinetic theory not merely has, but is an history, and to evaluate it is to evaluate how it has fared in this large variety of encounters. Which of these have been victories, which defeats, which compounds of victory and defeat, and which not classifiable under any of these headings? To evaluate a theory, just as to evaluate a series of theories, one of Lakatos's research programs, is precisely to write that history, that narrative of defeats and victories.

This is what Lakatos recognised in his paper on *History of Science and Its Rational Reconstructions.*[6] Methodologies are to be assessed by the extent to which they satisfy historiographical criteria; the best scientific methodology is that which can supply the best rational reconstruction of the history of science and for different episodes different methodologies may well be successful. But in talking not about history, but about rational reconstructions Lakatos has still not exorcised the ghosts of the older Popperian belief in methodology; for he was quite prepared to envisage the rational reconstruction as 'a caricature' of actual history. Yet it matters enormously that our histories should be true, just as it matters that our scientific theories make truth one of their goals.

Kuhn interestingly and perhaps oddly insists against Lakatos on truth in history (he accuses Lakatos of replacing genuine history by "philosophy fabricating examples"), but yet denies any notion of truth to natural science other than that truth which attaches to solutions to puzzles and to concrete predictions. In particular he wants to deny that a scientific theory can embody a true ontology, that it can provide a true representative of what is 'really there'. "There is, I think no theory-independent way to reconstruct phrases like 'really there'; the notion of a match between the ontology of a theory and its 'real' counterpart in nature now seems to me illusive in principle."[7]

This is very odd; because science has certainly shown us decisively that some existence-claims are false just because the entities in question are *not* really there — whatever *any* theory may say. Epicurean atomism is not true, there are no humours, nothing with negative weight exists; phlogiston is one with the witches and the dragons. But other existence-claims have survived exceptionally well through a succession of particular theoretical positions: molecules, cells, electrons. Of course our beliefs about molecules, cells, and electrons are by no means what they once were. But Kuhn would be put into a very curious position if he adduced this as a ground for denying that some existence-claims still have excellent warrant and others do not.

What however, worries Kuhn is something else: "in some important respects, though by no means in all, Einstein's general theory of relativity is closer to Aristotle's mechanics than either of them is to Newton's."[8] He therefore concludes that the superiority of Einstein to Newton is in puzzle solving and not in an approach to a true ontology. But what an Einstein ontology enables us to understand is why *from the standpoint of an approach to truth* Newtonian mechanics is superior to Aristotelian. For Aristotelian mechanics as it lapsed into incoherence could never have led us to the special theory; construe them how you will, the Aristotelian problems about time will not yield the questions to which special relativity is the answer. A history which moved from Aristotelianism directly to relativistic physics is not an imaginable history.

What Kuhn's disregard for ontological truth neglects is the way in which the progress toward truth in different sciences is such that they have to converge. The easy reductionism of some positivist programs for science was misleading here, but the rejection of such a reductionism must not blind us to the necessary convergence of physics, chemistry, and biology. Were it not for a concern for ontological truth the nature of our demand for a coherent and convergent relationship between all the sciences would be unintelligible.

Kuhn's view may, of course, seem attractive simply because it seems consistent with a fallibilism which we have every reason to accept. *Perhaps* Einsteinian physics will one day be overthrown just as Newtonian was; perhaps, as Lakatos in his more colourfully rhetorical moments used to suggest, all our scientific beliefs are, always have been, and always will be false. But it seems to be a presupposition of the way in which we do natural science that fallibilism has to be made consistent with the regulative ideal of an approach to a true account of the fundamental order of things and not vice versa. If this is so, Kant is essentially right; the notion of an underlying order — the kind of order that we would expect if the ingenious, unmalicious god of Newton and Einstein had created the universe — *is* a regulative ideal of physics. We do not need to understand this notion quite as Kant did, and our antitheological beliefs may make us uncomfortable in adopting it. But perhaps discomfort at this point is a sign of philosophical progress.

I am suggesting, then, that the best account that can be given of why some scientific theories are superior to others presupposes the possibility of constructing an intelligible dramatic narrative which can claim historical truth and in which such theories are the subject of successive episodes. It is because and only because we can construct better and worse histories of this kind, histories which can be rationally compared with each other, that we can compare theories rationally too. Physics presupposes history and history of a kind that invokes just those concepts of tradition, intelligibility, and epistemological crises for which I argued earlier. It is this that enables us to understand why Kuhn's account of scientific revolutions can in fact be rescued from the charges of irrationalism levelled by Lakatos and why Lakatos's final writings can be rescued from the charges of evading history levelled by Kuhn. Without this background, scientific revolutions become unintelligible episodes; indeed Kuhn becomes — what in essence Lakatos accused him of being — the Kafka of the history of science. Small wonder that he in turn felt that Lakatos was not an historian, but an historical novelist.

A final thesis can now be articulated. When the connection between narrative and tradition on the one hand, and theory and method on the other, is lost sight of, the philosophy of science is set insoluble problems. Any set of finite observations is compatible with any one out of an infinite set of generalizations. Any attempt to show the rationality of science, once and for all, by providing a rationally justifiable set of rules for linking observations and generalizations breaks down. This holds, as the history of the Popperian school shows, for falsification as much as for any version of positivism. It holds, as the history of Carnap's work shows, no matter how much progress may be made on detailed, particular structures in scientific inference. It is only when theories are located in history, when we view the demands for justification in highly particular contexts of a historical kind, that we are freed from either dogmatism or capitulation to scepticism. It therefore turns out that the program which dominated the philosophy of science from the eighteenth century onwards, that of combining empiricism and natural science was bound either at worst to break down in irrationalism or at best in a set of successively weakened empiricist programs whose driving force was a deep desire not to be forced into irrationalist conclusions. Hume's Disease is, however, incurable and ultimately fatal and even backgammon (or that type of analytical philosophy which is often the backgammon of the professional philosopher) cannot stave off its progress indefinitely. It is, after all, Vico, and neither Descartes nor Hume, who has turned out to be in the right in approaching the relationship between history and physics.

NOTES

1. Bruno Bettelheim, *The Uses of Enchantment* (New York: Alfred A. Knopf, 1976), pp. 74-75.

2. Ibid., p. 47.

3. David Hume, *Treatise of Human Nature*, ed. L. A. Selby-Bigge (London: Oxford University Press, 1941), Bk. I, iv, vii, pp. 267-69.

4. Letter to his sister Valli, in *I Am a Memory Come Alive*, ed. Nahum N. Glatzer (New York: Schocken Books, 1974), p. 235.

5. Richard M. Burian, "More than a Marriage of Convenience: On the Inextricability of History and Philosophy of Science," *Philosophy of Science*, 44 (1977), 1-42.

6. I. Lakatos, "History of Science and Rational Reconstructions," in Boston Studies in the Philosophy of Science, Vol. VIII, ed. Roger C. Buck and Robert S. Cohen (Dordrecht-Holland: D. Reidel Publishing Co., 1974).

7. Thomas S. Kuhn, *The Structure of Scientific Revolutions*, 2d ed. (Chicago: University of Chicago Press, 1970), p. 206.

8. Ibid., pp. 206-7.

ACCIDENTAL ('NON-SUBSTANTIAL') THEORY CHANGE AND THEORY DISLODGMENT

WOLFGANG STEGMÜLLER

1. THE TENSION BETWEEN SYSTEMATIC AND HISTORICAL APPROACHES IN THE PHILOSOPHY OF SCIENCE

The philosophy of science as initiated and developed in this century mainly by empiricists was purely systematic in its orientation. Increasing attention to the history of science and to the psychological and sociological aspects of its practice should have, one might have thus expected, meant a welcome addition to the logic of science. Whoever entertained such hopes was, however, in for a bitter disappointment. In particular, with the appearance of Professor Kuhn's work on scientific revolutions it became dreadfully clear that the results achieved in the different branches did not even yield a *consistent* overall picture of science. The fledgling student of the philosophy of science appeared to be faced with having to choose between two *incompatible paradigms*: the logical or the psychological-historical.

Indeed, the situation was even somewhat more aggravated; for the discussion was being conducted at two different levels with the pendulums swinging in opposite directions at each level. At the more concrete level of the philosophy of science the tendency was more and more toward Kuhn's way of looking at things. At the more abstract level of *general* epistemological investigations things looked entirely different. A number of penetrating thinkers attempted to show that even if Kuhn himself did not so intend it, his conception of natural sciences inevitably leads to a form of subjectivism as well as of irrationalism and of relativism, and thus, to positions which for philosophical reasons are untenable or even absurd. Indeed, Kuhn himself often emphasized that these *supposed* consequences of his ideas must be based on misunderstandings. Since, however, it was apparently not possible to pin down the sources of these misunderstandings, these critics did not believe Kuhn.

Thus, young philosophers of science were driven into a sort of intellectual schizophrenia. On one hand they found the Kuhnian approach uncommonly attractive, on the other, if they took Kuhn's critics seriously, they felt forced to regard it as in need of fundamental revision.

It has been my firm conviction for a long time now that this represents a wholly impossible situation, and that it is absolutely imperative to bridge the gap between the historically and the systematically oriented approaches. The attempts in this direction to date appeared to me unsatisfactory for many reasons. As I came across Sneed's book it became abruptly clear that at the bottom of Kuhn's theses lies a *theory* concept which is totally different from the one then current among philosophers of science.

For a long time, indeed, for *too* long a time, metamathematics has furnished the model to which philosophers of science turned and on which they attempted to pattern their investigations of theories. For logicians and metamathematicians it goes without saying that theories are classes of sentences. This interpretation had proven so fruitful for handling all problems in these areas that it was never questioned. Philosophers of science adopted this view of theories as a matter of course, and with it, the tacit assumption that in their discipline, too, the logical reconstruction of theories as classes of sentences would prove fruitful. Today, I no longer believe this assumption to be correct. We will gain a better understanding of scientific theories if we give up this statement view. In this connection I should like to follow Bar-Hillel in referring to the new conception positively as the *structuralistic conception of theories*. I hope this short autobiographical excursus will prove helpful in understanding what follows.

In order to forestall false expectations I should like to make two observations before going any further: (1) the task of a logical reconstruction also includes indicating the *limits* of what can be logically comprehended and explained. In regard to the problems at hand, I am convinced that these limits must be much more narrowly drawn than most 'empiricists' and 'rationalists' believe. (2) Although I will at times be dealing with special phenomena, including those which Kuhn calls "normal science" and "scientific revolutions," detailed analyses are not my primary goal here. First and foremost I want to deal with the objections mentioned above, such as irrationalism, subjectivism, and relativism, thus contributing to the clarification of questions belonging to the abstract epistemological level.

I would like to specify more closely which systematic approach will be taken here. I have purposely elected the one which presumably lies the furthest from Kuhn's, and is so dissimilar to it that one can scarcely imagine how the two can be brought into touch, namely, the axiomatic method as developed by P. Suppes. The only thing which I was able to discover common to the approaches of Kuhn and Suppes was that both were the target of the most bitter attacks from philosophical quarters, even if for wholly different reasons. While Kuhn reaped the protests already mentioned, Suppes' procedure drew objections primarily on grounds that it is so abstract and so general that it precludes a discussion of a host of problems central to the philosophy of science. Essentially, these objections culminate in the challenge to specialize Suppes' method in such a way that the epistemological problems in question can be discussed. It appears to me that Sneed has achieved this to a great extent. Each one of the realistic, pragmatic steps taken by Sneed in the process of specializing the Suppes approach constitutes simultaneously a step toward the erection of a new pillar for the bridge leading to the historically oriented philosophy of science.

Let me state the essential points of Sneed's account. First, the idea of a single 'cosmic' application of a physical theory is scrapped in favor of the thesis that each such theory has *several partly overlapping applications*. Second, these intersections lead to the important *differentiation between laws and constraints*. While laws hold in some one, or possibly all applications, constraints establish more or less strong 'cross-connections' between the particular applications. Third, it should be remembered that the *special laws* holding only for certain applications must be differentiated from the basic law which is to be incorporated into the core of a theory. A fourth point appears to me to be of utmost importance, namely, the *theoretical-nontheoretical dichotomy*. I should like to remind you that this distinction is handled quite differently than it was within the framework of empiricism. The scientific language is not divided into a 'fully understandable observational language' and a theoretical language which is 'only partly interpretable' by means of correspondence rules. Instead, the theoretical terms of a theory T are distinguished on the basis of a criterion. The measurement of theoretical functions depends upon a successful application of just this theory T. Thus, one can say that these quantities are T-determinable, and one must henceforth speak of 'T-theoretical quantities', not simply 'theoretical quantities'. It appears to me that only in this way do we find an answer to "Putnam's challenge," namely, to show 'in what way theoretical terms come from theories'. The theoretical terms 'come from the theory' in the sense that their values are measured in a theory-dependent way. This leads to Sneed's problem of theoretical terms whose only known solution to date is the Ramsey-method.

The contrast to the traditional way of thinking becomes abundantly clear where two different physical theories T_1 and T_2 are formulated in the same language. One and the same term of this language can then be simultaneously theoretical and non-theoretical; i.e. theoretical in relation to T_1 and non-theoretical in relation to T_2.[1] Later I will consider a fifth point, *the method of paradigmatic examples.*

2. THE STRUCTURALISTIC THEORY CONCEPT: THEORIES, THEIR EMPIRICAL CLAIMS, HOLDING A THEORY

I would now like to examine more closely the structuralistic view of theories. Compared with traditional ideas identifying theories with classes of sentences, this structuralistic conception offers five important advantages: (1) With it a concept corresponding to Kuhn's notion of *"normal science"* can be introduced in an unforced natural way. (2) With it a *concept of progress* can be introduced which also covers the revolutionary cases. (3) The phenomenon of the immunity of theories to 'recalcitrant experience' can be made clear and understandable. (4) It permits an elegant simplification of what Lakatos intended his *theory of research programmes* to achieve. (5) It removes the danger—and this is perhaps the main advantage—of falling into a rationality monism and, thus, into the *rationality rut* of assuming there could be but *one single* source of scientific rationality.

We now turn again to the central question of what may be understood as a *theory*. Sneed has distinguished between

(1)   a theory as an entity based on a theory element$<K, I>$, whereby K is a theory core and I is the set of intended applications,

and

(2)   the empirical claims of a theory, which have the form $I \in A(N^*)$ with N^* being the core-net induced by the theory-net N.[2]

If it is asked whether (1) or (2) applies to *that which a scientist considers a theory,* the concrete answer in the most cases will be neither. The scientist will be thinking of something much less abstract, something with flesh and blood involving people, their convictions and their knowledge. This third concept we will call *holding a theory.*

Perhaps the following analogy to the philosophy of language will help to make this somewhat clearer. Sneed occasionally character-ized theories and empirical claims as *products*. Linguistic objects, words and sentences, can also be seen as products, and speech act theory has shown that the extremely important dimension of the performative modi is lost from this point of view. Similarly, theories and empirical claims stand in much the same relation to *acts of holding* a theory as do linguistic products to speech acts.

The concept of holding a theory can be introduced in a broader or in a narrower sense. Further, one can give it a more objective or a more subjective accent. For all these definitions one needs extra-logical concepts such as 'person', 'believes that', 'has supporting evi-dence for', as well as a variable t ranging over historical times. Instead of formal precision I will attempt here an intuitive gloss.[3] In order to introduce the *weak* objective variant, we will assume a theory T in the earlier sense to be given. The statement that a per-son p holds a theory T (in the weak sense) at time t (abbreviated $H_w(p, T, t)$) means that there is a net N based on specializations of the basic core K_b of T such that p believes $I \in A(N^*)$ at t, furthermore, that p has supporting evidence for this proposition, and finally that p believes N to be a *strongest* existing net such that $I \in A(N^*)$. If one likes, one can also incorporate into this concept the person's be-lief that using this theory will yield progress. The phrase 'has sup-porting evidence for' implicitly contains the confirmation problem. Since we are going to disregard this problem here, we will use the abbreviation 'p knows that Y' to mean 'p believes that Y and p has data supporting Y'.

3. 'NORMAL SCIENCE' AND 'SUBJECTIVISM'

Before sketching other variants, I would like to indicate how the con-cept of holding a theory can be used to explicate the notion of nor-mal science. The idea is this: *if several persons hold the same theory, they will be said to belong to the same normal scientific tradition.* This means that the persons in question do indeed use the same theory to construct their hypotheses, but couple it to a variety of different convictions and assumptions. Thus, the theory T remains unchanged, while the empirical claims attached to it may change at any time. I would like to propose calling all those changes not in-volving the theory itself *accidental theory changes*, since one can draw an illuminating comparison with the ancient substance-accident dichotomy: the basic core $K = <M_p, M_{pp}, M, C>$ is the immutable substance underlying change, while the core specializations represent the constantly changing accidents.

But now I am anticipating. To actually arrive at a viable concept of normal science in Kuhn's sense, several important factors must still be considered. To this end I must briefly say something about the concept of *paradigm*. What Wittgenstein had in mind and wanted to illustrate with the example "game" was as follows: Neither an explicit extensional characterization of the predicate G for *game* via a listing *of all* games, nor a precise definition of G by the stipulation of sufficient and necessary conditions for membership in G is possible. Instead, we must limit ourselves to effectively specifying a sub-set G_0 of G, the *list of paradigms* (or *paradigmatic examples*) *of games*. Elements will then be admitted to the difference set $G - G_0$ only if they exhibit a significant number of properties common to most elements of G_0. This formulation underscores the irremediable vagueness adhering to a set determined by paradigmatic examples.

In our case, though, the general concept of a paradigm will only be used for a very special purpose: The set I of intended applications of a theory is not completely specified from the very beginning by means of a list or a strict definition; it is an *open* set for which the theory's creator has stipulated a sub-set I_0 of paradigmatic examples, and which can be changed (through additions and cuts) in the course of working with the theory provided the condition $I_0 \subseteq I$ is met. Thus, for instance, Newton specified the paradigms for the application of his theory by designating examples such as the solar system, certain parts thereof, the tides, pendulum motion, and free falling bodies near the earth's surface.

This idea can be utilized for our explication attempt as follows:[4] We exand the present theory concept to a concept of a theory in the strong sense, i.e. to what Sneed called a Kuhn-theory, and require that there once existed a person p_0 who at time t_0 successfully applied the core K of the theory, i.e. $I_0 \in A(K)$. We then modify the concept of holding a theory by taking "theory" to mean this strong theory concept and requiring that the person p holding the theory also choose the set I_0 as the set of paradigms for I. This establishes the *historical source* of the theory in its inventor, as well as the *paradigm* concept and the *historical continuity* between all those persons holding the theory. The resulting *concept of holding a theory in the strong sense*, $H_{st}(p, T, t)$, could be taken as an explication of the Kuhnian concept of normal science, at least of its objective variant.

This objective variant can be replaced by a subjective one. The only difference is that *some existential quantifiers and the epistemic* *operators 'believes that' and 'knows that' are switched around.* Whereas previously we always spoke of the existence of a net N and a set I about which the person p knows or believes something, we now say that p knows of a net N and a set I that $I^0 \subseteqq I$ and $I \in A(N^*)$, and that as far as far as p knows N is a strongest net and I a largest set of its kind. If under 'subjectivism' nothing other is meant than a philosophical temperament which prefers this subjective to the objective variant, this would be a quite viable subjectivism.[5]

4. RATIONALITY AND PROGRESS BRANCHING IN NORMAL SCIENCE

What about the rationality of the normal scientist? In principle this question is easy to answer; indeed, without having to go into the problem of whether, and how, criteria for scientific rationality can be formulated. For whether these criteria are inductivistic, deductivistic or something else, their satisfaction, or violation, pertains only to empirical claims, and thus turns completely on the word 'knows'. In any case the normal scientist, i.e. the scientist holding a given theory, *can* satisfy any of these rationality criteria.

Normal science allows for *two sorts of progress*. One consists in expanding the set of intended applications, the other in further specializations of the basic core K_b.

Their counterparts are the corresponding types of *setbacks* which a normal scientist often experiences; namely, being forced to retract an attempted expansion of the range of application or an attempted core specialization.

I would also like to mention two interesting complications. Wherever we have used a superlative to characterize the concept of holding a theory, it was always with the *indefinite*, not the definite article. The reason lies in the following possibility:

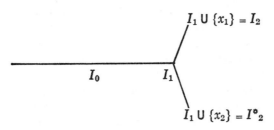

$$I_1 \cup \{x_1\} = I_2$$

$$I_0 \qquad I_1$$

$$I_1 \cup \{x_2\} = I^*_2$$

The branching is intended to indicate that a given core specialization is applicable either to I_2 or to $I^*{}_2$ but *not* to I_1 U $\{x_1\}$ U $\{x_2\}$. In such a situation neither the theory, nor experience, nor logical reasoning can help. The scientist must *decide* on the basis of value judgments.

Another kind of branching is also possible. The scientist can at a given time be faced with the choice of either expanding his current range of application I at the expense of additional expansions of his net, or leaving I unchanged in order to gain a further core specialization.

Typical situations of this kind could be called *progress branching in normal science*. In these branches we have located a juncture where value judgments are unavoidable in deciding which way to proceed. Should someone regard *this* as subjectivism, the *only* correct reply is that *this is a species of subjectivism which we can not evade*.

5. HOLISM OF EMPIRICAL CLAIMS. THE THEORY-LADENNESS OF OBSERVATIONS

In connection with this reconstruction sketch for the concept of normal science, I should like to make a few short remarks about two concepts which appear often in the current literature. The expression *"holism"* can be used in relation to theories as well as empirical hypotheses. In relation to empirical content the holistic standpoint can be formulated as follows (and this is a true statement): *the empirical content of a theory at a certain time is not exhibited by numerous special hypotheses constructed on the basis of this theory, but by one single big empirical claim: $I_t \in A (N^*{}_t)$.*

Concerning the second item, the so-called *theory-ladenness of observations*, I would like to point out an equivocation which has caused much confusion. It is maintained, for example, that the description of the facts relevant for a theory itself requires a theory. This is in most cases true. But it is also harmless, and creates no special problem. For the theory required is, of course, not the same as that *for which* the facts are being described, but a more elementary, underlying theory. Some authors want, though, to maintain something much stronger than this, namely, that the facts for a theory T are determined *by this theory itself*. This appears to be the meaning of such phrases as 'theories define their own facts'. Yet even this stronger version of the thesis is not only intelligible, but correct *if confined to T-theoretical terms*. And in this case it creates a serious problem, namely, the problem of theoretical terms as formulated by Sneed for which only the Ramsey-solution is currently known.[6]

6. THEORY DISLODGMENT WITHOUT FALSIFICATION. THE THREEFOLD IMMUNITY OF THEORIES. THEORY CHOICE AND RATIONALITY

The concept of holding a theory, which served to define the notion of normal science, or at least an important aspect of this notion, was only the first step toward de-irrationalizing the current image of the Kuhnian conception of science. Now what about scientific revolutions? Can the logician also contribute to a better understanding of *this* phenomenon? Here I should like to begin with a confession so that you will not be too terribly disappointed with the following remarks: The logician can actually accomplish far less in this case than in the case of the phenomenon which Kuhn called normal science. This is not because scientific revolutions are in fact thoroughly irrational processes, but simply because many aspects of these phenomena lie outside the competence of the logician.

First we will try to characterize that aspect of the phenomenon described by Kuhn which again shocked many readers and led to charges of irrationalism, subjectivism, and this time relativism as well. All empiricist philosophers, and the modern rationalists too, agreed until quite recently that a theory which founders on experience must be discarded.

As opposed to this, Kuhn's thesis is that even a theory plagued with ever so many anomalies is not discarded because it has foundered on experience. Instead, it is jettisoned only when another theory is available to take its place. This prima facie curious phenomenon may be called *'theory dislodgment by a superseding theory'*, or briefly *'theory dislodgment'*. I will attempt to show that in this case, too, the structuralistic view of theories enables us first, to gain a basic logical understanding of the situation; second, to produce a plan for a viable concept of scientific progress in revolutionary changes; and thus, third, to deliver something like a logical test for the correctness of Kuhn's thesis. Concerning the first point we must focus our attention upon a certain particular aspect of theories, namely, their *steadfastness in the face of 'recalcitrant data'*. This is expressly emphasized by Kuhn and felt by many to be especially shocking.

Such an immunity does actually exist and, indeed, in three different respects. The by far most important of these, the *first kind of immunity*, arises when one considers the relationship between the *core* of a theory and the specializations of this core. As you will remember, the empirical claims of a theory with the basic core K_b

have the form: $I_t \in A(N^*{}_t)$ (whereby 't' is a historical time index). As an empirical claim this 'central empirical statement' of a theory can be refuted by experience. The refutation does not, however, directly effect the theory itself, for the falsification of the empirical claim only proves that *certain* specializations of the core are not suitable. Indeed, *the same holds for every finite number of such unsuccessful attempts.* We can, by paralleling Popper's argument proving the non-verifiability of strict universal quantifications, obtain the following proof for the unrefutability of a theory on the basis of a finite number of refuted empirical claims: *since the number of possible specializations of a theory-element is potentially infinite, no number, be it ever so large, of unsuccessful attempts to specialize a given theory-element can be considered conclusive proof that a successful specialization of this element is impossible.* Thus, we are not forced to give up the theory; there might just be a still undiscovered specialization which would prove successful when discovered.

If we place ourselves in the 'normal scientist's' situation, i.e. in the situation of one who already holds a theory, we will realize that this scientist is always working with theories whose cores have in the past repeatedly served well. When, therefore, a member of the community is not successful in working with the core, it is natural and understandable that he, and not the theory, be blamed.

Many philosophers have thought that the description of the phenomenon of theory dislodgment indicated a rationality gap. In particular, Kuhn's thesis that the decision to scrap a theory *is always simultaneously a decision in favor of a new theory* was thought to imply something irrational and, thus, logically incomprehensible.[7] To support this, their second charge of irrationalism, they argued that there must be something like a *critical level* at which a theory must be rejected regardless of whether a new one is available or not. Here again we clearly discern the influence of the statement view, namely in the attempt to put scientific theories in the same category with *statistical* hypotheses, if not deterministic laws. As the brief logical analysis has shown, there is no critical level at which a theory must be discarded. Stipulating such a level would be a purely arbitrary act.

Concerning the second half of Kuhn's thesis we need only add a psychological truism to the immunity already established in order to comprehend this situation, namely, the elementary insight that people do not throw away tools which have served well as long as they possess no better substitutes. Or to take a more drastic example which better depicts the situation of a crisis-ridden scientific theory:

Would someone who was freezing not seek shelter in a hut simply because it was awfully ramshackle? Were he not to, this would mean he prefers sure death to mere danger.

That the philosopher has overstepped his competence here by resorting to *empirical generalizations* is a charge I could not accept. The situation seems to me similar to that of the ordinary-language philosopher. He does not base his analyses on statistical surveys concerning the use of language, but on his own linguistic competence. In respect of psychological truisms like the one just mentioned, we have at least the same degree of competence. As a *human being* I am competent to evaluate certain reactions as *typically human* without having to resort to generalizations, which properly ought to be called 'hypothetical'.

These two forms of understanding, based on the linguistic competence of the native speaker and on the competence of our judgments concerning spontaneous human reactions respectively, could be called *elementary hermeneutic understanding*. If we accept this choice of terminology, we can say that in order to gain an accurate grasp of the phenomenon of theory dislodgment, logical and hermeneutic understanding must work together.

Such cases must, however, be carefuly distinguished from those situations in which a negative decision is made in relation to certain parts of the range of application of a theory. In order to see this clearly we must take a look at the *second kind of theory immunity*. To this end we recall once again the relationship between I_0 and I. I_0 is the explicitly given extensional sub-set of I consisting of the paradigmatic examples. This sub-set can never be changed. With the exception of this minimal requirement, I is an open set. Should the scientific community in trying to apply the theory to some $a \in I - I_0$ experience fundamental difficulties, stretching perhaps over generations of research, and thus, conclude that this application is not possible, it need not, *contrary to falsificationism*, hold the theory responsible. Instead, it can decide to deny a's membership in the theory's range of application.

Here we come in sharp conflict with the demands of the 'critical rationalists'. For according to their notion of critical attitude, a scientist should make his theory *as sensitive as possible* to potential refutation. In our present case that would mean stipulating sharp criteria for membership in I and, consequently, rejecting the theory. I would like to counter this demand with the following observation: it appears that no physicist has ever been willing to assume the risk of falsification involved in stipulating sufficient and necessary conditions for membership in I. When optical phenomena could not be explained with the help of Newton's particle mechanics, as he hoped they could, his work was not pronounced invalid; instead it was concluded in accord with Maxwell's conception that light did not consist of particles. As I have not approached science via a preconceived over-all conception of scientific rationality I am unable to perceive anything irrational in such a decision.

But what happens when the fundamental law of the theory fails in I_0? Here we meet the *third* kind of immunity of theories. It is a consequence of two particular features of physical theories: first, the occurrence of theoretical terms in the core, and second, what I have called the holism of empirical claims. Instead of analyzing the general case we will illustrate with a simple example. Assume we agree to take Newton's second law as the only fundamental law of his theory. Then accepting this law means nothing more than being committed to promise that suitable force and mass functions satisfying this law exist in all intended applications, functions which take special forms in certain applications and are connected across these applications by certain constraints. It is the near vacuousness of this wide-ranging promise which precludes its empirical refutation.

7. THEORY HOLISM AND 'PROPAGANDA'. THE ROLE OF VALUE JUDGMENTS

In view of these three forms of irrefutability it is understandable that even a theory caught in a crisis will almost always be retained until a promising new theory is constructed. Here another viable form of *holism* takes its place along side the holism of empirical claims. This 'theory holism' could be briefly formulated as follows: the decision to accept a theory is always *an all-or-nothing-decision*, and it *cannot be replaced by any rules nor dictated by a so-called experimentum crucis*.[8]

8. OVERCOMING THE RELATIVISM CHARGE. PROGRESSIVE REVOLUTIONS

Following this attempt to de-irrationalize and de-subjectivize the current picture of Kuhn's conception of science, I must now take up the *charge of relativism*. It seems to contain a grain of truth.

For the sake of illustration I will briefly formulate the relativism charge against Kuhn as sharply as possible: 'An actual change of theories is described by Kuhn in sociological-psychological language.

In this way one gets the impression of a complete parallel with religious and political power struggles. Assume further that to this picture be added the thesis of the incommensurability of the old and the new theories. All this adds up to *relativism*.'

We want, now, to illustrate this objection with the following possible-world picture: Let T_1 and T_2 be two theories designed to solve the same kind of problems but having different theoretical terms. Initially theory T_1 prevails in the possible world w_1 but is subsequently dislodged by theory T_2 after having run into a crisis. Exactly the opposite transpires in possible world w_2. Here T_2 prevails initially, is beset by crisis and subsequently dislodged by T_1. One can well imagine this happening given different psychological and sociological conditions suitable to each case. In both worlds the proponents of the new theory are convinced they have brought progress. Thus, left alone with the psychological-sociological progress criterion, we must admit *that in both worlds there has been, by definition, progress*. This appears fully unacceptable to us. 'Revolutionary progress' *cannot designate a symmetrical relation*.

It is important not to misunderstand my point. I do not deny that two such events could *happen*, nor that in both cases those involved *believe* progress has been served. My thesis is simply that in at least one of these two worlds the agents of the *alleged* progress must be mistaken; real progress can only have taken place in one of the two worlds.

Thus we have located the heart of the problem. The 'missing link' by Kuhn is not a 'critical rejection level'[9]; it is the *introduction of an adequate concept of scientific progress for the case of theory dislodgment*. Only in this way, it appears to me, can we avoid the Scylla of teleological metaphysics and the Charybdis of relativism.

Today I believe that Kuhn himself wanted to point out this difficulty. The last pages of his book can be understood as a challenge to the systematic philosophy of science to come up with a viable concept of scientific progress not infected with a teleological metaphysics. In my opinion Sneed's reduction concept offers the best start in this direction to date, if not yet the final solution. It also appears to me that the late Professor Lakatos had something similar in mind with his concept of sophisticated falsification. Sneed's reduction concept is especially interesting because it permits *a comparison of theories with fully heterogeneous conceptual apparatus*.

In cases of radical theory change a complete reduction is presumably not possible. Here one must be satisfied with the notion of the *approximative imbedding* of one theory in another. Sneed's reduction concept must be correspondingly expanded and liberalized. Concerning this extra-ordinarily important approximation problem there is, as far as I know, only one single interesting preliminary work. I mean a book from Günther Ludwig.[10] Ludwig works with '*blurred*' functions and relations, indeed, even with '*blurred*' objects. This idea may be successfully incorporated into the Sneedian conceptual apparatus as my collaborator and former student Moulines has shown. In this way it becomes possible to work with *blurred* models and possible models, even with *blurred* partial possible models.[11] Nevertheless I must admit that this is not yet a fully developed theory.

I must append a qualifying remark to this discussion of theory dislodgment. I have for simplicity's sake considered only the case of '*radical*' theory change; i.e., the case where the basic core K_b is replaced by another. The construction of theory nets makes it possible to give an analogous account of a 'mini-revolution' such as Kuhn calls attention to in the appendix to the 2nd edition of his book. We have this kind of 'small revolution' when the 'pyramid point' K_b remains unaltered but a specialization *at a relatively high place in the pyramid* is replaced by another. On the other hand it is also possible that during the course of the development of a theory not only the 'pyramid point' K_b but also certain specializations remain unaltered.

9. IS PROGRESS BRANCHING POSSIBLE IN REVOLUTIONARY THEORY DISLODGMENTS? THE 'EVOLUTIONARY TREE'

Is there such a thing as revolutionary progress branching? Concerning this question I would like to present a provoking thesis. According to teleological conceptions of scientific progress there surely can be no such thing. But the concepts of reduction and approximative imbedding were intended primarily to serve in formulating an *immanent* progress criterion which dispenses with all such 'metaphysical conceptions'. Assume now for the sake of argument that such progress concepts are available. It is then quite conceivable that we run across situations of the following kind:

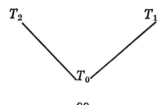

This diagram is to be interpreted as follows: a theory T_0 can be dislodged by either T_1 or T_2, whereby T_0 is either *reducible to or approximatively imbeddable in both*. T_1 and T_2 are nevertheless neither equivalent, nor is either one reducible to the other because although both T_1 and T_2 explain the phenomena explained by T_0, the totality of phenomena which the one accounts for only *partially overlaps* those explained by the other. In perfect analogy to the case of normal scientific progress branching, we have here a juncture at which *ultimate*, not provisional, *value judgments* must decide which route to take, or whether both such paths should be pursued.

Add this possibility to the two forms of normal scientific progress branching already described and we see that from a logical point of view nothing can be urged against the picture of a branching '*evolutionary tree*' which shocked so many. Nevertheless, many philosophers will object that the mere belief in the *conceivability* of such a situation implies a scientific relativism. To this I would reply: if by definition any interpretation of scientific progress not logically producing linearity is to be called 'relativism', indeed, even when an adequate progress concept is available, *then this is presumably a form of relativism which we must swallow*. My initial position must then be re-formulated. It is true that I tried to de-irrationalize and de-subjectivize the picture of Kuhn's conception of theory change shared by philosophers of quite different persuasions. On the other hand, though, I have not only not furnished the means for overcoming a certain variant of what some call *relativism*, but I have attempted to show that this form of relativism is *defensible*. If, however, it is asked whether, and how often, such branching has actually occurred, the logician, *qua logician*, is unable to say anything and must pass the question along to his colleagues in other fields. But it must not be overlooked that no matter what the answer, there would still remain a problem to be solved. For even if progress branching has occurred, it was presumably quite rare. But why? I know of no general answer. We are faced with a somewhat paradoxical situation: the prima facie shocking idea of progress producing a branching evolutionary tree proves under closer analysis to be epistemically harmless. The *real* problem here is to explain *why such branching is much more rare than one would expect*. I have only the vague idea that an adequate answer will involve peculiarities of human nature as well as internal and external factors.[12]

Let me make a concluding remark. I cannot hope that the material presented by Sneed and myself will suffice to convince you. On the one hand you may have the impression of having been bombarded with too many novelties. On the other, we have for the time being only a meager basis, namely, the theories of mathematical physics. Whatever a logician may have to say about a topic like 'theory change', it is sure to be dry as bones compared with the fascinating vividness and colorful richness of Kuhn's writings.

Since the logic of science is still in its infancy very much remains to be done before the bridge between it and the history of science can be completed. Future success depends, however, not only on our efforts and skills, but on something else too. In those fields of knowledge dealing with human affairs one can observe in recent times an unfortunate trend. The representatives of various schools of thought do not even listen to one another any more.[13] This trend has begun to catch hold in the philosophy of science too, and seems to gain momentum the more opinions diverge.

This need not be, since it has not always been so. Ancient philosophers differed in their opinions no less than philosophers today. But no matter how vigorously they attacked each other they never refused to talk it out. The future situation in the philosophy of science will depend to a great extent on whether we succeed in regaining this virtue of the ancient Greeks, namely, of listening to each other.

NOTES

*A version of this paper was published in advance in *Erkenntnis* **10** (1976), 147-178.

1. The concept 'pressure' offers an example if we take mechanics as T_1 and phenomenological thermodynamics as T_2.

2. (Editor's note) The technical terms in (1) and (2) are taken from J. D. Sneed's paper, "Describing Revolutionary Scientific Change: A Formal Approach," which was read at the same symposium as the Stegmüller paper and appeared in the same volume. For Sneed, a *theory-core* (K) is the ordered quadruple, $<M_p, M_{pp}, M, C>$. He explains the intuitive ideas involved in this identification as follows: "First, there is a distinction between theoretical and non-theoretical components. Roughly, M_p is the set of all possible models of the *full* conceptual apparatus of the theory including theoretical components, while M_{pp} is the set of all models obtained by simply 'lopping-off' the theoretical components leaving only the non-theoretical part of the conceptual apparatus. I have called these respectively 'partial models' and 'potential partial models'. Second, there is the idea of laws formulated with theoretical components. This is captured by M which picks out [from] the set of all possible models of the full conceptual apparatus just those which satisfy certain laws. Third,

there is the idea that different applications of the theory-element are interdependent in the sense that one may not—at least for theoretical functions—employ values of functions in one application of the theory without regard for some of the values of the same functions in other applications. This is captured by the constraints C on M_p. These have the effect of ruling out certain combinations of theoretical function values in different applications." (p. 251-2). The set I of *intended applications* is what the theory-element (i.e., the ordered pair, $<K, I>$ is about. The notion of a *theory-net* is introduced as follows: "First we define the notion of a 'specialization' of a theory-core. Intuitively, a specialization of $K = <M_p,$ $M_{pp}, M, C>$ assigns to some sub-set of M_{pp} certain special laws represented as further restrictions on the set M together perhaps with some constraints associated with these laws—represented as further restrictions on C. . . . Next we define a 'theory-net' as a set of theory elements together with the specialization relation. We also require that cores appearing in the net be uniquely associated with their intended applications" (254). Just as a theory has an associated theory-core, so too a theory-net has an associated core-net (N°). The core-net is said to be "induced" by the theory-net. Sneed says "Intuitively, N° picks out just those members of Pot (M_{pp}) [the power set of M_{pp}, i.e., the set of all M_{pp}'s subsets] whose elements may be supplied with theoretical functions in ways which satisfy special laws and constraints in applications where they are postulated to apply, as well as those laws and constraints which are postulated to apply, in applications standing above them in the net—including, of course, those of K" (256). The set picked out in this way by N° is called $A(N^\circ)$.

3. For formal definitions cf. Sneed, [10], p. 266, and Stegmüller, [11], p. 194.

4. For technical details cf. Sneed, [10], p. 294, and Stegmüller, [11], pp. 221ff. The deviation of the latter from Sneed's definition is due to the attempt to eliminate the 'platonistic' character of the set *I*. This was done by way of an auxiliary definition (D15, p. 221) in which the applications of a theory *T* accepted by a person at a given time were defined.

5. For a more exact formulation of this *subjective variant* cf. Stegmüller, [12].

6. Cf. Stegmüller, [11], holistic thesis (III), p. 272 and its discussion p. 276.

7. This view was advocated, e.g., by J. Watkins in [13], as well as originally by I. Lakatos in [5].

8. Cf. Sneed, [10], pp. 90ff. and Stegmüller, [11], pp. 271ff. Three further kinds of 'holism' may be distinguished from the two mentioned here ('holism of empirical claims' and 'holism of empirical theories'). Sometime the thesis of the '*theory-ladenness of observations*', according to which 'a theory defines its own facts', is included as a part of this thesis (cf. Stegmüller, [11], holistic thesis (III) pp. 272ff.). Besides these, there is also what could be called the '*holism of refutation and confirmation*'. According to it only an entire scientific system can be confronted with 'experience' and supported or falsified by it. A detailed examination of this form of holism is a task for confirmation and test theory. But in any case,

one can extract a certain concession to this conception from the 'holism of empirical claims' described in Section I. Finally, there also appears to be something like a *'methodological holism'*. According to it one must answer all questions in the philosophy of science simultaneously. Theories, for example, cannot be investigated in isolation, but only in the context of the entire theory hierarchy. Or the problem of scientific explanation must be dealt with together with the problems of concept and theory construction, and these in turn with those of confirmation and testing. This fifth form of holism is unacceptable for the simple reason that it makes superhuman demands on philosophers.

9. Were there one, the phenomenon of theory dislodgment as such would have to be regarded either as an irrational process or as an incomplete description of a rational process. The present location of the "missing link" is such that it need neither contest the phenomenon of theory dislodgment nor regard it as an incomplete description.

10. G. Ludwig, [7], pp. 71ff.

11. This theory, which uses quite strong topological concepts, cannot be sketched here. The starting point is the concept of *uniform filters* as introduced by G. Ludwig, op. cit., p. 76f.

12. Internal factors would, for example, be pre-systematic intuitive considerations of analogy or simplicity. The external factors would include, among other things,, available technology and the dominating Weltanschauung. Concerning the latter, cf. also K. Hübner, 'Zur Frage des Relativismus und des Fortschritts in den Wissenschaften, Imre Lakatos zum Gedächtnis', *Journal for the Philosophy of Science*, 5, (1974 285-303.

13. An impressive account of this deplorable situation within social philosophy has been given by Kurt v. Fritz in his booklet: *The Relevance of Ancient Social and Political Philosophy for our Times. A short Introduction to the Problem.* Berlin-New York, 1974.

BIBLIOGRAPHY

[1] Kuhn, T. S.: 1970, *The Structure of Scientific Revolutions* 2nd ed.), University of Chicago Press, Chicago.
[2] Kuhn, T. S.: 1970, 'Logic of Discovery or Psychology of Research?', in I. Lakatos and A. Musgrave (eds.), *Criticism and·the Growth of Knowledge*, Cambridge University Press, Cambridge, pp. 1-23.
[3] Kuhn, T. S.: 1970, 'Reflections on My Critics', in I. Lakatos and A. Musgrave (eds.), *Criticism and the Growth of Knowledge*, pp. 231-278.
[4] Kuhn, T. S.: 1973, 'Objectivity, Value-Judgment, and Theory Choice', The Franklin J. Machette Lecture, Furman University.
[5] Lakatos, I.: 1970, 'Falsification and the Methodology of Scientific Research Programmes', in I. Lakatos and A. Musgrave (eds.), *Criticism and the Growth of Knowledge*, pp. 91-195.
[6] Lakatos, I.: 1972, 'History of Science and Its Rational Reconstruction', *Boston Studies in the Philosophy of Science*, Vol. VIII, D.

Reidel Publishing Company, Holland, pp. 91-136.
[7] Ludwig, G.: 1970, *Deutung des Begriffs "physikalische Theorie" und axiomatische Grundlegung der Hilbertraumstruktur der Quantenmechanik durch Hauptsätze des Messens*, Springer-Verlag, Berlin-Heidelberg.
[8] Moulines, C.-U.: 1975, *Zur Logischen Rekonstruktion der Thermodynamik*, Diss., Universität München.
[9] Moulines, C.-U.: 1975, 'A Logical Reconstruction of Simple Equilibrium Thermodynamics', *Erkenntnis* 9, 101-130.
[10] Sneed, J. D.: 1971, *The Logical Structure of Mathematical Physics*, D. Reidel Publishing Company, Dordrecht.
[11] Stegmüller, W.: 1973, *Probleme und Resultate der Wissenschafts theorie und Analytischen Philosophie, Band II, Theorie und Erfahrung: Zweiter Halbband, Theorienstrukturen und Theoriendynamik*, Spring-Verlag, Berlin-Heidelberg. English Translation Springer-Verlag, New York, 1976.
[12] Stegmüller, W.: 1975, 'Structures and Dynamics of Theories. Some Reflections on J. D. Sneed and T. S. Kuhn', *Erkenntnis* 9, 75-100.
[13] Watkins, J.: 1970, 'Against 'Normal Science',' in I. Lakatos and A. Musgrave (eds.), *Criticism and the Growth of Knowledge*, pp. 25-37.

II. SOCIAL SCIENCES

REASON, TRADITION, AND THE
PROGRESSIVENESS OF SCIENCE

M. D. KING

The sociology of knowledge is concerned with "the relationship between human thought and the social context in which it arises."[1]
So, on this reading, the sociology of science may be taken to be concerned with the analysis of the social context of scientific thought.
But scientific thought, most sociologists concede, is distinguished
from other modes of thought precisely by virtue of its immunity
from social determination — insofar as thought is scientific it is governed by reason rather than by tradition, and insofar as it is rational
it escapes determination by "non-logical" social forces. If the rationality of science in this sense is admitted, what can we hope to learn
by studying scientific ideas in their social context? The majority of
sociologists of science have implicitly or explicitly answered this
question by drawing a sharp distinction between science as a "system of ideas" governed by an "inner logic" and science as a "social
system" shaped by non-logical forces, and by arguing that though
sociological analysis can add little or nothing to our appreciation of
the former, it is the obvious means of understanding the latter. They
have, in other words, accepted a clearly drawn division of labor.
Science as a system of knowledge is, they accept, simply not their
business; it is the province of the history or perhaps the philosophy
of science. The aim of these disciplines is to exhibit the internal structure and intellectual affinities of scientific ideas, rather than their
social origins or influences. They seek to comprehend ideas within
an intellectual rather than a social context, to exhibit their "cognitive" rather than their "behavioral" antecedents and consequences.
Sociologists, on the other hand, are concerned with science as a
social activity or, to choose at random some of the available phrases,
with "science as a social system," or as "a particular sort of behavior,"
with "the human side of science," or with its "communal" character.[2]
And so sociology, from this view, seeks to explain the behavior of
scientists—whether toward one another or toward outsiders—and, in
line with the functionalist thinking which has dominated the field,
to explain it chiefly in terms of the values and norms to which scien-

tists *qua* scientists are committed. The majority of sociologists appear, then, to have accepted that there is no intrinsic connection between the ideas scientists hold and the way they behave, that scientists' choice of ideas is governed by reason while their behavior is dictated by a non-logical tradition, and that the latter may be understood without reference to the former.

This division between the history of scientific ideas and the sociology of scientific conduct, between the study of science as "a particular sort of knowledge" and as "a particular sort of behavior" has met with the ready consent of historians and sociologists alike. One can see why such a division of labor should appear so attractive to both sides—whatever its intellectual justification. It saves intellectual historians from the indignity of being told that the "real" causes of scientific growth lie beyond their professional comprehension; and it relieves sociologists of the necessity of understanding scientific ideas.

However, at least one figure has spoken out against this "divorce of convenience." T. S. Kuhn in his book *The Structure of Scientific Revolutions*[3] moves freely backward and forward across the boundary between the history of ideas and the sociology of scientific behavior. Whatever the merits of the particular account he gives of scientific change, his work forces us to reopen the question of whether its intellectual and social dimensions can be properly understood in isolation from one another.

... The "behavioral" or "functional" approach to the sociology of science [can be traced] back to its roots in R. K. Merton's efforts to weld together an anti-rationalistic sociology and a rationalistic view of science.... This approach is rooted in an extended analogy between science and economic activity: thus it treats science as "work," scientists as workers, and scientific ideas as commodities or as "products" of scientific research. Accordingly, it sees the social system of science as a system for the production and dissemination of scientific ideas, and it postulates the virtual bifurcation of scientific "product" and the processes of scientific "production," of scientific ideas and the concrete practices which give rise to them.[4] By thus treating as extrinsic the connection between the practice of science and the knowledge it produces, sociologists have been able to undertake a sociological interpretation of the former without concerning themselves with the question of the social determination of the latter. Further, they have used the parallel with economic life to suggest precisely in what sense the practice of science might be thought of as being socially determined: both science and the economy are, according to this view, alike in being propelled by "non-logical" social sentiments, values, and motivations, while being finally governed by an inflexible a-social logic. This logic is in the one case expressed in fixed canons of scientific methodology and, in the other, in the "iron laws" of economic science.

... Kuhn's analysis of scientific development raises serious doubts concerning the validity of this account of the relationship of scientific practice and scientific ideas. In particular it challenges the view that the practice of science is structured around a universal a-social logic of procedure, and instead treats it as being governed by concrete, discrete, "local" traditions which indeed resist rationalization.

... What kind of sociology of science might be developed from Kuhn's conception of research traditions? Significantly, as we shall see, Kuhn himself when speaking of the social character of science draws his terms not from economics—the domain of the "rational"—but from politics, law, and religion where "tradition" still enjoys at least a measure of respect. He points the way to a sociology of scientific authority, consensus, and commitment rather than to a Mertonian sociology of scientific production, distribution, and exchange. We may put the difference simply, if rather crudely, by saying that Kuhn's thesis suggests that choosing a scientific theory is more like choosing a political philosophy or religion, and less like choosing some economic product like a television set or a refrigerator than Merton's approach allows....

To bring out the significance of Kuhn's work we will begin by contrasting the way he and Merton approach the study of priority disputes; for Merton's now famous paper on this subject set out for a whole generation of sociologists the main guidelines for the "normative" analysis of the internal organization of science.

MERTON'S "ECONOMIC" SOCIOLOGY OF SCIENCE: SCIENCE AS A SYSTEM OF PRODUCTION

The main argument of Merton's paper[5] can be briefly summarized thus: The history of science is punctuated by innumerable disputes between scientists over claims to priority of discovery. Why are these disputes so frequent and so often harsh? They cannot be explained fully as simply providing evidence of the over-developed egotism of the men attracted to science, for in reality they often involve men who are personally both modest and unambitious. Moreover, the disputes are often conducted not by the rival discoverers themselves but by their friends and followers who personally stand to gain little or nothing from having established the claims of their candidates. It appears, then, the answer must lie elsewhere than in the personalities of scientists, namely in the institutional character of science (a classic piece of Durkheimian reasoning this!). It is the case that the institutional order of science singles out originality as a supreme value and generously rewards it, for it is through the cumulation of original contributions that knowledge advances. So that scientists who pursue claims for priority of discovery are not exercising their over-developed egos, they are responding to normative pressures and acting out their social roles. If a scientist hesitates to assert his own priority, then his friends will step in and so affirm the values which govern their collective life. Recognition of a discoverer's claim by the scientific community is testimony to the fact that he has met the most exacting demand placed upon him by his vocation, and appropriate rewards will follow. In sum, then, priority disputes in science are generated by social pressures not by personal dispositions; that they are frequent and often acrimonious provides evidence of the strength of these pressures, i.e., of the social norms of science and of the sentiments these norms inculcate, not of the egotism of scientists.

Notice that here again Merton looks for the explanation not in the character of science as an intellectual enterprise, but in its social nature. However, his argument still requires us to accept a positivistic view of science. For from this view scientific discoveries are bound, by the very nature of science, to be almost invariably "multiple" and therefore occasions for dispute. If science is a collective activity which advances linearly through the accumulation of "discoveries," then—given that scientists have broadly the same intellectual and technical resources at their disposal—any number of them will be bound to reach the point at which a discovery becomes inevitable at about the same time. Thus the *intellectual* structure of science, insofar as it ensures simultaneity of discovery, provides unlimited occasions for wrangles over priority—but *occasions* only. It is the *social* structure of science that ensures that scientists turn these occasions for dispute into actual disputes. Here, as in his Protestant-Science thesis, Merton's argument depends on that dissociation of the social and intellectual dimensions of science which comes naturally to the positivist position.

Now consider how Kuhn approaches the same problem in his paper on the "Historical Structure of Scientific Discovery."[6] His whole analysis of the structure of scientific growth is grounded on the belief that this positivistic view of incremental accumulation of unit discoveries is fundamentally misconceived. It serves the needs of the scientific community rather than those of the historians of science. Positivistic history of science provides a charter for the social arrangements of the community of scientists; it does not give a picture of the past as it really happened. Kuhn, in effect, virtually reverses Merton's argument: he maintains that it is precisely because, as Merton has shown, the scientific community confers so much prestige upon a scientist who makes a significant discovery that scientists picture discoveries as the kind of events that can be attributed to a particular individual, at a particular time and place, and conceive the history of science as a thread along which such unit discoveries are strung like beads. In a word, the positivist view of science is the product of social pressures; it is an ideology for a highly status-conscious community, not a true account of its intellectual character.

Kuhn's own thesis on the structure of scientific growth is too well known for me to need to give an account of it here. All we have to ask is how does it bear upon Merton's analysis for priority disputes, and upon the sociology that has stemmed from that analysis?

Kuhn concedes that a certain number of discoveries do fit into the positivists' scheme. They are typical of what he calls normal science —that is, scientific inquiry aimed at filling in an established view of nature. Under these conditions discoveries are clearly circumscribed events. They can be anticipated in the light of existing knowledge— this is the case with, say, the discovery of an element which fits into a gap of the periodic table—so that scientists know in advance more or less what they are looking for, and are consequently able to say precisely when it has been found and by whom. Science of this kind fits Merton's pattern. And certainly it may give rise to priority disputes, but these are not likely to be very prolonged or very fierce. For if it is in the nature of such discoveries that it is possible to say who made them where and when, then disputes over priority can be settled finally by reference to the historical record.

But Kuhn distinguishes a second class of discoveries, typical of what he calls "revolutionary" phases in scientific development, which cannot be located in time and space with such exactitude. It is these that are likely to give rise to prolonged and bitter wrangles, for rival claims cannot easily be adjudicated. Discoveries of this kind—Kuhn gives as examples, oxygen, electric currents, X-rays—were not, and could not have been, predicted from established theory. They arose as anomalies whose significance emerged only slowly, and which were fully assimilated only after more or less radical adjustments

were made in theory. When is such a discovery made? When someone first catches a glimpse of the unanticipated phenomenon, or
when its full meaning has been realized? Kuhn maintains that the
attempt to date this kind of discovery or to attribute it to an individual must be in the last analysis arbitrary "just because discovery
of a new sort of phenomenon is necessarily a complex process which
involves recognizing both that something is and what it is."[7]

Surely these are the discoveries that will tend to give rise to
priority disputes. Moreover, they are not merely, as Merton would
have it, *occasions* for conflict; they inevitably generate it. Merton,
true to his positivism, does not allow that disputes might arise over
the intellectual question of precisely *what* has been discovered when
a discovery is made; all discoveries, for him, are of Kuhn's first type.
For him, the point at issue is the social and historical one: *who* discovered it and *when?* What is at stake is a social matter: namely,
the individual scientist's property rights in discoveries, and the prestige that accrues to him as a "propertyholder." Priority disputes are
social facts, requiring explanation in terms of other social facts. But
what Kuhn's position implies is that for certain discoveries, at least,
the intellectual debate over what has been discovered and the social
dispute as to who discovered it are inextricably intertwined. The
one issue cannot be resolved in isolation from the other: to concede
priority to a discoverer is to acknowledge as authoritative his interpretation of the discovery or, in Kuhn's terms, to treat his work as
paradigmatic.

Kuhn, acknowledging his debt to Merton, accepts also the notion
that the recognition of priority is the recognition of a property right.
This is certainly a suggestive analogy. But both Merton and Kuhn
follow the dominant school in American sociology in treating property as an emblem of status rather than a source of power. Discovery
from this view confers prestige. But I would argue that Kuhn's analysis of the intellectual structure of discovery requires a more radical
departure from Merton's position than perhaps even he realizes.
More than prestige is at stake in the case of discoveries which do not
merely block in some part of a bounded discipline, but which break
through to new fields. In this latter case recognition of priority is
recognition of *intellectual authority*—of the right of the discoverer
or his epigoni to set out research strategies for the new field of inquiry. To use Merton's own example of what he describes as the
second rank of eponymy[8]—the long list of scientists who are credited
with having fathered a new science or branch of science: To confer
upon someone the title of "Father of this or that science" or sub-

science is not merely to recognize that he has earned our esteem by playing a crucial role in its birth, it is to concede that he (and perhaps more often his intellectual heirs) have earned the parents' right to be heard on questions concerning its future development. What is at stake is not simply the prestige of a "father," but his authority, and the intellectual commitments of his heirs. To cite a case near at home: if we acknowledge that Comte was the "Father of Sociology," we commit ourselves to the view that sociology is more or less what Comte was doing.

A great deal of the sociology of science of the last decades has been conducted under Merton's paternal eye. But I believe that his work in both its "externalist" and "internalist" phases is vitiated by his acceptance of a narrowly positivistic view of science. This meshes quite smoothly with his functionalist sociology, but it means that he has approached the study of science as "a particular sort of behavior," to use Storer's phrase, with a narrowed view of its character as an intellectual enterprise. This, I believe, is the part of A. R. Hall's charge against the sociology of science that sticks. However, Kuhn's arguments seem to me to suggest that Hall's conclusion—that it would be better all around if sociology gave up the pretence of understanding the intellectual side of science and confined itself to studying "the public force of science and the public reaction to scientists"[9]—is bad advice. Kuhn's brief analysis of priority disputes suggests very strongly that their significance as indices of social forces does not come fully to light until their cognitive structure has been carefully explored. If this is the case, then it might be expected that Kuhn's analysis of the structure of scientific change will point to lines of inquiry which have hitherto been obscured by sociologists' adoption of a position that radically dissociates scientific knowledge and the social activity which gives rise to it, and so sidesteps the whole question of the social significance (both within science and outside it) of the scientists' claim to intellectual authority.

In what remains of this paper I will try to indicate how Kuhn's work illuminates this issue, and provides a language in which it can be discussed.

T. S. KUHN'S "POLITICAL" SOCIOLOGY OF SCIENCE:

SCIENCE AS A SYSTEM OF "TRADITIONAL" AUTHORITY

The two key elements of Kuhn's thesis—his attack on the positivistic view of scientific change and his notion of a "paradigm"—involve significant departures from the Mertonian sociology of science.

Positivism treats tradition and science as natural enemies. Traditional beliefs and practices exercise a magical power over men which protects them from the critical appraisal of common sense. Science demystifies tradition; it penetrates the enchanted defenses of tradition and exposes its cognitive and technical absurdities. Merton breaks down this tradition/science antithesis. On the one hand, he underlines the "reasonableness" of traditional beliefs and practices by looking beyond their cognitive and technical failure to their "expressive" and "functional" success, i.e., their success in giving expression to profound non-logical sentiments and in contributing to the maintenance of social order. On the other hand, while accepting the rationality of science as a system for producing knowledge in conformity to a fixed logic of procedure, he breaks with positivism by asserting that as a social system science is governed by a non-logical normative tradition.

Kuhn adopts a more radical position. He questions what Merton, no less than the positivists, simply takes for granted: that the cognitive development of science is a rational process governed by timeless rules of procedure. In fact, he denies that such standards exist and maintains that the practice of science is monitored not by universal rules but by "local" traditions of thought which define for a particular group of practioners precisely what problems, methods, theories are to count as scientific, and where the boundaries of their scientific authority are to be drawn. Where Merton directs sociologists' attention to the normative tradition governing scientific behavior as such, Kuhn is concerned with the socio-psychological processes through which specific authoritative traditions of scientific thought and practice are established, perpetuated, elaborated, and, in time, undermined and displaced. Central to this task is his notion of a paradigm—a tradition-defining piece of scientific work to which a community of scientists is committed. What is the nature of the authority exercised by or through such paradigms? How is it exercised? And how does it come to be overthrown? These appear to be the questions which draw Kuhn's analysis of the structure of scientific growth into contact with sociological thought; notice that contact is made with the sociological analysis of areas of life in which tradition is still accepted as a positive force, namely politics, law, and religion, rather than the "liberated" or "rationalized" field of economics.

Any account of the sociological significance of Kuhn's work must, then, center upon his critique of the rationalistic view of science and his idea of a paradigm as a repository of scientific authority. He has been heavily attacked on both these fronts—chiefly by philosophers of science.[10] But here we are concerned only with the *sociological* significance of the position he has adopted, and of the criticisms launched against it.

The rationality of science

First let us consider the sociological implications of the controversy surrounding his views concerning the limits of scientific rationality. The essence of Kuhn's position can be put in a few words: scientific knowledge is not gained simply by escaping the spell of tradition and viewing the world "objectively" or "rationally." It comes from seeing the world from a particular point of view, or rather from a succession of points of view—each point of view constituting a self-authenticating tradition of thought. Rules for doing science or standards of scientific judgment are not therefore absolutes, they are relative to a particular theoretical viewpoint. This means that when scientists are faced with a choice between alternative articulations of the same fundamental perspective, they have common standards to guide them; but if they are forced to choose between alternative incommensurable world views, there are no over-arching criteria to which they can appeal. So scientific choices are only rational within the context of a single viewpoint of unquestioned authority; choice between alternative viewpoints, though constrained by logic and observation, necessarily involves "an element of arbitrariness,"[11] it is in the last resort a nonrational social act, an act of faith likened by Kuhn to religious conversion.

Though Kuhn insists that choices between alternative world views are not in the last analysis rational, he is anxious to show that they are nonetheless *progressive*. Having cut himself from the notion that progressiveness of science is rooted in its logical character or in its methodology, Kuhn seeks to show that it is guaranteed or at least virtually guaranteed by its social character—by the nature of science as a social system. For him the final constraint upon scientific choice is a social rather than a logical one: the final arbiter is the professional judgment of the scientific group. If a scientific community can be persuaded of the necessity of relinquishing their commitment to one fundamental standpoint, or one tradition of practice, in favor of another, then this in itself is sufficient to provide a "virtual guarantee' that change will be progressive: "What better criterion than the decision of the scientific group could there be?"[12]

105

This attempt to ground the progressiveness of science on the collective psychology of the scientific community has met with severe criticism from philosophers of science like Shapere and Lakatos.[13] Where positivism treats scientific choice, commitment, and consensus as functions of truth, Kuhn appears to wish simply to reverse the equation and to take consensus of scientific opinion as a measure of scientific merit. This would seem to replace epistemology with sociology—hence the understandable hostility of the philosophers. But it seems to me that this is one issue that sociologists *can* sidestep.

Commitment and scientific merit are distinguishable. Commitment is a state or attitude of mind which can be attributed to a particular individual or group at a particular point in time; it is a socio-psychological fact. Scientific merit, on the other hand, is an attribute —whether judged by absolute or relative standards, whether recognized by a particular group of men or not—of propositions. Positivism is a theory of science which, by equating recognized merit with truth and supposing that scientists commit themselves only to what is judged to be true in terms of a-social standards of truth, makes a sociology of scientific commitment simply superfluous. Kuhn, in contrast, wishes to abandon the idea of truth as an absolute, to anchor judgment of the relative merits of scientific theories and therefore the progressiveness of conceptual changes in the conviction of the scientific community, and so to use a sociology of scientific commitment as a foundation for (or even a substitute for) a theory of knowledge. But I would maintain that we can learn from Kuhn's sociology without using it to find answers to epistemological problems. Provided only that it is conceded that as a matter of historical fact scientists' commitments to theories are not in the first instance (whether or not they are in the last) dictated by explicit a-social standards of judgment, then room is left for a sociological account of the processes by which changing patterns of consensus are formed and reformed.

In fact, I would argue that the force of Kuhn's sociological analysis of scientific change is greatly weakened when he seizes upon it to rescue his thesis from the *epistemological* difficulties which arise out of his denial of the claim that scientific choices are dictated by impersonal standards. When, in other words, he directs it toward finding a social explanation for the *overall* progressiveness of science rather than to the task of illuminating the processes through which actual historical instances of conceptual change impress themselves upon a scientific group. Let me, then, try to show in what ways Kuhn's sociology appears to be thrown off its course by his treatment of this question of progressiveness.

Paradigms

Kuhn's conception of the constraints under which the scientist works—the constraints that make his work "science," and guarantee its progressiveness—can, I think, be illuminated with the help of a distinction made in sociological jurisprudence, namely, the distinction between declared laws and the "living law," that is, between formulated rules and precepts collected together in legal codes, and the law as it actually lives and is lived in society, and put to work in the courts.[14] Merton is concerned to identify the social pressures which add sanction to the a-social methodological rules of scientific investigation, and so endow them with the power to shape a way of life. Kuhn, in contrast, concentrates his attention upon the "living law" embodied in the day-to-day practices of actual groups of scientists. He believes that the growth of science stems finally from the character of this "working law" rather than from the operation of methodological canons of the kind enunciated by positivists and "socialized" by Merton.

Indeed, it might not be too extravagant to push still further the parallel between Kuhn's treatment of scientific progress and the analysis of legal development undertaken by sociologically-influenced legal theorists like the American realists. Characteristically, the legal realists—inspired by the distinguished working judge Oliver Wendell Holmes and greatly influenced by the pragmatism of William James and John Dewey—placed the center of gravity of legal development in the *practice* of law in the courts, rather than in its enactment or codification by the state, or in its rationalization by legal scholars. They maintained that the growth of the "living law" can only be traced by studying the day-to-day decisions of the courts rather than by reading the statute books or legal texts. And further, they argued that these decisions could be understood by treating them not as the necessary outcome of the logical extension of established principles of law, but as reflections of the professional judgment of the legal community. The legal realists were, in brief, concerned more with the life of the law than with its logic, and so tried to illuminate its growth by studying the sociology of the legal profession rather than by exhibiting the structure of legal reasoning. Kuhn's work seems to me to reflect much the same "pragmatic" spirit. While Merton tries to explain the conformity of practice to logic, Kuhn is concerned to give priority to practice over logic—to concrete ways of doing science over abstract codes of procedure. In consequence he provides an account of scientific development which

107

gives a much larger measure of free play for the scientist in deciding the merit of scientific theories than positivism allows, and which, further, accentuates the social rather than logical constraints upon his judgment. In fact, Kuhn's scientist begins to look very much like the legal realists' judge: a man engaged in the interpretation, elaboration, modification, and even on occasions overthrow of a professional tradition of practice, rather than an automaton whose activities are finally monitored by a fixed inexorable logic.

The analysis of the formation, transmission, articulation, and eventual breakup of research traditions is surely a task that sociologists should be equipped to undertake. However, the conceptual scheme developed by Merton cannot handle it: to postulate a commitment on the part of scientists to highly abstract and generalized values may appear to explain their dedication to "scientific method," but it can do little to illuminate the rise and fall of the concrete traditions which govern the day-to-day practice of science. And yet paradoxically though Kuhn sets out with the aid of his concept of a paradigm to do just this, he works himself by degrees into a position very like that of Merton.

Thus the argument in his book *The Structure of Scientific Revolutions* rests on the proposition that a scientific community is distinguished by its members' commitment to a particular way of doing science as exemplified in certain "accepted examples of actual scientific practice" or paradigms. But a later paper on this subject concludes with the assertion that scientific progress is to be explained by scientists' commitment to certain "paramount values" which plainly have priority over paradigms—in fact the latter are given only passing consideration in the text.[15] Why has Kuhn shifted the locus of scientific commitment from (transitory) concrete paradigms to stable abstract values? To answer this question we must look at the use he makes of the notion of a paradigm in his attempt to show that to deny the rationality of science is not necessarily to deny its progressiveness.

Kuhn contends that a research tradition (the "living law" of a scientific community) springs from what he calls paradigms. But his critics have pointed out that the notion of a paradigm is highly ambiguous.[16] In places Kuhn appears to use the term to refer to what Toulmin has called "ideals of natural order" or "master-theories"—i.e., "the rational ideas or conceptions of the regular order of Nature" into which the scientist must fit the phenomena he is studying to render them intelligible.[17] But elsewhere Kuhn states emphatically that the term "paradigm" denotes not a world-view but a specific example of actual scientific practice which serves as a model for a research community and implicitly defines the legitimate problems and methods of a research field for successive generations of practitioners. In fact, he is at pains to distinguish sharply between exemplary, tradition-defining, scientific achievements of this kind and "the various concepts, laws, theories and points of view that may be abstracted from them."[18]

Kuhn's insistence on his distinction is in accord with his rejection of scientific rationalism; where "rationalists" maintain that scientists judge the value of a piece of scientific work against general and fully articulated standards of merit, Kuhn asserts that the definitive quality of a paradigmatic study impresses itself directly upon scientists, unmediated by explicit rules and standards. Paradigms, not theories of methodological rules, are the final repositories of scientific authority; they are the (uncodified) charters of scientific communities, the focal point of the complex of theoretical, methodological, and instrumental commitments that give coherence to a scientific field. Faithfulness to the traditions which spring from paradigms or sets of paradigms is the hallmark of genuine "science." To break faith with established tradition is to risk being labelled a crank, a charlatan, or being made an "outlaw."

A sociologist reading Kuhn's attack on scientific rationalism can hardly fail to be struck by how closely it resembles Oakeshott's famous onslaught against political rationalism; Kuhn's science like Oakeshott's politics is subject to authority of concrete traditions rather than that of abstract "reason."[19] Both are seen as practical activities that, to use Oakeshott's distinction, involve not merely technical knowledge (or technique) which "is susceptible of formulation in rules, principles, directions, and maxims" and which may therefore be learned from a book and thereafter "applied," but also practical knowledge which cannot be reduced to rules, cannot be written down and therefore "can neither be taught nor learned, but only imparted."[20] Knowledge of this latter kind whether in science or politics is according to Oakeshott expressed in "a customary or traditional way of doing things . . . it exists only in practice, and the only way to acquire it is by apprenticeship to a master—not because the master can teach it (he cannot), but because it can be acquired only by continuous contact with one who is perpetually practising it."[21] This surely is the essence of Kuhn's notion of a paradigm—that science is governed by tradition rather than reason; that it is learned directly from models not through mastery of theories and technical rules; that the progress of science depends not on the scientists'

openness of mind, independence, skepticism, and rejection of authority, but upon their submission to the authority vested in these
models; that, in short, the progressiveness of science stems from its
coherence, coherence which does not derive from the fact that scientists pursue a single end (the "truth") by means selected in accordance with common standards (scientific method), but from the
fact that the practice of scientists springs up within what Oakeshott
calls a common "idiom of activity." It follows that the practice and
development of science is to be understood not by trying to show
that it conforms to the means/end scheme of positivistic theories of
action, but by comprehending the "idiom" (or idioms) in which it is
practiced. It would not be difficult to go on drawing parallels between Oakeshott and Kuhn, but more illuminating for our present
purpose are two significant contrasts. First, Kuhn does not appear to
share Oakeshott's reverence for tradition. Oakeshott seeks not only
to deflate the pretensions of rationalists—mere political *parvenus*—
but to restore the sacred character of tradition, to reinvest it with
mystery. What was said by the radical Major Cartwright of Burke's
view of the constitution holds also for Oakeshott's writings on tradition—that he could never speak of it "but in trope or figure, in
simile, metaphor, or mysterious allusion." Kuhn's language is more
direct. His aim is not to surround tradition with mystery, but subject it to intellectual analysis. Secondly, Oakeshott conceives science
as a single tradition, and scientists as engaged in a single "conversation," conducted, down the years, in a single idiom.[22] Kuhn is forced
by his contention that research traditions stem from paradigms, i.e.,
from particular pieces of scientific work, to see the history of science
in terms of a succession of discrete traditions each defined by a
paradigm or set of paradigms, each with its own distinctive idiom,
each holding the undivided attention of a community of scientists
for a certain period of time, and each destined eventually to be
discarded. Science, for Kuhn, is not a single conversation, but a
medley of conversations conducted in different idioms, the speakers
in one idiom not being able to comprehend fully speakers in another,
for, as Kuhn himself puts it, "those who subscribe to alternative,
incommensurable paradigms are bound to a degree to talk past each
other."[23]

This picture of science must raise doubts about its overall progressiveness: if "normal" science progresses because scientists submit to being governed by a paradigm, what guarantee is there that
changes from one paradigm to another, one "idiom" to another, will
also be progressive?

Normal science as Kuhn conceives it is progressive almost by definition. Its reigning paradigms define for a community of scientists what problems, procedures, and solutions are admissible, or in other words what, for them, is counted as science. Further, the whole institutional apparatus of a normal scientific community— controlling as it does the training and socialization of recruits, access to research facilities and channels of communication and publication, and the distribution of rewards—is geared toward keeping the practice of science within the bounds set by the ruling paradigms, and thus preventing the energies of scientists from being dissipated by their engaging in interminable disputes over basic assumptions, or tackling insoluble problems, or engaging in debates with "deviants" who do not accept the rules of the game. Consequently, insofar as it has the power to enforce conformity to its paradigms, the scientific community is "an immensely efficient instrument for solving the problems or puzzles that [these] paradigms define."[24]

The progressiveness of science, in its normal phase, depends therefore on the vigor with which the authority of paradigms is asserted so as to channel available resources into finding solutions for a limited range of problems. However, science does not always progress "normally." In the history of science periods of normal development, according to Kuhn, are separated by comparatively brief "revolutionary" upheavals—extraordinary episodes during which a scientific community loses confidence in the ability of its governing paradigms to generate research strategies that will solve all the legitimate problems before them, casts around for alternative models, and finally transfers its loyalties to a new paradigm which promises better. But what guarantee is there that such paradigm changes are progressive? Kuhn maintains that choices between paradigms are not dictated by logic or by evidence. Consequently if they are progressive then the explanation must be psychological or sociological; it must lie in the character of the scientific community that makes them. However, Kuhn is at pains to stress that choices between paradigms that characterize "extraordinary" science are very different in kind from the choices that face practitioners of "normal" paradigm-dominated science; the former are made, and justified, without the possibility of a final appeal to principle or precedent. In fact, he likens them to such phenomena as gestalt-switches or religious conversion; they are intrusions into normality, rather than outgrowths from it.

So we end with the paradox that the scientific community which ensures the progressiveness of *normal science* by the single-mindedness with which it enforces conformity to its reigning paradigms, also guarantees the progressiveness of *extraordinary science* by the qualities it brings to the task of discrediting these paradigms and putting others in their place. Kuhn extracts himself from this paradox by changing his original position, a change which may or may not give a convincing explanation of the progressiveness of science, but which clearly, in my view at least, greatly detracts from the sociological value of his account of scientific change. Having at the outset asserted that the scientists' primary commitment is to the concrete ways of doing science exemplified in paradigms, Kuhn finally maintains that scientists have a yet more basic commitment to certain "paramount values," which underwrites their acceptance of particular paradigms, and sees them through the uneasy periods when the authority of these paradigms is wavering. In effect, Kuhn maintains that science is governed by a kind of political culture which prevents scientists from losing their heads during periods of crisis.[25]

Kuhn's scientists are thoroughgoing constitutionalists. They are reformers, not revolutionaries. They are devoted to finding solutions to problems within the framework of an established tradition of thought, not to undermining its foundations. They are by nature and training ingenious puzzle-solvers who will only lose faith in accepted procedures if they continually fail to produce solutions. Only then will they look around for alternative ways of playing the game; and only when they can see that an alternative promises a settled future of puzzle-solving will they commit themselves to it.

Scientific revolutions, on this account, may be intellectually momentous affairs, but socially they generally prove to be pretty innocuous. Scientists have no stomach for disorder. They will not cut themselves off from the old order until the new is clearly before their eyes. But as soon as this is the case, they make the change without much friction. They quickly adopt the new ways of play and regroup themselves into puzzle-solving communities, leaving behind only a few diehards. Thus the intellectual discontinuity of the paradigm-switch is compensated for by the continuity of the "political culture," their paramount commitment to unanimity and to normality. Therein, according to Kuhn, lies the final guarantee of the progressiveness of scientific revolutions: scientists will only take up a new paradigm if they are convinced that it will not require them to negate the achievements of the past, and will enable them to return to the satisfying routines of normal science. Scientists will not entertain a new way of doing science unless it can produce consensus and normality. To accuse Kuhn, as Lakatos does[26] of making scientific progress the hostage of mob psychology may be excusable as rhetoric but it misrepresents the spirit of Kuhn's argument: collective psychology perhaps, but the collective psychology of a group of men whose very activity engenders a respect for order, a group more akin to a body of lawyers than to a revolutionary mob.

Whether or not Kuhn's recent account of the paramount values of science stands as a socio-psychological explanation of the progressiveness of science in general, I doubt very much that it contributes as much to our understanding of particular instances of scientific change as does the notion of a paradigm. Indeed it leads us away from the latter problem. If we assert that scientists at the last are committed not to any particular pattern of normal science but merely to "normality" as such, and not to any one particular scientific community but merely to "group unanimity," as such, then the problem of explaining changes in the mode of practice and the social structure of science virtually disappears; for what is made to strike the eye is not the changes but the continuity in paramount values.

It is remarkable how close Kuhn's epistemological interest in explaining progressiveness drives him to Merton's sociological position. Merton makes scientific values lend social weight to the a-social canons of scientific method which guarantee the progressiveness of science; Kuhn dispenses with such methodological canons, but gets out of difficulty by recruiting his "paramount values"—which finally are no less abstract and a-historical than Merton's logic of procedure —to stand in their place. This is a great pity; it comes from bending sociology for epistemological reasons to an "essentialist" or "necessitarian" view of science with the aim of catching its "spirit" or driving force and so explaining its progressiveness. This is to repeat once again Merton's confusion of an account of the essence or meaning of science with an explanation of its historical development over a particular period of time. More valuable is Kuhn's original conception that the day-to-day practice of science is governed by concrete research traditions, by "living law," rather than by abstract rules, values, or essences. This opens a whole new field for sociological inquiry. It invites us to study the *contingent* relationships between the rise and decline of such tradition-bound ways of doing science, the movement of more or less rationally-supported ideas, and the development of socially-constrained scientific institutions. The way ahead for the sociology of science, I would argue, lies not in the elaboration of theories of scientific man, whether we give him the appearance of Merton's rational "methodist" or Kuhn's puzzle-solving constitutionalist, but in the study of the interrelations of modes of thought, work-styles, and the social positions of scientific men, employing as Kuhn does the notion of scientific authority—rational or "traditional," intellectual or social—as the key-linking concept.

I have tried to show in this paper that writers like Merton and Kuhn who have allowed their sociology of science to be dictated by the problem of finding a social basis for the rationality or, as in Kuhn's case, the progressiveness of science have been forced to assert that the scientist's ultimate commitment is to a set of highly abstract values, values which are supposed to generate or confirm a constant mode of life which remains undisrupted by changes in scientific thought. I would argue that to postulate the existence of such a value system does little to illuminate the actual course of scientific change. Rather the reverse—to the extent that scientists are represented as being able to alter on demand their patterns of thought and practice without doing violence to these ultimate commitments, scientific changes appear to be unproblematic. Scientific values come to be seen as a kind of frame within which any "scientific" picture of the world can be fitted without strain. For Merton such a picture is bound to fit, because the frame was pre-formed to accommodate the products of rational scientific activity; for Kuhn it fits, because only pictures that *do* fit count as scientific.

However, to assume, in the interests of epistemology, a spontaneous alignment between scientific values, practice, and thought is to deny oneself the means of comprehending the real course of scientific change. What I would advocate is a kind of "epistemological agnosticism," similar to the attitude of "methodological atheism" taken up by Berger in his sociology of religion, which would give sociologists the opportunity of developing the kind of approach that serves more to illuminate actual historical processes of change in the patterns of thought, mode of practice, and social situation of scientists, than to meet the demands of epistemology.

Kuhn's *Structure of Scientific Revolutions* sketches in the broad outlines of this approach. But, as I have tried to show, more recently he has appeared to alter the terms of his analysis, perhaps to meet the criticism levelled against him by the philosophers of science. However there is a weakness even in the earlier study. It fails to live quite up to its title. It does not present a convincing analysis of the *internal* structure of scientific revolutions; indeed it concedes that they are intrinsically unanalyzable events by likening them to gestalt-switches or acts of religious conversion. As a consequence Kuhn does not succeed in developing a sociological theory of scientific change. He fails to do so because from the outset he separates scientific growth into distinct phases. In periods of "normal" science, scientists' basic commitments—conceptual, methodological, technical—are virtually constant. During the intervals of "extraordinary" science there is a complete switch-around in these commitments. In the normal phase the emphasis falls on the stability of commitments, and upon the tradition-bound authority structure that underwrites them. In periods of revolution, on the other hand, scientists break with one set of commitments and adopt another. In the one case change is marginal; in the other it is represented as an unanalyzable mutation.

Sociologists cannot, then, expect to find in Kuhn's work a ready-made theory of scientific change. But what Kuhn has done is to show how such a theory might be developed by attacking the problem of how concrete ways of doing science, or more specifically the authority structures that uphold them, are modified, disrupted, and perhaps overthrown in the face of changes in scientific thought and technique.

NOTES

1. Peter L. Berger and Thomas Luckman, *The Social Construction of Reality* (London, 1967), 16.

2. See, for instance: N. W. Storer, *The Social System of Science* (New York, 1966), in which science is described as "a particular sort of behavior"; John Ziman, *Public Knowledge: The Social Dimension of Science* (Cambridge, 1968), 130, asserts that "The true sociology of science is ... [concerned] with the social interactions between a scientist and his colleagues ..."; cf. Stephen Cotgrove, "The Sociology of Science and Technology," *British Journal of Sociology* 21 (1970), 1-15.

3. T. S. Kuhn, *The Structure of Scientific Revolutions* (Chicago, 1962).

4. This is a striking point of overlap between Merton and Marxist historians of science from B. Hessen and J. D. Bernal to Christopher Hill. They share the inclination to assimilate science to "work," and to stress the spontaneous alignment of the interests of the scientific movement and of the groups they regard as being economically the most progressive at any given point in time, be they capitalists in the seventeenth century or the workers in the twentieth century. See my discussion of J. D. Bernal in "Science and the Professional Dilemma" in *Penguin Social Sciences Survey*, ed. Julius Gould (London, 1968), 51-68.

5. R. K. Merton, "Priorities in Scientific Discovery: A Chapter in the Sociology of Science," *American Sociological Review* 22 (1957), 635-659.

6. T. S. Kuhn, "Historical Structure of Scientific Discovery," *Science* 136 (1962), 760-764.

7. Ibid., 762.

8. Merton, "Priorities," 643.

9. Hall, "Merton Revisited," 13-14.

10. See especially, Imre Lakatos, "Criticism and the Methodology of Scientific Research Programmes," *Proceedings of the Aristotelian Society,* n.s., 69 (1968-69), 149-186; and Dudley Shapere, review of *The Structure of Scientific Revolutions* in this volume.

11. Kuhn, *Structure of Scientific Revolutions,* 4.

12. Ibid., 169.

13. See note 10.

14. See W. Friedmann, *Legal Theory,* 4th ed. (London, 1960), Chap. 23, on which my account largely rests.

15. T. S. Kuhn, "Logic of Discovery or Psychology of Research" in *Criticism and the Growth of Knowledge,* ed. Imre Lakatos and Alan Musgrave (Cambridge, 1970).

16. See especially Shapere in this volume, esp. p. 29; and Stephen Toulmin, "Conceptual Revolutions in Science," in *Boston Studies in the Philosophy of Science,* ed. R. S. Cohen and M. W. Wartofsky (Dordrecht, 1967), III, 337-341.

17. S. Toulmin, *Foresight and Understanding* (London, 1961), Chaps. 3 and 4.

18. Kuhn, *Structure of Scientific Revolutions,* 11.

19. Michael Oakeshott, "Rationalism in Politics" (1947) reprinted in *Rationalism in Politics* (London, 1962), 1-36.

20. Ibid., 10.

21. Ibid., 11.

22. See the essay on "Rational Conduct" (1950) reprinted in *Rationalism in Politics,* 80-110. On pp. 102-103 there is a discussion of the nature of scientific activity which is strikingly similar to that of Kuhn.

23. Kuhn, *Structure of Scientific Revolutions,* 147.

24. Ibid., 165.

25. The notion of "paramount values" is introduced by Kuhn in the final sections of his paper "Logic of Discovery or Psychology of Research." See note 15.

26. I. Lakatos, "Criticism and the Methodology of Scientific Research Programmes," 181.

THE PARADIGM CONCEPT AND SOCIOLOGY: A CRITICAL REVIEW

DOUGLAS LEE ECKBERG and LESTER HILL, JR.

INTRODUCTION

Undoubtedly one of the more influential and controversial scholarly books to emerge in the last few decades is Thomas S. Kuhn's (1962; 1970a) *The Structure of Scientific Revolutions.* The impact of this work has been felt in such diverse fields as history, philosophy, political science, anthropology, sociology, theology, and even art (Hollinger, 1973). Students of each of these disciplines, in assessing the relevance of the paradigm concept for their own concerns, have begun arguments which continue to this time (see, for example, the wry account in Perry, 1977).

Although these discussions are interesting in their own right, it is the discussion among sociologists that is of primary concern here. There have been several attempts to use Kuhn's scheme of scientific structure to analyze the development of sociology. The results of these attempts have been far from satisfactory. In fact, there are almost as many views of the paradigmatic status of sociology as there are sociologists attempting such analyses. As we will demonstrate, sociology is seen as possessing anywhere from two to eight paradigms, depending on which analyst one chooses to cite.

One explanation of this phenomenon is that a number of sociological theorists have misused the paradigm concept. The result of this misuse has been that the concept has come to be used in ways which Kuhn never intended. In some cases it has taken on attributes which he specifically disavows. Multiple interpretations of the term have had the effect of allowing sociologists to cite Kuhn as a source while, at the same time, they are not taking seriously the implications of his position.

We use the term "misuse" advisedly. As we will show later, Kuhn's original paradigm formulation left considerable room for variance in interpretation. Still, two aspects were central to the term even prior to 1962 (for example, Kuhn, 1957: ix): the cognitive nature of para-

117

digms and the community structure in which they appear. Moreover, the writers discussed here were largely aware of Kuhn's (1970a) later explication of the concept. When they miss either aspect of paradigm, they misuse the concept in a technical sense, even when their arguments are otherwise compelling. Their general positions may command respect, but their reliance on Kuhn is ill-founded.

In this paper we shall (1) provide a clear explication of the paradigm concept by following definitions and uses of the term by Kuhn (1962; 1970a; 1970b; 1974) and Masterman (1970), (2) show the various ways in which sociologists have used the concept, (3) attempt to ascertain just why such a theoretically important contribution has been so misused, and (4) provide our own version of the paradigmatic status of sociology. This paper will not consider the validity of Kuhn's overall position.

COGNITIVE ASPECTS OF PARADIGMS

In one respect it is not surprising that the paradigm concept has been misconstrued. Kuhn himself admits that his original explication was obscure (Kuhn, 1970a:181). Even a sympathetic critic (Masterman, 1970) suggests that Kuhn uses the term in at least twenty-one different ways, but she also notes that the various usages fall into three main categories: metaphysical, sociological, and construct paradigms. By the time the concept found its way into general sociological discourse, Kuhn had made several efforts to clarify its meaning. Others, however, seemed more intent on stretching it. As Perry (1977:40) notes, ". . . if Kuhn has been concerned to delimit the meaning of his key terms, others have been engaged in extending them" (see Heyl, 1975:62).

Without necessarily agreeing with the specific labels employed, we can agree with Masterman that paradigm refers to beliefs at three different levels. At the broadest level of generality (corresponding to what Masterman calls "metaphysical paradigms," or "metaparadigms") are unquestioned presuppositions. Kuhn does not overtly grant such usage, but Masterman finds it abundant in his work, and it is the only kind of paradigm to which his philosophical critics have referred (Masterman, 1970:65).

More restrictive is Kuhn's disciplinary matrix (corresponding roughly to Masterman's sociological paradigm), which represents the shared commitments of any disciplinary community, including symbolic generalizations, beliefs, values, and a host of other elements (Kuhn, 1970a:182ff.). A disciplinary matrix may be seen as

118

the special subculture of a community. It does *not* refer to the beliefs of an entire discipline (e.g., biology), but more correctly to those beliefs of a specialized community (e.g., phage workers in biology). This is an important point which will be discussed in more detail below.

The most restrictive use of paradigm is reserved for what Kuhn calls an "exemplar." Corresponding to what Masterman labels an "artifact" or "construct" paradigm, this term refers, first of all, to the concrete accomplishments of a scientific community. What many of his critics (and supporters) have failed to see is that it is the exemplar which is the most central meaning of paradigm for Kuhn. Compared with disciplinary matrix, for example, he states that exemplar is the deeper of the usages (Kuhn, 1970a:175; 1974:463, 471ff.).

Since the crucial meaning of the paradigm concept for Kuhn is the exemplar, it is important that we understand in detail what he means by this term. By "exemplar," Kuhn means "initially, the concrete problem-solutions that students encounter from the start of their scientific education, whether in laboratories, or examinations, or at the ends of chapters in science texts" (1970a:187). To such problem-solutions, Kuhn adds "at least some of the technical problem-solving found in the periodical literature that scientists encounter during their post-educational research careers and that also show them by example how their job is to be done" (1970a:187).

Masterman helps us to begin to unravel some of the confusion associated with the paradigm concept by noting that a "paradigm is a concrete 'picture' of something, A, which is used analogically to describe a concrete something else, B" (1970:77). Masterman is telling us that the important question is not what an exemplar *is* (such that one can enumerate it) so much as what it *does*. Kuhn never quite succeeds in making this point explicit, which may explain some of the confusion surrounding his argument. Where he has failed, however, Masterman (1970:70) succeeds:

> [if] we ask what a Kuhnian paradigm *is*, Kuhn's habit of multiple definition poses a problem. If we ask, however, what a paradigm *does*, it becomes clear at once ... that the construct sense of "paradigm," and not the metaphysical sense ... is the fundamental one. *For only with an artifact can you solve puzzles.* (emphasis in original)

Again:

> What Kuhn must be feeling his way to, in talking about an arti-

fact which is also a "way of seeing," is an assertion, not about the *nature* of his artifact, but about its *use*: namely, that being a picture of one thing, it is used to represent another. . . . (Masterman, 1970:76-7, emphasis added)

It was following Masterman's comments that Kuhn began making more explicit the *function* of an exemplar:

The resultant ability to see a variety of situations as like each other . . . is, I think, the main thing a student acquires by doing exemplary problems. . . . After he has completed a certain number, which may vary from one individual to the next, he views the situations that confront him as a scientist in the same gestalt as other members of his specialists' group. (Kuhn, 1970a:189)

The term, paradigm, is taken from linguistics, where it refers to patterns of declension, conjugation, and so forth, of types of words, such that a given word will make sense in different contexts of use (e.g. amo, amas, amat). Kuhn's most straightforward demonstration of a paradigm element involves the various derivations of Newton's $f = ma$, such that in various contexts the formula comes to be $mg = md^2/sdt^2$, $mgSin\Theta = -md^2/sdt^2$, $m_1d^2s_1/dt_2+k_1s_1 = k_2(dt \; s_2-s_1)$, and so on (Kuhn, 1974:464 and passim). The point is that symbolic (and other) generalizations in science are applied in areas where it is nowhere immediately apparent that they fit. Fitting is accomplished through a series of examples given to a student which indicate that generalization A can be modified to become generalizations A', A'', A''', and so forth, as the situation changes. All of these make sense in terms of the base generalization which spawned them.

The function, then, of an exemplar is to permit a way of seeing one's subject matter *on a concrete level*, thereby allowing *puzzle solving* to take place. This is central for Kuhn because it is the basis for his notion of normal science, and normal science is the basis for his demarcation between science and nonscience (Kuhn, 1969; 1970b: 245-6). For a discipline to be a science it must engage in puzzle-solving activity; but puzzle solving can only be carried out if a community shares concrete puzzle solutions, or exemplars. It is the *exemplar* that is important, not merely the disciplinary matrix, and certainly not merely the general presuppositions of the community. The latter may be important (see Holton, 1973; 1975), but they do not direct ongoing, day-to-day research.

Something more should be said about the interrelationships among the three levels of paradigm. Perhaps the most important point is that they are embedded one within the other. That is, the greater structure (the metaphysical paradigm) acts as an encapsulating unit, or framework, within which the more restricted, or higher-order, structures develop.[1] A specific disciplinary matrix will not develop within just any arbitrary *Weltanschauung*. An exemplar will be even further restricted. Before exemplars could develop, say, in sociology, one would have to accept some basic sociological presuppositions. It must be stated immediately that the presence of a disciplinary matrix does not guarantee in any way that normal science will develop. Kuhn is attempting to describe the structure of a science, not give guidelines for its accomplishment. In Kuhn's (1970b:245) own words:

> ... I claim no therapy to assist the transformation of a proto-science to a science, nor do I suppose that anything of the sort is to be had.... If... some social scientists take from me the view that they can improve the status of their field by first legislating agreement on fundamentals and then turning to puzzle solving, they are badly misconstruing my point.

Returning to the interrelationships among the three levels of paradigm, we find that each lower level has directive power over the next higher level such that the development of the higher level can be seen as an articulation of the lower. There *is* a reflexive side to the relationship, however. A "revolution" is that reconceptualization of a lower order belief made necessary by the presence of anomalies in the next higher level. Anomalies are possible only because each higher level of belief is more constrained than the previous level. When we reach the level of the exemplar we are speaking of almost purely concrete applications of a highly structured body of belief. It is at this level that inconsistencies can and do become apparent. Such inconsistencies appear in the course of active puzzle solving.

STRUCTURAL ASPECTS OF PARADIGMS

As the foregoing discussion illustrates, "paradigm" (more precisely, "exemplar") indicates a quite specific type of cognitive framework. What is equally important, however, is the structure of the group which collectively holds a paradigm (see Kuhn, 1970a:176-81; 1970b:251-3). Specifically, a paradigm presupposes an integrated community of practitioners. Ongoing puzzle solving, in fact, occurs only when a group exists which shares a consistent body of belief such that a consensus emerges with regard to the phenomena one investigates, the methods one uses, and so forth.

Kuhn's discussion of the training of new scientists exemplifies this group context of research. New students in a discipline are painstakingly taught the matrix of beliefs which mark the discipline. The change from confused undergraduate to sophisticated scientist is a massive one. Students first learn a basic sort of knowledge, then begin learning applications of it. Later they begin learning the specialized body of knowledge which constitutes their scientific specialties.

In all cases, the neophyte scientists are dependent on their texts and professors for explication of what may at first appear incomprehensible. A relatively unproblematic learning process is possible only where there is a lack of dispute over what constitutes real knowledge, the "truth" of the situation. It is only after long-term tutelage that students learn where to look for puzzles—research topics to which paradigms virtually guarantee a solution.

Thus, a paradigm locks its practitioners together within a fairly rigid, highly elaborated framework of beliefs. This is not a serendipitous overlapping of elements from various perspectives. It is made of the consensual beliefs of a self-contained community. No analysis which neglects the *communal* nature of a paradigm can capture the essence of the concept. It is so important that Kuhn claims that if he were to rewrite *The Structure of Scientific Revolutions* he would "*open* with a discussion of the community structure of science" (Kuhn, 1970a:176, emphasis added). What is truly surprising is the number of sociologists who have not seen or have preferred to ignore "the sociological base of [Kuhn's] position" (Kuhn, 1970b:253).

SOCIOLOGISTS AND THE USE OF THE PARADIGM CONCEPT

As we have seen, a paradigm refers to that thing which allows scientists to go about solving the puzzles they continually generate. When used by sociologists, however, the term comes most often to mean no more than a general theoretical perspective, or even, as we shall see, a collection of elements from several more or less distinct perspectives. As such, the paradigms spoken of by sociologists are nebulous, shifting entities, indicating whatever one wishes them to indicate, and are limited only by the theorist's imagination. While a specialized scientific community can be readily isolated on the basis of (1) quite specific beliefs concerning subject entities and (2) professional relationships among active scientists, perspectives can be formed at will, depending only upon which elements in intellectual discourse one wishes to emphasize. To put it another way, the sociological pie can be sliced many ways, but it is problematical as to whether any of these slicings indicate paradigmatic structure.

Table 1 presents twelve different sets of authors who view the organization of sociology in at least ten fundamentally different ways —each claiming to present "Kuhnian paradigms." The earliest among these authors is R. W. Friedrichs (1970; 1972) who makes quite clear his debt to Kuhn, and whose initial description of paradigms follows Kuhn's closely (Friedrichs, 1970:4). In application, however, Friedrichs radically revises the concept. Having admitted that Kuhn's original scheme was not intended to be used in the analysis of social science (e.g., 1962:ix-x), Friedrichs (1970:18-9) proceeds to attempt just such an analysis. He concedes that there is no dominant paradigm in sociology (of the kind necessary for normal science), and that such may not be possible. (Of course, from Kuhn's perspective, paradigms, or exemplars, are not seen as being discipline-wide in the first place.) He then spends much space arguing about the distinctive nature of social science, and later in his work actually criticizes Kuhn for failing to notice the difference (Friedrichs, 1970:324-5).

Friedrichs' basic contention is that in sociology there are two orders of paradigm. On one level are those paradigms which Friedrichs sees as much like those in natural science. Two of these are primary: (1) the system, or consensus paradigm (Friedrichs, 1970:25) and (2) the most popular contender, the conflict paradigm (Friedrichs, 1970: 45). This type of paradigm is supposed to correspond to the "fundamental image a discipline has of its subject matter" (Friedrichs, 1970: 55, emphasis removed).

However, according to Friedrichs, this primary order of paradigms is *not* the most crucial one for the social sciences. There is a "more fundamental paradigmatic dimension" in the social sciences, and that is the "image the social scientist has of *himself as scientific agent*" (Friedrichs, 1970:55, emphasis in original. For an evaluation of this "paradigm as a form of personal salvation," see Perry, 1977: 42-4). Friedrichs contends that this level of paradigm is the more basic and has a controlling power over paradigms of the other order. Finally, Friedrichs maintains that there are two fundamental paradigms: the priestly and the prophetic. The choice between them determines the choice between the conflict and consensus paradigms (1970:290-1; also see Westhues, 1976, for an elaboration and extension of this argument).

123

Considering Friedrichs' lower-order paradigms, it is evident at once that they correspond, at *best*, to disciplinary matrices, and perhaps not even to that level of paradigm, as they are *discipline-wide* and do not divide sociology by our community criterion. Friedrichs' higher-order paradigms are even more metaphysical. We do not argue that such cognitive sets do not exist. We *do* hold that they are not group-bounded and that they affect no more than minimally the *direction* of research. Neither order of paradigm is of a concrete enough quality to support a puzzle-solving tradition. Postulation of such a structure implies that research is *not* strictly paradigmatic, that it does *not* utilize artifacts. Here, science (or at least social science) comes to be seen as a purely political undertaking in which research traditions and anomalous findings play no active parts. Such implications are quite different from those associated with Kuhn's notion of paradigm.

An important point that Friedrichs disregards is that Kuhn is interested in scientific activity as revolving about a technical or instrumental knowledge. Concern with oneself as an actor is concern with something fundamentally different. It is not surprising that the behavior postulated to accompany such divergent concerns would be strikingly different. The question is how an author could premise such differences yet state that the same model of behavior underlies both concerns.

It might be noted that Friedrichs (1972) does take note of Kuhn's clarification of the paradigm concept. Following Kuhn's discussion of the importance of exemplars in the development of a discipline, Friedrichs develops an idea for a type of exemplar for sociology which he calls "the dialectic." However, he once again so revises the concepts that they lose their original content. In this case he argues that a stream of articles in major journals functions in the same way as do concrete accomplishments within a coherent research tradition. There are, of course, similarities between the two, but unless the streams themselves are part of a research tradition they do not lend themselves to technical puzzle solving.

Friedrichs is not alone, of course, in contending that the consensus/functional approach is one of the major paradigms in sociology. Lehman and Young (1974), Kuklick (1972), and Bottomore (1975) all claim that functionalism (along with various competitors) is a paradigm in sociology. The same argument against Friedrichs advanced above applies here. Functionalism and its contenders are simply *not* paradigms in the sense that Kuhn intended. They are not widely recognized achievements which practically and conceptually define the course of future research. If we read Kuhn correctly, the exemplar concept (paradigm) must indicate a much more imposing authority (cf., Bryant, 1975:356ff.).

In each of the cases cited above the focus has been on what might be termed discipline-wide "paradigms"; they are not specific to substantive areas. Sociologists, with few exceptions, have stuck to this level of analysis. One writer goes so far as to claim that true specialties are not possible in sociology, that general ideas are of the greatest importance (Urry, 1973:466). Be this as it may, the greater number of theorists reviewed here have offered just such broad analyses (see, for example, Sherman, 1974; Walsh, 1972; and Wilson, 1970).

Although the sociologists cited above feel that there are, or have been, paradigms in sociology, there are others who feel that the discipline is still preparadigmatic. Among these are Denisoff et al. (1974:2-3), who contend that while sociology does not yet have a paradigm, there are certain *paradigmatic assumptions* underlying sociological work. From their discussion it is evident that they accept a broad definition of paradigm in that what they portray is an overarching matrix of beliefs (Denisoff et al. 1974:3-7).

Another author, Andrew Effrat (1972), feels that a rigorous application of the paradigm concept forces us to conclude that sociology is preparadigmatic. In his discussion of the concept, Effrat explicitly chooses to employ a "[c]onsiderably looser and more generous use of the criteria," and holds that such usage suggests "that there have been a number of reigning paradigms" (Effrat, 1972:11fn.). Having chosen this path, Effrat (1972:12-4) offers what is perhaps the most elaborate method yet for generating paradigms in sociology. Specifically, he employs a typology based upon the interaction of two dimensions: (1) level of analysis (micro vs. macro) and (2) substantive component emphasized (material, affective, interactional, and idealist or symbolist). He thus generates eight paradigms for political sociology alone, and he admits that there may still be more.

At the end of a complexity spectrum away from Effrat is Michael Carroll (1972), who presents us with a series of assumptions which he contends underlie the "analysis of variance paradigm." While not maintaining that this is the only paradigm in sociology, Carroll does state that it is extremely widespread. As is the case with most of the writers discussed above, Carroll deals only with discipline-wide ideas. He is also concerned with the methodological, rather than the substantive, assumptions of the perspective (though he shows interrelationships between the two). Moreover, while Kuhn concerns himself with the functions of paradigms, Carroll is concerned exclusively with their dysfunctions. In addition, Carroll's discussion does not directly consider the generation of puzzles, but rather the treatment of puzzles arising from other sources (cf. Kuhn, 1961). As an over-arching generalization, Carroll's paradigm *may* be seen as a component of a disciplinary matrix, but *not* as an exemplar.

A view of paradigms similar to that of Carroll is the one presented by Jack D. Douglas (1971). Douglas holds that a hypothetical-statistical paradigm overlays most of sociology, infusing those com-peting paradigms which are, indeed, attached to substantive con-cerns. He argues that a difference between natural and social science lies in the fact that in natural science paradigm choice exists only between areas of specialization, while in the social sciences it exists across specialties (thus, they are "multiple paradigm"). Yet, following this, he states that the hypothetical-statistical method is seen to be "*the* valid paradigm for research methods in *any* area of specializa-tion" (Douglas, 1971:46). His concern is closely related to that of Carroll and, in trying to place it in a Kuhnian framework, he opens himself to the same criticisms.

We come now to what may be the most mixed attempt to apply Kuhn's paradigm concept to sociology—that of George Ritzer (1975). Ritzer's analysis is at once promising and frustrating. It is promising because, in the abstract, Ritzer understands the concept, understands that it has been misunderstood by sociologists, and concerns himself with the *functions* of paradigms (e.g., Ritzer, 1975:5). It is frustrating because, having once grasped the concept, Ritzer then lets it escape him entirely.

As far as we know, Ritzer is the only sociological theorist who makes a clear distinction between disciplinary matrix and exemplar, and he is one of the few who recognizes that a paradigm need not apply to a discipline as a whole. Having seen all of this, Ritzer pro-ceeds to act as if just the opposite were the case. First, his paradigms are discipline-wide. Secondly, and more important, Ritzer *dismisses* the importance of exemplars and self-assuredly asserts that "[t]he paradigm is the broadest unit of consensus within a science" (Ritzer, 1975:7). We have already seen how broad definitions lose the essen-tial features of paradigm for us. Of course, it is perfectly admissible to analyze science in terms of metaparadigms: E. A. Burtt (1954) did so in the 1920s. The problem with such an analysis in this particular instance is that it misses the puzzle-solving/puzzle-producing, com-munity-based nature of exemplars, and gains nothing new for us. Kuhn does not present us merely with the old idea that metaphysical assumptions structure perceptions in science; rather, he presents us with an analysis of the *place* of such assumptions in the *social organization* of science.

Ritzer's analysis then, like most others, lacks a necessary specificity of referent. For if paradigms are the broadest units of consensus, how can they serve "to differentiate one scientific community (*or sub-community*) from another" (Ritzer, 1975:7)? The broadest unit of consensus in science will be some form of western scientistic world view, or perhaps a linguistic organization of the world such as those discussed by sociolinguists since Whorf (1956).

In this regard, Ritzer's division of sociology into "social facts," "social behavior," and "social definitions" paradigms must be seen as arbitrary, while his statement that each paradigm has "an" exemplar is naive in terms of puzzle-solving traditions. Interestingly, what were seen as conflicting paradigms by others—structural functionalism and conflict theory—are, in Ritzer's scheme, incorporated into a single social facts paradigm (e.g., Ritzer, 1975:57).

It might be asked how perspectives seen as so diverse by others can be placed within a single paradigm. The answer must lie with the theorists. We can only assert that paradigms are *unified* bodies of belief shared by a cohesive *community*. Ritzer joins what others put asunder, and he is far from alone in this regard. The sociological literature on paradigms is strewn with different pie-slicing arrangements. Friedrichs might argue that all three of Ritzer's paradigms fall within the consensus (or priestly) mode. Walsh and Wilson put all of the above (with the possible exception of social definitions) into a positivistic paradigm, while Friedrichs could hold that both positivistic and phenomenological paradigms are priestly. Sherman might assert that the two are separate paradigms joined by a third, emancipatory paradigm, and Douglas seems to argue that a statistical paradigm underlies all three of Ritzer's groups.

Those theorists who generate paradigms on the basis of arbitrary schemes miss *both* the cognitive and the structural aspects of the paradigm concept. Those who speak of conflicting schools of thought (e.g., Kuklick, 1972; and Westhues, 1976) are at least in the same ballpark as Kuhn. They, at least, recognize that his argument concerns structured groups.

In this context, the work of Nicholas Mullins (1973) deserves mention. Mullins is one of a number of sociologists of science who have applied the paradigm and related concepts to analyses of group structure in scientific communities. Recently he has used sociometric techniques developed for such studies (supplemented with a goodly supply of intuition) to indicate that there definitely are coherent theory groups within sociology. The groups he finds do not correspond, in any simple way, with those postulated above. Mullins contends that the variables he employs indicate that the structure of these groups corresponds rather well with that of theory groups in natural science.

Although we are getting ahead of our argument, it is relevant to inquire here if the kinds of *ties* operating within natural science groups are at work within sociological groups. There is reason to doubt that the cognitive content shared by a sociological theory group is precisely the same as that indicated by the term paradigm. Mullins' analysis is directed at group structure rather than at cognitive ties. He admits that his techniques are useful for constructing indicators of group cohesiveness rather than for presenting the group relationships themselves. His roots are more in Derek Price's (1963) invisible colleges than they are in Kuhn's paradigms. Moreover, while occasionally mentioning "paradigmatic content," Mullins is content to call his structures "theory groups." Furthermore, he notes that while sociology seems to fit the model of group structure found in the natural sciences to a decent degree, there *are* some differences. Notably, (1) there is a lack of delineation between different stages of group development within sociology, but not in natural science, and (2) sociology appears to have a looser social and intellectual organization than does natural science (Mullins, 1973:130-6). More will be made of this later.

A problem with analyses such as that presented by Mullins (1973: 321) is related to his admission that his methods merely present indications of social ties. These social ties might be concrete indicators of communities, and could, therefore, serve as evidence for the existence of paradigms. They are, however, necessary but not sufficient conditions for paradigms. In our search for paradigms in sociology then, Mullins' techniques can indicate the structure, but not the content, of theory groups. What is certain is that we cannot be sure that (1) sociology has the same structure as does natural science, or that (2) the patterns that do exist are indicative of paradigm-sharing or paradigm-bounding.

MISUSE OF THE CONCEPT—WHY SOCIOLOGISTS?

If Thomas Kuhn is to be believed, paradigmatic status is determined by the workings of a unified group of specialists. If such is the case, one cannot divide a discipline freely into paradigms, but must be constrained by both group structure and cognitive consensus. Why then do sociologists appear to feel free to divide their discipline into various, inconsistent perspectives and call these divisions "paradigms?" It appears that we can look in two directions for the source of this dilemma: either to Kuhn himself or to the sociologists who have attempted to use his framework.

The simplest answer might be that Kuhn has failed to define his concept clearly enough, and that writers have been victims of ambiguity on his part (for criticisms of Kuhn's position in various respects see Lakatos and Musgrave, 1970; Shapere, 1971; Scheffler, 1967; and Trigg, 1973). This answer has some merit especially if we remember Kuhn's early multiple use of the term (see Masterman, 1970). Moreover, one of Kuhn's most detailed reassessments of the concept was not published until recently (Kuhn, 1974). However, with the lone exception of the hardback edition by Friedrichs, all of the people herein cited mention Kuhn's (1970a) postscript, his (1970b) article in the Lakatos and Musgrave (1970) reader, Masterman's (1970) article, or some combination of the three. Several merely cite, and then disregard, Kuhn's later works. As was stated above, where Kuhn has attempted to delimit the meanings of his terms, others have tried to extend them.

The above observation indicates that we should look in the direction of the sociologists in order to understand the confusion associated with the paradigm concept. A very important clue that can help us to get started is the longstanding concern among sociologists regarding the *scientific status* of the discipline. This is a concern which dates back at least to Comte. The idea implies that the standard by which to measure social science is the success of natural science (Douglas, 1972:52-3). This concern has been fueled by Kuhn's simultaneous references to limited rationality and to science. He speaks of science in terms which have long been applied to sociology. With such a parallel, it has required only a small impetus to move some sociologists from seeing their discipline as sharing some elements with natural science to seeing it as being equal to natural science "paradigmatically."

The wish here is father to the thought, for it is only by disregarding Kuhn's warning that the differences between natural and social science communities served to crystallize his thoughts (Kuhn, 1962:x) that one can say, as does Friedrichs,

if one were to apply Kuhn's posture to the behavioral sciences, it would be possible to conceive of the divisive struggle currently being waged within sociology not as *humiliating proof* of the discipline's relative immaturity, but as evidence of its *coming of age* (Friedrichs, 1970:2, emphasis added).

Friedrichs adds that taking such a stand will allow us to "ignore the *incessant demand* that we profess ourselves worthy of the label 'scientific'." Such a stance will allow us to keep from "running in embarrassment" when our fundamental differences are pointed out (Friedrichs, 1970:2-3, emphasis added; also see Lachenmeyer, 1971).

Thus, sociologists find paradigms scattered across sociology, but only by corrupting Kuhn's model of science. The discovery of paradigms across the field of sociology have been made possible only by redefining the concept (Heyl, 1975:64-5; Perry, 1977; and Pocock, 1971:14fn.). Analysis, however, requires strict usage of terms. It is only by being strict that we come to understand the dynamics about which Kuhn intends to speak. Emphasis on discipline-wide paradigms must be seen as misplaced:

> Paradigms pertain to fields like the study of heat, optics, mechanics, etc.; *there are not and cannot be* paradigms of physics or chemistry. In other words paradigms are not discipline-wide but sub-disciplinary. Their span is likely to be coterminous with that of specialties: conversely, specialities will be paradigm-bonded social systems (Martins, 1972:19, emphasis added).

If this point is missed, we lose one of Kuhn's most fundamental contributions to discourse on the nature of scientific inquiry.

THE PARADIGMATIC STATUS OF SOCIOLOGY

What, then, is the paradigmatic status of sociology? An attempt to answer that question, especially after a critique of others who have tried the same, may be gratuitous. The important analysis is that of the paradigm concept itself, and of the prospects and limits of its use. Still, the status of sociology in this regard is intrinsically interesting, and such an analysis may help clarify the applicability of the concept.

Perhaps the first point to stress is that the general question as to whether sociology has paradigms at the discipline-wide level is moot; *all* disciplinary groups have paradigms (disciplinary matrices) of this sort (see Kuhn, 1970a:179; 1970b:272fn; and 1974:460fn.). At this level it seems that crisis, or, at least, conflict is inevitable. There is probably no need for a monolithic perspective at this level, and it could be unhealthy were one to emerge (see Merton, 1975:28). Here, a Kuhnian paradigm approach is inapplicable, for no truly extended research can take place at this level. Problems abound, but no real puzzles can be found. To the extent that this *is* sociology, it can be said to be a nonspecialized science (Urry, 1973). If this in essence is sociology, then it certainly does not progress by means of sequential concrete examples.

In this respect, of course, it can be (and is) argued that sociology is different from the natural sciences. If this argument is valid, however, then Kuhn's framework cannot be used to analyze the paradigmatic status of the discipline, and we "nonnatural" scientists should concentrate on doing whatever we are supposed to "nonnaturally." However, the consensus seems to be that sociology is, or will become, a science of the natural variety. If this position is adhered to, and if we are to use Kuhn's framework, then it is in the substantive areas of sociology that we must look for paradigms (exemplars). *If* they exist, they will be found in such areas as political socialization, status attainment,[2] ethnic relations, and so forth, *not* in functionalism, conflict theory, and symbolic interactionism. Those who state so emphatically that there are paradigms in sociology must support their assertions by showing that there is at least one area of research that is guided by concrete examples of scholarship, which serve to generate and to solve puzzles. What we often actually find is research modeled upon no other research at all, upon a short, soon-extinguished line of research or upon a single theorist's speculations. There is little extended puzzle solving. There are few instances in the literature where an important puzzle has been solved. Indeed, there are few puzzles, mostly problems. If a problem is considered important, it is never solved at all, but serves as a point of contention among variant perspectives.[3] We find constant arguing, bickering, and debate, but very little agreement. This lack of agreement affects operationalization and manipulation of concepts, such that different research requires different, often incommensurable data. The concepts themselves seem to change from study to study.

Let us be explicit. Although we see the present situation in sociology as being unsettled, we are *not* arguing that there can be no exemplary research in social science. For example, we feel that in the *substantive* area of attitude change paradigmatic research has long been conducted under the cognitive dissonance school of thought. This school has a strong research tradition. Countless puzzles have been generated and solved within it, and the necessary modeling process apparently has occurred. It should be noted immediately, however, that the schools of sociology are not similar to the school of cognitive dissonance. They are more loosely organized. Very loosely. A greater burden falls on the shoulders of a young sociologist than on those of a physicist. The sociologist is not provided with a set of clear normative guidelines followed by those in a tightly organized group.

The conclusion seems inescapable. If paradigms (exemplars) exist in the discipline of sociology, they are difficult to find. Moreover, if they do exist, they (1) must not be discipline-wide, (2) must be found within substantive areas of research, (3) must have communities of practitioners which coalesce around them, and (4) must be used to both generate and solve puzzles and thus generate a visible research tradition.

Table 1. Twelve Sets of Sociological "Paradigms"

Carroll (1972)	Douglas (1972)	Friedrichs (1970)
ANOVA	(1) Hypothetical-Statistical (2) Phenomenological (?)	(1) Priestly (2) Prophetic
Lehman & Young (1974)	Walsh (1972)	Westhues (1976)
(1) Conflict (2) Consensus	(1) Positivistic (2) Phenomenological	(1) Class (2) Organization
Kuklick (1972)	Ritzer (1975)	Sherman (1974)
(1) Structural-functionalism (2) Ecological-interactionism (3) Operationalism	(1) Social Facts (2) Social Definitions (3) Social Behaviors	(1) Nomological (2) Interpretive (3) Critical

Bottomore (1975) | **Denisoff, Callahan & Levine (1974)**

(1) Structural-functionalism
(2) Historical
(3) Structuralism
(4) Phenomenological

(1) Microsociology
(2) Social Evolutionism
(3) Functionalism
(4) Conflict Theory
(5) Nominalism/Voluntarism

Effrat (1972)

(1) Marxism
(2) Cultural and Personality School
(3) Durkheimian
(4) Weberians/Parsonians/Cyberneticists

(5) Exchange/Utilitarianism
(6) Freudianism
(7) Symbolic Interactionism
(8) Phenomenology/Ethnomethodology

Table 2. Nicholas Mullins' (1973) Empirically Grounded Sociological Theory-Groups

(1) Standard American Sociology
(2) Symbolic Interactionism
(3) Small Group Theory
(4) Social Forecasters
(5) Ethnomethodology
(6) New Causal Theory
(7) Structuralists
(8) Radical-Critical Theory

NOTES

1. In this discussion "higher" refers to more restricted levels of belief-consensus. Shared exemplars, for example, are at the highest level of consensus, while metaparadigms are low. Lower orders of belief, here, serve as bases upon which the higher orders are constructed.

2. We should note here the current debate over the theoretical status of status attainment research (see, for example, Horan, 1978). Indeed, two anonymous referees suggested that this research is paradigm-based in the Kuhnian sense. It is not our purpose to enter into this debate in this paper. We do feel that those who seek paradigms in substantive areas such as status attainment are at least looking in the right direction. However, they still must show that the paradigms they find contain *both* the cognitive and the structural characteristics discussed above.

3. Regarding this discussion, it is relevant to note that many analyses of the paradigmatic status of sociology might be seen more accurately as thematic analyses in the sense discussed by Holton (1975). Holton (1975: 334) explicitly warns us of the danger of confusing thematic analyses with such things as paradigms and world views. He then quickly notes two major differences between paradigms and themata. First of all, "...thematic oppositions persist during 'normal science,' and themata persist through revolutionary periods" (Holton, 1975:334). The point here is that thematic oppositions (e.g., order vs. conflict) are never resolved in the sense that a puzzle is solved, but are argued over endlessly. A second major difference between paradigms and themata is that "[t]o a much larger degree than ... paradigms ... thematic decisions seem to come more from the individual than from the social surrounding" (Holton, 1975: 334). Hence, different individuals using a thematic perspective will slice the sociological pie in numerous ways.

ECKBERG AND HILL

REFERENCES

Ben-David, Joseph
1973 "The state of sociological theory and the sociological community: a review article." Comparative Studies in Society and History 15:448-72.

Bottomore, Tom
1975 "Competing paradigms in macrosociology." Pp. 191-202 in Alex Inkeles, James Coleman, and Neil Smelser (eds.), Annual Review of Sociology. Palo Alto: Annual Reviews.

Bryant, C. G. A.
1975 "Kuhn, paradigms, and sociology." British Journal of Sociology 26:354-9.

Burtt, Edwin Arthur
[1924] The Metaphysical Foundations of Modern Physical Science.
1954 New York: Anchor Books.

Carroll, Michael P.
1972 "Considerations on the analysis of variance paradigm." Pacific Sociological Review 15:443-59.

Crane, Diana
1972 Invisible Colleges. Chicago: University of Chicago Press.

Denisoff, R. Serge, Orel Callahan, and Mark H. Levine
1974 Theories and Paradigms in Contemporary Sociology. Itasca, Illinois: F. E. Peacock.

Douglas, Jack D.
1971 "The rhetoric of science and the origins of statistical thought: the case of Durkheim's Suicide." Pp. 44-57 in Edward A. Tiryakian (ed.), The Phenomenon of Sociology. New York: Appleton-Century-Crofts.

Effrat, Andrew
1972 "Power to the paradigms: an editorial introduction." Sociological Inquiry 42:3-34.

Friedrichs, Robert W.
1970 A Sociology of Sociology. New York: Free Press.
1972 "Dialectical sociology: an exemplar for the future." Social Forces 50:447-55.

Heyl, John D.
1975 "Paradigms in social science." Society 12:61-7.

Hollinger, David A.
1973 "T. S. Kuhn's theory of science and its implications for history." American Historical Review 78:370-93.

Holton, Gerald
1973 Thematic Origins of Scientific Thought. Cambridge, Mass.: Harvard University Press.
1975 "On the role of themata in scientific thought." Science 188:328-34.

134

Horan, Patrick M.
  1978 "Is status attainment research atheoretical?" American Socio-
        logical Review 43:534-41.
King, M. D.
  1971 "Reason, tradition, and the progressiveness of science." History
        and Theory 10:3-32.
Kucklick, Henrika
  1972 "A 'scientific revolution': sociological theory in the United
        States." Sociological Inquiry 43:2-22.
Kuhn, Thomas S.
  1957 The Copernican Revolution. Cambridge, Mass.: Harvard Uni-
        versity Press.
  1961 "The function of measurement in modern physical science." Isis
        52:161-93.
  1962 The Structure of Scientific Revolutions. Chicago: University of
        Chicago Press.
  1969 "Comment (on the relationship between science and art)." Com-
        parative Studies in Society and History 2:403-12.
  1970a The Structure of Scientific Revolutions. 2nd ed. Chicago: Uni-
        versity of Chicago Press.
  1970b "Reflections on my critics." Pp. 231-78 in Imre Lakatos and
        Alan Musgrave (eds.), Criticism and the Growth of Knowledge.
        Cambridge, Eng.: Cambridge University Press.
  1974 "Second thoughts on paradigms." Pp. 459-82 in Frederick Suppe
        (ed.), The Structure of Scientific Theories. Urbana: University of
        Illinois Press.
Lachenmeyer, Charles W.
  1971 The Language of Sociology. New York: Columbia University
        Press.
Lakatos, Imre and Alan Musgrave (eds.)
  1970 Criticism and the Growth of Knowledge. Cambridge, Eng.:
        Cambridge University Press.
Lehman, T., and R. T. Young
  1974 "From conflict theory to conflict methodology: an emerging
        paradigm for sociology." Sociological Inquiry 44:15-28.
Martins, Herminio
  1972 "The Kuhnian 'revolution' and its implications for sociology."
        Pp. 13-58 in T. J. Nossiter, A. H. Hanson, and Stein Rokkan
        (eds.), Imagination and Precision in the Social Sciences. London:
        Faber and Faber.
Masterman, Margaret
  1970 "The nature of a paradigm," Pp. 59-90 in Imre Lakatos and Alan
        Musgrave (eds.), Criticism and the Growth of Knowledge. Cam-
        bridge, Eng.: Cambridge University Press.
Merton, Robert K.
  1975 "Structural analysis in sociology." Pp. 21-52 in Peter M. Blau
        (ed.), Approaches to the Study of Social Structure. New York:
        Free Press.

Mullins, Nicholas C.
1973 Theories and Theory Groups in Contemporary American Sociology. New York: Harper and Row.
Perry, Nick
1977 "A comparative analysis of 'paradigm' proliferation." British Journal of Sociology 28:38-50.
Phillips, Derek
1973 "Paradigms, falsification, and sociology." Acta Sociologica 16:13-30.
Pocock, John G. A.
1971 Politics, Language and Time: on Political Thought and History. New York: Atheneum.
Price, Derek J. de Solla
1963 Little Science, Big Science. New York: Columbia University Press.
Ritzer, George
1975 Sociology: A Multiple Paradigm Science. Boston: Allyn and Bacon.
Shapere, Dudley
1971 "The paradigm concept." Science 172:706-9.
Scheffler, Israel
1967 Science and Subjectivity. New York: Bobbs-Merrill.
Sherman, L. W.
1974 "Uses of the masters." American Sociologist 9:176-81.
Suppe, Frederick
1974 The Structure of Scientific Theories. Urbana: University of Illinois Press.
Trigg, Roger
1973 Reason and Commitment. Cambridge, Mass.: Cambridge University Press.
Urry, John
1973 "Thomas S. Kuhn as sociologist of knowledge." British Journal of Sociology 24:462-73.
Walsh, David
1972 "Sociology and the social world." Pp. 15-36 in Paul Filmer, Michael Philipson, David Silverman, and David Walsh (eds.), New Directions in Sociological Theory. Cambridge, Mass.: M.I.T. Press.
Westhues, Kenneth
1976 "Class and organization as paradigms in social science." American Sociologist 11:38-48.
Whorf, Benjamin
1956 Language, Thought, and Reality. Cambridge, Mass.: M.I.T. Press.
Wilson, Thomas P.
1970 "Conceptions of interaction and forms of sociological explanation." American Sociological Review 35:697-710.

KUHN VERSUS LAKATOS, OR
PARADIGMS VERSUS RESEARCH PROGRAMMES
IN THE HISTORY OF ECONOMICS

MARK BLAUG

In the 1950s and 1960s economists learned their methodology from Popper. Not that many of them read Popper. Instead, they read Friedman, and perhaps few of them realized that Friedman is simply Popper-with-a-twist applied to economics. To be sure, Friedman was criticized, but the "Essay on the Methodology of Positive Economics" nevertheless survived to become the one article on methodology that virtually every economist has read at some stage in his career. The idea that unrealistic "assumptions" are nothing to worry about, provided that the theory deduced from them culminates in falsifiable predictions, carried conviction to economists long inclined by habit and tradition to take a purely instrumentalist view of their subject.

All that is almost ancient history, however. The new wave is not Popper's "falsifiability" but Kuhn's "paradigms." Again, it is unlikely that many economists read *The Structure of Scientific Revolutions* (1962). Nevertheless, appeal to paradigmatic reasoning quickly became a regular feature of controversies in economics and "paradigm" is now the byword of every historian of economic thought.[1] Recently, however, some commentators have expressed misgivings about Kuhnian methodology applied to economics, throwing doubt in particular on the view that "scientific revolutions" characterize the history of economic thought.[2] With these doubts I heartily concur. I will argue that the term "paradigm" ought to be banished from economic literature, unless surrounded by inverted commas. Suitably qualified, however, the term retains a function in the historical exposition of economic doctrines as a reminder of the fallacy of trying to appraise particular theories without invoking the wider metaphysical framework in which they are embedded. This notion that theories come to us, not one at a time, but linked together in a more or less integrated network of ideas, is however better conveyed by Lakatos' "methodology of scientific research programmes." The main aim of my article is indeed to explore Lakatos' ideas in application to the history of economics.[3]

The task is not an easy one. Lakatos is a difficult author to pin down. His tendency to make vital points in footnotes, to proliferate labels for different intellectual positions, and to refer back and forth to his own writings—as if it were impossible to understand any part of them without understanding the whole—stands in the way of ready comprehension. In a series of papers, largely published between 1968 and 1971, Lakatos developed and extended Popper's philosophy of science into a critical tool of historical research, virtually resolving a long-standing puzzle about the relationship between positive history of science and normative methodology for scientists. The puzzle is this. To believe that it is possible to write a history of science "wie es eigentlich gewesen" without in any way revealing our concept of sound scientific practice or how "good" science differs from "bad" is to commit the Inductive Fallacy in the field of intellectual history; by telling the story of past developments one way rather than another we necessarily disclose our view of the nature of scientific explanation. On the other hand, to preach the virtues of *the* scientific method while utterly ignoring the question of whether scientists now or in the past have actually practiced that method seems arbitrary and metaphysical. We are thus caught in a vicious circle, implying the impossibility both of a value-free, descriptive historiography of science and an ahistorical, prescriptive methodology of science.[4] From this vicious circle there is, I believe, no real escape, but what Lakatos has done is to hold out the hope that the circle may be eventually converted into a virtuous one.

Enough said by way of introduction. Let us look briefly at Popper and Kuhn, before putting Lakatos' "methodology of scientific research programmes" to work in a field such as economics.

1. FROM POPPER TO KUHN TO LAKATOS

Popper's principal problem in *The Logic of Scientific Discovery* (1935) was to find a purely logical demarcation rule for distinguishing science from nonscience. He repudiated the Vienna Circle's principle of verifiability and replaced it by the principle of falsifiability as the universal a priori test of a genuinely scientific hypothesis. The shift of emphasis from verification to falsification is not as innocent as appears at first glance, involving as it does a fundamental asymmetry between proof and disproof. From this modest starting point, Popper has gradually evolved over the years a powerful anti-inductionist view of science as an endless dialectical sequence of "conjectures and refutations."[5]

A hasty reading of *The Logic of Scientific Discovery* suggests the view that a single refutation is sufficient to overthrow a scientific theory; in other words, it convicts Popper of what Lakatos has called "naive falsificationism" (Lakatos and Musgrave 1970, pp. 116, 181; Lakatos 1971, pp. 109-14). But a moment's reflection reminds us that many physical and virtually all social phenomena are stochastic in nature, in which case an adverse result implies the improbability of the hypothesis being true, not the certainty that it is false. To discard a theory after a single failure to pass a statistical test would, therefore, amount to intellectual nihilism. Patently, nothing less than a whole series of refutations is likely to discourage the adherents of a probabilistic theory. A careful reading of Popper's work, however, reveals that he was perfectly aware of the so-called "principle of tenacity"—the tendency of scientists to evade falsification of their theories by the introduction of suitable ad hoc auxiliary hypotheses —and he even recognized the functional value of such dogmatic stratagems in certain circumstances.[6] Popper, in other words, is a "sophisticated falsificationist," not a "naive" one.[7]

In general, however, Popper deplores the tendency to immunize theories against criticism and instead advocates a bold commitment to falsifiable predictions, coupled with a willingness and indeed eagerness to abandon theories that have failed to survive efforts to refute them. His methodology is thus plainly a normative one, prescribing sound practice in science, possibly but not necessarily in the light of the best science of the past; it is an "aggressive" rather than a "defensive" methodology because it cannot be refuted by showing that most, and indeed even all, scientists have failed to obey its precepts.[8]

In Kuhn's *Structure of Scientific Revolutions*, the emphasis shifts from normative methodology to positive history: the "principle of tenacity," which for Popper presents something of an exception to best-practice science, becomes the central issue in Kuhn's explanation of scientific behavior. "Normal science," or problem-solving activity in the context of an accepted theoretical framework, is said to be the rule, and "revolutionary science," or the overthrow of one "paradigm" by another in consequence of repeated refutations and mounting anomalies, the exception in the history of science. It is tempting to say that for Popper science is always in a state of "permanent revolution," the history of science being the history of continuous "conjectures and refutations"; for Kuhn, the history of science is marked by long periods of steady refinement, interrupted on occasions by *discontinuous* jumps from one ruling "paradigm" to another with no bridge for communicating between them.[9]

To judge a dispute such as this, we must begin by defining terms. In the first edition of his book, Kuhn frequently employed the term "paradigm" in a dictionary sense to stand for certain exemplary instances of scientific achievement in the past. But he also employed the term in quite a different sense to denote both the choice of problems and the set of techniques for analyzing them, in places going so far as to give "paradigm" a still wider meaning as a general metaphysical *Weltanschauung*; the last sense of the term is, in fact, what most readers take away from the book. The second edition of *The Structure of Scientific Revolutions* (1970) admitted to terminological imprecision in the earlier version[10] and suggested that the term "paradigm" be replaced by "disciplinary matrix"; " 'disciplinary' because it refers to the common possession of the practitioners of a particular discipline; 'matrix' because it is composed of ordered elements of various sorts, each requiring further specification" (Kuhn 1970, p. 182). But whatever language is employed, the focus of his argument remained that of "the entire constellation of beliefs, values, techniques and so on shared by the members of a given community," and he went on to say that if he were to write his book again, he would start with a discussion of the professionalization of science before examining the shared "paradigms" or "disciplinary matrices" of scientists (p. 173).

These are not fatal concessions for the simple reason that the distinctive feature of Kuhn's methodology is not the concept of paradigms that everyone has seized on, but rather that of "scientific revolutions" as sharp breaks in the development of science, and particularly the notion of a pervasive failure of communications during periods of "revolutionary crises." Let us remind ourselves of the building bricks of Kuhn's argument: the practitioners of "normal science," although widely scattered, form an "invisible college" in the sense that they are in agreement both on the "puzzles" that require solution and on the general form that the solution will take; moreover, only the judgment of colleagues is regarded as relevant in defining problems and solutions, in consequence of which "normal science" is a self-sustaining, cumulative process of puzzle solving within the context of a common analytical framework; the breakdown of "normal science" is heralded by a proliferation of theories and the appearance of methodological controversy; the new framework offers a decisive solution to hitherto neglected "puzzles" and this solution turns out in retrospect to have long been recognized but previously ignored; the old and new generations talk past each other as "puzzles" in the old framework become "counterexamples" in the new; conversion to the new approach takes on the nature of a religious experience, involving a "gestalt switch"; and the new framework conquers in a few decades, to become in turn the "normal science" of the next generation.

The reader who is acquainted with the history of science thinks immediately of the Copernican Revolution, the Newtonian Revolution, or the Einstein-Planck Revolution. The so-called Copernican Revolution, however, took a hundred and fifty years to complete and was argued out every step of the way; even the Newtonian Revolution took more than a generation to win acceptance throughout the scientific circles of Europe, during which time the Cartesians, Leibnizians, and Newtonians engaged in bitter disputes over every aspect of the new theory; likewise, the switch in the twentieth century from classical to relativistic and quantum physics involved neither mutual incomprehension nor quasi-religious conversions, at least if the scientists directly involved in the "crisis of modern physics" are to be believed.[11] It is hardly necessary, however, to argue these points, because in the second edition of his book Kuhn candidly admits that his earlier description of "scientific revolutions" suffered from rhetorical exaggeration: paradigm changes during "scientific revolutions" do not imply absolute discontinuities in scientific debate, that is, a choice between competing but totally incommensurate theories; mutual incomprehension between scientists during a period of intellectual crisis is only a matter of degree; and the only point of calling paradigm changes "revolutions" is to underline the fact that the arguments that are advanced to support a new paradigm always contain ideological elements that go beyond logical or mathematical proof (Kuhn 1970, pp. 199-200).[12] As if this were not enough, he goes on to complain that his theory of "scientific revolutions" was misunderstood as referring solely to major revolutions, such as the Copernican, Newtonian, Darwinian, or Einsteinian; he now insists that the schema was just as much directed at minor changes in particular scientific fields, which might not seem to be revolutionary at all to those outside "a single community [of scientists], consisting perhaps of fewer than twenty-five people directly involved in it" (pp. 180-81).

In short, in this later version of Kuhn, any period of scientific development is marked by a large number of overlapping and interpenetrating "paradigms"; some of these may be incommensurable but certainly not all of them are; "paradigms" do not replace each other immediately and, in any case, new "paradigms" do not spring up full-blown but instead emerge as victorious in a long process of

141

intellectual competition. It is evident that these concessions considerably dilute the apparently dramatic import of Kuhn's original message, and in this final version the argument is difficult to distinguish from the average historian's account of the history of science. What remains, I suppose, is the emphasis on the role of values in scientific judgments, particularly in respect of the choice between competing approaches to science, together with a vaguely formulated but deeply held suspicion of cognitive factors like epistemological rationality, rather than sociological factors like authority, hierarchy, and reference groups, as determinants of scientific behavior. What Kuhn has really done is to conflate prescription and description, deducing his methodology from history, rather than to criticize history with the aid of a methodology. Kuhn does his best, of course, to defend himself against the charge of relativism and to explain "the sense in which I am a convinced believer in scientific progress" (Kuhn 1970, pp. 205-7), but the defense is not altogether convincing. Actually, a wholly convincing defense would reduce his account of "scientific revolutions" to a nonsense.

Which brings us to Lakatos.[13] As I read him, Lakatos is as much appalled by Kuhn's lapses into relativism as he is by Popper's ahistorical if not antihistorical standpoint.[14] The result is a compromise between the "aggressive methodology" of Popper and the "defensive methodology" of Kuhn, but a compromise which stays within the Popperian camp;[15] Lakatos is "softer" on science than Popper, but a great deal "harder" than Kuhn, and he is more inclined to criticize bad science with the aid of good methodology than temper methodological speculations by an appeal to scientific practice. For Lakatos, as for Popper, methodology has nothing to do with laying down standard procedures for tackling scientific problems; it is concerned with the "logic of appraisal," that is, the normative problem of providing criteria of scientific progress. Where Lakatos differs from Popper is that this "logic of appraisal" is then employed at one and the same time as a historical theory which purports to retrodict the development of science. As a normative methodology of science, it is empirically irrefutable because it is a definition. But as a historical theory, implying that scientists in the past did in fact behave in accordance with the methodology of falsifiability, it is perfectly refutable. If history fits the normative methodology, we have reasons additional to logical ones for subscribing to fallibilism. If it fails to do so, we are furnished with possible reasons for abandoning our methodology. No doubt, Hume's Guillotine tells us that we cannot logically deduce ought from is or is from ought. We can, however, influence ought by is and vice versa: moral judgments may be altered by the presentation of facts, and facts are theory-laden so that a change of values may alter our perception of the facts. But all these problems lie in the future. The first task is to reexamine the history of science with the aid of an explicit falsificationist methodology to see if indeed there is any conflict to resolve.

Lakatos begins by denying that isolated individual theories are the appropriate units of appraisal; what ought to be appraised are clusters of interconnected theories or "scientific research programmes" (SRP). Duhem and Poincaré had argued long ago that no individual scientific hypothesis is conclusively verifiable or falsifiable, because we always test the particular hypothesis in conjunction with auxiliary statements and therefore can never be sure whether we have confirmed or refuted the hypothesis itself. Since any hypothesis, if supplemented with suitable auxiliary assumptions, can be maintained in the face of contrary evidence, its acceptance is merely conventional. Popper met this "conventionalist" argument by distinguishing between "*ad-hoc*" and "*non-ad-hoc*" auxiliary assumptions: it is perfectly permissible to rescue a falsified theory by means of a change in one of its auxiliary assumptions, if such a change increases the empirical content of the theory by augmenting the number of its observational consequences; it is only changes which fail to do this that Popper dismissed as "*ad-hoc*."[16] Lakatos generalizes this Popperian argument by distinguishing between "progressive and degenerating problem shifts." A particular research strategy or SRP is said to be "*theoretically* progressive" if a successive formulation of the programme contains "excess empirical content" over its predecessor, "that is, ... predicts some novel, hitherto unexpected fact"; it is "*empirically* progressive if this excess empirical content is corroborated" (Lakatos and Musgrave 1970, p. 118). Contrariwise, if the programme is characterized by the endless addition of ad hoc adjustments that merely accommodate whatever new facts become available, it is labeled "degenerating."

These are relative, not absolute distinctions. Moreover, they are applicable, not at a given point in time, but over a period of time. The forward-looking character of a research strategy, as distinct from a theory, defies instant appraisal.[17] For Lakatos, therefore, an SRP is not "scientific" once and for all; it may cease to be scientific as time passes, slipping from the status of being "progressive" to that of being "degenerating" (astrology is an example), but the reverse may also happen (parapsychology?). We thus have a demarcation rule between science and nonscience which is itself historical, involving the evolution of ideas over time as one of its necessary elements.

The argument is now extended by dividing the components of an SRP into rigid parts and flexible parts. "The history of science," Lakatos observes, "is the history of research programmes rather than of theories," and "all scientific research programmes may be characterized by their 'hard core,' surrounded by a protective belt of auxiliary hypotheses which has to bear the brunt of tests." The "hard core" is irrefutable by "the methodological decision of its protagonists"—shades of Kuhn's "paradigm"!—and it contains, besides purely metaphysical beliefs, a "positive heuristic" consisting of "a partially articulated set of suggestions or hints on how to change, develop the 'refutable variants' of the research-programme, how to modify, sophisticate, the 'refutable' protective belt" (Lakatos and Musgrave 1970, pp. 132-35).[18] The "protective belt," however, contains the flexible parts of an SRP, and it is here that the "hard core" is combined with auxiliary assumptions to form the specific testable theories with which the SRP earns its scientific reputation.

If the concept of SRP is faintly reminiscent of Kuhn's "paradigms," the fact is that Lakatos' picture of scientific activity is much richer than Kuhn's. Furthermore, it begins to provide insight as to why "paradigms" are ever replaced, a mystery which is one of the central weaknesses of Kuhn's work. "Can there be any objective (as opposed to socio-psychological) reason to reject a programme, that is, to eliminate its hard core and its programme for constructing protective belts?" Lakatos asks. His answer, in outline, is that "such an objective reason is provided by a rival research programme which explains the previous success of its rival and supersedes it by a further display of heuristic power" (Lakatos and Musgrave 1970, p. 155; also Lakatos 1971, pp. 104-5). He illustrates the argument by analyzing Newton's gravitational theory—"probably the most successful research programme ever"—and then traces the tendency of physicists after 1905 to join the camp of relativity theory, which subsumed Newton's theory as a special case.[19] The claim is that this move from one SRP to another was "objective," because most scientists acted as if they believed in the normative "methodology of scientific research programmes" (MSRP). Lakatos goes on to advance the startling claim that all history of science can be similarly described; he defines any attempt to do so as "internal history" (Lakatos 1971, pp. 91-92).[20] "External history," in contrast, is not just all the normal pressures of the social and political environment that we usually associate with the word "external," but any failure of scientists to act according to

MSRP, as, for example, preferring a degenerating SRP to a progressive SRP on the grounds that the former is more "elegant" than the latter, possibly accompanied by the denial that it is degenerating.[21] The claim that all history of science can be depicted as "internal" may of course be difficult to sustain in the light of historical evidence, but Lakatos recommends that we give priority to "internal history" before resorting to "external history." Alternatively, what we can do is "to relate the internal history *in the text*, and indicate in the footnotes how actual history 'misbehaved' in the light of its rational reconstruction" (Lakatos 1971, p. 107), advice which Lakatos himself followed in his famous Platonic dialogue on the history of Euler's Conjecture on Polyhedrons (Lakatos 1964).

In reply to Lakatos, Kuhn minimized the differences between them :"Though his terminology is different, his analytic apparatus is as close to mine as need be: hard core, work in the protective belt, and degenerating phase are close parallels for my paradigms, normal science, and crisis (Lakatos and Musgrave 1971, p. 256). Kuhn insisted, however, that "what Lakatos conceives as history is not history at all but philosophy fabricating examples. Done in that way, history could not in principle have the slightest effect on the prior philosophical position which exclusively shaped it" (Kuhn 1971, p. 143). This seems to ignore Lakatos' deliberate attempt to keep history as such separate from "philosophy fabricating examples" and provides no resolution of the dilemma which surrounds the historiography of science: either we infer our scientific methodology from the history of science, which commits the fallacy of induction, or we preach our methodology and rewrite history accordingly, which smacks of "false consciousness."[22]

Lakatos, replying to Kuhn, tries to score a logical victory for his own approach to the historiography of science by claiming that it is perfectly capable of postdicting novel historical facts, unexpected in the light of the extant approaches of historians of science. In that sense, the "methodology of historiographical research programmes" may be vindicated by MSRP itself: it will prove "progressive" if and only if it leads to the discovery of novel historical facts (Lakatos 1971, pp. 116-20). The proof of the pudding is therefore in the eating. It remains to be seen whether the history of a science, whether natural or social, is more fruitfully conceived, not as steady progress punctured every few hundred years by a scientific revolution, but as a succession of progressive research programmes constantly superseding one another with theories of ever-increasing empirical content.[23]

2. SCIENTIFIC REVOLUTIONS IN ECONOMICS

Both Kuhn and Lakatos jeer at modern psychology and sociology as pre-paradigmatic, proto-sciences, and although economics seems to be exempted from the charge, Lakatos seems to think that even economists have never seriously committed themselves to the principle of falsifiability: "The reluctance of economists and other social scientists to accept Popper's methodololgy may have been partly due to the destructive effect of naive falsificationism on budding research programmes" (Lakatos and Musgrave 1970, p. 179 n). It is perfectly true that a dogmatic application of Popper to economics would leave virtually nothing standing, but it is a historical travesty to assert that economists have been hostile to Popper's methodology, at least in its more sophisticated versions. What is the central message of Friedman's "as-if" methodology if not commitment to the idea of testable predictions? And indeed, the pronouncements of nineteenth-century economists on methodology, summed up in John Neville Keynes' magisterial treatise *The Scope and Method of Political Economy* (1891), are squarely in the same tradition even if the language is that of verification rather than falsification plus or minus a naive Baconian appeal to "realistic" assumptions. The real question is whether the "principle of tenacity" does not figure much more heavily in the history of economics than in the history of, say, physics.[24] Analytical elegance, economy of theoretical means, and generality obtained by ever more "heroic" assumptions have always meant more to economists than relevance and predictability. They have in fact rarely practiced the methodology to which they have explicitly subscribed, and that, it seems to me, is one of the neglected keys to the history of economics. The philosophy of science of economists, ever since the days of Senior and Mill, is aptly described as "innocuous falsificationism."[25]

Let us begin by reviewing the attempts to apply Kuhn's methodology to economics. What are the ruling "paradigms" in the history of economic thought? According to Gordon, "Smith's postulate of the maximizing individual in a relatively free market...is our basic paradigm"; "economics has never had a major revolution; its basic maximizing model has never been replaced...it is, I think, remarkable when compared to the physical sciences that an economist's fundamental way of viewing the world has remained unchanged since the eighteenth century" (Gordon 1965, pp. 123, 124). Likewise, Coats asserts that economics has been "dominated throughout its history by a single paradigm—the theory of economic equilibrium via the market mechanism," but, unlike Gordon, Coats singles out the so-called Keynesian Revolution as a paradigm change, a Kuhnian "scientific revolution," and subsequently he has claimed almost as much for the so-called Marginal Revolution of the 1870s (Coats 1969, pp. 292, 293; Black, Coats, and Goodwin 1973, p. 38; but see p. 337). Benjamin Ward, a firm believer in Kuhn's methodology, also dubs the Keynesian Revolution a Kuhnian one, and furthermore he claims that the recent postwar period has witnessed a "formalist revolution" involving the growing prestige of mathematical economics and econometrics, which leaves him wondering why such a radical change should have made so little substantive difference to the nature of economics (Ward 1972, pp. 34-48). Lastly, Bronfenbrenner, after defining a "paradigm" as "a mode or framework of thought and language," goes on to cite Keynesian macroeconomics, the emergence of radical political economy, the recent revival of the quantity theory of money, and the substitution of the Hicksian IS-LM cross for the Marshallian demand-and-supply cross as cases in point, a procedure which falls into the trap set by Kuhn himself (Bronfenbrenner 1971, pp. 137-38). Bronfenbrenner identifies three revolutions in the history of economic thought: "a laissez-faire revolution," dating from Hume's *Political Discourses* in 1752; the Marginal Revolution of the 1870s as a "second possible revolution"; and the Keynesian Revolution of 1936.

If we had not previously recognized the inherent ambiguities in Kuhn's concepts, this brief review would suffice to make the point. Be that as it may, it appears that if economics provides any examples at all of Kuhnian "scientific revolutions," the favorite example seems to be the Keynesian Revolution, which at any rate has all the superficial appearance of a paradigm change. It is perfectly obvious, however, that the age-old paradigm of "economic equilibrium via the market mechanism," which Keynes is supposed to have supplanted, is actually a network of interconnected subparadigms; in short, it is best regarded as a Lakatosian SRP. It is made up, first of all, of the principle of constrained maximization, "Smith's postulate of the maximizing individual in a relatively free market," or what Friedman calls for short the "maximization-of-returns hypothesis." The principle of maximizing behavior subject to constraints is then joined to the notion of general equilibrium in self-regulating competitive markets to produce the method of comparative statics, which is the economist's principal device for generating qualitative predictions of the signs rather than the magnitudes of his critical variables.

The "hard core" or metaphysical part of this programme consists of weak versions of what is otherwise known as the "assumptions" of competitive theory, namely, rational economic calculations, constant tastes, independence of decision making, perfect knowledge, perfect certainty, perfect mobility of factors, etcetera. If they are not stated weakly, they become refutable by casual inspection and cannot, therefore, be held as true a priori. The "positive heuristic" of the programme consists of such practical advice as (1) divide markets into buyers and sellers, or producers and consumers; (2) specify the market structure; (3) create "ideal type" definitions of the behavioral assumptions so as to get sharp results; (4) set out the relevant ceteris paribus conditions; (5) translate the situation into an extreme problem and examine first- and second-order conditions; etcetera. It is evident that the marginalists after 1870 adopted the "hard core" of classical political economy, but they altered its "positive heuristic" and provided it with a different "protective belt."

Keynes went still further in tampering with the "hard core" that had been handed down since the time of Adam Smith. First of all, Keynes departed from the principle of "methodological individualism," that is, of reducing all economic phenomena to manifestations of individual behavior. Some of his basic constructs, like the propensity to consume, were simply plucked out of the air. To be sure, he felt impelled by tradition to speak of a "fundamental psychological law," but the fact is that the consumption function in Keynes is not derived from individual maximizing behavior; it is instead a bold inference based on the known, or at that time suspected, relationship between aggregate consumer expenditure and national income. On the other hand, the marginal efficiency of capital and the liquidity-preference theory of the demand for money are clearly if not rigorously derived from the maximizing activity of atomistic economic agents. Similarly, and despite what Leijonhufvud would have us believe, Keynes leaned heavily on the concepts of general equilibrium, perfect competition, and comparative statics, making an exception only for the labor market, which he seems to have regarded as being inherently imperfect and hence always in a state, not so much of disequilibrium as of equilibrium of a special kind.[26]

The really novel aspects of Keynes, however, are, first of all, the tendency to work with aggregates and indeed to reduce the entire economy to three interrelated markets for goods, bonds, and labor; secondly, to concentrate on the short period and to confine analysis of the long period, which had been the principal analytical focus of his predecessors, to asides about the likelihood of secular stagnation; and thirdly, to throw the entire weight of adjustments to changing economic conditions on output rather than prices. Equilibrium for the economy as a whole now involved "underemployment equilibrium," and the introduction of this conjunction, an apparent contradiction in terms, involved a profound change in the "hard core" of nineteenth-century economics, which undoubtedly included the faith that competitive forces drive an economy towards a steady state of full employment. Furthermore, the classical and neoclassical "hard core" had always contained the idea of rational economic calculation, involving the existence of certainty equivalents for each uncertain future outcome of current decisions. Keynes introduced pervasive uncertainty and the possibility of destabilizing expectations, not just in the "protective belt" but in the "hard core" of his programme. The Keynesian "hard core," therefore, really is a new "hard core" in economics. The Keynesian "protective belt" likewise bristled with new auxiliary hypotheses: the consumption function, the multiplier, the concept of autonomous expenditures, and speculative demand for money, contributing to stickiness in long-term interest rates. It is arguable, however, whether there was anything new in the marginal efficiency of capital and the saving-investment equality. Keynesian theory also had a strong "positive heuristic" of its own, pointing the way to national income accounting and statistical estimation of both the consumption function and the period multiplier. There is hardly any doubt, therefore, that Keynesian economics marked the appearance of a new SRP in the history of economics.

Furthermore, the Keynesian research programme not only contained "novel facts" but it also made novel predictions about familiar facts: it was a "progressive research programme" in the sense of Lakatos. Its principal novel prediction was the chronic tendency of competitive market economies to generate unemployment. Now, the fact that there was unemployment in the 1930s was not itself in dispute. Orthodox economists had no difficulty in explaining the persistence of unemployment. The government budget in both the United States and Britain was in surplus during most years in the 1930s. It did not need Keynes to tell economists that this was deflationary. It was also well known that monetary policy between 1929 and 1932 was more often tight than easy; at any rate, neither the United States nor the United Kingdom pursued a consistent expansionary monetary policy. Furthermore, the breakdown of the international gold standard aggravated the crisis. There was, in other words, no lack of explanations for the failure of the slump to turn into a boom, but the point is that these explanations were all *"ad hoc,"* leaving intact the full-employment-equilibrium implications of standard theory. The tendency of economists to join the rank of the Keynesians in increasing numbers after 1936 was therefore perfectly rational; it was a switch from a "degenerating" to a "progressive" research programme, which had little to do with contentious issues of public policy.

This assertion is likely to arouse consternation because we all have been taken in, to a greater or lesser extent, by the mythology which has come to surround the Keynesian Revolution. According to the Walt Disney version of interwar economics, the neoclassical contemporaries of Keynes are supposed to have believed that wage cutting, balanced budgets, and an easy-money policy would soon cure the Great Depression. It comes as a great surprise to learn from Stein (1969) and Davis (1970) that no American economist between 1929 and 1936 advocated a policy of wage cutting; the leaders of the American profession strongly supported a programme of public works and specifically attacked the shibboleth of a balanced budget. A long list of names, including Slichter, Taussig, Schultz, Yntema, Simons, Gayer, Knight, Viner, Douglas and J. M. Clark, concentrated mainly at the universities of Chicago and Columbia but with allies in other universities, research foundations, and government and banking circles, declared themselves in print well before 1936 in favor of policies that we would today call Keynesian. Similarly, in England, as Hutchison (1968) has shown, names such as Pigou, Layton, Stamp, Harrod, Gaitskell, Meade, E. A. G. and J. Robinson came out publicly in favor of compensatory public spending. If there were any anti-Keynesians on questions of policy, it was Cannan, Robbins, and possibly Hawtrey, but definitely not Pigou, the bogeyman of the *General Theory*.[27] This, by the way, explains the reactions of most American and British reviewers of the *General Theory*: they questioned the new theoretical concepts, but dismissed the policy conclusions of the book as "old hat."

A fair way of summarizing the evidence is to say that most economists, at least in the English-speaking countries, were united in respect of practical measures for dealing with the depression, but utterly disunited in respect of the theory that lay behind these policy conclusions. What orthodoxy there was in theoretical matters extended only so far as microeconomics. Pre-Keynesian macroeconomics in the spirit of the quantity theory of money presented an incoherent mélange of ideas culled from Fisher, Wicksell, Robertson, Keynes of the *Treatise*, and Continental writers on the trade cycle. In a sense then the Keynesian theory succeeded because it produced the policy conclusions most economists wanted to advocate anyway, but it produced these as logical inferences from a tightly knit theory and not as endless epicycles on a full-employment model of the economy.[28]

It would seem that certain puzzles about the Keynesian Revolution dissolve when it is viewed through Lakatosian spectacles. The attempt to give a Kuhnian account of the Keynesian Revolution, on the other hand, creates the image of a whole generation of economists dumbfounded by the persistence of the Great Depression, unwilling to entertain the obvious remedies of expansionary fiscal and monetary policy, unable to find even a language with which to communicate with the Keynesians, and, finally, in despair, abandoning their old beliefs in an instant conversion to the new paradigm. These fabrications are unnecessary if instead we see the Keynesian Revolution as the replacement of a "degenerating" research programme by a "progressive" one with "excess empirical content." Moreover, in this perspective, we gain a new insight into the postwar history of Keynesian economics, a history of steady "degeneration" as the Keynesian prediction of chronic unemployment begins to lose its plausibility. In the 1950s, the contradiction between cross-section and time-series evidence of the savings-income ratio, the former yielding a declining and the latter a constant average propensity to save, spawned a series of revisions in the Keynesian research programme, from Duesenberry's relative income hypothesis to Friedman's permanent income hypothesis to Modigliani's life-cycle theory of saving. Simultaneously, Harrod and Domar converted static Keynesian analysis into a primitive theory of growth, a development which discarded principal elements in the Keynesian "protective belt" and more or less the whole of the "hard core" of the original Keynesian programme. Friedman's monetarist counterrevolution went a good deal further, and for a few years in the late 1960s it almost looked as if Keynes had been decisively repudiated. The efforts of Patinkin, Clower, and Leijonhufvud to give a disequilibrium interpretation of Keynesian economics, and thus to integrate Keynesian theory into a more general neoclassical framework with still greater "excess empirical content," would seem to constitute a "progressive" research programme, superseding both static pre-Keynesian microeconomics and static Keynesian macroeconomics. Keynes' General Theory is now a special case, and this is scientific progress in economics, perfectly analogous to the absorption of Newton as a special case in the general theory of relativity.

It is possible to give a similar "internalist" account of the so-called Marginal Revolution as further demonstration of the applicability of MSRP to economics. The difficulties in the standard notion that marginalism was a new "paradigm" in economics were thoroughly thrashed out at the Bellagio Conference (see Black, Coats and Goodwin 1973) and it is only necessary to add that the innovations of Menger, Jevons, and Walras are more suitably described, not as a new SRP, but as a "progressive problem shift" in the older research programme of classical political economy. As frequently happens in such cases, there was "loss of content" as well as gain. What was lost, such as theories of population growth and capital accumulation, had become by the 1860s an incoherent body of ideas, virtually empty of empirical implications. The reaction against the Classical School was more a reaction against Ricardo than against Adam Smith. The Ricardian system was itself a "progressive problem shift" in the Smithian research programme, motivated by the experiences of the Napoleonic Wars and designed to predict the "novel fact" of the rising price of corn, leading in turn to rising rents per acre and a declining rate of profit. The "hard core" of Ricardo is indistinguishable from that of Adam Smith, but the "positive heuristic" contains elements which would have certainly surprised Adam Smith, and this explains the difficulties that many commentators have experienced in identifying disciples of Ricardo who were not also disciples of Adam Smith.[29]

I once argued that the distinctive feature of the Ricardian system was, not the labor theory of value, not Say's law, not even the inverse relation between wages and profits, but "the proposition that the yield of wheat per acre of land governs the general rate of return on invested capital as well as the secular changes in the distributive shares" (Blaug 1958, p. 3). The notion that Ricardo is at one and the same time the heir of Adam Smith and his principal critic can be conveyed succinctly in the language of MSRP. All the leading British classical economists up to Jevons and even up to Sidgwick subscribed to the basic Ricardian link between the productivity of agriculture and the rate of capital accumulation, and it is in this sense that we can speak of a dominant Ricardian influence on British economic thought throughout the half-century from Waterloo to the Paris Commune. There are unmistakable signs after 1848 of "degeneration" in the Ricardian research programme, marked by the proliferation of "ad hoc" assumptions to protect the theory against the evidence that repeal of the Corn Laws in 1846 had failed to bring about the effects predicted by Ricardo (Blaug 1968, pp.

227-28).[30] On the other hand, the Ricardian research programme was by no means dead by 1850 or even 1860. Cairnes' work on the Australian gold discoveries and Jevons' study *The Coal Question* (1865) showed that there was still unrealized potential in the Ricardian system. Nevertheless, Mill's "recantation" of the wages fund theory in 1859 expressed a widely felt malaise, typical of those who find themselves working within a steadily degenerating SRP.

The trouble with this line of argument is that Ricardo did not exert a preponderant influence on Continental economic thought. There is absolutely no evidence of any widespread sense of increasing discomfort in France or Germany around 1870 with classical economic doctrine, conceived broadly on the lines of Adam Smith rather than of Ricardo. What was missing in the British tradition, it was felt, was the utility theory of value, which had roots on the Continent going back to Condillac, Galiani, and even Aristotle. What we see in Menger and even more in Walras, therefore, is the attempt to concentrate attention on the problem of price determination at the expense of what Baumol has called the "magnificent dynamics" in Smith, Ricardo, and Mill, in the course of which due emphasis was given to the neglected demand side. This could be seen, and indeed was seen, as an improvement rather than an outright rejection of Adam Smith. There was no room in this schema for the specifically Ricardian elements, except in afterthoughts about long-run tendencies. In the Continental perspective, that is, the whole of the Ricardian episode in British classical political economy was regarded as something of a detour from the research programme laid down by Adam Smith. In other words, whatever we say about Jevons and the British scene, there was no Marginal Revolution on the Continent: there was a "problem shift," possibly even a "progressive problem shift," if predictions about "the price of an egg" may be regarded as more testable than predictions about the effects of giving free rein to the workings of "the invisible hand."

Clearly, economists after 1870, or rather 1890, reassessed the nature of the facts that economics ought to be concerned with. It is conceivable that this "gestalt switch" can only be explained in terms of "external history." If so, and particularly if we lack any independent corroboration for this historical explanation, we have a refutation of MSRP as a metahistorical research programme. I have been arguing, however, that an "internalist" account makes it unnecessary to resort to "external factors." It would be premature, however, to arrive at that conclusion on the basis of my crude sketch of historical developments. Only a series of detailed case studies of the spread of marginalism on the Continent after 1870 could settle that question.[31] What I want to insist here is simply that MSRP gives us a powerful handle for attacking these problems. ...

NOTES

1. Similarly, sociologists have seized avidly on the Kuhnian apparatus: See, e.g., Ryan 1970, pp. 233-36, Martins 1972, and the collection of essays in Whitley 1974.

2. See Coats 1969, Bronfenbrenner 1971, and Kunin and Weaver 1971.

3. I dedicate this paper to the memory of Imre Lakatos, Professor of Logic and the Philosophy of Science at the London School of Economics, who died suddenly at the age of fifty-one on February 2, 1974. We discussed an early draft of this paper a number of times in the winter of 1973 and, for the last time, the day before his death. He promised me a rebuttal, which now alas I will never read.

4. One of Lakatos' fundamental papers (1971, p. 91) opens with a paraphrase of one of Kant's dictums, which perfectly expresses the dilemma in question: "Philosophy of science without history of science is empty: history of science without philosophy of science is blind."

5. Not to mention his formulation of a political philosophy, generated by the same conception. For a splendid, if somewhat hagiographic, introduction to the wide sweep of Popper's work, see Magee 1973.

6. For example: "In point of fact, no conclusive disproof of a theory can ever be produced; for it is always possible to say that the experimental results are not reliable, or that the discrepancies which are asserted to exist between the experimental results and the theory are only apparent and that they will disappear with the advance of our understanding" (Popper 1965, p. 50; see also pp. 42, 82-83, 108); in the same spirit, see Popper 1962, II, 217-20, Popper 1972, p. 30, and Popper in Schilpp 1974, I, 82.

7. Economists will recognize immediately that Lipsey really was a "naive falsificationist" in the first edition of his *Introduction to Positive Economics* and only adopted "sophisticated falsificationism" in the third edition of the book: see Lipsey 1966, pp. xx, 16-17.

8. I owe the vital distinction between "aggressive methodologies" and "defensive methodologies" to Latsis (1974). Popper does make references to the history of science, and clearly Einstein is his model of a great scientist. Nevertheless, he is always insistent on the metaphysical and hence irrefutable basis of the falsifiability principle (see, e.g., Schilpp 1974, II, 1036-37).

9. See the revealing criticism of Popper by Kuhn and the equally revealing criticism of Kuhn by Popper (Lakatos and Musgrave 1970, pp. 14-15, 19, 52-55).

10. Masterman (Lakatos and Musgrave 1970, pp. 60-65) has in fact

identified twenty-one different definitions of the term "paradigm" in Kuhn's 1962 book.

11. Toulmin 1972, pp. 103-5. Of all the many critiques that Kuhn's book has received (Lakatos and Musgrave 1970, and references cited by Kunin and Weaver 1971), none is more devastating than that of Toulmin (1972, pp. 98-117), who traces the history of Kuhn's methodology from its first announcement in 1961 to its final version in 1970. For an extraordinarily sympathetic but equally critical reading of Kuhn, see Suppe 1974, pp. 135-51.

12. This is almost obvious because if two "paradigms" were truly incommensurable, they could be held simultaneously, in which case there would be no need for a "scientific revolution": the strong incommensurability thesis is logically self-contradictory (Achinstein 1968, pp. 91-106). What Kuhn must have meant is "incommensurability to some degree," and the new version is simply a belated attempt to specify the degree in question.

13. My sketch of recent developments in the philosophy of science omits discussion of such influential writers as Feyerabend, Hanson, Polanyi, and Toulmin, who have each in his own way challenged the traditional positivist account of the structure of scientific theories. But see Suppe (1974), whose masterful essay of book length covers all the names mentioned above. Lakatos, however, is deliberately omitted in Suppe's account (Suppe 1974, p. 166 n.).

14. See the characteristic reaction of Popper to Kuhn: "to me the idea of turning for enlightenment concerning the aims of science, and its possible progress, to sociology or to psychology (or ... to the history of science) is surprising and disappointing" (Lakatos and Musgrave 1970, p. 57).

15. Bloor (1971, p. 104) seems wide of the mark in characterizing Lakatos' work as "a massive act of revision, amounting to a betrayal of the essentials of the Popperian approach, and a wholesale absorption of some of the most characteristic Kuhnian positions."

16. Although Popper's distinction succeeds in refuting "conventionalism," it tends to erode the fundamental asymmetry between verification and falsification which is the linchpin of his philosophy of science: see Grünbaum 1973, pp. 569-629, 848-49. Archibald 1967 illustrates the problem of distinguishing ad hoc auxiliary assumptions in testing the Keynesian theory of income determination.

17. If the term "scientific research programmes" strikes some readers as vague, it must be remembered that the term "theory" is just as vague. It is in fact difficult to define "theory" precisely, even when the term is employed in a narrow sense: see Achinstein 1968, chap. 4.

18. Lakatos' "hard core" expresses an idea similar to that conveyed by Schumpeter's notion of "Vision"—"the preanalytic cognitive act that supplies the raw material for the analytic effort" (Schumpeter 1954, pp. 41-43)—or Gouldner's "world hypotheses," which figure heavily in his explanation of why sociologists adopt certain theories and reject others (Gouldner 1971, chap. 2). Marx's theory of "ideology" may be read as a particular theory about the nature of the "hard core"; Marx was quite right in believing that "ideology" plays a role in scientific theorizing but

he was quite wrong in thinking that the class character of ideology was decisive for the acceptance or rejection of scientific theories.

19.   However, he is not committed to the belief that every progressive SRP will be more general than the degenerate SRP which it replaces. There may well be a Kuhnian "loss of content" in the process of passing from one SRP to another, although typically the overlap between rival programmes will be larger than either the content-loss or content-gain.

20.   This is what Suppe (1974, pp. 53-56) has called the "thesis of development by reduction," namely, that scientific progress comes largely, and even exclusively, by the succession of more comprehensive theories which include earlier theories as special cases. The thesis, even in its weaker version, has been hotly debated by philosophers of science for many years.

21.   Lakatos holds that one cannot rationally criticize a scientist who sticks to a degenerating programme if, recognizing it is degenerating, he is determined to resuscitate it. This is somewhat contradictory. Feyerabend (1975, pp. 185-86) seizes on this weakness and others in a penetrating but sympathetic critique of Lakatos from the standpoint of epistemological anarchism (ibid., chap. 16, pp. 181-220).

22.   The dilemma in question is widely recognized by philosophers of science, as well as historians of science: see, e.g., Lakatos and Musgrave 1970, pp. 46, 50, 198, 233, 236-38; Achinstein's comments on Suppe (Suppe, 1974, pp. 350-61); and Hesse's essay in Teich and Young 1973.

23.   Contrast Kuhn 1957 and Lakatos and Zahar 1975 on the so-called Copernican Revolution. See also Zahar 1973 and Feyerabend 1974 on the Einsteinian Revolution and Urbach 1974 on the IQ debate. Several other case studies applying Lakatos' MSRP to the history of physics, chemistry, and economics, presented at the Nafplion Colloquium on Research Programmes in Physics and Economics, September 1974, are published in C. Howson (ed.), *Method and Appraisal in the Physical Sciences* and S. J. Latsis (ed.), *Method and Appraisal in Economics*, Cambridge University Press, 1976. Also see Latsis 1972, discussed below.

24.   "It may be said without qualification," Keynes wrote in *Scope and Method*, "that political economy, whether having recourse to the deductive method or not, must begin with observation and end with observation ... the economist has recourse to observation in order to illustrate, test, and confirm his deductive inferences" (Keynes 1955, pp. 227, 232). But it is characteristic that most of chapters 6 and 7, from which these sentences are drawn, is about the difficulties of verifying deductive inferences by empirical observations; we are never told when we may reject an economic theory in the light of the evidence or indeed whether any economic theory was ever so rejected.

25.   I owe this happy phrase to an unpublished paper by A. Coddington.

26.   The best single piece of evidence for this statement is Keynes' reaction to Hick's famous paper, "Mr. Keynes and the Classics." "I found it very interesting," he wrote to Hicks, "and really have next to nothing to say by way of criticism." Since Hicks's IS-LM diagram ignores the labor market, the reaction is hardly surprising. On Leijonhufvud's reading of Keynes, see Blaug 1975 and the references cited there.

27. I ignore the Stockholm School, which developed, independently of any clearly discernible influence from Keynes, most of the concepts and insights of Keynesian macroeconomics before the publication of either the *General Theory* (1936) or *The Means of Prosperity* (1933): see Uhr 1973. For Ohlin's recollections of the impact of Keynes of the Stockholm theorists, see Ohlin 1974, pp. 892-94.

28. Keynes himself put it in a nutshell. Writing to Kahn in 1937 with reference to D. H. Robertson and Pigou, he observed: "when it comes to practice, there is really extremely little between us. Why do they insist on maintaining theories from which their own practical conclusions cannot possibly follow? It is a sort of Society for the Preservation of Ancient Monuments" (Keynes 1973, p. 259). A hint of the same argument is found in the *General Theory*: a footnote in the first chapter refers to Robbins as the one contemporary economist to maintain "a consistent scheme of thought, his practical recommendations belonging to the same system as his theory."

29. See, e.g., O'Brien (1970), who shows that even John Ramsay McCulloch, Ricardo's leading disciple, never succeeded in resolving the conflict in his mind between Smith and Ricardo.

30. In an illuminating paper on Ricardo's and John Stuart Mill's treatment of the relationship between theory and facts, de Marchi (1970) argues that Mill did not, as I have alleged, evade refutations of Ricardo's predictions by retreating into an unspecified ceteris paribus clause; he was simply careless with facts and declined to reject an attractive theory merely because it predicted poorly. The issue between us is one of subtle distinctions and, as I am going to argue later on, these distinctions still plague modern economics. Suffice it to say that a defensive attitude to the Ricardian System is increasingly felt in successive editions of the *Principles* and even more in the writings of Cairnes and Fawcett (Blaug 1958, pp. 213-20).

31. Black, Coats, and Goodwin (1973) provide a few of such case studies which seem to me to strengthen the internalist thesis.

REFERENCES

Achinstein, P. 1968. *Concepts of Science*. Baltimore.
Archibald, G. C. 1967. "Refutation or Comparison?" *British Journal for the Philosophy of Science*, vol. 17.
Black, R. D. C., A. W. Coats, and C. D. W. Goodwin, editors. 1973. *The Marginal Revolution in Economics: Interpretation and Evaluation*. Durham, N.C.
Blaug, M. 1958. *Ricardian Economics*. New Haven.
————. 1968. *Economic Theory in Retrospect*. 2d edition. Homewood, Ill.
————. 1975. "Comments on C. J. Bliss, 'Reappraisal of Keynesian Economics.'" In *Current Economic Problems: The Proceedings of the Association of University Teachers of Economics Conference, 1974,*

edited by M. Parkin and A. R. Nobay. London.

Bloor, D. 1971. "Two Paradigms for Scientific Knowledge." *Science Studies*, vol. 1.

Bronfenbrenner, M. 1971. "The 'Structure of Revolutions' in Economic Thought." *History of Political Economy*, vol. 3, Spring.

Coats, A.W. 1969. "Is There a 'Structure of Scientific Revolutions' in Economics?" *Kyklos*, vol. 22.

Davis, J. R. 1971. *The New Economics and the Old Economists*. Ames, Iowa.

de Marchi, N. B. 1970. "The Empirical Content and Longevity of Ricardian Economics." *Economica*, vol. 37, August.

Feyerabend, P. K. 1974. "Zahar on Einstein." *British Journal for the Philosophy of Science*, vol. 25.

_____. 1975. *Against Method. Outline of an Anarchistic Theory of Knowledge*. London.

Gordon, D. F. 1965. "The Role of the History of Economic Thought in the Understanding of Modern Economic Theory." *American Economic Review*, vol. 55, May.

Gouldner, A. W. 1971. *The Coming Crisis of Western Sociology*. London.

Grünbaum, A. 1973. *Philosophical Problems of Space and Time. Boston Studies in the Philosophy of Science*, ed. R. S. Cohen, and M. Wartofsky. Dordrecht-Holland.

Hicks, J. 1965. *Capital and Growth*. Oxford.

Hutchison, T. W. 1968. *Economics and Economic Policy in Britain, 1964-1966*. London.

Keynes, J. M. 1973. *The Collected Writings of John Maynard Keynes: XIV. The General Theory and After*, Part II. London.

Keynes, J. N. 1955. *The Scope and Method of Political Economy*. 4th edition. New York.

Kuhn, T. S. 1957. *The Copernican Revolution*. Cambridge, Mass.

_____. 1970. *The Structure of Scientific Revolutions*, 2d edition. Chicago.

Kunin, L., and F. S. Weaver. 1971. "On the Structure of Scientific Revolutions in Economics." *History of Political Economy*, vol. 3, Fall.

Lakatos, I. 1964. "Proofs and Refutations, (I), (II), (III), (IV)." *British Journal for the Philosophy of Science*, vol. 14.

_____. 1971. "History of Science and Its Rational Reconstruction." In *Boston Studies in Philosophy of Science*, VIII, edited by R. S. Cohen, and C. R. Buck.

_____, and A. Musgrave, editors. 1970. *Criticism and the Growth of Knowledge*. London.

_____, and E. Zahar. 1975. "Why Did Copernicus' Programme Supersede Ptolemy's?" In *The Copernican Achievement*, edited by R. S. Westman, University of California Press.

Latsis, S. J. 1972. "Situational Determinism in Economics." *British Journal of the Philosophy of Science*, vol. 23.

_____. 1974. "Situational Determinism in Economics." Ph.D. Dissertation. University of London.

Lipsey, R. G. 1966. *An Introduction to Positive Economics*. London.

Magee, B. 1973. *Popper.* Fontana Modern Masters. London.

Martins, H. 1972. "The Kuhnian 'Revolution' and Its Implications for Sociology." In *Imagination and Precision in Political Analysis*, edited by A. H. Hanson, T. Nossiter, and S. Rokkau. London.

O'Brien, D. P. 1970. *J. R. McCulloch: A Study in Classical Economics.* London.

Ohlin, B. 1974. "On the Slow Development of the 'Total Demand' Idea in Economic Theory: Reflections in Connection with Dr. Oppenheimer's Note." *Journal of Economic Literature*, vol. 12, no. 3, Sept.

Popper, K. R. 1962. *The Open Society and Its Enemies.* 4th edition. London.

————. 1965. *The Logic of Scientific Discovery.* New York.

————. 1972. *Objective Knowledge: An Evolutionary Approach.* Oxford.

Ryan, A. 1970. *The Philosophy of the Social Sciences.* London.

Schilpp, P. A., editor. 1974. *The Philosophy of Karl Popper.* Library of Living Philosophers, Vol. XIV. 2 vols., LaSalle, Ill.

Schumpeter, J. A. 1954. *History of Economic Analysis.* New York.

Stein, H. 1969. *The Fiscal Revolution in America.* Chicago.

Suppe, F. 1974. *The Structure of Scientific Theories.* Urbana, Ill.

Teich, M., and R. Young, editors. 1973. *Changing Perspectives in the History of Science.* Dordrecht-Holland.

Toulmin, S. 1972. *Human Understanding.* Oxford.

Uhr, C. G. 1973. "The Emergence of the 'New Economics' in Sweden: A Review of a Study by Otto Steiger." *History of Political Economy*, vol. 5, Spring.

Urbach, P. 1974. "Progress and Degeneration in the 'IQ Debate' (I), (II)." *British Journal for the Philosophy of Science*, vol. 25.

Ward, B. 1972. *What's Wrong with Economics?* New York.

Whitley, R. 1974. *Social Processes and Scientific Development.* London.

Zahar, E. 1973. "Why Did Einstein's Programme Supersede Lorentz's?" *British Journal for the Philosophy of Science*, vol. 24.

PARADIGMS AND POLITICAL THEORIES

SHELDON S. WOLIN

The status of political theory has been a perennial subject of controversy. In recent years the debate in the United States has focused upon methodological considerations. This was probably inevitable, given the intention of a sizable group to transform the study of politics into a "science of politics modelled after the methodological assumptions of the natural sciences."[1] In pointing to the model of scientific inquiry as the appropriate one for political and social science; by claiming that reliable political knowledge was to be acquired only by emulating scientific procedures of observation, data-gathering, classification, and verification; and by insisting that precise knowledge was identical with the transformation of "metaphysical" or "normative" statements into empirically verifiable ones, the exponents of science succeeded in restricting the debate to procedural matters. On this ground they encountered only scattered opposition. An occasional critic might charge social scientists with the mistake of treating philosophical questions as empirical ones,[2] but as resistance dwindled it was increasingly assumed that the case had been proven for applying scientific methods to the study of politics, that it was indeed science that was being applied, and, consequently, that the time was not distant when political science would enjoy the two main benefits of science, precise and cumulative knowledge. It is now commonplace to encounter in the literature of political and social science a statement like the following which occurs almost as an afterthought: "Everything we have said already has been based on the assumption that social science is not only possible but even essentially the same as natural science."[3]

There are two features of the case for a scientific politics which I wish to examine here. As suggested above, the advocates of science have set for themselves the objective of developing a theory which will serve as a guide for empirical inquiry. They state explicitly that this theory is intended as a substitute for "traditional" (i.e. prescientific) theory. The nature of the substitute has two aspects: it involves the application of a different method, that of science, and a different set of questions. The idea of a substitute presupposes a critical judgment about the shortcomings of traditional theory. A representative example of such a judgment would be the following: "Theorizing, even about politics, is not to be confused with metaphysical speculation in terms of abstractions hopelessly removed from empirical observation and control."[4] This is the first feature of the case which I propose to examine. It will be my contention that the nature of traditional theory has been misunderstood and that this misunderstanding has been read back so as to mislead the political scientist about the nature, consequences, and possibilities of his own enterprise.

The second feature is closely connected with the first. The scientific critique has charged that traditional political theory has failed to produce cumulative knowledge. The response of the defenders of the tradition has been surprisingly weak. Sometimes they have contended that it is no longer possible to produce an original theory about politics. Most of the important things, it is alleged, have already been said. Other times the defenders of the tradition have argued that each age or society has been concerned with its own peculiar political problems, and hence political knowledge has been and always will be local and restricted. The political scientist has taken advantage of these uncertainties and, by pointing to the successful example of science, has argued that one of the boons of scientific methods is the promise of creating an expanding body of reliable knowledge. Under this heading, I wish to examine the possibility that the idea of scientific progress has been misconceived.

To a considerable extent, the two aspects are related. The political scientist[5] contends that *because* traditional theory was preoccupied with metaphysical or "normative" concerns, it was unable to produce a cumulative body of knowledge. In addressing questions about the nature of justice, authority, rights, and equality and in formulating these questions in terms of projective models of a good society which were supposed to embody the true form of justice and authority, traditional theory saddled itself with a type of inquiry in which it was impossible to progress, or, indeed, even to specify what a cumulative advance would look like. The usual objection made by political scientists is that traditional theory abounds in assertions which are in principle untestable. In those cases, such as in the writings of Machiavelli, where the statements are amenable to empirical proof, theorists have been satisfied with examples or illustrations rather than systematic evidence.

The contemporary political scientist is determined to avoid these

161

pitfalls by following a different prescription: "Whether [a] proposition is true or false depends on the degree to which the proposition and the real world correspond."[6] If theory is to produce reliable political knowledge it must subject its assertions to systematic testing. In the past the failure to develop methods of empirical verification and to formulate statements which, in principle, are testable, has deprived theory of the means for resolving conflicting assertions about politics or for establishing a reliable foundation of knowledge upon which succeeding research might build. By rejecting scientific procedures, earlier theorists had closed off the possibility of cumulative knowledge and had condemned the enterprise to an anarchic condition in which no problem is ever solved, no issue ever closed, and no assertion, however bizarre, ever refuted. Although on occasion the dissenting voice of a Hobbes might protest the scandalous contrast between the static condition of theory and the progressive course of science, the situation remained unremedied for centuries. A few decades ago, a contemporary political scientist expressed exactly the same judgment as Hobbes: that political science had not as yet advanced beyond the stage of Aristotle.[7]

According to its critics, the non-cumulative character of traditional theory is inherent not only in its preoccupations and methods but in its strategy as well.

> A science of politics [we are told], which deserves its name must build from the bottom up by asking simple questions that can, in principle, be answered; it cannot be built from the top down by asking questions that, one has reason to suspect, cannot be answered at all, at least not by the methods of science. An empirical discipline is built by the slow, modest, and piecemeal cumulation of relevant theories and data.[8]

The history of science is said to demonstrate that cumulative knowledge has been the result of cooperative effort. Ideally, therefore, theories should be akin to battle-plans which permit numerous researchers to push ahead, each adding his own advance to the previously consolidated position and preparing the way for a fresh push after his own assignment has been completed. Traditional theory, in contrast, has produced its solitary heroes, inspired by the dream of creating *the* theory which would stand perfect and complete for all time, consciously designed not to encourage modifications or improvements. Our contemporary conception of the strategic implementation of theory was first announced by Bacon, who had mocked classical philosophy — "it can talk, but cannot generate" — and had spread before men's eyes a vision of organised and strategically directed research that is now taken for granted:

> For I well know that axioms once rightly discovered will carry whole troops of works along with them, and produce them, not here and there one, but in clusters. . . . Consider what may be expected . . . from men abounding in leisure, and from association of labours, and from successions of ages: the rather because it is not a way which only one man can pass at a time (as is the case with that of reasoning) but one in which the labours and industries of men (especially as regards the collecting of experience) may with the best effect be first distributed and then combined. For only then will men begin to know their strength, when instead of great numbers doing all the same things, one shall take charge of one thing and another of another.[9]

The case for the scientific study of politics is based on the contention that traditional theory was "trans-empirical,"[10] more concerned with transcending the world of facts than with formulating propositions which could be tested against the world of facts. This misunderstanding of the nature of theory has foreclosed the possibility of cumulative knowledge. One solution, which has met with widespread approval, is to distinguish "normative theory," which would comprise the traditional preoccupations with "values," ideal political orders, and the history of political theory, from "empirical theory" which would concentrate upon employing scientific procedures in the acquisition of reliable knowledge and building a growing body of steadily more inclusive generalisations.[11]

The view of science and scientific progress held by political scientists is not unwarranted by prevailing conceptions of science. According to one authority, ". . . the most dynamic, distinctive, and influential creation of the western mind is a progressive science of nature. Only there in the technical realm does the favorite western idea of progress hold any demonstrable meaning."[12] The question which I wish to raise is whether these prevailing conceptions are the only ones. Are there other conceptions of science and scientific progress which present more striking analogies, not with scientific political inquiry as it is now understood, but with traditional political theory as it used to be practised? Are there conceptions which assign a different role to theory and research and which, as a consequence, cast a different and even disturbing light on the understanding of scientific progress and, more significantly, on the intellectual and material conditions necessary to promote scientific knowledge? Is the particular relationship between fact and theory, which seems to lie at the basis of the hopes for a scientific politics, so straightforward a matter in science? If there are disturbing complexities, what is their import for the relationship between political theories and political facts?

It may seem bizarre to suggest parallels between scientific theory and traditional political theory,[13] yet this objection may be overcome if one consideration, which is apt to be forgotten by political scientists, is recalled. To describe science as a cumulative body of knowledge, that is, knowledge acquired incrementally over time, is to suggest that important things can be learned about the practice of science when it is interpreted as an historical enterprise. This is the assumption of the historian of science who attempts to explain how discoveries have occurred and why some errors proved fruitful and others unproductive.[14] Until very recently the historical approach was the preferred method of studying and teaching political theory. The justification of the historical method, however, was rarely that it enabled the student to become acquainted with theories which were progressively truer. A few interpretations did suggest that earlier theories had prepared the way for the truth embodied in a particular theory (e.g. Thomism or Marxism), but on the whole these interpretations have been treated as inspired by the same sort of suspicious motives which once led Christian writers to describe the ancient religions as a *praeparatio evangelica* for Christianity. Instead, the study of the major theories from the Greeks onwards is defended either as a means for improving one's understanding of politics by exposing it to the diversity of ideas embodied in the history of theory; or as a means for becoming acquainted with "ageless" theories;[15] or, finally, as a way of analysing the relationships between a particular theory and its social, political, and philosophical milieu.[16] What has not been argued is that the student of theory should investigate Plato, Aristotle, Machiavelli, and Marx in the same spirit as the student of chemistry examines the work of Boyle, Black, Cavendish, Priestley, and Lavoisier, that is, as a movement towards a progressively truer theory.

All of this seems commonplace and scarcely worth the effort of stating it, except for the fact that many of the great theorists held a different view of their work. They believed that their theories had advanced political knowledge past the point achieved by their predecessors. "I depart very far from the methods of others," Machiavelli wrote, "but since my aim is to write something useful to him who understands it, I have decided to concentrate on the truth of the matter rather than with any fanciful notion."[17] The precise sense in which Machiavelli considered his own work to be an advance over the past is a complicated question and while it is easy enough to distinguish it from a claim to having added to the previous state of knowledge, it is not so easy to say whether Machiavelli considered his own theories to have superseded completely those of the past, or only some of the past theories, or only some parts of past theories. At any event, the idea of theoretical advance is present and it is stated in a way that invites historical inquiry.

If it is granted that in some as yet unspecified sense the historical dimension is relevant both to scientific theory, which has displayed cumulative advance, and to political theory, which has not, at least apparently not in the same way, then we might consider some of the unsettling possibilities which are being suggested by the newer ways of analysing the history of science. The contemporary be-haviourist, who confidently entertains a hard distinction between traditional or pre-scientific political theories and contemporary scien-tific ones, must surely experience some uncertainty when he reads that historians of science are experiencing

> growing difficulties in distinguishing the "scientific" component of past observation and belief from what their predecessors had readily labelled "error" and "superstition." The more carefully they study, say, Aristotelian dynamics, phlogistic chemistry, or caloric thermodynamics, the more certain they feel that those once current views of nature were, as a whole, neither less scientific nor more the product of human idiosyncrasy than those current today. If those out-of-date beliefs are to be called myths, then myths can be produced by the same sort of methods that now lead to scientific knowledge.[18]

To take one more example of special interest to those neo-Hobbesians who look upon traditional political theories as the principal reason for the non-cumulative state of political knowledge: We are told that historians of science now entertain "profound doubts about the cumulative process" and "rather than seeking the permanent con-tributions of an older science to our present vantage, they attempt to display the historical integrity of that science in its own time."[19]

In the remaining pages I wish to consider the possible bearing of these new interpretations of science on our understanding of both contemporary and traditional political theory. The specific issues and suggestions which I wish to consider can be most readily understood by restating briefly the major argument advanced in one recent book, *The Structure of Scientific Revolutions* by Professor Thomas Kuhn. Although Kuhn's argument is addressed to historians and philosophers of science, much of what he says has a relevancy and special poignancy for the scientifically minded political scientist. Few political scientists are trained as scientists and few are interested in investigating for themselves the logical basis or the historical development of the sciences. For the most part their conceptions of science, its methods, and its history have no other basis than some view which they believe to be authoritative. Wanting nothing more than to be allowed to get on with the work of empirical investigation, they are not anxious to engage in disputes concerning the theoretical foundations which support and justify their work. Their hope is that the meaning of science has been settled. This lends a special irony to the heroic charge which Hobbes had laid on his inheritors: if words are valued "by the authority of an Aristotle, a Cicero, or a Thomas, or any other doctor whatsoever, if but a man," they "are the money of fools." The value of Kuhn's book is that it takes direct issue with certain specific notions concerning scientific progress which are a vital part of the justifications accepted by political scientists.

Kuhn disputes the view of scientific progress as a form of incremental advance which is made possible because scientists scrupulously adhere to certain practices governing theorising. He argues against the notion that scientific progress results from the way that scientists build on the achievements of their predecessors; and that scientific theories are discarded when new knowledge has disproved them, or when they fail to conform to commonly accepted standards of scientific explanation and proof. It is not Kuhn's intention to destroy these notions of scientific progress, only to object to their being identified with the whole of scientific activity and theory construction. The cumulative growth of scientific knowledge and the process whereby a particular scientific theory is modified as a result of research are part of what Kuhn characterises as "normal science." To convey his meaning he adopts socio-political language. Normal science is a particular form of activity carried on by a "community" of scientists. Students of seventeenth-century political thought will find Kuhn's analysis of the scientific community familiar: it is a community based on an agreement which extends not only to the rules governing inquiry and to stipulations concerning what shall qualify as a scientific question and count as a scientific answer, but it extends as well to the particular theory which is accepted as true by the members in their research and investigation. The particular theory which dominates a scientific community is designated a "paradigm." From a sociological viewpoint, a paradigm provides a consensual basis which consolidates the loyalties and commitments of the members. Paradigms are "universally recognised scientific achievements that for a time provide model problems and solutions to a community of practitioners" (p. x). As the acknowledged arbiter of what constitutes significant scientific activity a paradigm guides the community in its choice of problems; the community, in turn, has as its task the solution of the puzzles set by the paradigm. Scientific progress consists in fulfilling the promise of a paradigm. Generally, a paradigm is worked out in three main ways. First, scientists seek to establish in rigorous fashion the class of facts subsumed under the paradigm. Second, they test the predictions of the paradigm with the facts disclosed by investigation: .they "match" fact and theory to ascertain the extent of correspondence or "fit." Finally, they seek to articulate the theory by undertaking factual investigations designed to clarify problems suggested by the paradigm (pp. 24-7).

As Kuhn would have it, the crucial mark of a mature science consists of a paradigm recognised as such by the scientific community. Recognition means not only that the community agrees to conduct research along lines determined by the paradigm, but that it is willing to enforce the paradigm on its members. Scientific progress is critically dependent upon the ability of a community to develop effective means of enforcement. The achievements of science are testimony to the skill with which scientists have solved the political problem of organisation. "In its normal state . . . a scientific community is an enormously efficient instrument for solving the problems or puzzles that its paradigms define" (p. 165).[20] A scientific community develops means for concerting the energy, resources, and attention of the members and directing them unremittingly towards the elaboration of a designated theory. Among these means are the rules and practices entailed by the paradigm; members of the community are expected to conform to these norms of scientific behaviour and non-conformance is usually met by sanctions. Deviant behaviour, to use the current idiom, does not normally take the form of rejecting scientific methods but of directing them to problems which do not lie within the province of the accepted paradigm or of applying them in a way which suggests a view of the world different from that implied by the reigning paradigm.

Normal scientific activity, the activity in which most scientists inevitably spend almost all their time, is predicated on the assumption that the scientific community knows what the world is like. Much of the success of the enterprise derives from the community's willingness to defend that assumption, if necessary at considerable cost. Normal science, for example, often suppresses fundamental novelties because they are necessarily subversive of its basic commitments (p. 5).

Social scientists who are impressed by the seeming fertility of the scientific imagination in producing new theories may be sobered by Kuhn's emphatic assertion that one of "the most striking features" of normal science is "how little" it aims "to produce major novelties, conceptual or phenomenal" (p. 35). Scientific progress, far from arising out of the concerted quest for endless theoretical novelties, seems to require the suppression of competing viewpoints.[21] The enforcement of a paradigm permits the normal scientist to get on with his work without being distracted by the need to defend the basic principles of the paradigm, its canons of inquiry, or the view of the world which it embodies (pp. 162-3). As we shall note later, novel theories have their place, but they tend to be restricted to times of trouble when the scientific community undergoes a crisis in belief regarding its paradigm. The scientific community prospers best when crisis and novelty are rare. Unlike other communities which experience a crisis in belief and seek gropingly to adjust, the scientific community rapidly adapts itself to a new paradigm, quickly redefines its membership, and efficiently disposes of of the old believers.

> There are always some men who cling to one or another of the older views, and they are simply read out of the profession, which thereafter ignores their work. The new paradigm implies a new and more rigid definition of the field. Those unwilling or unable to accommodate their work to it must proceed in isolation or attach themselves to some other group (p. 19).[22]

The enforcing power, seemingly so vital to scientific advance, presupposes a membership willing and predisposed to acquiesce in the observance of the norms of the community. Just as other communities develop means of inducting citizens into the practices and beliefs of the community and seek to internalise the values of the community, the scientific community has also understood that the exercise of coercive authority can be made cheaper, more efficient, and less obtrusive if the modes of initiation and education of the members predispose them towards the loyal behaviour needed in paradigm-workers. Kuhn describes the process of initiation as partly a matter of winning the loyalty of a new generation of scientists to the view of the world embodied in a paradigm, and partly as a matter of enforcing the authority of the paradigm and of its community of practitioners upon the initiates. The major vehicle is scientific education which trains the student in the methods and outlook of the dominant paradigm. The use of scientific textbooks plays a strategically significant part in the education of scientists; they are a major means "for the perpetuation of normal science." The student is made to rely upon textbooks until this third or fourth year of graduate study and, as Kuhn wryly notes, he is rarely exposed to "the creative scientific literature" that made the textbook possible (p. 164). In its customary form, the textbook contributes powerfully to the view that the history of science is a record of cumulative advance. Textbooks "refer only to that part of the work of past scientists that can be easily viewed as contributions to the statement and solution of the texts' paradigm problems." "Partly by selection and partly by distortion" earlier scientists "are implicitly represented as having worked upon the same set of fixed problems and in accordance with the same set of fixed canons that the most recent revolution in scientific theory and method has made seem scientific" (pp. 136-7). Kuhn concludes that "it is a narrow and rigid education, probably more so than any other except perhaps in orthodox theology. But for normal-scientific work, for puzzle-solving within the tradition that the textbooks define, the scientist is almost perfectly equipped" (p. 165).

Thus political scientists who envy the organisation of the scientific community and the results of its research, should have a special interest in Kuhn's observations on the process whereby that community institutes one paradigm rather than another. The contemporary political scientist finds himself assailed by a variety of paradigms competing for support, material as well as intellectual and emotional. Is there an objective way for deciding between the competing claims of game theory, bargaining theory, equilibrium models, systems theory, communication theory, functional theory, or structural-functional theory? Kuhn offers little comfort on this score. Up to a certain point, what matters is not which is the "truer" paradigm, but which is to be enforced. In the early development of most sciences, diverse theories competed for acceptance; the eventual losers were not adjudged to be less scientific, nor was the winner decided by appealing to impersonal standards of observation or experience. "An apparently arbitrary element" operates in the selection of one paradigm over another (p. 4). "Philosophers of science have repeatedly demonstrated that more than one theoretical construction can always be placed upon a given collection of data." Alternative scientific theories are easy to invent, Kuhn remarks, but scientists rarely permit themselves this form of indulgence, because it diverts energy and resources from on-going work. "Retooling is an extravagance" (p. 76).

The arbitrary element in the choice of paradigms is best revealed during crises when an existing paradigm is being challenged. When the challenge is successful and a new paradigm displaces the old, the scientific community has undergone what Kuhn characterises as a revolution. He finds this to be a recurrent experience in the development of the mature sciences. His discussion is relevant to the political scientist who finds himself in the midst of the "behavioural revolution." The relevance of a scientific revolution does not lie in the repetition of a word, but in what the scientific experience discloses about the relationship between fact and theory or, more precisely, about the criteria used in discarding one theory for another.

In Kuhn's view, normal science is characterised by a close "fit" between theory and fact. In the practice of normal science, the truth or falsity of statements is determined by confronting the operative paradigm with facts disclosed or amassed by investigation and observation (p. 80). The intimate relation between theory and fact is closely connected with, and even made possible by, the kind of activity decreed in the working out of a paradigm. Kuhn describes this activity as a species of puzzle-solving. The research problems of normal science are set by its paradigm: the problems are to the paradigm as pieces are to a puzzle. The solution "exists" but has yet to be worked out; or, stated differently, the outcome is anticipated, but the way of achieving it remains in doubt. What may be an unsolved puzzle for one paradigm may not even exist for another (p. 80).

> ... one of the things a scientific community acquires with a paradigm is a criterion for choosing problems that, while the paradigm is taken for granted, it can be assumed to have solutions. To a great extent these are the only problems that the community will admit as scientific or encourage its members to undertake.... One of the reasons why normal science seems to progress so rapidly is that its practitioners concentrate on problems that only their lack of ingenuity should keep them from solving (p. 37).

170

The assumption that solutions exist to the puzzles of a paradigm gives rise to expectations about what will be found through research. As long as these expectations are mostly fulfilled, science is said to proceed normally. When the expectations are frustrated; when inquiry discloses facts which cannot be squared with the paradigm, the scientific community undergoes a crisis in belief. Its confidence in the reigning paradigm is shaken. Kuhn introduces the concept of "anomaly" to describe these findings of normal science which cannot be reconciled with the paradigm, despite efforts made at adjusting the paradigm (pp. 52-3). Kuhn finds it difficult to advance a simple explanation as to why or when a particular anomaly provokes a crisis in theory. "There are always some discrepancies" between a theory and nature, and normal science is able to function effectively despite "persistent and recognized anomaly." At one time, the existence of an anomaly will prove so compelling that it "call(s) into question explicit and fundamental generalisations of the paradigm." At another time a crisis may develop when the anomaly appears to obstruct certain practical aims, as when astrology inhibited the design of calendars and the resulting dissatisfaction helped to prepare the way for the acceptance of the Copernican paradigm (pp. 81-2).

When anomalies reach the stage of "crisis" the repercussions on the scientific community are profound. In the face of repeated failures to solve the puzzles set by the paradigm, the scientist feels insecure and his insecurity is reflected in a certain loosening of discipline and a relaxation of the rules governing research (pp.67-8, 83). "Divergent articulations" of the paradigm begin to appear and are encouraged by a growing realisation that what had been thought to be merely a particularly stubborn puzzle is something unaccountable under the terms of the old dispensation. The few scientists who had first dared to question the paradigm are joined by others who commit themselves to resolving the crisis. Soon normal science gives way to "extraordinary" science which signifies a determination to look at the world anew and uninhibited by the frowning presence of the old paradigm. Once the old paradigm has been doubted, its authority-structure is weakened and the resultant crisis "loosens the rules of normal puzzle solving in ways that ultimately permit a new paradigm to emerge" (p. 80).

No paradigm is overthrown unless an alternative lies at hand; but once the new paradigm has been proclaimed, the scientific community quickly institutionalises it, employing all of its means for enforcement and compliance. The rigidity of the community, which had previously discouraged novel alternatives, now becomes a powerful asset for consolidating the new theory. The fact that it truly possesses an "establishment" enables the scientific community to make its paradigm-switch quickly and efficiently. Above all, once the decision to switch has been taken, the authority and power of the community are available for insuring compliance (pp. 164-5).

The decision itself is not easily achieved, given the formidable apparatus of enforcement behind the existing paradigm and the fact that a paradigm is maintained by destroying its rivals and suppressing alternatives. Indeed, Kuhn appears most uncertain in the matter of explaining why it is that a paradigm is ever successfully challenged. At one point he suggests that the arbitrary element inherent in the choice of any paradigm makes it likely that normal research will encounter anomalies which will eventually provoke a crisis (p. 5). Elsewhere he simply notes that the rigidity of the scientific community may prevent insiders from challenging the paradigm but since its writ does not extend to "outside" fields, there is always the possibility of the scientific equivalent to l'étranger proposing a new paradigm, a possibility that has occurred frequently in the history of science (pp. 143, 164). In the face of the resistance that any challenging paradigm is likely to encounter, Kuhn's uncertainty edges towards despair and his conclusion echoes the same doubts that haunted the medieval defenders of another kind of paradigm: "But so long as somebody appears with a new candidate for paradigm — usually a young man or one new to the field — the loss due to rigidity accrues only to the individual" (p. 165).

The question of most interest to the political scientist is, what induces the scientific community to reject its reigning paradigm and to choose another? It is not enough to suggest that a theory is discarded when it is falsified. No theory ever fits the facts completely and every theory is capable of being falsified. A theory maintains its hold over its practitioners, not because it has resisted falsification or because it fits the facts as a glove fits the hand, but because the scientific community agrees that the theory fits the facts "better" *when* the facts are viewed from the perspective of *that* theory (pp. 144-6).

Most political scientists tend to assume that the decision to change paradigms is analogous to a fact-finding proceeding in which, *per curiram*, scientists review new "facts" and on the basis of logic, evidence, and experiment solemnly decide that the old theory has been superseded by a "higher" form of explanation.[23] In Kuhn's description, a decision between paradigms appears more like an adversary proceeding, more competitive than deliberative.[24] What is at issue are new cognitive and normative standards, not new facts. A new theory embodies a new way of looking at phenomena rather than the discovery of hitherto inaccessible data. It represents a break with the existing tradition of scientific practice and proclaims new standards of legitimate activity; it proposes somewhat different rules for inquiry, a different problem-field, as well as different notions of significance and of what constitutes a solution. Neither the new paradigm nor the old can provide neutral procedures for deciding between their respective merits, because each paradigm has its own distinctive procedures. Because "each group uses its own paradigm to argue in that paradigm's defense," the neutrality of each is impugned and there is no *tertium quid* available.

The lack of a neutral arbiter becomes all the more intriguing if it is recalled that established facts are susceptible to diverse explanations and that no theory provides a perfect fit with the facts.[25] The "arbitrary" element mentioned earlier should not be taken to imply a total lack of accepted criteria for judging between paradigms. At a minimum, a new paradigm must hold out the promise of being able to transform the old anomalies into new puzzles. It must also be capable of generating new puzzles for research. Above all, a further reduction in the arbitrariness accompanying the decision to switch follows from the fact that the decision will be made by those most qualified rather than by "outsiders."[26] After these qualifications have been duly noted, it remains the case that the decision concerning the future possibilities of a particular paradigm is one that "can only be made on faith" (p. 157).

Kuhn's analysis may produce some anxieties in the political scientist who had believed that scientific theories were, in some simple sense, symbolic reproductions of reality. These anxieties may provoke him to protest that "nature" represents a "reality" that, after all is said and done, is *there*; hence it would be misleading to suggest that the enforcement of a paradigm merely proves that a theory works, not that it is true. The reality of nature sets limits to what would be considered an admissible candidate for paradigm-adoption. The way that Kuhn treats this objection is not likely to dispel the anxieties of the political scientist. He puts it in the form of a question: "what must nature ... be like in order that science be possible at all?" His answer suggests that "nature" does not constitute an obvious limit at all: "Any conception of nature compatible with the growth of science..." will do (p. 172), which would seem to be tantamount to saying that it is the requirements of scientific advance, rather than anything permanent about nature, which are determining.

II

Customarily, the historical study of political theories seeks to trace the evolution of political ideas either by demonstrating how the characteristics of the theories of one age differ from those of another, or by specifying the continuities which persist from one age to another. In the pages which follow, I should like to borrow from Kuhn's discussion in order to suggest a different way of thinking about the history of political theory. In particular, I should like to draw on his conception of the role of paradigms in the history of science and to show that a comparable phenomenon has been present in the history of political theory. My purpose is not to argue that political theory is a species of scientific theory, but rather that political theories can be best understood as paradigms and that the scientific study of politics is a special form of paradigm-inspired research. Necessarily, my references to the history of political theory will be cryptic.

When the idea of paradigms is applied to the history of political theory, it is surprising to discover many theorists have considered theorising to be an activity aimed at the creation of new paradigms. One of the most familiar expressions of this sort of self-consciousness is represented by Machiavelli's boast that "I have determined to enter upon a path not yet trodden by anyone."[27] The path to which he refers is, of course, one which leads to a new theory. In *The Prince* his sarcastic allusion to those who "have fancied for themselves republics and principalities that have never been seen or known to exist in reality" was clearly intended to evoke the paradigm of utopian theories and to make it obvious to all that he was offering an alternative.[28] The same pretensions were evident in Hobbes's announcement that he had distilled "rules" for "making and maintaining commonwealths ... which rules neither poor men have the leisure, nor men that have had the leisure, *have hitherto* had the curiosity, or the method to find out."[29] Like Machiavelli, Hobbes was self-conscious to the point of arrogance about the novelty of his paradigm: "... how different this doctrine is from the greatest practice of the world, especially of the western parts, that have received their moral learning from Rome and Athens ..."[30] Hobbes surpassed Machiavelli in his determination to destroy previous paradigms, especially those associated with the names of Aristotle, Cicero and St. Thomas.[31]

Self-consciousness in paradigm-innovation was not the peculiarity of ironic iconoclasts, such as Machiavelli and Hobbes, or the result of the sharpened historical consciousness of modern writers. Thucydides had taken pains to distinguish his own methods of inquiry from the techniques of poets and chroniclers — the true rivals of the historian and philosopher in ancient Greece — and had recommended his methods to those "who desire an exact knowledge of the past as an aid to the interpretation of the future."[32] Polybius had explicitly taken issue with Plato's paradigm of philosophical knowledge and had proposed instead a form which would combine the knowledge of the historian and the practical statesman.[33]

When applied to the history of political theory, Kuhn's notion of a paradigm, "universally recognised scientific achievements that for a time provide model problems and solutions to a community of practitioners," invites us to consider Plato, Aristotle, Machiavelli, Hobbes, Locke, and Marx as the counterparts in political theory to Galileo, Harvey, Newton, Laplace, Faraday, and Einstein. Each of the writers in the first group inspired a new way of looking at the political world; in each case their theories proposed a new definition of what was significant for understanding that world; each specified distinctive methods for inquiry; and each of the theories contained an explicit or implicit statement of what should count as an answer to certain basic questions. Kuhn's criterion, that a paradigm should provide "model problems and solutions," is approximated in the way that one theorist will adopt major elements from another. When Aquinas refers to Aristotle as "the philosopher" and proceeds to incorporate certain key Aristotelian notions, such as *physis* and *polis*, and to put them to work, we have a striking analogy with what Kuhn calls "paradigm-adoption." Many other instances could be introduced to show that the tradition of political theory displays a high degree of self-consciousness about the role and function of paradigms. Harrington's political ideas were elaborated in reference to two main paradigms, that of "ancient prudence" as represented by Aristotle and that of "modern prudence" by Machiavelli.[34] One could also point to the paradigmatic influence of Locke upon eighteenth-century political writers in America and France;[35] of Hobbes upon later writers such as Benthan, James Mill, and Austin; of Marx and Max Weber upon political and social writers of the last hundred years.

In pointing to the unique status of certain major political theories, I am not suggesting that later writers merely borrowed from them or were influenced by them. The point is more substantial, namely,

175

that major theories have served as master-paradigms enabling later and lesser writers to exploit them in a manner comparable to that of "normal science." This was the manner in which the Aristotelian paradigm was used by medieval writers, such as John of Paris or Ptolemy of Lucca, and, if we allow paradigmatic status to the Aristotelian-Thomistic synthesis, the same can be said of Hooker and the Spanish writers of the sixteenth century, such as Victoria and Suarez. One might also point to all of the lesser Machiavellis listed in Meinecke's *Staatsräison*, in Acton's introduction to Burd's edition of *Il Principe*, or in Benoist's ponderous volumes on *le Machiavélisme*. This matter might be stated differently by saying that one of the main reasons why students of political theory continue to read Locke instead of those writers, such as Hunton of Lawson, who are reputed to have anticipated or influenced him, is that Locke spawned Lockians who set to work using his ideas to solve political problems.[36]

These examples raise the possibility that there have been important instances of cumulative knowledge in the history of political theory. What is curious is that historians of political theory have been so reluctant to explore this possibility. In most textbooks and university courses on the subject, the method of instruction is designed to produce exactly the opposite effect of texts in the natural sciences. Instead of interpreting past theories as preparing the way for the next phase of political theories, commentators and lecturers tend to underscore the differences between the great theorists. The inevitable result is an emphasis upon discontinuity and novelty. At the same time, almost no attention is paid to the numerous and nearly anonymous followers who have busied themselves working out the master-theory. Instead of being considered "normal scientists," they are dismissed as tiresome and repetitious epigoné. If we remember that theoretical originality is not the hallmark of normal science, the historian of political theory who ignores the dilative work of the under-labourers, has closed off a whole range of questions, the most interesting of which is: what sorts of intellectual operations occur when a political theory is put to work in circumstances different from those which inspired it?

One of the functions of a paradigm is to enable its users to solve puzzles generated by the paradigm when it is applied to nature. Although, as I have contended, an analogous process has been at work in political theory, most commentators have implicitly denied that this has been the case. They have generally viewed the process either as a form of mimesis and hence not deserving of attention, or as an example of distortion. The second response is interesting, because it can be related to Kuhn's point that a paradigm is not intended to solve all puzzles in advance, but to supply the means for solving them, even if they have not been anticipated. When the historian of political theory encounters the case of a paradigm being applied to unexpected puzzles, his instinctive reaction is to suspect that the paradigm is being distorted for partisan ends. For example, following the reception of Aristotle in the thirteenth century, it was the common practice of medieval political writers to press him into service in the great polemical controversies concerning church-state relationships. In the hands of a master, such as Marsilius of Padua, the Aristotelian paradigm was not applied mechanically to matters forseen by the paradigm, but to unanticipated puzzles.[37] As is well known, Marsilius countered the papal claims to secular authority by relying on Aristotelian arguments concerning the self-sufficient nature of the political community and its possession of all necessary means for the maintenance of internal peace and order. At the outset of his great work, *Defensor Pacis*, he announced that he would investigate the major cause of disorder and that this cause was one that "Aristotle could not have known."[38] Like a loyal paradigm-worker, Marsilius was not put off by the fact that Aristotle had not envisaged the medieval Church, but rather proceeded on the assumption that if Aristotle were truly "the master of those that know" his paradigm would furnish the resources for solving a new problem.

Instead of considering this practice as a form of creative adaptation, the modern scholar responds with the finicky criticism that Aristotle's conception of a *polis* had not been intended for the much larger and dualistically organised medieval political society. Of one such attempt by James of Viterbo, an early fourteenth-century papalist, Mr. John B. Morrall writes that "one would guess that the Greek philosopher himself would have regarded this development with suspicion; the medieval territories would have seemed to him far too large to fit his conception of a true political community."[39] It is not my intention to discredit the historian's concern with deviations from the texts, but only to protest that it has closed off some potentially fruitful ways of thinking about political theories. One of these ways involves viewing the function of a theory as directing its users to new puzzles, unresolved or even unforeseen by the theory itself. In fact this conception of a theory is in accord with the practice of some historians, as is illustrated by Professor Ullmann's remark about Aquinas: "... Thomas was the one writer who not only fully understood the Philosopher, but who also, precisely because he so fully understood Aristotle, perceived the potentialities of his doctrines."[40]

Admittedly, an Aquinas or Marsilius can hardly be classified as paradigm-workers; they are more like paradigm-creators who combined elements of the old with distinctive additions of their own. In this respect Kuhn's remark applies to them: "new paradigms are born from old ones" and borrow much from the conceptual and manipulative apparatus of the traditional paradigm, "although they seldom employ these borrowed elements in quite the traditional way" (p. 148). In political theory the line is not always easy to draw between paradigm-workers and paradigm-creators, as the example of the Marxian paradigm shows. Under which category does Lenin's theory of revolution fall? or Hilferding's studies on imperialism? or Trotsky's analysis of revolution in an "underdeveloped" society? Are these examples of normal science or of extraordinary science? Whatever conclusion one might arrive at, it seems clear that in generating a wide range of problems, in supplying a distinctive world-view, in indicating criteria of significance and canons of inquiry, Marxism has been one of the most extraordinary paradigms in the history of Western political thought.

Having pressed this far with the analogy between political theory and scientific paradigms, we must next inquire whether the history of theory reveals anything comparable to the highly efficient enforcement powers of the scientific community. Once the history of political theory is examined with this question in mind, a surprising amount of affirmative evidence turns up. Plato's Academy, for example, was instituted to extend the master's paradigm into many areas of knowledge, among which politics was one of the most important. The same might be said for Aristotle's Lyceum, although the political motive was less marked than in the Academy.[41] One could also mention the example of Calvin's Geneva and the enforcement of the Puritan paradigm in the Massachusetts Bay Colony. An outstanding modern example is the official status of Marxism in the Soviet Union. It is also possible that other examples might be revealed by historical research. There is some ground for believing that certain paradigms were enforced among communities of Renaissance scholars; the circle which included Erasmus and More might be investigated from this point of view. Or the activities of the eighteenth-century French Encyclopedists might serve equally well.

With the possible exception of Marxism, it appears that political theorists have had only indifferent success in generating communities which, on an institutionalised basis, could enforce paradigms and guide research. The question which then suggests itself is, have political theorists sought a different way of enforcing their theories? Here the answer is overwhelmingly affirmative, and a brief exploration of this theme discloses significant differences between political theorists and scientists. In contrast to the scientist, who seeks to elicit acceptance of his theory from his fellow-scientists, the political theorist has viewed this form of acceptance as a secondary matter. The reason is not simply that a genuine "community" of theorists has been a rarity, but rather that the kind of power which the theorist seeks is to be found in the political community itself. By means of his theory the scientist hopes to transform the outlook of the members of the scientific community and to gain the support and power of that community for the application of his theory to the investigation of nature. The aim of many political theorists has been to change society itself: not simply to alter the way men look at the world, but to alter the world. This is the viewpoint that tempted Plato to journey to Syracuse, where he hoped to "capture" Dionysius II and convert him into an instrument for changing a political society in accordance with the principles of Plato's theory.[42] If the authenticity of the Platonic letters is too dubious, the same preoccupation with using power to transform society reappears in the *Republic* (v, 473) where Plato alluded to that "one change" which might pave the way for radical reform, the uniting of "political power and philosophy" in one man.

A similar impulse informed Machiavelli. The Dedication to *The Prince* made plain his intention of "discussing and directing the government of princes." Machiavelli's *Discourses* was even bolder, for it not only projected a new political system but hinted that the old one would have to be overthrown to make way for the new.

A final example is provided by Hobbes. His political objectives are recognisable in the closing lines of his Introduction to *Leviathan*:

> ... He that is to govern a whole nation must read in himself, not this or that particular man; but mankind: which though it be hard to do, harder than to learn any language or science; yet when I shall have set down my own reading orderly, and perspicuously, the pains left another, will be only to consider, if he also not find the same in himself.

By declaring that the theory of *Leviathan* had been prepared for "he that is to govern a nation," Hobbes was confronted with the same problem as Plato: how to persuade the ruling authority to enforce his paradigm? That Hobbes conceived the problem to be the same is verified by the way in which he invokes the *memoria Platonis:*

> ... considering ... how much depth of moral philosophy is required in them that have the administration of the sovereign power, I am at the point of believing this my labour, as useless, as the commonwealth of Plato.

Hobbes buoyed his sagging spirits with the belief that none had succeeded before him in reducing political knowledge to a set of simple theorems and hence there was still hope that

> this writing of mine may fall into the hands of a sovereign ... and by exercise of entire sovereignty, in protecting the public teaching of it, convert this truth of speculation into the utility of practice.[43]

The successors to this tradition of paradigm enforcement are too numerous to mention. One thinks of Rousseau with his constitutions for Corsica and Poland; Bentham's appeals to the despots of Europe; Saint-Simon's efforts to gain the attention of Napoleon; and the numerous attempts made during the nineteenth century to found small communities on the basis of explicit theories. If one is impressed only by the failure of these theories, he might wish to consider how successfully a theorist's paradigm has been enforced in the Soviet Union.

It would be misleading to conclude that the only possibility open to the political theorist is either to follow the model of Plato and seek to educate a ruler or to follow the model of Marx and work for a revolution. Another method of paradigm enforcement, one which is consonant with the present *locus* of political theory in universities, is a distinct alternative. Hobbes was probably the first theorist to envision these possibilities. He recommended that his own paradigm be converted into a kind of official theory and taught at the universities, which might then become like "the fountains of civil and moral doctrine" from which "the preachers and the gentry" might draw such water as ought to be sprinkled upon the people.[44]

Today the modern American university offers an even more enticing prospect, for to the natural educational influence at its disposal there has been added the power of foundations. In concert they provide a powerful mechanism for enforcing paradigms and subsidising research. Until recently, one vital ingredient has been lacking in political science departments—the paradigm itself. Previously, most departments had practised a tolerant attitude, ad-mitting a wide diversity in methods and assumptions. Now the situation has changed dramatically. The growth of social science and the successful behavioural revolution have supplied the missing element, and there appears to be a convergence between a paradigm, a mechanism of enforcement, and ample resources for carrying on paradigm-directed research. A remarkable insight into this process is furnished, perhaps unintentionally, in David Easton's recent book, *A Framework for Political Analysis*. His description of the origins of the behavioural revolution "in political theory" seems like an echo of Hobbes's dictum that "the first truths were arbitrarily made by those that first of all imposed names upon things. . . ."[45] According to Easton, behaviouralism involves "more" than just the adoption of scientific methods for the study of politics, and "it is only partly correct to see in it an ideological weapon lending color and vigor to the movement of a diffuse and informal group of academic rebels against tradition." The "name" itself, political behaviouralism, "can be considered an accident," produced by a desire to placate a committee of the United States Senate which had been conducting hearings for a proposed national science foundation "to stimulate and provide funds for scholarly research." The "representatives of the social sciences" were dismayed to learn that some senators had their own name for the social sciences, "the socialistic sciences," and hence were understandably reluctant to underwrite this particular type of research. Accordingly, the name "behavioural science" was coined by its supporters "to identify those aspects of the social sciences that might come under the aegis of a foundation devoted to the support of hard science." The tactic proved successful and when, by virtue of another "accidental" turn of events the Ford Foundation decided "at about the same time" to institute a Behavioural Sciences Division, the "name" was well on the way to becoming a movement.[46]

In striking ways, the behavioural movement satisfies most of Kuhn's specifications for a successful paradigm. It has come to dominate the curricula of many political science departments throughout the country; a new generation of students is being taught the new methods of survey analysis, data processing, and scaling; behavioural textbooks are increasingly in evidence; and there are even signs that the past is being reinterpreted in order to demonstrate that the revolution is merely the culmination of "trends" in political science over the past few decades.[47] Whether there has occurred a phenomenon similar to that reported by Kuhn—those with other loyalties "are simply read out of the profession, which

181

thereafter ignores their work" — will not be discussed, except to note that some of the most interesting political theories are the work of *les étrangers*, uncommitted and marginal figures, such as Eric Hoffer, Hannah Arendt, and Bertrand de Jouvenel, who are largely ignored.[48]

At a later point we shall consider briefly the kind of paradigmatic activity represented by behaviourism, but now it will be useful to fasten upon one peculiarity of the revolution by returning to some questions posed by Kuhn: why do paradigm-revolutions occur? what kinds of anomalies are apt to provoke a search for new modes of explanation in political theory? In one respect the behavioural revolution forms a close analogue with Kuhn's description of scientific crisis. The dissatisfaction which scientists are said to express over the inability of a paradigm to solve puzzles was duplicated in the severe criticism which political scientists directed at traditional political theories. The classics could not furnish the "operational" hypotheses for investigating specific problems, such as what determines how and whether voters will vote, the sources of voter attitudes, the extent to which beliefs deemed fundamental to the persistence of the system are shared, who makes decisions in a democratic system, and the degree of control actually exercised by citizens over their governors. The results of this dissatisfaction are familiar to most, readers, but what is less obvious is the contrast between the new paradigm and the theories of the past.

Many of the great theories of the past arose in response to a crisis in the world, not in the community of theorists. It was not a methodological breakdown that prompted Plato to commit himself to the *bios thereotikos* and to produce the first great paradigm in Western political thought; it was, instead, the breakdown of the Athenian *polis*. Again, it was not a simple desire to replace theological with Aristotelian methods that led to the *Defensor Pacis*, but a continuing crisis in the relations of church and state. There is no need to multiply the instances: the paradigms of Machiavelli, Bodin, Harrington, Hobbes, Locke, Tocqueville, and Marx were produced by a profound belief that the world had become deranged. The intimate relation between crisis and theory is the result not only of the theorist's belief that the world is deeply flawed but of his strategic sense that crisis, and its usual accompaniments of institutional collapse and the breakdown of authority, affords an opportunity for a theory to reorder the world. This was the theme of Plato's *Republic*; of the last chapter of Machiavelli's *Prince* and the preface to Book II of the *Discorsi*; of Hobbes's *Leviathan*; and of virtually all that

182

Marx wrote. In each case political crisis was not the product of the theorist's hyper-active imagination but of the actual state of affairs. Greek democracy *was* undergoing its final, agonising crisis; the Florentine republic was being transformed by the Medici into a personal government; the English civil wars did lead to the break-down of authority; industrial capitalism did produce profound social and political dislocation and did raise the question of the bour-geoisie's competence to govern. In each instance the theorist's re-sponse was not to offer a theory that would correspond to the facts, or "fit" them as snugly as the glove does the hand. Derangement in the world signified that the facts were skewed. A theory corre-sponding to a sick world would itself be a form of sickness. Instead, theories were offered as symbolic representations of what society would be like if it could be reordered.

If, for a moment, we were to retrace the discussion to the point where it mentioned certain historical crises which have actually occurred, it might be suggestive to consider these crises in society from the viewpoint of Kuhn's conception of "anomaly." It will be recalled that an anomaly presupposes a theory which is being worked out and, in the process, certain phenomena are encountered which cannot be accounted for by the theory. If we were to con-sider political crises as situations in which ruling authorities cannot account for certain happenings, in the sense of being unable to deal with them effectively, we might designate these situations as anom-alous. But *pace* Kuhn, in what sense do they constitute theoretical anomalies? What is the theory whose expectations are being violated or contradicted?

The obvious response is to say that Kuhn's conception of paradigms seems out of place when it is applied to a context for which it had not been devised. Instead of accepting this objection I should like to try to amend the concept so that it can be made useful for analysing actual political societies. My proposal is that we conceive of political society itself as a paradigm of an operative kind. From this viewpoint society would be envisaged as a coherent whole in the sense of its customary political practices, institutions, laws, struc-ture of authority and citizenship, and operative beliefs being or-ganised and interrelated. A politically organised society contains definite institutional arrangements, certain widely shared under-standings regarding the location and use of political power, certain expectations about how authority ought to treat the members of society and about the claims that organised society can rightfully make upon its members. In some societies many of these features are explicitly set forth in a written constitution. In saying that the practices and beliefs of society are organised and interrelated, that its members have certain expectations and share certain beliefs, one is saying that that society believes itself to be one thing rather than another, a democracy rather than a dictatorship, a republic rather than a monarchy, a directed society rather than a free one. This *ensemble* of practices and beliefs may be said to form a paradigm in the sense that the society tries to carry on its political life in accordance with them. Further, in its agencies of enforcement and in its systems of rules, a political society possesses the basic instrumentalities present in Kuhn's scientific community and employs them in an analogous way. Society, too, enforces certain types of conduct and discourages others; it, too, defines what sorts of "experiments" — in the form of individual or group actions — will be encouraged, tolerated, or suppressed; by its complex organisation of politics through legislatures, political parties, and the media of opinion, society also determines what shall count in determining future decisions.

In the natural course of its history a society undergoes changes which impose strains upon the existing paradigm. A society may find the paradigm being challenged directly, or it may experience difficulty in coping with the results of change. New social classes may have emerged; new economic relationships may have developed; or new racial or religious patterns may have appeared. In much the same way that a scientific community will seek to adjust its paradigm to account for "novelty," a political society will seek to adapt its system to the new developments brought by change. To the degree that a society succeeds in adapting, its efforts might even be likened to a form of puzzle-solving. For example, given the political culture of early nineteenth-century England, its professions of being a society with representative institutions and guaranteed liberties, the ways in which that society adjusted its paradigm to accommodate the growing self-consciousness among the working classes and the accompanying demands for suffrage reforms provide an example of the adaptation of a political paradigm to new "facts." The paradigm has to be changed, because, if there is to be accommodation, the "facts" must be viewed differently: in this case, not as they had been viewed at Peterloo but as they were to be viewed during the passage of the successive Reform Bills. Once the "facts" are viewed differently and the paradigm is altered accordingly, the consequence is a change in the facts themselves. In the case of the suffrage reforms in nineteenth-century England, new voters were created and some old grievances disappeared.

If we now shift our attention to a different political paradigm and at the same time recall Kuhn's remark that some phenomena may not constitute an anomaly under one paradigm but will under another, we may consider the status of suffrage demands relative to the paradigm of nineteenth-century Russian Czarism. In this case the rising demands for representative institutions and the extension of the ballot appeared as anomalies, not, as they did in England, as puzzles. Given the political paradigm of Czarism, the demands for change could not be accommodated without radically altering the paradigm. In the end, the "facts" proved to be too much for the theory.

It is also possible to think of a third type of situation which would build on Kuhn's remark that some puzzles impugn the ability of the scientist rather than the paradigm (p. 80). The relative failure of liberal administrations to deal effectively with the condition of the American Negro, at least not until very recently, can be treated as an instance of Kuhn's point. The fault lay not with the democratic paradigm but with its "scientists"; the most embarrassing aspect of the Negro protest movement was its reminder that some of the basic elements of the paradigm, such as the Constitution and the Declaration of Independence, were more consistent with the demands of the protestants than with the actions of the guardians of the paradigm.

III

If space permitted, it would be possible to extend the discussion of political paradigms to examine the problem of revolution as a species of paradigm change. In the remaining pages, however, I should like to direct attention once more at the "normal" political paradigm. As long as a political society can handle its "puzzles" and make minor adjustments in the paradigm to accord with the new "facts" brought by social change, that society is proceeding in a way reminiscent of "normal science." Now one of the interesting points made by Kuhn is that when normal science is busily and successfully at work, it tends to be impatient of philosophy and, in fact, does not need it. Philosophy has a tendency to question accepted assumptions and to reopen issues which were thought to be closed. In the eyes of normal science, philosophy appears as a distraction and a potential diversion of energies away from puzzle-solving activity. Similarly, we might say that when political societies are operating normally, they will envince little interest in political philosophy, except perhaps to eye it with sceptical disapproval if it should appear interested in questioning fundamental assumptions. Society, too, is more preoccupied with resolving the practical "puzzles" of politics in accordance with the prescriptions of its paradigm. It also finds "retooling an extravagance."

Society's indifference towards theory is matched by the indifference of theorists. Throughout the history of Western political theory we find that most of the major theories have been produced during times of crisis, rarely during periods of normalcy. This phenomenon suggests that the major theories resemble "extraordinary science": they are produced when the operative political paradigm is encountering, not puzzles, but profound anomalies. Further, the major theories exhibit the same feature of extraordinary science: they seek to discredit the existing operative paradigm. One need only recall Plato's criticism of democracy, Machiavelli's strictures on princes in the *Discorsi*, Locke's indictment of royal absolutism, and Marx's critique of capitalist society. Obviously no one will pay much attention to these attacks if they do not feel bothered by the operation of the existing paradigm. People much prefer to concentrate upon enjoying the benefits or exploring the possibilities of the prevailing system. This indifference is not the expression of a choice between having a theory or living without one. A society which is operating fairly normally has its theory in the form of the dominant paradigm, but that theory is taken for granted because it represents the consensus of the society.

Thus one can think in terms of two kinds of paradigms. There is the extraordinary type represented in the major political theories and there is the normal one embodied in the actual arrangements of a political society. Earlier an analogy had been drawn between the enforcement of a political paradigm and the enforcement of a scientific one. By extending this analogy a bit further it may be possible to locate behavioural studies and to say something about their theoretical status. As we have noted, normal science works on the paradigm provided and enforced by the scientific community; in this sense, normal science is the extension of the community's paradigm into the form of research. Turning now to behavioural studies, one of the most striking characteristics among the numerous studies on voting, community power, political participation, and decision-making is their acceptance of the prevailing political paradigm as the frame of reference and as the source of research problems. Most, if not all, of these problems are only problems because the operative paradigm suggests that they are. Among the questions being investigated are: What determines the attitudes and preferences of voters? What accounts for the apathy of voters? What is the functional value of non-participation? To what extent do political élites dominate decision-making and to what degree are they responsive to the citizenry? What effect does membership in many and often conflicting groups have upon the stability of a political system?

Since it is difficult to imagine these questions as problems under any except a liberal or democratic regime, they suggest that political behaviourism, like normal science, proceeds by an understanding of the world as defined by the dominant paradigm. To be sure, the dominant paradigm does not dictate the specific methods of inquiry, but it does influence the criteria of significance and does set limits around what is to be considered useful inquiry. Thus the contrast between behavioural theory and traditional theory comes to resemble the difference between normal and extraordinary science. Traditional theory, like extraordinary science, is preoccupied with possible rather than actual worlds and, as a consequence, it jeopardises rather than repairs the regnant paradigm.

In the case of behavioural theory and traditional theory a contrast need not imply a divorce. One of the most interesting and disturbing features of behavioural findings is their subversiveness. Many of the common notions about the quality of the democratic electorate have been shaken. The same might be said about prevailing beliefs about the democratic character of politics, decision-making in American communities, and the representativeness of elected officials. Some evidence seems to suggest that a democratic system will enjoy greater stability if certain segments of the electorate did not vote; other evidence hints that the poorer elements of the population possess attitudes which might be dangerous to the political order.[49] On the basis of these findings one might speculate that normal science may be in the process of exposing anomalies rather than puzzles. If this is the case, and if the anomalies were to become more persistent and widespread, the paradigm might be in trouble; and if this should happen, then we might expect that extraordinary science would reappear.

NOTES

1. D. Easton, *A Framework for Political Analysis* (Englewood Cliffs, New Jersey: Prentice-Hall, 1965), p.8.
2. P. Winch, *The Idea of a Social Science* (London: Routledge and Kegan Paul, 1956), *passim*.
3. B. Barber, *Science and the Social Order* (New York: Collier Books, 1962), p. 311.
4. H. D. Lasswell and A. Kaplan, *Power and Society: a Framework for Political Inquiry* (New Haven: Yale University Press, 1950), p. x.
5. I use interchangeably the words "political," "social," and "behavioural" science. Inasmuch as most political scientists aspire to be "social" or "behavioural" scientists, my usage is not arbitrary. My comments are directed primarily at American political science.
6. R. Dahl, *Modern Political Analysis* (Englewood Cliffs, New Jersey: Prentice-Hall, 1963), p. 8.
7. H. Simon, ' "The decision-making schema": a reply', *Public Administration Review*, vol. 18 (1958), p. 63.
8. H. Eulau, *The Behavioral Persuasion in Politics* (New York, Random House: 1963), p. 9.
9. *The Great Instauration* (from "The plan of the work"; *Novum Organum*, Bk. I, cxiii. Quotations are from the edition by H. G. Dick, *Francis Bacon: selected Writings* (New York: Random House, 1955), pp. 447, 525.
10. See Dahl, *op. cit.* p. 102.
11. This distinction is defended by Dahl, *op. cit.* pp. 101 ff. and W. C. Runciman, *Social Science and Political Theory* (Cambridge, 1963), p. 2. Some of the implications of this distinction had been anticipated by Bacon's contrast between "one method for the cultivation, another for the invention of knowledge." The former referred to the "received philosophy" and was useful "for supplying matters for disputations or ornaments for discourse, – for the professor's lecture and for the business of life." The latter was for exploring the "untried and unknown." *Novum Organum*, Preface. *Selected Writings*, pp. 458-9.
12. C. C. Gillespie, *The Edge of Objectivity* (Princeton, 1960), p. 8.
13. Throughout this essay "traditional political theory" is intended to refer to the major writers in the Western tradition of political theory. Marx, whose writings are full of a fine ambivalence towards the older modes of theorizing, constitutes a convenient dividing line.
14. The fruitfulness of error has been emphasised by K. Popper, *Conjectures and Refutations* (London: Routledge and Kegan Paul, 1963), especially essays 1, 3, 4, and 10. See also J. Agassi, "Towards an historiography of science," *History and Theory*, Beiheft 2 (1963), pp. 4-54.
15. Justifications based upon diversity and agelessness have been advanced by J. Plamenatz, *Man and Society*, 2 vols. (New York: McGraw-Hill, 1963), vol. 1, p. xxi.

16. G. H. Sabine, *A History of Political Theory*, 3rd ed. (New York: Holt, Rinehart and Winston, 1961), pp. v-vi.

17. *Il Principe*, ch. 15. In this context there is great relevancy to Marx's constant effort to indicate his debts to his predecessors as well as to demonstrate the precise nature of his advance beyond them.

18. T. Kuhn, *The Structure of Scientific Revolutions* (Chicago: University of Chicago Press, 1964; first edition 1962), p. 2. This viewpoint is implicit in the earlier work of E. A. Burtt, *The Metaphysical Foundations of Modern Science* (1924); see his discussion of the Copernican revolution (New York: Doubleday Anchor, 1954), pp. 38 ff.

19. Kuhn, *op. cit.* p. 3.

20. Compare the above with the account of a social scientist: "... science rejects the imposition of any truth by organized and especially by non-scientific authority. The canons of validity for scientific knowledge are also individualistic: they are vested not in any formal organization but in the individual consciences and judgments of scientists who are, for this function, only informally organized." Barber, *op. cit.* p. 99.

21. An instructive case-study of the rigidity of the scientific community is "The politics of science and Dr. Velikovsky," *American Behavioral Scientist*, vol. VII, no. 1 (September, 1963).

22. Kuhn's phrase, a "more rigid definition of the field," is employed in the context of a discussion of the crisis-phase when a paradigm tends to loosen and dissolve.

23. This appears to be the assumption underlying the following statement about "interdisciplinary" progress in social science theory: "What some have felt to be fruitless and wasteful inquiries into the theoretical boundaries of our discipline have simply represented a groping toward at least the gross units in terms of which political life can be identified, observed, and analyzed ... Slay the dragon of disciplinary redefinition as we may, it insists upon rearing its head in a new form each time and to higher levels of conceptual sophistication." Easton, *op. cit.* p. 22.

24. Kuhn writes: "Competition between segments of the scientific community is the only historical process that ever actually results in the rejection of one previously accepted theory or in the adoption of another" (p. 8).

25. Compare the following: "... Knowledge is to be a [conceptual] reproduction of the external world ..." V. Gordon Childe, *Society and Knowledge* (New York: Harper, 1956), p. 54.

26. Kuhn does not consider the question of whether these decisions may have been influenced by governmental authorities or industrialists.

27. *Discorsi*, I, Pref.

28. In the same vein Bodin wrote: "We aim higher in our attempt to attain, or at least approximate, to the true image of a rightly ordered government. Not that we intend to describe a purely ideal and unrealisable commonwealth, such as that imagined by Plato or Thomas More ... We intend to confine ourselves as far as possible to those political forms that are practicable." *Six Books of the Commonwealth*, Bk. I, ch. 1, tr. M. J. Tooley (Oxford: Blackwell), p. 2.

29. *Leviathan,* ch. 20, ed. Oakeshott (Oxford: Blackwell), p. 136.

30. *Ibid.* ch. 3 (p. 242).

31. This was most strikingly illustrated in *De Cive* (Preface to the Reader). Hobbes carefully arranged his targets, beginning with Socrates ("The first who truly loved this civil science") and proceeding through the later classical authors ("After him comes Plato, Aristotle, Cicero, and other philosophers, as well Greek, as Latin").

32. *History,* 1, 21-2.

33. *Histories,* XII, 28. 2-3.

34. Bacon had acknowledged being "much beholden to Machiavel." *Works,* ed. Spedding, Ellis and Heath, vol. 3, p. 430. Pareto remarked that "many maxims of Machiavelli . . . hold as true today as they were in his time." *The Mind and Society,* 3 vols. (New York: Dover, 1963), vol. 4, pp. 1736-7. Finally: "The present work is much closer to the straight-forward empirical standpoint of Machiavelli's *Discourses* or Michel's *Political Parties.*" Lasswell and Kaplan, *op. cit.* p. x.

35. On the working out of the Lockean paradigm in America see L. Hartz, *The Liberal Tradition in America* (New York: Harcourt, Brace, 1955).

36. C. H. McIlwain, *Constitutionalism and the Changing World* (Cambridge, 1939), ch. IX (on Hunton); A. H. Maclean, "George Lawson and John Locke," *Cambridge Historical Journal,* IX (1947), 69-77.

37. Without reference to the theme of this essay, Professor Ullmann has written that "the Aristotelian orientation of the later Middle Ages can perhaps be compared with the reorientation effected through a Galileo or a Newton." *Principles of Government and Politics in the Middle Ages* (London: Methuen, 1962), p. 244.

38. Dictio I, cap. 1, 7.

39. *Political Thought in Medieval Times* (New York: Harper, 1962), p. 88.

40. Ullman, *op. cit.* p. 243.

41. See W. Jaeger, *Aristotle,* 2nd ed. (Oxford: Oxford University Press, 1962), pp. 54, 286, 314 ff. Also the essay by W. Anderson on the differences between the Academy and the Lyceum in *Teaching Political Science,* ed. R. H. Connery (Durham: Duke University Press, 1965).

42. See Epistle VII. The story of Plato's encounter with Dionysius was transmitted to later centuries by Plutarch. More's *Utopia* and Elyot's *Governor* made explicit reference to it.

43. *Leviathan,* ch. 31 (p. 241).

44. *Ibid.* (p. 467).

45. *English Works,* I, 91.

46. Easton, *op. cit.* pp. 4-13. It should be added that Easton suggests that the story may be apocryphal. Inasmuch as he introduces it in order to illustrate the same theme of power being brought to support a particular form of inquiry, the literal truth of the story is not critical.

47. See, for example, R. A. Dahl, "The behavioral approach," *American Political Science Review,* vol. 55 (1961), pp. 763-72. A more ambitious claim is made by H. Eulau, *op. cit.* p. 7: ". . . the behavioral persuasion represents an attempt, by modern modes of analysis, to fulfill the quest

for political knowledge begun by the classical political theorists."

48. Ironically, Arthur Bentley, who is widely regarded among scientifically oriented political scientists as one of their great forerunners, was a truly marginal figure, even to the point of eccentricity.

49. S. M. Lipset, *Political Man* (New York: Doubleday Anchor 1963), pp. 87 ff.

III. HUMANITIES

T. S. KUHN'S THEORY OF SCIENCE
AND ITS IMPLICATIONS FOR HISTORY

DAVID A. HOLLINGER

Not since the publication of R. G. Collingwood's *Idea of History* has a work of "theory" won from historians the amount of interest recently accorded Thomas S. Kuhn's *The Structure of Scientific Revolutions*.[1] If historians are conventionally aloof from philosophy of history, they are even less attentive to philosophy of science—yet contemporary footnotes prove that Kuhn's theory of *science* speaks to, and for, historians as few works of philosophy of *history* ever have. Even the revered Collingwood, for all his influence upon intellectual historians during the 1940s and 1950s, served to stop discussions as often as to advance them; a citation to Collingwood's profound but forbidding "Epilegomena"[2] enabled historians to perform an act of calm defiance: "we historians are on to something basic and complicated about human experience, which you can read about in Collingwood, and if you can't understand what he says, well, that's your problem." This defiant use of Collingwood may have been appropriate in some cases, and Collingwood will presumably continue to serve historians in this way without coming down off the shelf he now shares with a more mobile junior partner. Kuhn, unlike Collingwood, is being read carefully by many practicing historians.

Not since the time of Charles Beard has any guild historian attracted an audience among the academic intelligentsia as extensive as Kuhn's. Collingwood, too, was a historian, but he always remained the peculiar possession of historians and of a handful of philosophers; *The Structure of Scientific Revolutions* has become a major text for interdisciplinary discourse and has been acclaimed by the *cognoscenti* that reads Lévi-Strauss, Piaget, Erikson, Laing, Lucács, and Chomsky.[3] Kuhn's audience beyond history and philosophy comes to

Of the several persons who made useful suggestions on the basis of an early draft of this article, I wish to acknowledge the help of Max Black, Robert W. Gordon, Joan Heifetz Hollinger, Georg Iggers, Louis O. Mink, Charles Pailthorp, Ronald G. Walters, and especially Thomas S. Kuhn, commentator at a session of the annual meeting of the American Historical Association before which the paper was read, New York, Dec. 28, 1971.

him for what he says, or implies, about the relation of permanence to change, knowledge to culture, and history to value. This interest in Kuhn constitutes, among other things, a quickening of interest in insights that have long been vouchsafed to historians, for Kuhn's vision of these relationships owes much to the professional subculture of history. Hence Kuhn's relation to historians is simultaneously that of outsider and insider; he is a philosopher of science from whom historians can learn and a historian who may help clarify the historian's outlook for the benefit of an era that has long since turned to sociologists, scientists, psychologists, and literary critics for definitions of whatever issues engage the intelligentsia as a whole.

The meaning Kuhn's work has for history can best be clarified by answering three questions. First, To what extent can Kuhn's description of the behavior of scientific communities function heuristically, as a methodological postulate, in the study of communities organized for purposes other than that of doing science? More specifically, How, if at all, can Kuhn's sense of historical development enrich political, cultural, and intellectual history and other fields outside the history of science? Second, What are the normative implications of Kuhn's philosophy of science—his sense of validity—for the attempt to improve the quality of the "knowledge" historians produce? Third, What stake, if any, do historians in general have in the controversy between Kuhn and many philosophers over the nature of science?

The Structure of Scientific Revolutions excites the imagination of working historians chiefly because much of what it says about scientific communities seems to apply so strikingly to other kinds of communities. David H. Fischer asserts that Kuhn is "relevant to all fields" of history, and any number of manifestoes have announced the applicability of Kuhn to general intellectual history and its subdisciplines.[4] In practice, Kuhn's terms have been employed explicitly by historians of art, religion, political organization, social thought, and American foreign policy, in addition to their more predictable use by historians of the social sciences and the natural sciences.[5] It is Kuhn's sense of historical development that attracts all this attention; specifically, historians are moved by Kuhn's sense of what a tradition is, what conditions sustain it, and what the relation is between tradition and innovation. Kuhn acknowledges that his view of historical development owes much to the conventional historiography of politics and the arts,[6] but *The Structure of Scientific Revolutions* has made such a distinctive contribution that two of our most methodologically sophisticated historians of political thought—J. G. A.

Pocock and Sheldon Wolin—have gone all the way to the history of science to find, in Kuhn, the theory of change satisfactory to them.[7] Most uses of Kuhn by historians overlook or minimize the prior kinship with Kuhn that in fact makes rapport so possible; Kuhn's terms are often imported, in toto, from their context in the history of science, so that Kuhn enters the discourse of historians as entirely an outsider, as yet another emissary from sociology whose newfangled ideas the historian feels obliged to summarize before "applying them to history." The result is that many "applications" of Kuhn take the somewhat incongruous form of analogies between science and non-science; a Kuhnian "scientific revolution" is explicitly compared to the American decision to withdraw from Vietnam under the pressure of antiwar demonstrations at the Pentagon and at Chicago.[8]

The problem is that Kuhn's striking achievement in the history of science has made what we might call the species-specific aspects of his sense of historical development so available and compelling that we have difficulty getting through the species back to the genus of which Kuhn's theory is a part. Yet it is the generic in Kuhn that historians have been trying to employ, and this accounts for the fumbling apologies that so often accompany attempts to show that the history of society is, for all practical purposes, "just like" the history of tightly organized, technically equipped scientific communities. Insofar as *The Structure of Scientific Revolutions* can enrich historiography beyond the sciences, insofar as the book's sense of historical development can function heuristically as a methodological postulate, it will do so less awkwardly if historians achieve a more comfortabe relation with Kuhn, if they themselves seize more effective control over what they have found in Kuhn.[9] This requires a clear, general understanding of the sense of historical development that is embedded in *The Structure of Scientific Revolutions*.

Kuhn's notion of the "paradigm," his most celebrated and maligned term,[10] embodies the sense that activities are defined and controlled by tradition, and that tradition consists of a set of devices, or principles, that have proven their ability to order the experience of a given social constituency. An operative tradition provides a community with criteria to distinguish one activity from another, sets priorities among those activities, and enables the community to perform whatever common activities make it a community at all. Insofar as the community's common experience is contingent, that experience presents itself as a series of "problems" to be solved by the tradition, which validates itself by transforming the contingency of experience into something comprehensible and subject to maximum control.

197

Tradition, then, is socially grounded, and its function is that of organization. Organization may be achieved through a number of modes and devices, ranging from formal institutions to informal habits and from codes of abstract principles to concrete examples of how problems of a given class have been solved in the past. Whether it is conduct or perceptions that require organization, whether the task is prescriptive or cognitive, the organizing devices have enough flexibility to sustain them through successive, contingent experiences: to the extent that a tradition can expand and adapt, like the English common law, it is that much more likely to retain its constituency.

But traditions do lose their constituencies sometimes, and it was of course the transition from one research tradition to another in scientific communities that Kuhn was especially concerned to explain. Kuhn's notions of "normal science," "anomaly," "crisis," and "paradigm-shift" (or "revolution") manifest an integrated set of senses concerning the relation of tradition to change. Change is possible within the terms of an operative tradition, as we have seen, insofar as the elements of the tradition are, like principles or precedents in the common law, able to expand their implications enough to deal with new experiences while not losing their identity. Such innovation within a tradition is energized by an essentially conservative instinct, to maintain the viability of tried-and-true ways of acting and thinking. However tenacious a tradition, its constituency may still find itself surrounded with problems that defy solution. Traditional organizing devices, even when stretched, may fail to control and comprehend the experiences that apparently fall within their province. This failure can occur in a variety of ways. The community may be suddenly subject to conditions radically different from those in effect when the reigning traditions were institutionalized; another culture may have set up housekeeping next door, thereby creating a constant source of novel stimuli too immediate and concrete to be ignored even by those who would prefer not to acknowledge the novelty's existence. Or the community's activities in one area may be affected by upheavals in another: perhaps a political upheaval, replacing one governing elite with another, or replacing oligarchy with democracy, will produce new criteria for what counts as the satisfactory understanding and control of otherwise unchanged religious or economic life. The discovery of problems unsolved by the tradition may even result from a dynamism within the tradition itself: endemic tenacity may extend and refine organizing devices to such a degree of precision that they can recognize as "unorganizable" something that cruder, less demanding devices might treat as routine.[11] Whatever the path to crisis, a community thus disorganized must come up with a way to put things in order, and here the pioneering instinct comes into play. Attempts to refurbish the old tradition are replaced by the conscious search for new and more functional devices of organization; tenacity and singleness of purpose are replaced by the intentional proliferation of alternatives. A community's entire store of cultural resources may be ransacked before a consensus begins to emerge that certain proposed devices are superior to others. The more complete the consensus, the greater the stability the community enjoys, and the more likely it is that the new organizing devices will become traditional. Certain communities may go through a full cycle of (1) secure tradition, (2) novelty and confusion, (3) disagreement over whether to resist innovation or encourage it, and if the latter, in what direction, (4) coalescence around a candidate that might become (5) another secure tradition. Other communities may never achieve the unanimity necessary for this "cycle" to come about; rather their traditions may be less secure, their confusion and conflict more permanent, and their "revolution" less pronounced, if ever worthy of the name.

Once this sense of historical development is abstracted from *The Structure of Scientific Revolutions* it sounds like a set of truisms. This fact only serves to illustrate a point Kuhn has insisted upon: concrete examples, like Kuhn's achievement in the history of science, have a staying power distinct from that of the general principles they embody. Had Kuhn written the foregoing two paragraphs instead of having written *The Structure of Scientific Revolutions*, it is doubtful that he would have inspired so many attempts to "apply Kuhn's ideas to history." Yet the foregoing may enable historians to recognize and control just what it is that Kuhn seems to say for them. Once defined generically, the sense of development found in Kuhn can be more easily distinguished from other ideas about historical development and evaluated comparatively. And one man's "truism" can be another's enlightenment: theorists of social change, for example, now treat Kuhn as a significant and original contributor to that field.[12]

Among genera of theories of historical development, the one to which *The Structure of Scientific Revolutions* belongs acquires some of its distinctness from its indifference to the overall pattern and ultimate character of history. Connected to no total cosmic scheme, the theory stands somewhat apart from "speculative philosophy of history." There is no determinate life cycle, no implication that cer-

199

tain changes are "natural" for a cultural unit at certain times, no insistence that traditions will or will not attain a certain degree of stability, no reason, in principle, why a given tradition might not live forever. The theory neither holds that change is always gradual, cataclysmic, or dialectical nor insists that change is generated by elements exclusively within or outside of "social systems." The theory offers a thoroughly nonteleological view of change: no idea of progress is implied, nor one of decline; there is no sense that Athenian political organization was superior in the second century B.C. to what it had been in the fifth, no sense that New England's religious ideas were better, or worse, in 1730 than in 1630. No golden age stands behind or beyond, no *élan vital* energizes history, and no deities preside over it. Hence the generic sense of development that informs Kuhn's work is aloof from many of the concerns that drive the classical theorists surveyed recently by Bruce Mazlish and Robert A. Nisbet.[13]

Kuhn's general vision of change carries with it a minimum of anthropological and social theory. It does not specify as "natural" any particular relationships among the various psychosocial and economic drives that are served by organizing devices; it does not connect art and religion with economic needs, for example, nor does it suggest that all human activities have their being within a grand struggle between Eros and Thanatos. It depicts stability, equilibrium, and integration as goals, but these echoes of functionalist sociology are muted somewhat by the absence of anything like that school's emphasis on stasis: "the purposive end" of social systems, for the functionalists, is "the mere persistence and perpetuation of the system itself."[14] The Kuhnian vision emphasizes instead the terms on which a tradition justifies itself or loses its binding power: according to its ability to organize the community's contingent, historical experience. What is left open in the Kuhnian theory, considered generically, is the fundamental constitution of what is being stabilized and integrated. The aims of natural science help fill this gap for Kuhn in *The Structure of Scientific Revolutions*, but these are clearly "species-specific."

While the limited scope of Kuhn's general sense of development is the basis for much of its distinctness and utility, this cuts both ways. A historian concerned to explain a given temporal episode might find that Kuhn's vision frees the historian from grand developmental formulas and enables him to focus more directly on that episode, in its particularity; yet this same historian must look beyond Kuhn for a body of theory that will help him formulate and answer the questions left unasked by the Kuhnian framework. The latter simply would not predict, for example, that internal conflicts over the adequacy of competing religious faiths will be found to be functions of economic conditions. But neither would the Kuhnian vision prevent the discovery, through auxiliary means, that this was the case in a particular community at a particular time. Historians must be prepared to see things Kuhn does not lead them to look for, but Kuhn's sense of historical development may be able to neutralize the biases of a number of social and anthropological theories without excluding them from the matrix of inquiry. Kuhn's sense of development is different in scope and emphasis from Marxist, Freudian, and even functionalist theories, but its relation to them is not necessarily that of a rival: it can serve as a control, as a qualifier, whereby the traditional and fruitful eclecticism of the historian can continue to draw upon diverse insights about the nature of man and society without being victimized by attendant prescriptions concerning the nature of change. To the extent that historians employ generalizations in order to understand the particulars of history,[15] historians are best served by a sense of development like Kuhn's, which excludes the fewest of possible relationships from vision and retains the most.

The distinctness and potential utility of Kuhn's sense of development are functions not only of its limited scope but of its positive attributes. In the dynamics of change, for example, Kuhn's emphasis is on the role of tradition in helping to define a given contingent experience and in responding to it; traditions are not passive entities, helplessly battered about by circumstance, capable only of adapting to a concrete, externally defined given. Yet the ordinance that cultural forms have over experience is not to be understood as the triumph of spirit over matter, nor even of "ideas" over "events": the Kuhnian vision replaces this source of materialist-idealist disputation with a dialogue between traditions and contingent experience, in order that the historian can more freely investigate the functions of cultural forms as organizing devices. One can say of Kuhn what Gordon Wood has said about Bernard Bailyn in another context: he brings together idealism and behaviorism by showing that men are as much "victims" of their ideas as beneficiaries of them; traditions prevent men from seeing in their experience phenomena that an alternative tradition might lead them to confront.[16]

Furthermore, Kuhn anchors traditions firmly in social subgroup constituencies, and thereby he distinguishes his work from history that inquires less rigorously into exactly who is served by given institutions and ideas. Constituencies can be identified with relative ease in the developed sciences, but this species-specific aspect of Kuhn's work serves to encourage historians in general to ask more insistently, "Whose experience in connection with what activity is being organized by what cultural forms?" Hence Kuhn both promotes and socializes the "radical contextualism" of much of contemporary intellectual history, in keeping with which great pains are being taken to see that the choices attributed to historical figures like Hobbes and Locke were authentically available to them, not imposed on their milieu by history's subsequent elaboration of alternatives to positions they took.[17] More sociological than metaphysical or psychological in orientation, Kuhn's vision of historical development depends absolutely on "communities," whose internal and external relations in any particular case require careful definitions.

Essential to Kuhn's sense of what communities do are his emphases on conflict and problem solving. Subgroups in a community may propose devices for organizing whatever activities they must perform in concert with the community as a whole; when this happens the relation between the subgroups is one of competition. The proponents of each device attempt to persuade or overpower opposing groups, and in the process they may refine their devices to the point that they become more obviously functional: in this sense, competition can be productive. The alternative devices are candidates for the job of "problem solving," a notion so dominant in Kuhn's sense of development that all other activities are, in effect, translated into its terms. The plausibility of Kuhn in the present context depends largely on whether one believes this translation can be effected comfortably, behind the scenes, without turning "problem solving" into another heavy, mechanical formula, and without ignoring aspects of a community's life that we regard as essential to its history.[18] Certainly the assertive effort of scientists to expand knowledge through solving the "puzzles" of normal science is "species-specific" to *The Structure of Scientific Revolutions*, but this manifests the more generic sense that contingent experience functions in relation to a tradition as a series of "problems" that must be solved in order that the activities of the community, whatever they are, may be carried out in an organized, satisfactory fashion. The notion that all thought and action participate in "problem solving" is of course a familiar one, at least since the time of John Dewey.

Finally, a positive aspect of Kuhn's sense of development is its emphasis on elements of tradition that are prior to, or even apart from, principles, laws, and other conventionally "rational" organizing devices. Certain specific, concrete achievements within the remembered history of a community may function as models for thinking and acting without first being transformed into abstract principles. Kuhn thus reinforces compellingly the historian's practice of looking for prototypes of this sort, especially when trying to explain the behavior of a community that seems not to be following any principles at all. For example, English colonists in America enslaved Africans long before the principle of lifetime, heritable, racial slavery was acknowledged by English Americans. The behavior of the colonists was influenced by precedents from social situations they regarded as analogous.[19]

If *The Structure of Scientific Revolutions* can inspire attempts to depict in its terms the history of nation-states, no wonder this work has led historians to compare their own guild to Kuhn's scientific communities. While not "a science," the discipline of history is at least an academically organized branch of inquiry; it resembles Kuhn's scientific communities more obviously than do many of the cultural units that are said to partake of the same pattern of historical development. Increasingly, historians offer new interpretations, or suggestions for new research, as "paradigm-proposals," and historians have begun to regard basic changes in common outlook as "paradigm-shifts."[20] The introduction of this vocabulary has been especially easy since histories of the profession have long been grounded, quite firmly, in some of the generic insights that inform *The Structure of Scientific Revolutions*. Conceivably historiography could profit by yet more attention to the role of certain concrete achievements in establishing professional traditions and to the role of these traditions in controlling the response of historians to changes in their own intellectual and social environment; but the impression persists that we already have an abundance of exactly this sort of information about ourselves. The best of our professional histories was written by John Higham, Leonard Krieger, and Felix Gilbert soon after Kuhn's book appeared, but the authors of *History* seem not to have required Kuhn's help to direct their attention to questions of this sort.[21] Hence, while one could no doubt deliberate at length over the extent to which Kuhn's analysis of the historical development of scientific communities can, or should, be taken to apply to the professional community of historians, this question is finally not very interesting. A much more important and difficult question presents itself as soon as we acknowledge one crucial distinction between our relation to our own profession and our relation to conventional objects of historical study.

What matters most about the discipline of history is its ability to distinguish good history from bad history, accuracy from confusion, truth from fraud. However diverse and complicated the aims of doing history, we are at least dependent upon this activity for knowledge about certain things. While we care about the ways in which history is relative, we care even more about the ways in which it is true. Suddenly the fact that Kuhn wrote about science becomes important, as it decidedly is not when his work is read for its general sense of historical development. To what extent does Kuhn's philosophy of science—his sense of validity—provide the discipline of history with prescriptions for the improvement of its services? This question is grounded, then, in our engagement with the community rather than in our detachment from it; and its pursuit requires that we cease to read Kuhn as we have until this point, as a describer of the behavior of groups and the individuals within them. We need now to look within and beyond Kuhn's sense of historical development to find his sense of validity, or objectivity.

The relevance to history of Kuhn's sense of how the sciences achieve validity is more complicated than the tired question, Is history a science? Kuhn's admirers among historians include those least inclined to discard history's traditional autonomy for the more scientific standing presumably afforded by methodological integration with the social sciences;[22] historians differ from the sociologists and political scientists who take up Kuhn as yet another model of science against which their own activities can be measured. The difference follows from history's conviction that it antedates and transcends social science, that history partakes of art as well as science, that history is too much a "craft" to be subsumed under science. Historians have been less eager than social scientists to attribute to themselves the practice of "normal science" under controlling "paradigms," the mark of a truly "developed" science.[23] Yet historians, whether we regard them as craftsmen, protoscientists, or whatever, do operate with a sense that their discipline can be practiced with varying degrees of success. Hence historians can look to *The Structure of Scientific Revolutions* not to learn about the aims and methods of the sciences, but to understand how those aims and methods are fulfilled. The question is not the extent to which history and science share abstractly defined aims and methods, but whether Kuhn's account of how validity is achieved in the sciences can clarify and/or improve the status of validity in history. Historians continue to term good scholarship "objective," long after pretensions to "scientific history" have been forsaken. Can Kuhn's sense of validity help us, as historians, to clarify what we mean by "objective," and does Kuhn prescribe any means of achieving greater objectivity?

Certainly, without Kuhn's help, we could say that in the idiom of historians an "objective" account of some experience or event is valid on an intersubjective basis. This is to say that the truth of the account will be recognized by virtually all reasonable people, if they understand what is supposed to be the purpose of the account, if they follow the steps of its argument, and if they follow the pattern of its evidence. The account is about the event or experience, not about something else, and it is true, not false. Obviously there are questions begged in what counts as a "reasonable person" and what counts as "an experience or event," and these are among the issues about which philosophers argue. Positions on these issues divide one sense of validity from another.

One such division is between Kuhn and his critics among philosophers of science, some of whom insist that Kuhn has no sense of validity at all. Kuhn, it is charged, has so relativized even the developed sciences as to deny their claims to objectivity; Kuhn's philosophy of science allegedly turns the decisions of scientific communities into matters for "mob psychology."[24] This reaction is sparked by Kuhn's profoundly sociological orientation. His sense of validity is essentially the following: a truth-claim becomes valid when the most learned practitioners of a technically sophisticated field agree that the theory on which the claim is based explains the range of phenomena under common scrutiny more satisfactorily than does any other known theory. This view of what counts as true differs from any simple correspondence-theory, according to which truth is a function of correspondence with something "out there." It also differs from the "justificationist" philosophies of science, according to which science is distinguished by its use of certain standards of rationality that are not culture-bound. But for Kuhn the crucial questions are: Whose word do we take concerning what's "out there" (in other words, which theory explains the relevant phenomena the most satisfactorily?), and whose sense of "satisfactory" do we employ? In both cases Kuhn's answer is that we take the word of the professional community; but when he says this he is referring to tightly organized, self-contained groups of experts bound together by rigorously defined questions and highly technical methods. Only these professional communities in the "developed

205

sciences" are given this extraordinary position "above the law," above all models of justification. Kuhn can ground objectivity itself in professional communities of this sort because they alone have produced an impressive supply of ideas about nature that work. Ideas "work" when they predict the behavior of natural phenomena so well that we are enabled to manipulate nature or stay out of its way. Within the store of ideas of this type, some "work" better than others, and the successive discovery of better and better ideas is the transition from one valid idea to another, not a transition from invalidity to validity. The fact that a truth-claim may be brushed aside by a later, more technically equipped generation does not detract from that original truth-claim's status as "valid science for its own time."[25]

What needs to be underlined here is that Kuhn's sense of objectivity, while it depends on agreement, is not entirely circular, as would be the case if the community's decision were taken in a vacuum. Rather the community has to take some account of the particulars that are observed under specified conditions. By thus acknowledging that there is something "out there" we do not reactivate the crude realism of the correspondence-theory; rather we recognize the obvious fact that any organized enterprise, however elaborate its working apparatus, must come to grips with its material conditions; politicians in need of money can be expected to accumulate a certain amount of knowledge about the political values of the rich. Surely there are no insuperable philosophical difficulties in recognizing that physical phenomena have considerable influence over what physicists do, that millionaires affect much of the behavior of impecunious politicians, and that primary documents from the reign of Henry II exercise some control over what Angevin constitutional historians do. As for how we know that a given glob of reality is, in fact, "physical," "a millionaire," or "a document from the reign of Henry II," it ought to be sufficient to say that while these judgments are, technically speaking, interpretations, only the most hopeless solipsist would deny that some "globs of reality" admit more easily than others of the sets of definitions on which physics, capitalism, and constitutional history are founded.

Now, what about the relation of Kuhn's sense of validity to the discipline of history? Insofar as historians have produced a body of knowledge that "works" to the satisfaction of everyone who cares, it consists largely of the semiautonomous, name-and-date "facts" that take up the pages of standard biographies, and that are only incidental to the questions historians try the hardest to answer.

The most strikingly successful "answers" to questions historians care about are proverbially and persistently unable to inspire the degree of support given to reigning doctrines in the natural sciences —even the unusually tight "research consensus" created by C. Vann Woodward's *Origins of the New South* cannot serve as evidence that history is one of those disciplines that are "beyond the law." Historians, including those within fairly narrow subfields, are continually involved in debate over exactly what questions should be asked—precisely the sort of discussion the developed sciences are freed from by their tightly constructed "paradigm." Historians, moreover, actively go about asking radically different kinds of questions, and they grant professional status to work controlled by a number of different ideologies and commitments. Grudging or not, this tolerance of diversity distinguishes history from Kuhn's developed sciences, which tolerate it only when they do not know what they are doing, when a "normal science" consensus breaks down. Furthermore, the very notion of a "professional" community applies only ambiguously to history and to some of the social sciences, for the constituency of these disciplines is hard to define. In history, especially, the evaluation of a scholarly work frequently involves the participation of readers who, while not "professional historians," are sufficiently cognizant of what historians do to make the latter seek the approval of this larger, more intellectually diverse constituency.

Fortunately Kuhn's sense of validity has a corollary for knowledge-producing communities that fall short of the tightly organized, clearly successful research consensus of the developed sciences. These "protosciences," as Kuhn calls disciplines like history and most of the social sciences, both generate and test—however imperfectly —"testable propositions."[26] The professional community of historians regularly applies intersubjective standards to the scholarship of its members. The "profession," even if this term is stretched to cover the educated nonprofessionals whose approval is important to historians, does make judgments, does provide an atmosphere of organized criticism. This remains true despite the fact that the touchstone of "'good history" is notoriously difficult for anyone to define: the entire notion of intersubjective validity in history must live alongside the suspicion, if not the conviction, that the knowledge-producing aim of history is secondary to, or in any case qualified by, the moral and esthetic aims that presumably distinguish it from all sciences, physical and social. Indeed some historians would deny that the term "knowledge" is useful for denoting the type of "meanings" that historians discover in (or assign to) things. It would be a mistake to look to Kuhn for the clarification of these persistent complexities in the aims of history, but his view of validity is potentially relevant to history so long as we stipulate that the "testability" of a proposition is not a function of the use of any single, specific model of justification. However we define the aims of history, it remains true that no work of scholarship in that field will be counted as "successful" unless it persuades its professional readers of the following: (1) that the questions it asks are comprehensible, and worth asking; (2) that the sources it has examined are indeed the ones most relevant to the inquiry, and (3) that its analysis of the sources has been rational. By "rational" we mean that the author's presuppositions about human nature, the behavior of groups, causation, etc. are either shared by his readers or are perceived by his peers as respectable competitors to the views of the readers. The "knowledge" produced by historians is clearly distinguished from statements about the past that fail to persuade professional readers in these ways.

Hence we end up saying in a slightly different way something that has often been said about history: it is "imperfect knowledge." But when philosophers refer to history as "imperfect knowledge," they generally have the covering-law model of explanation in mind. In that view the knowledge produced by historians is imperfect because historians have not been able to explain particular events through the use of highly confirmed "laws," as the cracking of a radiator on a cold night can be explained by general laws concerning what happens to water at different temperatures and to metals under stress. On the Kuhnian analysis, however, the covering-law model of explanation is merely one of a number of possible values that may form part of a discipline's working assumptions, and the presence or absence of complete hypothetico-deductive explanation is not, in itself, enough to establish the validity or lack of validity of a truth-claim presented in its name. This is where we can see Kuhn's sociological orientation the most dramatically. Kuhn might be willing to grant that most of the developed sciences do, as a behavioral fact, strive for hypothetico-deductive explanations, but "imperfect knowledge" in the Kuhnian sense is imperfect on the grounds of the extent of agreement about its truth and among whom it is agreed. The "explanation" that a community, or part of a community, accepts may derive its coherence from properties that cannot be translated, without remainder, into "laws" of any kind: the cogency with which vast amounts of material are made to fit together by a particular, concrete achievement like Perry Miller's *The New England Mind*, or, again, Woodward's *New South*, may persuade professional readers of a work's rationality.

Whatever the structure of rationality in the developed sciences, or in the "imperfect knowledge" of disciplines like history, the structure's sociological base has aroused in several philosophers the fear that Kuhn's effect is to encourage a protoscience to impose, arbitrarily, a tight research consensus upon its practitioners in order that the discipline might more nearly approximate the mature sciences. Kuhn, it is said, encourages intellectual retrenchment, pedantic specialization, the avoidance of logical rigor, and, if not mob rule, at least the unjustified refusal to join issue with arguments presented by professional minorities.[27] On this view Kuhn's implications for history would be as follows. In order to make their work more completely objective, historians may determine what kinds of questions can be answered without controversy and then confine research to these questions. The sure-fire means of getting reliable knowledge is the elaborating of truisms and the collecting of information that, however dubious its significance, is at least true. Or, if more ambitious questions are to be allowed, objectivity can be won by expelling from the profession anyone unwilling to accept a given ideology. This would assure that research done by the remaining members of the group would not be subject to debilitating methodological criticism.

This reading of Kuhn's implications for history, and for any knowledge-producing discipline, is mistaken, I believe, and on grounds that demand clarification. Kuhn in fact presupposes a balance within professional communities between the drive to "perfect" their knowledge—even through retrenchment and the imitation of the developed sciences—and the drive to answer the very questions whose difficulty has prevented the prior achievement of a tight research consensus. Had Kuhn acknowledged this presupposition more openly, some of the confusion concerning his normative implications might have been avoided. Even when challenged to explain why his views do not encourage the hasty and arbitrary legislation of fundamentals and the repression of minorities Kuhn's response has been cryptic. The protosciences should be patient, Kuhn says, for maturity comes only to those who "wait and struggle" for it. But waiting and struggling presumably proceed on certain terms. What are they? And how shall "waiting and struggling" apply to crafts like history, which share only ambiguously in social science's quest for the "maturity" of the developed sciences?[28] Had

Kuhn chosen to address these questions more directly, and had he outlined the normative implications of his philosophy of science for history, I believe he would have been bound to claim something like the following.

The professional community of history, or of any knowledge-producing enterprise, has available to it at all times the value-systems of other disciplines, including the developed sciences. Insofar as there is a loose consensus in the learned world as a whole about what it is to be "rational," history and similar communities are answerable to that consensus. As long as history claims to be a participant in learned discourse, history must maintain a substantial measure of rapport with what counts as "good sense" in this larger constituency. Within the learned world's vast store of vaguely compatible value-systems, historians will find a number of specific value-systems—including, for example, that embodied in the hypothetico-deductive model for explanation. Historians may take up these specific value-systems and see if they function well in the discipline of history, given the common aims that make it a community at all. Yet the "common aims of the community" are to some extent at issue when history, or any "protoscience," is trying to resolve a basic internal conflict or to choose among the various, specific value-systems available to the community. And Kuhn does not prescribe any *specific* standard for the resolution of such problems. Professional communities in the protosciences are not a "law unto themselves," to be sure, but they would seem to be under no more specific ordinance than the obligation to be reasonable. Kuhn's refusal to go farther than this, his refusal to endorse specific value-prescriptions for the protosciences greatly alarms his critics, but it makes sense once we recognize its connection to the trust Kuhn has in the motives men bring to inquiry in general.

Kuhn's *Structure of Scientific Revolutions* as well as his recent efforts to clarify the argument of that book reveal a willingness to grant legitimacy to the basic questions around which inquiry does, as a behavioral fact, develop. Kuhn seems to assume that physical inquiry, historical inquiry, philosophical inquiry, zoological inquiry, political inquiry, or whatever, whether or not they have become developed sciences, or whether they ever will, do possess a kind of primal validity: the drives that bring these inquiries into being provide their practitioners with something to stand on in terms of the aims of the professional communities that may form around these inquiries. Kuhn, therefore, does not prescribe basic aims for the branches of inquiry; these aims are there and can be trusted. Indeed Kuhn so took for granted the legitimacy of the aims of the developed sciences that at least one critic was moved to complain that Kuhn did not discuss "the aim of science." Kuhn's response to this has been that the developed sciences seek "to explain in detail a range of natural phenomena,"[29] an answer too vague, I am sure, to satisfy his critics. Kuhn is simply more willing than are many philosophers of science to entrust responsibility to people who are not philosophers of science. If this makes him an "irrationalist," I do not see how the charge can be refuted. The persons drawn to a given inquiry and acculturated into the organized community that has taken form around that inquiry are, Kuhn seems to imply, in a position to take the lead in evaluating the various approaches to their field that the surrounding learned world presents to the community. Kuhn assumes that these practitioners themselves are sufficiently loyal to their callings to look for answers that will neither abandon their basic questions nor repudiate what counts as "rationality" in the larger culture for whose benefit the inquiry is being conducted. Obviously, disciplines without a "normal science" consensus must live at all times in a state that approximates "crisis" in a developed science, and Kuhn assumes that the basic aims of such disciplines are compelling enough to enable their practitioners to endure the uncertainty and conflict that attend upon theory proliferation and energetic methodological criticism.

The scope of Kuhn's normative implications for history and other protosciences is thus extremely limited, encompassing chiefly the questions of who should decide what, to the relative satisfaction of whom? Some of the confusion about Kuhn's normative implications might have been eliminated, again, had Kuhn more boldly distinguished between prescriptions of this sort, which are intrinsic to his theory of science, and prescriptions that are in principle consistent with that theory although Kuhn himself does not make them. The latter could include prescriptions of almost any specific content, so long as they are generated, discussed, and adopted or rejected within the appropriate framework of relations among practitioners, their colleagues, and their larger constituencies in the learned world. The fact that Kuhn has chosen not to integrate specific value-prescriptions for sociology or theology into *The Structure of Scientific Revolutions* must not be taken to obscure his conditional approval of interdisciplinary dialogue concerning the ways in which the basic aims of various disciplines ought to be interpreted and pursued.[30] Kuhn does, of course, separate himself from the schoolmarmish practice of the positivists, according to which the branches of knowledge are treated as pupils, some to receive gold stars for the mastery of certain methods, some to wear the dunce cap for speaking nonsense.

Perhaps Kuhn's position can be brought out more distinctly if we compare it to each of the polar attitudes that have defined the analytical philosophy of history during the past twenty-five years. As Rudolph Weingartner has pointed out, philosophers have been divided between those who wish to provide an account of what historians ought to be doing and those who wish to provide an account of what they actually do.[31] The most conspicuous of the former are the followers of Carl Hempel, the covering-law theorists whose philosophy of history provides historians with a specific model for explanation that, if it could be brought into more complete operation in history, would perfect the knowledge historians produce. Opposed to the "Hempelians" are a number of philosophers who take the methods of historians as self-justifying and who seek to provide an adequate philosophical account of what historians do. Historians almost always prefer the latter style of philosophy, for it can be taken to legitimize aloofness on the part of historians from methodological discussions in the social sciences and humanities generally. Historians interested in justifying this aloofness will not get much help from Kuhn, however, for he implies that history, insofar as it expects to survive as a recognized branch of inquiry, cannot afford to ignore frequently made methodological complaints about its procedures. Yet Kuhn does imply that historians have, in their own sense of their common aims, a legitimate place to stand when entering theoretical discourse with nonhistorians. For example, Kuhn would surely defend the reluctance of historians to put aside narratives, even though this reluctance creates ambiguities in "historical explanation" that diminish the standing of history in the eyes of some philosophers and scientists, who would prefer that explanation by covering laws proceed in a more forthright fashion.

If Kuhn would not regard the discipline of history as free from the need to justify itself, neither would he free subgroups of historians with special "perspectives" from the need to justify their point of view to other historians. We often speak of a historian's perspective as much more than a limitation on his objectivity; we see it rather as a positive opportunity to observe things that are obscure from other perspectives.[32] *The Structure of Scientific Revolutions* certainly supports this understanding of the function of a "point of view," but Kuhn's sociological sense of what makes an idea true exercises an important control on "perspectivism," and prevents it from turning into the more complete relativism of "every man his own historian." To the extent that what historians do has a claim to knowledge, this claim is based on the existence of a community, however amorphous, that evaluates the various "perspectives" of its members, as well as the relation between a given perspective and what is allegedly "discovered" within it. The community distinguishes among points of view that are comprehensive, parochial, and incoherent.

Community sanction is thus essential to knowledge, even when "imperfect," but this does not necessarily imply the repression of points of view the profession as a whole regards as "parochial." On the contrary, these ostensibly "parochial" perspectives have the same relation to the professional community of historians that the latter has to the other branches of knowledge. Just as historians can refuse to do away with "narratives" and still be considered, by most of the learned world, as producers of knowledge, so can the advocates of a "parochial" vantage point like Marxism remain doggedly "parochial" and still be contributors to history. But the Marxists, to take them only as an example, remain second-class citizens in the community of history in the same sense that history is a second-class citizen in a learned world where the developed sciences set the standard for knowledge. If Marxists refuse to abandon their parochialism in order to become better acculturated as historians, their situation is again comparable to the historians, in their entirety, in relation to the larger learned community: the parochial Marxists and the redoubtable narrative historians each have a set of commitments too essential to their callings to be relinquished, and in each case, also, the recalcitrance of the minority is tolerated by the larger group. The learned world tolerates narratives because it suspects that what works in physical inquiry might not, after all, work for every kind of inquiry, and the historical profession tolerates the Marxists because it knows that its collective judgment is too "imperfect" to justify the expulsion of a parochial minority with as much empirical and theoretical foundation as the Marxists. In both cases, then, the minority is taken seriously because it can make a case for itself in terms that can be at least understood by the majority.

Does this suggest that the appropriate balance between the demands of minorities and majorities is achieved automatically? Does it mean that Marxist interpretations of history have gotten no more and no less than their share of attention from the profession as a whole, decade by decade, during the twentieth century? Would Kuhn prevent us from saying that professional communities make mistakes? Since the meaning of these queries depends on whether they are taken to presuppose a transcendent standard for judgment, we are led directly into Kuhn's attempt to release philosophy of science from the need for such a standard.

That the history of a thing can tell you something about its nature has always been a controversial assertion with reference to science, an activity that even the nineteenth century was unable to historicize completely. Historians of science have been expected to write the history of an activity whose nature was known, or was in any case the business of someone else to define; not until recently have they been called upon to clarify the nature of science. Kuhn has been the most insistent advocate of this new role for history since 1962, when he introduced *The Structure of Scientific Revolutions* with the claim that the historical study of science "could produce a decisive transformation" in views on the nature of science. These words gained some of their drama from their immediate context: Kuhn's volume was published as part of the *International Encyclopedia of Unified Science*, the *summa* of logical positivism, the movement that viewed the nature of science as the most strictly synonymous with its logic. Kuhn sought to historicize the most recalcitrant of subjects, science, and he threatened to drive the "Whig interpretation of history" out of its last well-defended enclave, the historiography of the sciences.[33] Kuhn would carry the insights of historiography into new territory.

Kuhn's assault on Whiggery in the history of science met with complaints very much like those raised by defenders of Whiggish history in other fields. We have often been told, for example, that the important thing about antebellum abolitionists is that they were right. Whatever the complex web of historical conditions that enabled the antislavery radicals to see the evil of slavery clearly and to act to try to end it, our rational and moral relation to these radicals can only be obscured by attempts to bring out those sustaining conditions in their full, historical, material complexity. Accounts of the psychosocial basis for the behavior of the abolitionists detract from its righteousness, the argument goes, just as a sociological orientation toward science obscures the two things about science that are truly important: its ideal logic of justification and its access to the objective natural order. The ideal structure of science and the morally right response of reformers are what we need to understand; we cannot be helped by studies that justify obfuscation and debunking in the name of "comprehensiveness and complexity." Certain ethical and logical ideals are so important to our survival, and so precariously held, that they need reinforcement, not the more complete "understanding" that risks the miring of these ideals in the swamps of human nature and history.

Oliver Wendell Holmes, Jr.'s attempt to historicize law produced a discussion similar to the one now surrounding Kuhn's work. Holmes's belief that the law was made by judges, that its life was "experience" instead of logic, that there was no "natural law" waiting to be discovered and declared, placed him in opposition to the brittle formalism of his generation's jurisprudence.[34] To be sure, the "legal realists" who claimed Holmes as their prophet went on to deny the influence of precedent and reason, of rules and logic, on the behavior of judges,[35] but the realists' relation to Holmes is analogous to the relation of Kuhn's followers in the "counterculture" to *The Structure of Scientific Revolutions*.[36] For from "irrationalism," Kuhn's view of science is remarkably like the conventional view of law, now that the Holmesian insights have been detached from the excesses of the realists: law (science) is part of culture, but culture brings great rational and moral resources to the improvement of law (science), and the lack of a transcendent standard does not endanger society's loyalty to law (science).

The controversy over Kuhn's work is even more strikingly reminiscent of the nineteenth-century *Angst* over the fate of the doctrine of design. In *The Structure of Scientific Revolutions* Kuhn predicted that the "main obstacle" to the historicization of science would be the same abstract convictions marshaled against Darwinian natural selection.[37] The subsequent decade has confirmed the prediction. Since certain organisms and their component parts were so supremely capable of doing their job, how could biologists explain their development without design? Since certain scientific theories work so well, how can any explanation of their development dispense with a theory-independent, objective, natural order? Today most of us believe that Darwin's opponents exaggerated evolution's threats to the integrity of civilization and to the identity of man; the defenders of design seem to have been motivated by a sense of permanence much too extreme and absolute. The present issue is whether Kuhn denies to science the stability of structure and environment required for its practice. Kuhn's critics charge, in effect, that Kuhn is naive about how great and abiding is our need for cosmic anchors, for ideals of perfection unsullied by social, psychological, and historical functionality.

Kuhn's theory of science dispenses with the idea of a fixed, permanent natural order that can function both as a standard for truth in the case of particular theories and as a goal for the progress of science. Kuhn also rejects the a priori methodological unity of science, according to which specific, formalized rules of verification are assumed to attend upon the basic aims of science. Scientific progress for Kuhn is not progress toward completeness via the accumulation of correct observations; it is, rather, "evolution *from* primitive beginnings," from what scientists agree upon to explanations that increase and refine their "understanding of nature."[38] This "progress" of science is made possible by a conjunction of (1) continuity in basic aims,[39] with (2) the mysterious fact that parts of the natural world turn out to be "knowable,"[40] which is to say that the object of knowledge presents problems that can be solved to the satisfaction of enough people to enable a tight research consensus to come into being. This consensus, in turn, promotes the microscopic specialization that allows scientists either to expand the range of phenomena explained by their theories or to discover anomalies. The eventual explanation of anomalies may require the community to choose among alternative revisions of theory, and choices made by individual members of the community are controlled by a complex of preferences enumerated in no existing "logic of explanation." What the community decides will in any case settle the matter, will determine which theory revision will count as a progressive step in science. Such is the theory of science that Sir Karl Popper believes to be giving comfort to the enemies of "our civilization."[41]

We must aim at truth, said the late Joseph R. Levenson, "even if the truth cannot be known."[42] The fate of Kuhn's theory of science depends partially on the extent to which this tension is in fact bearable. In the context of contemporary thinking about the cultural relations of science, Kuhn's work raises the following question: Is it a necessary condition of the successful pursuit of science that scientists and/or the societies to which scientists look for support, retain the conception of a "fixed permanent scientific truth"[43] as the goal of science? Kuhn himself has not confronted this question directly, but *The Structure of Scientific Revolutions* surely assumes that our ability to make judgments can survive the knowledge of how entangled those judgments are in our psychosocial matrix and that neither our reason nor our values are inappropriately threatened by a thoroughly historical perspective. To the extent that we see around us certain disciplines that abandon their callings for the academic equivalent of get-rich-quick schemes, Kuhn trusts that such hoaxes can be identified and criticized without a transcendent standard. In this view culture-bound standards are stable enough to define "mistakes," to sustain a critical attitude toward our intellectual environment, so long as we understand that the transition from transcendent objectivity to socially grounded objectivity need not be a substitution of terror and caprice for rationality. *The Structure of Scientific Revolutions* can be read as an invitation to forsake at last the fictional absolutes of natural theology.

Issues of such depth would not be raised by the historicization of science if this process were allowed to proceed within the terms of the now-classical distinction between the historical sociology of scientific knowledge and the philosophy of scientific justification.[44] In keeping with this distinction, conventional sociology of science does not attempt to integrate its sociological explanations of ideas about nature with an articulate interpretation of what makes such ideas valid or invalid.[45] Questions about the success with which science achieves its aims are supposedly beyond the scope of the discipline, as, indeed, they would be beyond the scope of any historical, psychological, or sociological study of science, if the above distinction were rigorously adhered to. Yet *The Structure of Scientific Revolutions* seeks explicitly to explain the success of science;[46] this work is clearly distinguished from historical approaches to science that ignore validity or translate it into entirely neutral terms. Kuhn's attempt to account for the validity as well as the relativity of science endows his work with a significance for historians that will be missed by those who look only at his sense of development, and then at his sense of validity, without seeing how the two are actually related in *The Structure of Scientific Revolutions* itself. For the "science" that Kuhn would historicize remains throughout his work the real thing, the explicitly successful explanation of natural phenomena. Kuhn's "science" is an activity that we value greatly, an enterprise upon which "our civilization," as Sir Karl would say, and properly, is crucially dependent. Its historicization therefore brings into bold relief as nothing else now can the question of history's relation to value. Does a historical understanding of the "problem-solutions" we rely upon inhibit significantly our ability to defend, criticize, alter, and defend again those very "problem-solutions," those answers to life's questions that we believe in? Responses to this query have always affected the extent to which the insights of historians are solicited, ignored, or resisted. The discipline of history has a stake of its own in the controversy over the full historicization of science.[47]

217

NOTES

1. R. G. Collingwood, *The Idea of History* (New York, 1946); Thomas S. Kuhn, *The Structure of Scientific Revolutions* (Chicago, 1962; 2d ed. 1970), 1.
2. Collingwood, *Idea of History*, 205-334.
3. See, as examples, the references to Kuhn in Arthur Koestler and J. R. Smythies, eds., *Beyond Reductionism* (Boston, 1970), especially 228, and in Jean Piaget, *Structuralism* (London, 1971), 132. Cf. Karl W. Deutsch *et al.*, "Conditions Favoring Major Advances in Social Science," *Science*, 171 (1971): 450-59.
4. David H. Fischer, *Historian's Fallacies: Toward a Logic of Historical Thought* (New York, 1970), 162; J.G.A. Pocock, *Politics, Language and Time* (New York, 1971), 15; George W. Stocking, Jr., *Race, Culture, and Evolution* (New York, 1968), 302; Harry W. Paul, "In Quest of Kerygma: Catholic Intellectual Life in Nineteenth-Century France," *AHR*, 75 (1969-70): 423; Arthur M. Schlesinger, jr., essay review of Robert A. Skotheim, *American Intellectual History and Historians*, in *History and Theory*, 7 (1968): 219-21; Hayden V. White, "The Tasks of Intellectual History," *Monist*, 53 (1969): 619.
5. E.g., James S. Ackerman, 'The Demise of the Avante Garde: Notes on the Sociology of Recent American Art," *Comparative Studies in Society and History*, 11 (1969): especially 372; Murray G. Murphey, "On the Relation Between Science and Religion," *American Quarterly*, 20 (1968): 275-95; Pocock, *Politics*, 13-41; Sheldon S. Wolin, "Paradigms and Political Theories," in Preston King and B. C. Parekh, eds., *Politics and Experience: Essays Presented to Professor Michael Oakeshott on the Occasion of His Retirement* (Cambridge, 1968), 125-52; Reba N. Soffer, "The Revolution in English Social Thought," *AHR*, 75 (1969-70): 1938-64; Bruce Kuklick, "History as a Way of Learning," *American Quarterly*, 22 (1970): 609-28. Two examples of Kuhn's use in the history of social science are of special interest to historiography generally: Stocking, *Race*, especially 7-8, 70, 111-12, 232, 237, 302-03; Nathan G. Hale, Jr., *Freud and the Americans: The Beginnings of Psychoanalysis in the United States, 1876-1917* (New York, 1971), especially 71-115. This article is not concerned with the applicability of Kuhn's work to the field for which it was designed, the historiography of the developed sciences, but historians outside that field should be aware of the skepticism expressed by some historians of science. See, for example, John C. Green, "The Kuhnian Paradigm and the Darwinian Revolution," in Duane H. D. Roller, ed., *Perspectives in the History of Science and Technology* (Norman, 1971), 3-25, but compare the persuasive defense of Kuhn by Leonard G. Wilson, "Commentary on the Paper of John C. Greene," *ibid.*, 31-37.
6. Kuhn, "Postscript" to 2d ed. of *Structure*, 208; Kuhn, "Comment" [on the relation between art and science], *Comparative Studies in Society and History*, 11 (1969): 409.

7. Pocock, *Politics*, 13-41; Sheldon S. Wolin, "Paradigms and Political Theories," 160-191, in this volume.

8. Kuklick, "History," 621.

9. Pocock, *Politics*, 13-41, is without question the most sophisticated and successful contribution to this effort yet to appear. Cf. the interesting essay by Randolph Starn, "Historians and 'Crisis,'" *Past and Present*, no. 52 (Aug. 1971): 3-22, especially 17-18.

10. One ostensibly friendly reader claimed to find twenty-one meanings for this word in *The Structure of Scientific Revolutions*: Margaret Masterman, "The Nature of a Paradigm," in Imre Lakatos and Alan Musgrave, eds., *Criticism and the Growth of Knowledge* (Cambridge, 1970), 59-89. Kuhn has subsequently distinguished between two senses of "paradigm": (1) the "disciplinary matrix" consists of "the entire constellation of beliefs, values, techniques, and so on shared by the members of a given community," including (2) "exemplars," the specific, "concrete puzzle-solutions which, employed as models or examples, can replace explicit rules as a basis for the solution of the remaining puzzles of normal science." See "Postscript," 175, 182, 187.

11. Kuhn's concentration on this one factor is species-specific to *The Structure of Scientific Revolutions* and follows from the relative insulation of scientific communities from contingent social conditions external to the traditions of the community.

12. E.g., Guy E. Swanson, *Social Change* (Glenview, Ill., 1971), 119-22, Isaac Kramnick, "Reflections on Revolution: Definitions and Explanation in Recent Scholarship," *History and Theory*, 11 (1972): 26-63; Robert A. Nisbet, *Social Change and History: Aspects of the Western Theory of Development* (New York, 1969), especially 324; and the attempt by the editors of *Comparative Studies in Society and History* to make Kuhn central to a discussion of "A General Theory of Innovation," 11 (1969): 369-432, especially 369.

13. Bruce Mazlish, *The Riddle of History: The Great Speculators From Vico to Freud* (New York, 1966); Nisbet, *Social Change and History*, especially 303-04.

14. Kramnick, "Reflections on Revolution," 48, whose discussion of functionalism I have found helpful.

15. On the role of theoretical "generalizations" as opposed to "laws" in historical inquiry, see Carey B. Joynt and Nicholas Rescher, "The Problem of Uniqueness in History," *History and Theory*, 1 (1961): 150-62; Maurice Mandelbaum, "Historical Explanation: The Problem of 'Covering Laws,'" *ibid.*, 229-42; C. J. Arthur, "On the Historical Understanding," *ibid.*, 7 (1968): 203-16; and Rudolph Weingartner, essay review of Morton White, *Foundations of Historical Knowledge*, in *History and Theory*, 7 (1968): 240-56, especially 255.

16. Gordon S. Wood, "Rhetoric and Reality in the American Revolution," *William and Mary Quarterly*, 3d ser., 26 (1966): 23.

17. See especially Quentin Skinner, "Meaning and Understanding in the History of Ideas," *History and Theory*, 8 (1969): 3-53, which is offered as an attempt to apply to the history of ideas a "set of concepts" similar to that applied to the history of science by Kuhn and to the history of art by E. H. Gombrich, *Art and Illusion* (Princeton, 1960); Skinner, 7. Cf. John

Dunn, *John Locke* (Cambridge, 1968); Stocking, *Race*, 1-12. Stocking discusses *The Structure of Scientific Revolutions* along with another contextualist classic, Joseph R. Levenson, *Confucian China and Its Modern Fate* (Berkeley, 1958-65).

18. But cf. Pocock, *Politics*, 14.

19. Winthrop D. Jordan, *White over Black: American Attitudes toward the Negro, 1550-1812* (Chapel Hill, 1968), 3-98.

20. Representative examples include Gene Wise, "Implicit Irony in Perry Miller's *New England Mind*," *Journal of the History of Ideas*, 29 (1968): especially 579-81, and papers given on December 28, 1968, at the meeting of the American Historical Association in Boston: Gene Wise, "Paradigm Formulation in Recent American Studies," and J. Rogers Hollingsworth, "A Paradigm for the Study of Political History." C. Vann Woodward interpreted the paradigm concept more strictly in his presidential address in 1969, when he observed that history, unlike the sciences, had never been endowed with a ruling paradigm: "The Future of the Past," *AHR*, 75 (1969-70): 726. Cf. John Higham's careful use of the term in his *Writing American History* (Bloomington, 1970), 172.

21. John Higham *et al.*, *History* (Englewood Cliffs, N.J., 1965).

22. E.g., J. H. Hexter, "The Rhetoric of History," *History and Theory*, 6 (1967): 12-13, and Schlesinger, review of Skotheim, 219-21.

23. Not all the social scientists who use Kuhn can be accused of simply wrapping themselves in "true science." An interesting example of restraint is Robert I. Watson, "Psychology: A Prescriptive Science," *American Psychologist*, 22 (1967): 436-40. Cf. David Truman, "Disillusion and Regeneration: The Quest for a Discipline," *American Political Science Review*, 59 (1965): especially 865-66. Yet even Truman, in his final paragraph (p. 873), seems to lean in the direction of the caricature of Kuhnian social scientists offered by Paul Feyerabend, "Consolations for the Specialist," in Lakatos and Musgrave, *Growth*, 198. Cf., as examples without Truman's restraint, Gabriel Almond, "Political Theory and Political Science," *American Political Science Review*, 60 (1966): especially 869, 875, and Robert T. Holt, "Comparative Studies Look Outward," in Fred W. Riggs, ed., *International Studies: Present Status and Future Prospects* (Philadelphia, 1971), especially 134-36.

24. E.g., Dudley Shapere, "The Paradigm Concept," *Science*, 172 (1971): 706; Israel Scheffler, *Science and Subjectivity* (Indianapolis, 1967); Karl Popper, "Normal Science and Its Dangers," in Lakatos and Musgrave, *Growth*, 56-57; Imre Lakatos, "Falsification and the Methodology of Scientific Research Programmes," in *ibid.*, especially 93, 115, 178-79. Cf. Alan Ryan, *The Philosophy of the Social Sciences* (London, 1970), especially 233-35, and Peter Munz, essay review of Robert W. Friedrichs, *A Sociology of Sociology*, in *History and Theory*, 10 (1971): especially 364.

25. This paragraph is based primarily on Kuhn, "Reflections on My Critics," in Lakatos and Musgrave, *Growth*, especially 238, 247, 254, 261-64. Cf. Kuhn, *Structure*, especially 144-59, and Kuhn, "Postscript," 198-200, 209-10.

26. Kuhn, "Reflections," 244-45.

27. For an especially willful expression of these fears, see Feyerabend, "Consolations," 198-99. Feyerabend's essay, incidentally, is one of

the most trenchant critiques of Kuhn yet written. It and Margaret Masterman's "The Nature of a Paradigm" (59-89) are the most readable and interesting contributions to the Lakatos and Musgrave volume, which is a
symposium on Kuhn's work and its relation to Karl Popper's philosophy of
science. For a lively analysis of this volume and of its place in contemporary philosophy of science, see Joseph Agassi, "Tristram Shandy, Pierre
Menard, and All That," *Inquiry*, 14 (1971): 152-64. The most reliable
guide to the differences between Kuhn and the Popperians, however, is
David Bloor, "Two Paradigms for Scientific Knowledge?" *Science Studies*,
1 (1971): 101-15. Bloor's sensitive analysis of how the Popperians, especially Lakatos, have revised their position to meet Kuhn's challenge helps
to correct the popular misconception that it is only Kuhn who has been led
to reformulate some of his claims since 1962.

28. Kuhn, "Reflections," especially 245, where attention is directed
only at the development of disciplines that seek to predict the behavior
of natural phenomena and thereby attain "maturity."

29. Feyerabend, "Consolations," 201; Kuhn, "Reflections," 245.

30. Kuhn does make these prescriptions, of course, for the disciplines
he practices, or is close to; see not only *Structure, passim*, but also "The
Relations between History and History of Science," *Daedalus*, 100 (1971):
271-304.

31. Rudolph Weingartner, "The Quarrel about Historical Explanation," in Ronald H. Nash, ed., *Ideas of History* (New York, 1969), 2:
140-57.

32. An excellent summary of what has been conventional wisdom for
historians during the past twenty years is found in Higham *et al.*, *History*,
135-44, especially 136 (since the 1950s the emphasis has been on "the
positive opportunities of the historian's observational position").

33. Kuhn has not been alone in these efforts, as he acknowledges in
Structure, especially 2-3, and in "History of Science," *International Encyclopedia of the Social Sciences* (New York, 1968), 14: 74-83. Cf. Kuhn,
"The Relations between History and History of Science," 288-91. Cf.
also two very helpful accounts of recent developments in the history and
philosophy of science: Arnold Thackray, "Science: Has Its Present Past a
Future?" in Roger H. Steuwer, ed., *Historical and Philosophical Perspectives of Science* (Minneapolis, 1970), 112-27, and Stephen Toulmin, "Re-
discovering History: New Directions in Philosophy of Science," *Encounter*,
Jan. 1971, pp. 53-64.

34. For Holmes and his intellectual environment, see Morton G.
White, *Social Thought in America: The Revolt Against Formalism* (New
York, 1949), 59-75. The comparison of Kuhn to Holmes is also made in an
essay I read only after this paper was well advanced, M. D. King, "Reason, Tradition, and the Progressiveness of Science," *History and Theory*,
10 (1971): 24-25.

35. Wilfrid E. Rumble, Jr., *American Legal Realism: Skepticism, Reform, and the Judicial Process* (Ithaca, 1968).

36. E.g., W. I. Thompson, "Alternative Realities," *New York Times
Book Review*, Feb. 13, 1972, where the view that scientific discoveries are
made by those "working outside the containers [of knowledge] in the dark
of the unknown..." is misleadingly attributed to Kuhn. Cf. the equally

dubious attempt to link Kuhn with the socioeconomic determinism of Engels and J. D. Bernal: James E. Hansen, "An Historical Critique of Empiricism," in David H. DeGrood *et al.*, *Radical Currents in Contemporary Philosophy* (St. Louis, 1971), 44, 48.

37. Kuhn, *Structure*, 171-72.

38. *Ibid.*, 170.

39. This continuity of basic aims (see *ibid.*, 168) is what I take Kuhn to be clarifying by his recent references to the "paramount" values of scientific communities. Kuhn, "Logic of Discovery or Psychology of Research?" in Lakatos and Musgrave, *Growth*, 21; "Postscript," especially 184-85; "Reflections," 262. These clarifications have been interpreted by some as an important change in Kuhn's position. E.g., King, "Progressiveness of Science," 29. In any case, further research on what scientific communities value, tolerate, and disdain is Kuhn's own chief desideratum. See "Reflections," 238.

40. Kuhn, *Structure*, 173.

41. Karl Popper, "Normal Science and Its Dangers," in Lakatos and Musgrave, *Growth*, 53; cf. Herbert Feigl, "Beyond Peaceful Coexistence," in Stuewer, *Perspectives*, 7.

42. Levenson, *Confucian China*, 3: 89.

43. The phrase is Kuhn's. *Structure*, 172.

44. See, as examples of the formulation and use of this distinction, Herbert Feigl, "Philosophy of Science," in Roderick M. Chisholm *et al.*, *Philosophy* (Englewood Cliffs, N.J., 1964), 472, and Popper, "Normal Science and Its Dangers," 56-58.

45. E.g., Bernard Barber, "The Sociology of Science," *International Encyclopedia of the Social Sciences* (New York, 1968), 14: 92-100; cf. Stephen Cotgrove, "The Sociology of Science and Technology," *British Journal of Sociology*, 21 (1970): 1-15.

46. Kuhn, *Structure*, v, 160-73; Kuhn, "Reflections," 236.

47. Two very important contributions to the controversy appeared just when this article was being completed, Stephen Toulmin, *Human Understanding: The Collective Use and Evolution of Concepts* (Princeton, 1972), and Jerome R. Ravetz, *Scientific Knowledge and Its Social Problems* (Oxford, 1972).

PARADIGMS IN SCIENCE AND RELIGION

IAN BARBOUR

I. PARADIGMS IN SCIENCE

1. COMMITMENT TO PARADIGMS

Of the exponents of new views of the relation of theories and observations, Thomas Kuhn has been the most influential. One discussion of his ideas lists thirty-six reviews of *The Structure of Scientific Revolutions* in journals whose fields range from philosophy and science to psychology and sociology.[1] Many scientists feel at home in the volume because it gives frequent concrete examples from the history of science and seems to describe science as they know it. But others hold that he gives far too much prominence to subjective aspects of science. Workers in new research fields in the natural sciences, and in areas of the behavioural sciences where basic concepts and fundamental assumptions are in dispute, often find Kuhn's writing illuminating. I will summarize four themes of his book as it originally appeared, and then indicate some of the criticisms it has evoked and his subsequent reply to his critics. The debate reveals a new understanding of the nature of science which has far-reaching implications.

1. *Paradigms dominate normal science.* Kuhn maintains that every scientific community is dominated by a cluster of very broad conceptual and methodological presuppositions embodied in the "standard examples" through which students learn the prevailing theories of the field. Because such examples also serve as norms of what constitutes good science, they transmit methodological and metaphysical assumptions along with key concepts. A paradigm, such as Newton's work in mechanics, implicitly defines for a given scientific community the types of question that may legitimately be asked, the types of explanation that are to be sought, and the types of solution that are acceptable. It moulds the scientist's assumptions as to what kinds of entity there are in the world (Newton was interested in matter in motion) and the methods of enquiry suitable for studying them.

"Some accepted examples of actual scientific practice — examples which include law, theory, application and instrumentation together — provide models from which spring particular coherent traditions of scientific research."[2]

Normal science, says Kuhn, consists of work within the framework of a paradigm which defines a coherent research tradition. Scientific education is an induction into the habits of thought and activity presented by text books, and an initiation into the practice of established scientists. It leads to the acquisition of "a strong network of commitments, conceptual, theoretical, instrumental, and methodological." Paradigms illustrate ways of attacking a problem — for instance, by analysis in terms of masses and forces. Thereby they guide the direction of normal research, which is "an attempt to force nature into the preformed and relatively inflexible boxes that the paradigm supplies."[3] Like solving a puzzle or playing a game of chess, normal science seeks solutions within an accepted framework; the rules of the game are already established. A shared paradigm creates a scientific community — a professional grouping with common assumptions, interests, journals and channels of communication. This stress on the importance of the community suggests parallels in the role of the religious community which will be explored later.

2. *Scientific revolutions are paradigm shifts.* Kuhn holds that in normal research fundamental assumptions are not questioned. Anomalies are set to one side, or accommodated by *ad hoc* modifications. Ptolemaic astronomy went on adding planetary epicycles to remove discrepancies; defenders of the phlogiston theory were driven to postulate negative chemical weights in order to maintain their paradigm. But with a growing list of anomalies, a sense of crisis leads the scientific community to examine its assumptions and to search for alternatives. A new paradigm may then be proposed which challenges the dominant presuppositions.

Kuhn shows that when a major change of paradigm does occur it has such far-reaching effects that it amounts to a revolution. Paradigms are incompatible. A new paradigm replaces the old; it is not merely one more addition to a cumulative structure of ideas. A revolution from Aristotelian to Newtonian physics, for instance, or from Newtonian physics to relativity, is "a transformation of the scientific imagination" in which old data are seen in entirely new ways. For a period, adherents of two different paradigms may be competing for the allegiance of their colleagues, and the choice is not unequivocally determined by the normal criteria of research. Kuhn writes:

Though each may hope to convert the other to his way of seeing his science and its problems, neither may hope to prove his
case. The competition between paradigms is not the sort of battle that can be resolved by proofs ... Before they can hope to
communicate fully, one group or the other must experience the
conversion that we have been calling a paradigm shift. Just because it is a transition between incommensurables, the transition
between competing paradigms cannot be made a step at a time,
forced by logic and neutral experience. Like a gestalt switch it
must occur all at once or not at all.[4]

Scientists resist such revolutions because previous commitments have
permeated all their thinking; a new paradigm prevails only when the
older generation has been "converted" to it, or has died off and been
replaced by a new generation. As Kuhn portrays it, a paradigm shift
is thus a highly subjective process. He claims that scientific revolutions, like political revolutions, do not employ the normal methods
of change.

3. *Observations are paradigm-dependent.* Kuhn agrees with Feyerabend and Hanson that there is no neutral observation language.
Paradigms determine the way a scientist sees the world. Galileo saw
a swinging pendulum as an object with inertia, which almost repeats its oscillating motion; his predecessors, inheriting the Aristotelian interest in progress towards final ends, had seen a pendulum as a constrained falling object, which slowly attains its final
state of rest. As with a gestalt switch, the same situation can be seen
in differing ways. Scientists with rival paradigms may gather quite
dissimilar sorts of data; the very features which are important for
one may be incidental to the other. Rival paradigms, says Kuhn,
solve different types of problems; they are, like Feyerabend's basic
theories, "incommensurable."[5]

4. *Criteria are paradigm-dependent.* Competing paradigms offer
differing judgments as to what sorts of solution are acceptable. There
are no external standards on which to base a choice between paradigms, for standards are themselves products of paradigms. One can
assess theories within the framework of a paradigm, but in a debate
among paradigms there are no objective criteria. Paradigms cannot be falsified and are highly resistant to change. Adoption of a
new paradigm is a "conversion." Each revolution, says Kuhn:

... necessitated the community's rejection of one time-honoured
scientific theory in favour of another incompatible with it. Each
produced a consequent shift in the problems available for sci-

entific scrutiny and in the standards by which the profession determined what should count as an admissible problem or a legitimate problem-solution. And each transformed the scientific imagination in ways that we shall ultimately need to describe as a transformation of the world within which scientific work was done.[6]

Yet in one of his final chapters Kuhn does state that there are reasons, even "hard-headed arguments," for the adoption of a new paradigm. Its proponents must try to show that it can solve the problems which led to the crisis of the old paradigm. They can sometimes point to quantitative precision or to the prediction of novel phenomena not previously suspected. But in the very early stages the enthusiasts for a new paradigm may have little empirical support to offer, while the traditionalists may have many solved problems to their credit, despite unresolved anomalies. And even at later stages there is seldom anything approaching a conclusive proof of the superiority of one paradigm over another.[7] This question of criteria for choice of paradigms is perhaps the most important issue in the controversy over Kuhn's book.

2. PARADIGMS RECONSIDERED

Since its first appearance, Kuhn's volume has provoked extensive discussion. He has had enthusiastic supporters and strenuous critics. Each of the four theses outlined above has been attacked:

1. *Criticisms of "normal science."* Kuhn's critics complain that his concept of paradigm is vague and ambiguous. Masterman lists twenty-one different senses of paradigm in the book. Kuhn's portrayal of the authoritarian character of normal science has also been challenged. Popper argues that in science there is continual criticism of fundamental assumptions; only beginning students or routine workers in applied science would uncritically accept dominant presuppositions. The scientist, he asserts, can challenge prevailing views whenever he wants to. "If we try, we can break out of our framework at any time." Feyerabend maintains that there is, and should be, a multiplicity of basic alternatives present at all times, rather than the exclusive monopoly by one paradigm which Kuhn describes and defends. Normal science is more diverse and more self-critical than Kuhn recognizes.[8]

2. *Criticisms of "scientific revolutions."* Apart from the difficulty in identifying when a change is a "revolution" and when it isn't, the sharp contrast between normal and revolutionary science has been

questioned. S. E. Toulmin finds frequent small changes more typical of science — "micro-revolutions" which do not fit either of Kuhn's two classifications. In addition, he alleges, the struggle of alternative views occurs not simply in rare crises but more or less continuously. There are many gradations between routine and extraordinary science, differences of degree rather than of kind. There is also more continuity across a revolution than Kuhn depicts; there may be changes in assumptions, instrumentation and data, but there are no total discontinuities.[9]

3. *Criticisms of "the paradigm-dependence of observations."* Even if a new paradigm directs attention to new problems and new variables, the old data need not be discarded and much of it may still be relevant. Dudley Shapere insists that under successive paradigms there are partly overlapping vocabularies; otherwise there could be no possibility of communication or public discussion. If two paradigms really were "incommensurable," they could not be "incompatible"; to be considered "rivals" they must at least apply to a jointly identifiable phenomenon, describable in predicates shared by both protagonists. Moreover, though a paradigm determines which variables to study, it does not determine what the values of those variables will be. It may be resistant to falsification, but an accumulation of discordant data cannot be dismissed if empirical testing is to be maintained.[10]

4. *Criticisms of "the paradigm-dependence of criteria."* If observations as well as criteria are paradigm-dependent, there is no rational basis for choice among competing paradigms. Each paradigm determines its own criteria, so any argument for it is circular. The choice seems arbitrary and subjective, a matter of psychology and sociology more than of logic. Lakatos writes:

> For Kuhn scientific change — from one "paradigm" to another — is a mystical conversion which is not and cannot be governed by rules of reason and which falls totally within the realm of the (*social*) *psychology of discovery*. Scientific change is a kind of religious change ... There are no rational standards for their comparison. Each paradigm contains its own standards. The crisis sweeps away not only the old theories and rules but also the standards which made us respect them. The new paradigm brings a totally new rationality. There are no super-paradigmatic standards. The change is a band wagon effect. Thus *in Kuhn's view scientific revolution is irrational, a matter of mob psychology.*[11]

It is on this point that Kuhn's critics are most vehement, accusing

227

him of *relativism, subjectivism,* and *irrationality.* Paradigm preference can be discussed only relative to a particular community. Watkins contrasts the dogmatism in Kuhn's "closed societies" with the continuous criticism in Popper's "open societies" and concludes: "My suggestion is, then, that Kuhn sees the scientific community on the analogy of a religious community and sees science as the scientist's religion."[12] Popper himself says: "The Myth of the Framework is, in our time, the central bulwark of irrationalism. . . . In science, as distinct from theology, a critical comparison of the competing theories, of the competing frameworks, is always possible."[13] Kuhn's portrayal of normal science as dominated by unchallenged dogmas, his failure to specify criteria for paradigm choice, and his talk of "conversion" and "persuasion" all seem to these critics to threaten the objectivity and rationality of the scientific enterprise.

In response to his critics, Kuhn has added a Postscript in the second edition of his book, and has written several essays, in which he clarifies his earlier views and at some points significantly modifies them. Since his final position does answer some of his critics' objections, his more recent treatment of each of the four themes presented above should be outlined:

1. *The diverse meanings of "paradigm."* Kuhn now tries to distinguish some of the various features of science which were formerly lumped together. Paradigms in their primary meaning are shared crucial examples, for which he suggests the term *exemplars.* One learns science by concrete examples of problem-solving, rather than by explicit rules. A formula, such as $f = ma$, is of little use until one learns how to approach a new situation so that it can be applied. One "learns to see situations as like each other," and to recognize similarities which have not been formalized. Kuhn holds that the extension of such similarities, embodied in exemplars, is important for normal research as well as for the science student.[14]

The more general "constellation of group commitments" Kuhn now wants to call *the disciplinary matrix.* One component consists of widely held *values,* such as simplicity, consistency, and predictive accuracy (these will be examined in connection with criteria below, since Kuhn acknowledges that they are widely shared among different scientific communities). Another component consists of metaphysical commitments transmitted by *particular models:*

> Re-writing the book now I would describe such commitments
> as beliefs in particular models, and I would expand the category
> models to include also the relatively heuristic variety: the elec-

tric circuit may be regarded as a steady-state hydrodynamic system; the molecules of a gas behave like tiny elastic billiard balls in random motion. Though the strength of group commitment varies, with non-trivial consequences, along the spectrum from heuristic to ontological models, all models have similar functions. Among other things they supply the group with preferred or permissible analogies and metaphors. By doing so they help to determine what will be accepted as an explanation and as a puzzle-solution; conversely, they assist in the determination of the roster of unsolved puzzles and in the evaluation of the importance of each.[15]

By introducing these distinctions, Kuhn has modified his earlier idea of the unity of a paradigm as a total coherent viewpoint, though it is not clear just how he thinks of the separate components of the disciplinary matrix as interacting with each other.

2. *The distinction between "normal" and "revolutionary" science.* Kuhn qualifies this distinction but still defends it. He now wants a "scientific community" to be identified sociologically (e.g. by its patterns of inter-communication) before its shared paradigms are studied. Some "communities" turn out to be quite small — as few as a hundred scientists. There can be considerable variation among competing "schools of thought." We are told that members of a community can disagree about some rather fundamental issues; nineteenth-century chemists did not all have to accept atomism as long as they all accepted the laws of combining proportions. Further, there can be "small-scale revolutions" and "micro-revolutions" (without a preceding crisis) affecting specialized subgroups within a larger community. Nevertheless Kuhn still maintains that the most fruitful strategy of normal science is to develop and exploit the prevailing tradition, extending its scope and accuracy; the examination of assumptions and the search for alternatives, he holds, seldom occurs except during major crises.[16]

3. *The "translation" of observations.* Kuhn has also qualified his "incommensurability" thesis, though he continues to maintain that there is no neutral observation language. Communication is by no means impossible between men with rival paradigms. "Both their everyday and most of their scientific world and language are shared. Given that much in common, they should be able to find out a great deal about how they differ."[17] Each can try to see a phenomenon from the other's viewpoint, and eventually even anticipate how he would interpret it. The problem, says Kuhn, is like that of translation between two language communities, which is difficult

but not impossible. This analogy allows Kuhn to retain some vestiges of his idea of "conversion" — for a person can go beyond translation to the actual adoption of a new language in which he thinks and speaks.

4. *The "rationality" of paradigm-choice.* Kuhn objects strongly to the charge of irrationality. If science is not rational, he asks, what is? But to understand what scientific rationality really requires, we have to look at science with care. Kuhn reminds his critics that he always has maintained that there are "good reasons" and "hardheaded arguments" for choosing paradigms. In his Postscript he spells out more fully the values which are shared by all scientists:

> Probably the most deeply held values concern predictions: they should be accurate; quantitative predictions are preferable to qualitative ones; whatever the margin of permissible error, it should be consistently satisfied in a given field; and so on. There are also, however, values to be used in judging whole theories: they must, first and foremost, permit puzzle-formulation and solution; where possible they should be simple, self-consistent, and plausible, compatible, that is, with other theories currently deployed. (I now think it a weakness of my original text that so little attention is given to such values as internal and external consistency in considering sources of crisis and factors in theory choice).[18]

Kuhn insists, however, that these shared values provide no automatic rules for paradigm choice, since there is inevitable *variation in individual judgment* in applying them. Moreover, not all persons will assign the same relative weights among these values. After stating that debates over fundamental theories do not resemble logical or mathematical proofs, Kuhn concludes:

> Nothing about that relatively familiar thesis implies either that there are no good reasons for being persuaded or that those reasons are not ultimately decisive for the group. Nor does it even imply that the reasons for choice are different from those usually listed by philosophers of science: accuracy, simplicity, fruitfulness, and the like. What it should suggest, however, is that such reasons function as values and that they can thus be differently applied, individually and collectively, by men who concur in honouring them. If two men disagree, for example, about the relative fruitfulness of their theories, or if they agree about that but disagree about the relative importance of fruitfulness and, say, scope in reaching a choice, neither can be convicted of a

mistake. Nor is either being unscientific. There is no neutral algorithm for theory-choice, no systematic decision procedure which, properly applied, must lead each individual in the group to the same decision.[19]

Kuhn offers a pragmatic justification for this variability of individual judgment. For if everyone abandoned an old paradigm when it first ran into difficulties, all effort would be diverted from systematic development to the pursuit of anomalies and the search for alternatives — almost all of which would be fruitless. On the other hand, if no one took alternative paradigms seriously, radically new viewpoints would never be developed far enough to gain acceptance. Variations in judgment allow a distribution of risks, which no uniform rules could achieve. Yet the fact that there are agreed values encourages communication and the eventual emergence of a scientific consensus. Finally, these values provide standards in terms of which one can see genuine progress as one looks at a succession of theories in history. "That is not a relativist's position, and it displays the sense in which I am a convinced believer in scientific progress."[20] Kuhn thus denies the allegations of irrationality and subjectivism.

Some of Kuhn's critics are still far from satisfied in this regard. Thus Shapere, in a review of Kuhn's recent writings, repeats his earlier epithets:

It is a viewpoint as relativistic, as antirationalistic, as ever ... He seems to want to say that there are paradigm-independent considerations which constitute rational bases for introducing and accepting new paradigms; but his use of the term "reasons" is vitiated by his considering them to be "values," so that he seems not to have gotten beyond his former view after all. He seems to want to say that there is progress in science; but all grounds of assessment again apparently turn out to be "values," and we are left with the same old relativism ... The point I have tried to make is not merely that Kuhn's is a view which denies the objectivity and rationality of the scientific enterprise; I have tried to show that the arguments by which Kuhn arrives at this conclusion are unclear and unsatisfactory.[21]

Shapere does not define "rationality," but he evidently identifies it with rule-governed choice. Kuhn is called "anti-rationalistic," it seems, because he still holds that the choice of paradigms is not unequivocally specified by the values accepted throughout the scientific community. Such name-calling, however, sheds little light on the question of how choices in science are or should be made.

3. CRITERIA OF ASSESSMENT IN SCIENCE

In this section, a view of criteria for scientific choice is proposed which incorporates what I take to be the most significant insights of Kuhn's reformulated position and the most important contributions of his critics. Such a position may be less exciting than either the early empiricists' "objectivism" or the "subjectivism" which many readers found in Kuhn's first edition. But hopefully it can better represent an accurate description of what scientists actually do and a fruitful prescription for the continuation of the distinctive achievements of science. Its implications for the critique of religion are analysed in the next section.

I will distinguish the following aspects of science:

(1) observations,

(2) theories and theoretical models,

(3) "research traditions" (Kuhn) or "research programmes" (Lakatos), over a span of time, embodied in key examples ("exemplars"), and

(4) metaphysical assumptions about the nature of entities in the world. . . .

Exemplars have an important practical function in this scheme; as key examples, rather than explicit rules, they serve to initiate the student into the methods of attacking a problem which are accepted within a research tradition, and they guide the projected research programme of a particular scientific community. But exemplars do not determine the criteria for theory choice, and they can be considered separately from metaphysical assumptions. Traditions influence the type of model which is proposed in a new situation. Particular theoretical models (such as the billiard ball model of a gas) are treated here along with the theories which they generate and by which they are tested. A number of my conclusions [developed in an earlier section not included here] can now be applied within this scheme.

First, *all data are theory-laden, but rival theories are not incommensurable.* There is no pure observation language; the distinction between theory and observation is relative, pragmatic, and context-dependent. But protagonists of rival theories can seek a common core of overlap in observation languages, on a level closer to agreed observations to which both can retreat. This seems a more accurate way of describing communication concerning observations during basic controversies (such as those over relativity and quantum theory) than Kuhn's recent analogy of "translation," which assumes no common terms. It also allows more continuity and carry-over at the level of observations and laws before and after a revolution, and hence a more cumulative history, than Kuhn and Feyerabend recognize.

Something rather like a *"gestalt* switch" does occur in moving from one comprehensive theory to another. Different features of the phenomenon are selected for attention; new problems, new variables, new relationships are of interest. A familiar situation is seen in a new way. Further, it may be necessary to challenge and reinterpret the interpretive component of observations; to that extent, the data can be said to change. But this usually involves a retreat to observations whose interpretive component is not in doubt. Even in a *gestalt* switch, after all, there are lines in the picture which remain unchanged. Unlike a *gestalt* switch, however, there are in science criteria for favouring one interpretation over another — though I will suggest that in the very early stages, when a comprehensive theory of wide scope is first proposed, these criteria seldom yield definitive conclusions.

Second, *comprehensive theories are highly resistant to falsification, but observation does exert some control over them.* There are no "crucial experiments" which can be specified in advance. But the degree of vulnerability to counter-instances varies considerably among the various components of science. If unsupported by a theory, a law stating relationships between variables which are relatively "observable" will be thrown into question by a few persistent discrepancies. Theories, especially comprehensive ones, are more resistant to falsification, but an accumulation of anomalies, or of *ad hoc* modifications having no independent experimental or theoretical basis, cannot be tolerated indefinitely. An accepted comprehensive theory is overthrown not primarily by discordant data but by an alternative theory; we should visualize not a two-way confrontation of theory and experiment, but a complex confrontation of rival theories and a body of data of varying degrees of susceptibility to reinterpretation. A research programme is even more resistant to change than a theory, but may eventually be abandoned in favour of a new programme which has greater promise of explaining known data, resolving anomalies, and predicting novel phenomena.

Commitment to a research tradition and *tenacity* in a research programme are scientifically fruitful (on this Kuhn and Lakatos agree). Only if scientists stick with a programme and do not abandon it too readily will its potentialities be systematically explored and exploited. What balance between criticism and commitment is possible and desirable? Here Kuhn's revised picture of normal science allows for considerable diversity within a scientific community — including the presence of rival small groups and competing "schools of thought." Popper's advocacy of "continual criticism" ("we can break out of our frameworks at any time") and Feyerabend's plea for a plurality of basic alternatives in every field at all times ("proliferation of theories," "perpetual revolution") seem unrealistic and, even if they could be achieved, wasteful of scarce scientific manpower. There is both historical and strategic justification for Kuhn's view that, for most scientists, fruitful work is achieved within a framework of accepted assumptions, except when major difficulties in dominant theories are evident.

Third, *there are no rules for choice between research programmes, but there are independent criteria of assessment.* Criteria are indeed acquired more from studying past exemplars than from learning explicit principles; but they are common to many exemplars and can be stated apart from any of them. A scientist usually has some training in several related fields and some familiarity with their exemplars; his criteria are not dependent on one tradition alone.[22] As outlined earlier, the most important criteria are simplicity, coherence, and the extent and variety of supporting experimental evidence (including precise predictions and the anticipation of the discovery of novel types of phenomena). But there are no rules, no specific instructions, that is, for the unambiguous application of the criteria; there is, in Kuhn's words, "no systematic decision procedure which must lead each individual in the group to the same decision." Yet the criteria provide what Kuhn calls "shared values" and "good reasons" for choice; they are "important determinants of group behaviour, even though the members of the group do not apply them in the same way."

In *the very early stages,* when a comprehensive theory and its development into a research programme are first proposed, empirical criteria seldom have a predominant role. To [cite an] historical example: in the history of the theory of relativity, the Michelson-Morley experiment did not play the determinative part most textbooks assign to it. In point of fact, all of the experimental evidence on which Einstein drew had been available for fifty years; he was unaware of the Michelson-Morley results until considerably later. He was interested primarily in simplicity and coherence — in particular, the symmetry of the forms of the equations for electrical and magnetic fields in motion.[23] The variability of individual weighting among various criteria, which Kuhn describes, is also most noticeable in the early stages of a new theory. Thus the inconsistency between Bohr's quantum theory and the assumptions of classical physics worried some physicists very much when it was first proposed, whereas others thought this inconsistency of little importance compared to the accuracy of the predictions which it yielded.

The criteria for assessing theories are relevant to the *evaluation of research programmes*, but they cannot be applied in any rigorous way. The decision to abandon an accepted programme will depend on judgments of the seriousness of the anomalies, inconsistencies, and unsolved puzzles in the old programme (these are sometimes more important than Lakatos admits), and the promise of a proposed new programme. As Lakatos maintains, there are no clear-cut rules for such decisions, and there are risks in either changing programmes too precipitously or too reluctantly. The decision may be vindicated only decades later — which does not help much during the scientific controversy itself. Yet because there are accepted criteria common to all scientists the decision can be discussed and reasons set forth, and an eventual consensus can be expected.

Theories and programmes, then, are not verified or falsified, but *assessed by a variety of criteria*. Especially in the early stages of controversial theories of great generality, and in the decision to abandon a well-developed research programme in favour of a promising but undeveloped new one, the assessment is an act of personal judgment. In such circumstances the scientist is more like a judge weighing the evidence in a difficult case than like a computer performing a calculation. The judgment cannot be reduced to formal rules, yet it is subject to rational argument and evaluation by commonly agreed criteria. The impossibility of specifying explicit rules is one of the reasons why editors of scientific journals and panels awarding research grants must have considerable discretionary power in evaluating new ideas.

Finally, *metaphysical assumptions* are one stage further from direct empirical verification or falsification, yet even these are not totally immune to change. I agree with Kuhn that the scientist does have beliefs about the kinds of entity there are in the world, and does have ontological commitments (and not merely methodological commitments for the sake of a fruitful research strategy, as Lakatos would have it). Because Newtonian mechanics was spectacularly successful, physicists not only used it as an exemplar of what a theory should be like, but also took its categories as indicative of the constituents of the universe. Additional assumptions were made concerning regularity, causality, action-at-a-distance, and other basic features of the world. The same conceptual categories and presuppositions proved to be powerful tools in many fields, from astronomy to chemistry and biology. Less legitimately, perhaps, these metaphysical commitments were extended to a total world-view of reality as matter in motion.

But several things can happen to change the dominance of a set of metaphysical assumptions. The selection of the particular features of the research programme which had been assumed to be responsible for its success may be reconsidered; the emphasis may be placed instead on other features of the programme. Again, research programmes in one field — or in several fields — may be replaced by new programmes using very different basic concepts. Interest may also shift to new scientific fields, or to new areas of human experience; the earlier extension of metaphysical assumptions from one field, as wider interpretive categories for a total world-view, may then be questioned. In the course of history such assumptions have also in response to changing views of other areas of human experience.

The position I have presented is consistent with *critical realism*. Naive realism is not plausible if the history of science provides evidence of major paradigm shifts rather than simple cumulation and convergence. Thus Mary Hesse writes:

> The history of science has already sufficiently demonstrated that successive acceptable theories are often in radical conceptual contradiction with each other. The succession of theories of the atom, for example, exhibits no "convergence" in descriptions of the nature of fundamental particles, but oscillates between continuity and discontinuity, field conceptions and particle conceptions, and even speculatively among different topologies of space.[24]

On the other hand, there is in the history of science more continuity than one would expect from Feyerabend or from Kuhn's earlier work, in which truth is entirely relative to a succession of self-contained language systems dominated by diverse paradigms. I have argued that observations and basic laws are retained through paradigm-shifts, at least as limiting cases under specifiable circumstances; a new theory usually explains why the older theory was as good as it was and why its limitations became evident.

To summarize: the scheme I have outlined accepts the three "subjective" theses that (1) all data are theory-laden, (2) comprehensive theories are highly resistant to falsification, and (3) there are no rules for choice between research programmes. It also preserves Kuhn's most distinctive contributions concerning paradigms: the importance of exemplars in the transmission of a scientific tradition, and the strategic value of commitment to a research programme. At the same time I have made three assertions which seem to me essential for the objectivity of science: (1) rival theories are not incommensurable, (2) observation exerts some control over theories, and (3) there are criteria of assessment independent of particular research programmes.

II. PARADIGMS IN RELIGION

1. COMMITMENT TO PARADIGMS

Let us now examine more closely some parallels between commitment to a religious paradigm and commitment to a scientific paradigm, understood as a research tradition transmitted by key historical examples or exemplars. First we may recall *the importance of the community* of scientists interacting over a period of time. Neither religion nor science is an individual affair. Religion is corporate; even the contemplative mystic is influenced by a historical tradition. No one adheres to science or religion in general; the initiate joins a particular community and adopts its modes of thought and action.

Next, *crucial historical events* are central in the transmission of a tradition. Newton's work in mechanics served as exemplar for classical physics. The key events remembered by a community help to define its self-identity. Kuhn seems to hold that the exemplars are edited and perhaps idealized versions of historical accomplishments which appear in textbooks, rather than the actual historical events themselves. Events in the lives of Moses, Buddha, and Christ play somewhat similar roles in the self-definition of religious communities. It is the edited narratives in the scriptures and the often idealized "lives of saints" which are influential — though here the attempt to recover authentic history is itself religiously significant, despite the limits of such an endeavour (biblical criticism, the quest for the historical Jesus, etc.). Furthermore, religious traditions, unlike scientific ones, are often totally and explicitly organized around the memory of their historical exemplars as individual persons. Particular aspects of their lives serve as norms for the community's life and thought.

I have discussed elsewhere the status of events in history which are taken by a religious community to be *revelatory*.[25] I cited the

237

view of several theologians that there is no uninterpreted revelation; we are given not revealed propositions, but a human record of historical events understood to have involved both man and God. Revelatory events are recognized today by their ability to illuminate present experience; the special event enables us to see what is universally present. The past provides clues for the interpretation of the present; particular points in history disclose the powers at work throughout history. The exemplars of a religious community are thus more determinative of its ongoing life than those of a scientific community.

It is sometimes said that the *commitment* characteristic of religion contrasts with the *tentativeness* of science. [Basil Mitchell has contended] that religious beliefs are "articles of faith," not "tentative hypotheses." But the contrast is not as great if religious traditions are compared with research traditions rather than with scientific hypotheses.[26] In the previous section I concluded that the scientist does have a commitment to a tradition and legitimately sticks to it with considerable tenacity, exploring its potentialities rather than abandoning it too readily. It will be recalled that for Lakatos this commitment is a deliberate methodological decision; the "core" of a programme is treated as unfalsifiable, in order to develop its "positive heuristic." In Kuhn's account, which seems to me more plausible, the commitment arises from the scientific community's unconscious assumptions, which influence all its ways of thinking.

Lakatos' view of scientific commitment as a deliberate methodological decision might be compared with *voluntarist views of religious faith*. William James speaks of "the will to believe"; a person must act as if religious beliefs were true in order to live out their positive possibilities. F. R. Tennant refers to the sustained effort of the will required in any voyage of discovery; religious faith, he says, is like the deliberate decision to undertake and carry through a research project.[27] Again, in the interests of practical effectiveness a man may resolve to act decisively, even when the evidence is incomplete; perpetual suspended judgment would paralyze action. I wonder, however, whether religious faith can be adequately represented as a purely pragmatic methodological decision. I suggest that, as in the scientific case, there are ontological commitments present in religion; in the absence of concern for the truth of one's beliefs, the path would be open to the arbitrary adoption of useful fictions. William James himself acknowledged that he should have spoken of "the right to believe" rather than "the will to believe," for he was aware of the danger that wishful thinking can restrict one's openness to new evidence.

In *religious faith* there are of course distinctive attitudes which are not present in commitment to a scientific tradition. In the biblical view, faith is personal trust, confidence, and loyalty. Like faith in a friend or faith in a doctor, religious faith is not "blind faith," for it is closely tied to experience. But it does entail risk and vulnerability in the absence of logical proof. Marriage is "a venture of faith," not simply because its success is not predictable, but because it requires trust and self-commitment. Biblical faith is also "faithfulness" and "fidelity." But all of these attitudes presuppose beliefs; one cannot trust God unless one believes he exists. As H. H. Price has shown, "belief in" a person is both an expression of attitudes and an affirmation of beliefs about him ("belief that"); it is not reducible to either personal attitudes or propositional beliefs alone.[28]

Participation in a religious tradition also demands a more total *personal involvement* than occurs in science. Religious questions are of ultimate concern, since the meaning of one's existence is at stake. Religion asks about the final objects of a person's devotion and loyalty, for which he will sacrifice other interests if necessary. Too detached an attitude may cut a person off from the very kinds of experience which are religiously most significant. Reorientation and reconciliation are transformations of life-pattern affecting all aspects of personality, not intellect alone. Religious writings use the language of actors, not the language of spectators. Religious commitment, then, is a self-involving personal response, a serious decision implicating one's whole life, a willingness to act and suffer for what one believes in.

Is there in religion an *absolute commitment* which makes evidence irrelevant? Is total trust compatible with self-criticism and acknowledgment of the possibility of error? To the believer, disbelief may appear to be "faithlessness," disloyalty, and personal betrayal. "True faith" is shown by complete trust even in adverse circumstances. Job could say, "Though he slay me, yet will I trust in him." St. Paul could proclaim that "neither death nor life...nor height, nor depth, nor any other creature, shall be able to separate us from the love of God, which is in Christ Jesus our Lord" (Rom. 8.39). Such passages express the conviction that even the personal experience of evil is not incompatible with religious faith. But does this imply that beliefs have no experiential basis or that they are immune to criticism?

I would submit that religious commitment can indeed be combined with *critical reflection*. Commitment alone without enquiry tends to become fanaticism or narrow dogmatism; reflection alone without commitment tends to become trivial speculation unrelated to real life. Perhaps personal involvement must alternate with reflection on that involvement, since worship and critical enquiry at their most significant levels do not occur simultaneously. It is by no means easy to hold beliefs for which you would be willing to die, and yet to remain open to new insights; but it is precisely such a combination of commitment and enquiry that constitutes religious maturity.[29]

If *faith* were simply the acceptance of revealed propositions or assent to propositions, it would be incompatible with *doubt*. But if faith means trust and commitment, it is compatible with considerable doubt about particular interpretations. Faith does not automatically turn uncertainties into certainties. What it does is take us beyond the detached speculative outlook which prevents the most significant sorts of experience; it enables us to live and act amid the uncertainties of life without pretensions of intellectual or moral infallibility. But it does not give us wisdom or virtue transcending the limitations of human existence. Doubt frees us from illusions of having captured God in a creed; it calls into question every religious symbol. We are dislodged from all the attempted securities on which we rely, including certainties of belief.

Self-criticism is called for if we acknowledge that no church, book, or creed is infallible, and no formulation is irrevocable. The claim of any human institution or theological system to finality must be questioned if we are to avoid absolutizing the relative. The prophets of all ages have reserved their harshest criticisms for their own religious communities. The distinctive character of commitment to a religious paradigm in short does not exclude critical reflection....

2. CRITERIA OF ASSESSMENT IN RELIGION

Before analysing criteria for cognitive claims, we should look for a moment at possible criteria for non-cognitive functions. One such criterion is the ability of a religious tradition to *fulfill social and psychological needs*. Desirable social goals might include group unity, community stability, and social harmony. Among psychological goals are self-understanding, maturity, and integration of personality. Religious faith may allay anxieties and impart a significant direction to an individual's life. Some authors have tried to derive an objective list of human needs from scientific analysis of man's nature; the fulfillment of such needs could then provide neutral criteria for assessing religious paradigms. It is dubious, however, whether formulations of such needs, and of their relative importance, can be made without value judgments which are culturally conditioned.

The results of religious beliefs in human life may also be judged by *ethical criteria.* "By their fruits ye shall know them." Religions could be assessed both by their professed ideals and by their capacity to inspire lives of compassion, creative love, and the enhancement of human relationships. William James claimed that religious experience is a source of moral power, inward peace, and saintliness. At the theoretical level, coherence among ethical values is supported by beliefs about the nature of reality and the destiny of man. More significantly, at the practical level, motivation to sustain action is a product of personal transformation and reorientation as well as commitment to a world-view. Religious beliefs can be judged by the ethical norms they uphold and their effectiveness in motivating ethical action.

Such ethical criteria are, of course, *paradigm-dependent.* Creative love and integration of personality are ideals endorsed by some traditions more strongly than others. There is an inescapable circularity in any attempt to assess the criteria of assessment. Criteria for non-cognitive functions are indeed internal to particular "language-games" and relative to particular communities. The goals of the life-affirming Western tradition cannot be assumed in evaluating the pragmatic results of Eastern philosophies of life, for instance. We must turn, then, to the cognitive beliefs which are presupposed in these non-cognitive uses, even though the latter are in practice more important in the life of the religious community.

We ask, then, whether criteria for religious beliefs might parallel those for scientific theories. In any system of thought *simplicity* is desirable (e.g., minimum number of independent assumptions and conceptual categories); but it is seldom a major consideration in either science or religion. *Coherence* involves both internal consistency (the absence of contradictions) and systematic interrelatedness (the presence of connections and implications between statements). But *supporting evidence* is the most important criterion. Religious beliefs must give a faithful rendition of the areas of experience taken to be especially significant: religious and moral experience and key historical events. But they must also adequately interpret other events in our lives as active selves. Hence *extensibility* of application (fruitfulness) can be listed as an additional criterion. Finally, *comprehensiveness* in the coherent ordering of diverse types of experience within a systematic metaphysics is desirable, though, in my opinion, secondary to other criteria.

But in the *choice between paradigms,* the application of these criteria is even more indirect, ambiguous, and debatable in religion

241

than in science. Variations in individual judgment as to the relative weight which should be given to various criteria are more pronounced; some people seek systematic coherence above all else, while others stress adequacy to experience. Theravada Buddhism is remarkable for its simplicity, but perhaps at the price of comprehensiveness, since numinous experience and worship are less strongly represented than in other religions. Hinduism and Christianity include a richer interweaving of many strands, but at the price of simplicity. Among traditions there are also divergent convictions as to which types of experience are most significant. Between competing religious traditions there seem to be fewer common assumptions and less clear-cut common data than there are between competing scientific traditions, even during a scientific revolution.

In particular, religion lacks the *lower-level laws* which are characteristic of science. The terms of such laws are relatively close to observations, their theoretical components are not in dispute, and they are relatively vulnerable to falsification by counter-instances. These laws often survive scientific revolutions or undergo qualifications so that they can be retained under a restricted range of conditions; but sometimes newly formulated laws are historically important in the overthrow of a dominant paradigm. The absence of such laws in religion severely limits the extent to which data can exert some control over higher-level theories and paradigms. Statements which appear to be "laws" (such as "Sincere prayer will be answered") are too vague, and the terms are too elastic, for any precise application.

There are no rules for deciding when to abandon a paradigm in science, but *an eventual consensus* emerges — even though there may be rival paradigms for protracted periods, and no paradigm can be considered permanent. The emergence of consensus in religion seems an unrealizable goal. There are differences in cultural context which are intertwined with religious beliefs; hopefully any future global civilization will preserve considerable cultural diversity, and with it, religious pluralism. Among adherents of competing scientific paradigms there are common goals, standards, and procedures, but among different religious communities such common methodological assumptions are seldom found.

In sum, each of the *"subjective"* features of science mentioned in the previous section is *more* evident in the case of religion: (1) the influence of interpretation on data, (2) the resistance of comprehensive theories of falsification, and (3) the absence of rules for choice among paradigms. Each of the corresponding *"objective"* features of science is *less* evident in the case of religion: (1) the presence of common data on which disputants can agree, (2) the cumulative effect of evidence for or against a theory, and (3) the existence of criteria which are not paradigm-dependent. It is clear that in all three respects religion is a more "subjective" enterprise than science. But in each case there is a difference of degree—not an absolute contrast between an "objective" science and a "subjective" religion.

There are several reasons for stressing that in religion there are at least minimally present such "objective" features as common experience, relevant evidence, and common criteria. First, if it is true that an accepted paradigm is not falsified but replaced by an alternative, then the possibility of assessing a religious paradigm must in practice be compared with the possibility of assessing *alternative religious or naturalistic paradigms* — regardless of what the possibility of assessment in science may be. The most that one can expect of any set of beliefs is that it will make more sense of all the available evidence than alternative beliefs. The choice is not between religion and science, but between theism, pantheism, and naturalism, let us say, as each is expressed in a particular historical tradition. No basic beliefs are capable of demonstrable proof. A set of beliefs must be considered as an organic network of interrelated ideas.

Second, the *self-criticism* of one's own basic beliefs is possible only if there are criteria which are not totally paradigm-dependent. Every person has such basic beliefs; the choice is not whether to hold them but which ones to hold. Decision and action express implicit if not explicit affirmations. Better, then, to hold beliefs critically than uncritically, even if there is ambiguity and risk in any such process of evaluation.

Third, *communication* between paradigm communities is impossible unless they partially share a common language. If there is no core of shared terms and no experiences common to both communities, their assertions are "incommensurable" and no genuine discussion can occur. The further presence of shared criteria greatly enhances the fruitfulness of the interaction. I would maintain that persons in diverse traditions can appeal to facets of each other's experience and can discuss together their interpretive frameworks. Intelligible reasons can be offered, rather than arbitrary "leaps of faith."

The explorers in Wisdom's parable can converse.[30] They confront together a common situation, in which each traces the patterns that he finds significant. Each underlines distinctive features whose cumulative effect has impressed him. As when literary critics evaluate a play, there are both data and criteria held in common which make possible a rational discussion even among those whose conclusions differ. There are no *proofs*, but there are good *reasons* for judgments which are not simply matters of personal taste or individual preference.

Fourth, *critical reflection* is not incompatible with *religious commitment*. The centre of religion is worship — not the acceptance of an interpretive hypothesis but the acknowledgment of that which is worthy of devotion. The necessity of personal involvement and the limitations of metaphysical speculation have been repeatedly emphasized. But these distinctive characteristics of religion need not exclude an attitude of self-critical questioning in the search for a truth beyond individual preference. As with the scientist, a commitment to honesty in the pursuit of truth is prior to commitment to a particular paradigm.

NOTES

1. Eugene Lashchyk, *Scientific Revolutions*, Ph.D. dissertation, University of Pennsylvania 1969.
2. Thomas S. Kuhn, *The Structure of Scientific Revolutions*, University of Chicago Press 1962, p. 10.
3. Ibid., p. 24.
4. Ibid., pp. 147, 149.
5. Ibid., chap. 10.
6. Ibid., p. 6.
7. Ibid., chap. 12.
8. Margaret Masterman, "The Nature of a Paradigm"; K. R. Popper, "Normal Science and its Dangers"; P. K. Feyerabend, "Consolations for the Specialist"; all in *CGK*.
9. S. E. Toulmin, "Does the Distinction between Normal and Revolutionary Science Hold Water?," in *CGK*.
10. Dudley Shapere, "Meaning and Scientific Change," in R. Colodny (ed.), *Mind and Cosmos*, University of Pittsburgh Press 1966. See also Scheffler, op. cit., chap. 4.
11. *CGK*, pp. 93, 178.
12. J. W. N. Watkins, 'Against "Normal Science," ' in *CGK*, p. 33.
13. *CGK*, pp. 56, 57.
14. Thomas Kuhn, *The Structure of Scientific Revolution*, 2nd ed. University of Chicago Press 1970, pp. 187-191. See also his "Second Thoughts on Paradigms," in Frederick Suppe (ed.), *The Structure of Scientific Theories*, University of Illinois Press 1973.
15. *Structure of Scientific Revolutions*, 2nd ed., p. 184.
16. Ibid., p. 181. Also Kuhn, 'Reflections on my Critics,' in *CGK*, p. 249.
17. *Structure of Scientific Revolutions*, 2nd ed., p. 201.

18. Ibid., p. 185.
19. Ibid., pp. 199-200.
20. Ibid., pp. 205-206. See also Kuhn, "Notes on Lakatos," in *Boston Studies in Philosophy of Science*, vol. 8, pp. 144ff.
21. Dudley Shapere, "The Paradigm Concept," *Science*, vol. 172, 1971, pp. 708-709.
22. See William Austin, "Paradigms, Rationality and Partial Communication," *Journal of General Philosophy of Science* 3 (1972).
23. F. Schillp (ed.), *Albert Einstein: Philosopher-Scientist*, Library of Living Philosophers 1949, p. 53.
24. Mary Hesse, "Models of Theory Change," in *Proceedings of the IVth International Congress of Logic, Methodology and Philosophy of Science, Bucharest, 1971.*
25. Barbour, *Issues in Science and Religion*, pp. 229-236.
26. See William Austin, "Religious Commitment and the Logical Status of Doctrines," *Religious Studies*, vol. 9, 1973, p. 39.
27. William James, *The Will to Believe*, Longmans, Green & Co. 1921; F. R. Tennant, *Philosophical Theology*, Cambridge University Press 1930.
28. H. H. Price, "Belief 'In' and Belief 'That'," *Religious Studies*, vol. 1, 1965, p. 1.
29. This paragraph and the following one are developed more fully in *Issues in Science and Religion*, pp. 226ff.
30. [Editor's note] The reference is to John Wisdom, "Gods," *Proceedings of the Aristotelian Society* 45 (1944), 187.

POLITICS AS METAPHOR:
CARDINAL NEWMAN AND PROFESSOR KUHN

RICHARD VERNON

My object in this paper is to compare two texts in the history of ideas which are, on the face of it at least, very different from one another. John Henry Cardinal Newman's *Development of Christian Doctrine* remains one of the classic expositions of an evolutionary thesis; T. S. Kuhn's *Structure of Scientific Revolutions* already ranks as a near-classic statement of a revolutionary case. The contrast is, I think, not quite as stark as may appear at first sight: though Kuhn writes of revolutions, his concern, no less than Newman's, is nevertheless with "development";[1] and though his subject matter is the history of science, his concern too is, or once was, with "dogma."[2] What I most want to stress, however, is not this verbal correspondence, which may as it stands be intriguing rather than convincing, but a series of substantive parallels which flow from a mode of argument common to both these texts: the extensive use of political imagery in defining the structures of ideas in question and in explaining the character of their history.

The political metaphors favored by Newman and Kuhn are interesting not only for themselves but also, as I hope to show, for the light which they help to throw upon ideas of change. They are of intrinsic interest because since Plato's *Republic* at least politics has very often figured as the *explanandum* of analogy, the obscure field to be illuminated in the borrowed light of navigation or medicine or cookery of other examples; indeed, the very notions of "evolution" and "revolution" are sometimes seen as cases of this, for their political use is sometimes thought—probably mistakenly—to derive from biological or cosmological analogies. Yet here we have two notable texts which reverse the direction of analogy, and thus revert to the more fundamental argument of the *Republic*—that politics itself supplies a metaphor for human life. More significantly, though, in resting their arguments very largely upon a common base of political imagery, Newman and Kuhn offer a perspective from which to approach the vexed question of the relation between evolution and revolution, continuity and discontinuity, in change. Newman sees in

246

politics a metaphor for the developmental continuity of thought; Kuhn, a metaphor for its revolutionary discontinuities. Yet their points of departure, as I shall try to show, are surprisingly similar; perhaps, then, in tracing the points of convergence and divergence of these two tests, we may shed some light upon the subject of political change itself.

The Development of Christian Doctrine is Newman's watershed essay, marking his adoption of the Catholic faith. In it (as he explains in his introduction) he sets out to demonstrate the continuity of contemporary Catholic belief with apostolic doctrine, and it is in the service of this end that his idea of "development" acquires its immediate point. He must show that continuity is compatible with change: indeed, he goes further, and suggests that continuity *requires* change, that an idea is unfolded only in contact with successive diverse circumstances and through the mediation of many minds. The content of an idea, as he says, is "elicited and expanded by trial," and its trials reveal its manifold aspects, rather as different spatial perspectives disclose different features of an object.[3]

Newman speaks of this unfolding of ideas as an extension of their "jurisdiction" or "sovereignty" over events, that is, of their inclusiveness and their explanatory range.[4] In these words, of course, the political analogy is displayed, as it is in the various passages in which illustrative use is made of political changes. But Newman's use of politics emerges more fundamentally in the very structure of the developmental process as he describes it: for Christianity, as he says, is a "polity,"[5] and it is very largely from this that the basic features of its development arise. "Polity," it is true, could be read as a rather loose synonym for "society" or "community" (terms which he also uses): but Newman's argument lends it a more precise sense. It is not simply the fact of intercourse (society) or identification (community) that characterizes religions, but rather, a *public* character that governs their evolution, as Newman explicitly says, and as his remarks about "perspective" make clear: "in proportion to the variety of aspects under which it presents itself to various minds is [an idea's] force and depth, and the argument for its reality."[6] Hence the development of doctrine is "not like an investigation worked out on paper, in which each successive advance is a pure evolution from a foregoing, but it is carried on through and by means of communities of men and their leaders and guides; and it employs their minds as their instruments, and depends upon them, while it uses them."[7] This is necessarily so, for a large truth cannot be comprehended "all at once": "It is a characteristic of our minds, that they

247

cannot take an object in, which is submitted to them simply and integrally."[8] It is, then, the structure of a *political* society or community that is linked to cognition, a linkage through which Newman reasserts the classical identification of politics and reason. We can reason only about *public* objects, on this view, the diversity of our perspectives upon them assuring us that they enjoy real existence.[9]

In proposing this conception Newman sets aside some other possible models for explaining the character of change. Change is not, as we have already seen, a "pure evolution" (in the earlier nineteenth-century sense), or an unfolding of logical implication, even though, once a change has been completed, its relation to the whole in which it figures must have a "logical character," that is, the new state of doctrine must be internally consistent.[10] The process of change itself is something for which logical inference supplies only a metaphor. Notions of congruity and appropriateness play an important part: "verisimilitude and analogy"[11] are of value, whatever the doubt cast upon them by the Baconian view of natural science. For the language of Scripture is "figurative and indirect": "It cannot, as it were, be mapped, or its contents catalogued."[12] On the other hand, if the strict notions of inference and entailment fall short of the truth, nor is development, so conceived, any sort of episodic sequence of contingently related events. "It is not that first one truth is told, then another; but the whole truth, or large portions of it are told at once, yet only in their rudiments, or in miniature, and they are expanded and finished in their parts, as the course of revelation proceeds."[13] And finally, if development is neither a pure evolution (in its root sense) nor a mere sequence, nor does it lend itself, as some theologians had thought, to an essentialist reading in which one part or feature of doctrine — a "leading idea" — dominates over the rest: "There is no one aspect deep enough to exhaust the contents of a real idea."[14] In short, the meaning of Scripture consists in a web of mutually supported and reciprocally tested elicitings of its sense, which together comprise its "development," and which cannot be reduced to a linear set of premises and deductions, to a temporal sequence, or to any simple notion of hierarchy. As a "polity," then, or as a community with objects that are common but not perceived in identical ways, Christianity has a mode of complex development which is distinct from that of a disembodied notion.

The "politics" which Newman has in mind, therefore, is neither rationalist nor empiricist nor ideological, if we may take these difficult words as convenient labels for the errors which he criticizes. The

political process which he assumes is not a matter of deducing conclusions from first principles, or doing this and then that piecemeal,
or of pursuing some readily articulated abstract priority, to use the
Oakeshottian language that so naturally comes to mind here.[15] It
can be understood only as something internal to a group, as the interactions of men who share a common situation and are prompted
by it: and its logic is that of a never-finished search for coherence.
The state of things at any point is "imperfect"; there are "difficulties"
in the application of received principles, "apparent objections to
them," "deficiency in their comprehensiveness," "want of neatness in
their working." With such things we must be "patient";[16] improvements can only be partial, for the simple reason that we can see only
partially, and the whole escapes our manipulation. Government is
necessary, in Newman's implicit political model, because we need
to conclude under conditions of imperfect understanding, just as in
doctrinal controversy authority is necessary "to ratify the successive
steps of so elaborate a process, and to secure the validity of inferences which are to be made the premises of more remote investigations."[17] There is, then, no conflict between reason and authority in
political as in religious matters: for rational men will accept authority, on this view, because they grasp the limitations of individual
reason and will.

Newman generally excepts the history of the natural sciences from
the scope of this picture of development, agreeing with Bacon that
"doubt" is to be set above "dogma" in this sphere.[18] To be sure, scientific truth, like religious doctrine, undergoes change and growth;
but the progress of science is wholly a product of the (incremental)
exercise of "our ordinary powers," while the truth of religion "comes
to us as a revelation, as a whole, objectively," and its development
is a matter of perfecting our understanding of what is already given,
not of adding substantive novelties to a stock of knowledge.[19] The
understanding of religious truth, moreover, must be achieved from
the inside, as it were, by men who share in the developing com-
monality of belief, while the scientific, on the contrary, "is common
property, and can be taken and made use of by minds who are personally strangers, in any true sense, both to the ideas in question and
to their development."[20]

Now what is of much interest here is that these alleged features
of science which call for its exclusion from Newman's model are just
those features which Kuhn believes are mistakenly attributed to it.
Kuhn denies that scientific advance is purely incremental in nature.
It is moved forward by exemplary achievements, termed "para-

249

digms," which are given "as a whole," in Newman's words, and which the scientist must explicate and extend. These paradigms point forward to a complete understanding of the field in question, but completeness is never achieved. Many puzzles remain to be resolved, many implications remain to be tested, many inelegancies await elimination. Newman's remarks, quoted above, fit Kuhn's picture of scientific research to perfection: "difficulties in application," "apparent objections ... drawn from other matters of fact," "deficiency in ... comprehensiveness," "want of neatness" — all these may be matched in Kuhn's account point for point. And the "patience" which Newman enjoins is likewise a cardinal virtue for Kuhn's scientist: "There are always some discrepancies. Even the most stubborn ones usually respond at last to normal practice. Very often scientists are willing to wait," and very often they are justified in doing so.[21]

More crucially still, Kuhn's central contribution is his insistence that scientific advance issues from a community of specialists, and is not to be (wholly) explained in terms of the possession of some set of skills or readily defined methods. "Methodological directives" are always insufficient.[22] There is not "some explicit or even some fully discoverable set of rules and assumptions" that serves to encompass scientific research; it proceeds by "resemblance and by modelling" (Newman's "congruity" and "analogy").[23] Hence what is fundamental is membership in a community which transmits demands and aspirations not fully reducible to rules; its members absorb them "often without quite knowing" what their content is.[24] A scientific community, like the "communion" which Newman describes, binds its members together "by influences and engagements which it is difficult for strangers to ascertain";[25] and Newman's view that scientific knowledge is accessible as "common property" is to "strangers," reflects — in a strikingly stark form — exactly the picture of science which Kuhn is concerned to reject, a picture which draws too sharp a line (he alleges) between the logics of "discovery" and "justification."

Kuhn makes it quite clear that the community he has in mind is very much like a political community, and that, like Newman's Christian "polity," it requires the exercise of authority. Moreover, Newman and Kuhn justify this requirement in quite comparable ways, taking issue with certain radically individualist conceptions which, they object, neglect the individual's dependence upon the institutions which embrace him. What we may call "the incompleteness of beginnings" is a theme common to both writers. Since any important idea requires elaboration by its adherents over time, "the corrections of many minds and the illustration of many experiences,"[26] at its beginnings its meaning is not fully comprehended by the individual mind. "Its beginnings are no measure of its capabilities, nor of its scope. At first no one knows what it is, or what it is worth," Newman wrote;[27] and Kuhn, likewise, contends that paradigms in science are taken as authoritative well in advance of all the detailed and extensive research which is needed to sustain them. Not "past achievement" but "future promise" justifies the faith which is placed in a paradigm, and the scope of its explanatory power will not be known at the moment of its adoption: "if a new candidate for paradigm had to be judged from the start by hardheaded people who examined only relative problem-solving ability, the sciences would experience very few major revolutions."[28] In science as in theology, in short, the need for authoritative beliefs arises from the fact that the individual's perspective is too limited to encompass the long-term requirements of an historically evolving community.

The authoritative character of beliefs resides essentially in their exemplary force. What drives a scientific community forward, in Kuhn's view, is not a set of propositions which are articulated fully enough to be clearly confirmed or disconfirmed, but the power of a striking achievement which holds "promise" for the future. The "development" which Kuhn speaks of, then, is, like Newman's, quite different from a process of logical deduction from fully specified premises. Political scientists and others who have taken Kuhn's "paradigm" to be essentially a "conceptual framework" or some such thing are seriously mistaken in their reading of the argument for paradigms. The constitutive beliefs of a science, as Kuhn argued in 1961, are much better viewed in terms of a "model achievement" than in terms of some body of explicit doctrine such as "framework," "model," "rule" and so on: for each of these terms "challenges its user to say what the corresponding framework, model, assumption or rule *is*, and that proves to be just what neither the scientist, philosopher nor historian can ever sufficiently discover."[29] In *The Structure of Scientific Revolutions* this argument is elaborated at length, and is set out along with a distinction between paradigms and rules which recalls quite clearly Newman's distinction between principles and doctrine.[30] The life of a community is drawn from the paradigm or principle which guides it without instructing it, while doctrines or rules are instructions which the community formulates for itself in drawing upon its central inspiration.

Thus Kuhn's conception, no less than Newman's, refuses the models of deduction, sequence, and hierarchy. It refuses the model of deduction because, very much as in Newman's argument, the reconstruction of changes to fit a logical order is seen as an *ex post facto* imposition,[31] the work of authors of textbooks; the model of simple sequence, because scientific work is normally not a series of discrete events but a progressive completion of an already-given picture; the model of hierarchy, because what guides the work of normal science is not a specifiable "leading idea" but an example with complex aspects, an example generating a "web," "nest" or "network" of mutually supportive beliefs.[32]

In 1961, as I have mentioned already, Kuhn described these beliefs as "dogmas." For reasons that one can only guess at, this perhaps too provocative term does not appear in the book published in the following year. But if "dogma" disappears from view in *The Structure of Scientific Revolutions*, nevertheless the beliefs constitutive of normal science retain all their authoritative force in this longer presentation. Their dogmatic character is explained and justified by Kuhn along lines which recall Newman's argument almost verbally. It is the "complicated" (Newman) or "complex" (Kuhn) nature of the subject matter of inquiry that obliges a community of inquirers to accept definite limits to their work, and which makes any notion of purely independent investigation quite inappropriate. Moreover, it is the case that more "remote" (Newman) or "recondite" (Kuhn) problems can be approached only on the basis of a secure mastery of more immediate and basic matters, and if enquiry is to advance the investigators must agree to close off discussion of the basic structure of their subject matter.[33]

Kuhn's critique of the Baconian view of natural science thus converges significantly with Newman's critique of Protestant notions of the sovereignty of conscience. Possibly it is this that Professor Watkins has in mind when he suggests that Kuhn's scientific community is like a religious one:[34] a polemical remark which, it must be said, is not very helpful if the *kind* of religious community in question — Zen monastery? Quaker meeting? — is not specified. But actually there is nothing at all specifically religious about these notions of community and development, any more than they are peculiarly scientific. They were first evolved, or at any rate first elaborated, in a political context. The antecedents of the Newmanian and Kuhnian models are to be found in Hume's critique of the contractual theory of the state, a critique which likewise insists that a collective development cannot be wholly encompassed by the conscious intentions of those who begin it:[35] in Burke's familiar remarks on the value of "prejudice"; in Tocqueville's rather parallel view that "In order that society should exist, and, *a fortiori*, that a society should prosper, it is required that all the minds of the citizens should be rallied and held together by certain predominant ideas; and this cannot be the case, unless each of them sometimes draws his opinions from the common source, and consents to accept certain matters of belief at the hands of the community."[36] In opposition to this mode of thinking, moreover, Kuhn's critics are themselves sometimes driven to draw from the contrary, radical political tradition, resorting to language reminiscent of Thomas Paine and the French Declaration when they insist upon "the *permanent right* to challenge ... authority";[37] and the apparent oddity here is that it is Kuhn, the revolutionist, who inherits Burke's case against Paine, or Tocqueville's against Robespierre.

All this is, of course, to pose a problem. The notion of development is one which insists upon continuity. A process "will not be a development," Newman wrote, "unless the assemblage of its aspects, which constitute its ultimate shape, really belongs to the idea from which they start. A republic, for instance, is not a development from a pure monarchy, though it may follow upon it; whereas the Greek 'tyrant' may be considered as included in the idea of democracy."[38] Kuhn's picture of science, however, is one in which discontinuities play a notable role, and in his view the progress of science is punctuated by and in part consists of those "extraordinary" episodes which he calls "revolutions." Many of his critics have doubted that such things take place. Just as Kuhn's picture of the conservative character of normal science is overdrawn, they say, so too his picture of revolutionary change is too stark in its suddenness and, so to speak, its violence.[39] In contrasting Newman's and Kuhn's views, then, we step straight into the center of some hotly contested ground.

It is indeed in relation to what Kuhn calls "normal science" that Newman's idea of development acquires its clearest relevance, and in considering the revolutionary episodes which intervene between periods of normality we may seem to depart from the developmental thesis entirely. Newman for normal science, we may be tempted to say, Marx (or Blanqui?) for extraordinary science. But what is meant by distinguishing between developments and revolutions?

Newman sets out and applies to his subject seven "Notes" or tests which, he contends, establish the presence or absence of continuity through change: and if we consider Kuhn's notion of change in the light of these, the difference between the developmental and revolutionary conceptions turns out to be more than a little unclear. Consider the third and sixth, "assimilative power" and "conservative action," respectively: here we find Newman setting down as tests of continuity some considerations which Kuhn connects, rather, with *dis*continuity. The assimilative power of Catholic belief is observed, Newman says, in certain episodes in which doctrine is reorganized and rethought: "Facts and opinions, which have hitherto been regarded in other relations and grouped around other centres, henceforth are attracted to a new influence and subjected to a new sovereign. They are modified, laid down anew, thrust aside, as the case may be. A new element of order and composition has come among them."[40] As for conservative action, Newman writes: "A true development . . . may be described as one which is conservative of the course of antecedent developments, being really those antecedents and something else besides them; it is an addition which illustrates, not obscures, corroborates, not corrects, the body of thought from which it proceeds."[41]

The first of these passages describes brilliantly something very familiar to readers of Kuhn, the much-discussed "paradigm-shift" or "Gestalt-switch" which constitutes a scientific revolution: it does so, moreover, in the language of political revolution ("a new sovereign") and in terms which allow for a degree at least of negation (facts are "thrust aside"). Kuhn's account of this echoes Newman's description of developmental change quite precisely. When the shift of paradigms takes place, data are placed in "a new system of relations with one another," a phrase from Butterfield which Kuhn accepts; and a little later Kuhn describes the same event in his own words as "a new way of giving order to data."[42] One may not be quite sure what is meant by "data." Does the term refer to phenomena defined in a lay or nontechnical sense, so that we might say (for example) that phlogiston and oxygen theorists, despite their differing conceptualizations of the event, nevertheless both explain "combustion"? Does it refer, perhaps, to indices established by some unchanging standard of mensuration, such as the gain of weight recorded by chemical balances after combustion has taken place? The text does not help us here, but clearly we are to think partly at least in terms of the "assimilation" of some established perceptions to some novel "system of relations" or "order."

Here we are led at once to Newman's sixth Note: something is indeed conserved. But what it is that is conserved is less than clear, for in giving due weight to the conservation of data we must also allow properly for Kuhn's stress upon destruction. Taking various passages in isolation, we may extract two rather different positions from Kuhn's text. For on the one hand, Kuhn wants to say, apparently, that everything changes: there is a "new" scientific community or even a new "world" once the switch of paradigms has taken place. The new order is incommensurable with the old.[43] Kuhn specifically denies the rather familiar view that a new paradigm simply contains the old, reducing it to a "special case" of a larger conception of things; the Newton who may be reconstructed in the light of Einstein is no longer the historical Newton.[44] On the other hand, Kuhn also wants to stress the element of conservation. To be acceptable, he says, a new paradigm must "promise to preserve a relatively large part" of the capacity of its predecessor. New paradigms "seldom or never" preserve *all* the explanatory capacity of the old, but they "usually preserve a great deal of the most concrete parts of past achievement."[45] Some such view — in, if anything, a less qualified form — would seem to be implied in Kuhn's view that revolutions are "episodes in scientific development," "developmental episodes," or part of a "developmental process" — or, to quote from a chapter heading, that "progress" is achieved "through" them; for if the old and new paradigms were simply incommensurable, one could scarcely speak of any development, let alone progress, in the transition from one to the other.

This problem will be familiar to anyone who has read Kuhn's critics. It is sometimes taken to provide a knockdown argument against the whole revolutionary thesis: if something thus persists, it is argued, how can one speak of discontinuities, new worlds, and so on? This seems a bit polemical. Even less than Kuhn's own argument, it does not offer any clear account of what *would* constitute a revolution, and what sort of evidence would convince us that one had taken place. In this context some of Newman's remarks are of considerable help, and suggest a potentially useful distinction. For Newman rightly separates what we may call the scope or depth from the rate and quality of change. Gradualness of rate and quality is no measure of scope and depth: "a gradual conversion from a false to a true religion, plainly, has much of the character of a continuous process, a development, *in the mind itself*, even when the two religions, which are the limits of its course, are antagonists."[46] Likewise, Rome's transition from republic to empire was a crucial one, "yet in appearance the change was small"; "On the other hand, when the dissimulation of Augustus was exchanged for the ostentation of Diocletian, the real alteration of constitution was trivial, but the appearance of change was great."[47] More explicitly still, in outlining his first Note of continuity, "preservation of type," Newman insists that continuity is compatible with "considerable alteration of properties and relations, as time goes on. . . . *Great changes* in outward appearance and internal harmony."[48]

Unity of type and of principle, and the other features of continuity which Newman's Notes lay down, apparently survive quite drastic exoteric changes. Newman denies that the English Reformation and the French Revolution were, from a secular standpoint, departures from their respective countries' "development":[49] and here, as elsewhere in Newman's beguiling account, we may begin to feel that any clear notion of identity and difference begins to dissolve — or at least, that the confrontation between evolution and revolution is somewhat eased in its blankness.

If Newman chooses to regard the French Revolution, or, for that matter, the development from the Old Testament to the New, as continuous transitions, while Kuhn chooses to regard the transition from a particle to a wave theory of light as a revolution, then nothing in the above discussion allows us to correct or to approve either one. It all depends, we might be tempted to say, upon the level of analysis chosen. But actually, we need not be led to quite so trite a conclusion. What Newman's discussion permits, or requires, is a clear separation between the retrospective assessment of change and the experiences of those who participate in it or suffer it. The participants' experiences have no *decisive* claim upon the historian's assessments, and essentially psychological conceptions such as the "Gestalt-switch," conceptual and perceptual changes "in the mind itself," in Newman's words, do not tell the historian what he needs to know. For a discontinuity of *development* is not an episode of doubt or excitement or both, but a rift in the fabric of a discipline which subsequent analysis cannot repair.

It is all very well for Kuhn to object to writing the history of science backwards, and to complain (no doubt justly) that scientists, like everyone else, tend too easily to imagine their discipline's growth in the light of immanent and uniform change.[50] Despite his strictures on this point, the notion of development on which he relies is one which is inescapably retrospective. What lends the victory of one paradigm over another its (allegedly) "revolutionary" quality is not the degree of anguish which accompanies it — which must obviously vary enormously from case to case — but the shift in structure which we know, from hindsight, to be crucial; indeed, even to identify a "paradigm" is a retrospective judgment, for we can scarcely assess the *exemplary force* of something in advance of eventual responses to it. Moreover, the essentially collective character of the normal-scientific enterprise, in particular the minute specialization in the division of labor among its practitioners, implies a view of "science" as something which — like revelation, according to Newman — can be "mastered" by no one mind, and which for that reason issues in an emergent history, irreducible to an aggregate of biographies. Kuhn distinguishes explicitly between the "scientific enterprise as a whole" and "the individual scientist," and likewise (in the case of Priestley) between acting scientifically as an individual and participating in a scientific community.[51] All this is entirely defensible, and probably necessary, too. But the existence of *revolutionary* phases is established in large part by switching illicitly to a nonretrospective history, a chronicle of the individuals' experience, and it is this juxtaposition of explanatory modes that creates so strong an appearance of sharp periodic disjunctions.

It is here, above all, that Newman's views about change demonstrate their utility. What Newman stresses is the *essentially* retrospective character of history, which must, in his view, adopt a temporal scale far exceeding that of the actor's experience; it is obliged to do so because the actors themselves can have only partial and corrigible views of the objects which concern them, and hence the nature of these objects is more fully disclosed when multiple successive experiences have revealed more of them. This conception of history, as we have seen, is faithfully reflected in Kuhn's treatment of normal science, which, indeed, if true, would stand as a striking corroboration of Newman's developmental thesis in the history of ideas. But it makes no sense to abandon this approach, at arbitrary intervals, for what is in effect a contrasting implied theory of historiography: a theory in which the recovery of the actor's own experience becomes the essential aim, and in which, consequently, the subjective reactions and practical dilemmas of the scientist acquire decisive significance.

The participants must indeed choose between alternative conceptualizations of their field. That two (or more) alternatives are (partially) consistent with the same data makes their choice no easier, for this only means that the evidence does not speak unambiguously: it is just this that makes their choice "revolutionary," for it is this that involves a suspension of the (so to speak) constitutional principle of evidential judgment. The choice to be made is in large part (though not of course wholly)a *decision* about how to proceed in the future, and the choices involved are exclusive in the sense that one cannot follow two diverging paths at once. But that does not mean that, at some later point, the *content* of the discarded paradigm cannot be shown to be contained within the new one, or to be translatable into the new conceptual language. To be sure, it is "only" (as Kuhn misleadingly says) by hindsight that this can be done;[52] but it is the retrospective standpoint that is the relevant one if our concern is with science conceived of as a "development" rather than with the biography of the scientist. Development is discerned, as Newman says, "afterwards," and discontinuity cannot be established by pointing to choices, however hard, which the actors themselves were obliged to make. One may legitimately pursue either course as a historian, and it would be folly to claim that the superiority of one or other approach to history has been demonstrated (though feelings run high on both sides); but what one should not do is to adopt both at once, or rather, in succession, without regard to the specific and contrasting logics of the two.

When the oxygen theory emerged as a rival to the phlogiston theory, Kuhn writes at one point, "few contemporaries hesitated more than a decade" before adopting the new paradigm.[53] Now to hesitate for *as much as* a decade is of course troubling to the point of trauma, and to write of it as lightly as Kuhn does here is clearly to adopt the retrospective standpoint of the reflective historian, for whom a decade is but an instant. If we set aside the essentially psychological notions of perceptual change, which do not fit at all well with the developmental thesis, what we have in Kuhn is something quite Whiggish, as Professor Butterfield defines the Whig view in his classic book. The proper political analogy for much of Kuhn's argument is not the Blanquist upheaval which the color of his language sometimes suggests, but, rather, patterns of constitutional development such as the Whig historians traced — patterns in which there are, indeed, periodic emergencies, but within which emergencies are to be understood not as discontinuities or interruptions but in terms of a larger progressive trend. And it is this that raises inescapably the question of the political meaning of revolution.

It is, of course Newman who speaks the constitutionalist language of "jurisdiction" and "sovereignty," while Kuhn favours the language of revolutionary violence: he speaks of "battle," "competing camps," and "total victory." Now the extent to which violence of this kind is *political* in any strict sense is very much open to question. Newman quite rightly excludes the phenomenon of naked violence from political development,[54] and regards political change as change which is essentially *internal* to a community: political competition is analogous to wranglings and polemics *within* a religion, rather than to conflicts *between* different religions.[55] He does indeed also describe it as a kind of "warfare,"[56] but it can be so only in the very loosest of analogical senses, for it rests not upon coercive power but upon competing appeals to "faith," "prejudice," and "interest," as warfare does not. Whether revolution is to be placed within or outside the category of political change, then, is not quite clear. It is, as Kuhn himself points out, a *failure* of political recourse.[57] We may perhaps speak of it as a *change in politics*, but refuse to describe it as a *politic change*.

Likewise, should we not distinguish between "changes in science" and "scientific change"? Kuhn's concern in *The Structure of Scientific Revolutions* is with the latter. He does not want at all to deny to these extraordinary episodes a scientific character; he wants, rather, to expand the meaning of science, and to include extraordinary as well as normal episodes within it. But to do this is, implicitly, to regard them as changes internal to a community, and hence to imply the existence of a wider community of science which is not delimited by the self-definitions of the loyal paradigm workers. As it happens, this theme is more than implicit in *The Structure of Scientific Revolutions*; for Kuhn wishes to remind the scientist that his more distant predecessors were not prescientific cranks or amateurs, that their questions and answers are to be read out of the discipline only on the basis of a blinkered perspective, and that they were scientists as much as he himself.

Political historians and political scientists have quite often suggested that the self-definitions of revolutionaries are in part deluded. At least since Tocqueville, and even more since Albert Sorel's great study of the continuity between the Old Regime and revolutionary France,[58] they have pointed to the envelope of longer-term constraints and dispositions which survive political violence. Today it may in fact even be rather commonplace to match Sorel's discussion of the French Revolution with observations on contemporary examples: to point out, for example, that Maoism repeated certain ambitions of the Confucian systems, or that the Soviet Russian practice of locking up dissidents in mental wards has Czarist antecedents. There is nothing really surprising about such things; if they do shock us, or if they have an air of paradox about them, that is only because we do not always separate from each other two pictures of revolution which are distinct. A political revolution (minimally defined) is an act of violence through which power is unconstitutionally transferred; such an event is connected only contingently, and may not be connected at all, with the sort of drastic and across-the-board change for which we also use the word "revolution." *This* "revolution" is very likely to take place over a fairly lengthy and also indefinite period of time, it is very likely to consist in connections and implications which are invisible to or imperfectly grasped by those who live through it, and in general it is something much more readily accessible to the reflective backward glance of the historian. At any rate it is not encompassed by the practical resolves of revolutionary actors; for it is not within their power to determine how much will change, how, and to what longer-term effect, as a result of their action, even though, of course, their action is likely to be sustained by some prospective account of the nature and direction of historical change. It was partly for this reason, incidentally, that Albert Sorel's more notorious cousin, Georges, declared that all revolutionaries were moved by myths, for what they will turn out to have done is not defined by what they think they are doing.[59]

Kuhn's first book, on the Copernican revolution, concerned what may be called a "revolution in science," a change so complex, massive and far-reaching that we may say that science itself was changed by it: Kuhn spoke here of "major upheavals in the fundamental concepts of science."[60] At several points he claims to be building upon this conception in *The Structure of Scientific Revolutions*;[61] but the "scientific revolutions" of his title are not, I have suggested, the same thing as the "revolution in science" of his first book. There is a transition, to revert to the parallel models in political thought, from Marx to Locke. In Marx, or in the Marx now rather current, a revolution is an epochal change which is considered to be separable from any specific kind of political event or political behavior; it is defined by its outcomes, not by the means of its realization.[62] In Locke, on the other hand, a revolution is a political expedient; it is a temporary suspension of legality resorted to by practical men who have exhausted all the alternatives, and its object is to restore legality as quickly as possible. It is not a historical construct but a political category.

The tone of Kuhn's discussion, it is true, may often recall Marx, the Marx of 1848 in whose thinking the notion of epochal change was fused with the idea of political violence. Authority is disgraced, the centers of power — learned journals? — assailed, and the world is turned upside down. But on a more sober reading, it is the Lockean view of revolution that prevails. Kuhn's revolutionaries, like Locke's, are men who are deeply attached to order, and who will act unconstitutionally only when order has, against their will, been violated already. They are men who are willing to "trust," and who become distrustful only under severe provocation; only a "long train of abuses" (Locke) or recurring "anomalies" (Kuhn) will move them to withdraw their consent; and even then they will be acutely sensitive to the dangers inherent in revolt, and will demand that a new source of order and restraint be at hand. Being patient men, they will be prepared — as Locke's text seems to suggest — to hold their individual rights in abeyance, until the community at large is persuaded that abuses or anomalies have become intolerable,[63] and just as the English revolutionaries of 1688 sought to preserve a facade at least of legality, to put the interruption of continuity behind them as quickly as possible, so too Kuhn's scientists close their eyes to the discontinuities in their past, and strive to maintain the appearance of simple linear development. The textbook, as Kuhn describes it, is essentially a constitutional document, designed to impose patterns of legitimacy upon the contingencies of mere power.

Locke's revolution, unlike Marx's, *is* a "political revolution," a change internal to a community, and one self-consciously brought about for the sake of maintaining the community's survival and its effectiveness. Likewise, Kuhn's revolutions, in his second book, are "scientific revolutions," in the strictest sense, unlike the upheavals induced by Copernicus as he described them in his first. For this reason we may well wish to question that sharp disjunction between evolutionary and revolutionary change which Kuhn sometimes seems to adhere to and which his critics have seized upon. A political revolution, after all, may be an instrument of political evolution, and there is nothing in the notion of scientific revolution that excludes the idea of scientific development.

For there *is* a scientific community which survives revolution, in Kuhn's account, just as Locke's political community persists through rebellion. To be sure, Kuhn treats this community in a disarmingly residual manner; there are, he says, "ideological factors" which dispose the scientist to make the best possible sense of the data available to him, and it is only because of these "factors" that anomalies and difficulties are even perceived as problematic; it is because of these commitments that the scientist refuses to "slumber" in conservatism when his expectations have been violated by events.[64] Now to insist that the best possible sense should be made of things clearly involves a very strong commitment to rationality; and when Kuhn says that in situations of crisis "there is no standard higher than the assent of the relevant community,"[65] that remark must be subject to a very stringent qualification. It is not assent as such that makes their choice legitimate, but rational assent, assent controlled and guided by those ideological factors which place a premium upon intelligibility: just as Locke's revolutionaries act not by virtue of sheer will but in the light of unchanging principles of political right, which are bound up with the nature of the community as they see it. Temporary and provisional loyalties — to a particular prince, or to a particular paradigm — are overridden by the permanent ideologies of the community itself. We cannot, of course, point to any *institutional* basis for legitimacy other than consent; but that does not mean that there is no *standard* higher than consent, a view which belongs to a quite different notion of change, within which it would be impossible to make sense of either politics or science, for reality would be reduced to a sort of emanation of will.

"He that will with any clearness speak of the dissolution of government," Locke wrote, "ought in the first place to distinguish between the dissolution of the society and the dissolution of government. That which makes the community, and brings men out of the loose state of nature into one politic society, is the agreement which every one has with the rest to incorporate and act as one body, and to be one distinct commonwealth. The usual, and almost only way whereby this union is dissolved, is the inroad of foreign force making a conquest upon them."[66] It is this conception of revolution that underpins the "Whig" view that a political society persists through crises, and that its development may be served by occasional violations of the letter of legality in favor of its spirit. This view, which posits a linear continuity beneath the interruptions and violence of the past, has of course been much criticized; but it is not beyond defense, and indeed one may wonder whether so pervasive a model of change — "any historian," Butterfield said, may "fall into" it[67] — is wholly false. May we not *sometimes* read "the past with reference to the present," in Butterfield's phrase?

It would not be wide of the mark to regard Newman's argument in *The Development of Christian Doctrine* as a sophisticated defense of such a view of change, which, indeed, Newman would hold to be connected inseparably with the nature of politics itself. In judging and acting men anticipate and frame futures, and thus the backward glance of the historian retraces a path which, though not defined by the actors, is marked out or pointed to by the ideas which they entertain. The path leads in a direction which they cannot fully grasp, for there are unforeseen implications and unintended consequences; but these implications and consequences do not stand to the judgments or actions which produced them as an effect, in science, stands to a cause. Lenin neither foresaw nor intended Stalin: the English revolutionaries of 1688 neither foresaw nor intended the constitutional developments of the Hanoverian age: but it would, surely, be eccentric to deny that in either of these cases there is some discernible *logical* relation between the initial actions and the eventual outcome. Likewise, though less obviously, it would be a bold historian indeed who would deny that either of these revolutionary projects bore an intelligible relation to the political traditions from which they sprang. To say this is not of course to deny to political revolution any specific quality, as a violent act; but it is to deny that political revolution conceived of as an *event*, of however violent and irregular a kind, bears any necessary relation to historical discontinuity.

Kuhn, or so it was argued above, weakens his case by effectively conflating two pictures of revolution, and in treating the evidence for revolution in one sense as evidence for revolution in a quite different sense. In the style of John Locke, he envisages a "politic society" of science which survives change, and hence he regards revolution as at bottom an episode of (metaphorical) violence; yet in the style of Karl Marx, he also envisages revolution as epochal change, as a rift in the continuity of society itself, and not merely as an alteration of its (metaphorically) "governing" apparatus. But this latter theme is seriously undermined by the persistent though often apparently reluctant stress upon continuities which characterizes the argument of *The Structure of Scientific Revolutions*. In this connection, it may be added here, Kuhn's use of the term *crisis* displays the central thrust of his argument well: for crises arise for a group only if it anticipates and values a common future, and hence presuppose a degree of continuity. If a group could dissolve and reform itself at will, it would have no crises, but, rather, terminations. For a crisis is, in its root sense, an occasion for judgment; as such, it is not a pure negation, but a revelation of character, and although it obliges the actor to give up this or that aspiration or priority it cannot be said to transform his identity. The points of crisis in literature or drama, as Newman describes them, provide an apt parallel: "what constitutes a chief interest of dramatic compositions and tales is to use external circumstances ... as a means of bringing out into different shapes, and showing under new aspects, the personal peculiarities of character, according as either those circumstances or those peculiarities vary in the case of the personages introduced."[68] In this respect the making of choices is an essential feature of "development," understood as a progressively "exact and complete delineation of character": "Thus Aristotle draws the character of a magnanimous or munificent man; thus Shakespeare might conceive and bring out his Hamlet or Ariel; thus Walter Scott gradually enucleates his James, or Dalgetty, *as the action of his story proceeds.*"[69]

Although Newman makes this point by means of literary and dramatic analogies, it is the political analogy, nevertheless, that provides the most revealing single focus of his argument. As a community in which public objects, by definition, present themselves variously to individual minds, and are therefore contained in no single individual consciousness, a polity has a history which is irreducible to individual intentions; we may write its history as we trace the development of theological or scientific ideas, the individual actors figuring in it as bearers of a common process. From such a perspective, we will naturally be led to regard the crises undergone by communities not in terms of their contemporary color, as interruptions, but, in the light of a larger temporal context, as adaptations; and a revolution, understood in its political rather than its historical sense, is no more or less susceptible of such interpretation than any other kind of event. Needless to say, this argument leaves entirely open the question of whether or not there are *also* "revolutions" of an epochal kind, discontinuities in the very identity of a community: comprehensive and perhaps elastic though Newman's "Notes" or tests of continuity are, they do not wholly exclude such a possibility. But here, in a political context, the idea of revolution would become dependent upon larger judgments, perhaps ultimate ones: we would need to evaluate Locke's view that a community enjoys identity as a *"politic* society," for example, as against Marx's contention that its identity resides in its economic arrangements. And clearly, the concept of revolution itself would not settle anything here; it would merely raise all the difficulties anew.

One final point, implicit in all the above: under Plato's spell, political scientists still seek metaphors for politics, and the history and philosophy of science provide a rich supply. Kuhn's revolutionary thesis is a powerfully tempting model; but to adopt it as a metaphor for political change is to risk serious confusion, for it draws its own intelligibility from a political model, in which the public articulation of beliefs lends their history a distinctive character. Moveover, its difficulties, I have suggested, derive in part from its drawing ambiguously upon several different notions of political revolution, which are not consistent with one another in either their assumptions or their implications. Its metaphorical apparatus is tied to substantive problems about the nature of change, which political scientists have in the past pondered explicitly, and which are not separable from philosophical or ideological pictures of the nature of the political community. The moral, then, for the political scientist: "Beware! You have been here before." And for the political scientist who finds the Kuhnian picture of change persuasive, one could scarcely recommend a better corrective than Newman's essay, which draws upon political imagery for a contrary purpose, perhaps even more ingeniously, and in no less provocative a fashion.

NOTES

1. T. S. Kuhn, *The Structure of Scientific Revolutions* (Chicago, 1962), pp. 6, 91, 169.
2. T. S. Kuhn, "The Function of Dogma in Scientific Research," in *Scientific Change*, ed. A. C. Crombie (New York, 1963).
3. John Henry Cardinal Newman, *An Essay on the Development of Christian Doctrine* (London, 1909), p. 40.
4. *Ibid.*, 39.
5. *Ibid.*, p. 73.
6. *Ibid.*, p. 34.
7. *Ibid.*, p. 38.
8. *Ibid.*, p. 55.
9. Hannah Arendt, *The Human Condition* (Chicago, 1958), esp. pt. 2.
10. Newman, *Development of Christian Doctrine*, p. 190.
11. *Ibid.*, p. 113.
12. *Ibid.*, p. 71.
13. *Ibid.*, p. 64.
14. *Ibid.*, p. 35.
15. The views criticized by Newman are quite closely paralleled by those criticized by Michael Oakeshott in his "Political Education," in *Philosophy, Politics and Society*, ed. Peter Laslett (Oxford, 1956). The reader may well be reminded even more particularly of Oakeshott by Newman's remarks in *Development of Christian Doctrine* (p. 72).
16. Newman, *Development of Christian Doctrine*, p. 101.
17. *Ibid.*, p. 78.
18. *Ibid.*, p. 110.
19. *Ibid.*, p. 79.
20. *Ibid.*, p. 191.
21. Kuhn, *Structure of Scientific Revolutions*, p. 81.
22. *Ibid.*, p. 3; cf. Newman on the inadequacy of "tests" (*Development of Christian Doctrine*, p. 78).
23. Kuhn, *Structure of Scientific Revolutions*, p. 45.
24. *Ibid.*, p. 46.
25. Newman, *Development of Christian Doctrine*, p. 208.
26. *Ibid.*, p. 38.
27. *Ibid.*, p. 40.
28. Kuhn, *Structure of Scientific Revolutions*, pp. 156-57.

29. Kuhn, "Function of Dogma," p. 393.

30. Compare Newman, *Development of Christian Doctrine*, p. 178, and Kuhn, *Structure of Scientific Revolutions*, pp. 43-51.

31. Kuhn, *Structure of Scientific Revolutions*, p. 102.

32. *Ibid.*, pp. 41, 148.

33. Newman, *Development of Christian Doctrine*, p. 78; cf. Kuhn, *Structure of Scientific Revolutions*, pp. 15, 21, and "Function of Dogma," p. 363.

34. John Watkins, "Against Normal Science," in *Criticism and Growth of Knowledge*, eds. Imre Lakatos and Alan Musgrave (Cambridge, 1970), p. 33.

35. See Hume's essay "Of the Original Contract."

36. Alexis de Tocqueville, *Democracy in America*, ed. Phillips Bradley and trans. Henry Reeve (New York, 1955), II:9.

37. Stephen Toulmin, "Does the Distinction between Normal and Revolutionary Science Hold Water?" in *Criticism and Growth of Knowledge*, p. 40 (emphasis added).

38. Newman, *Development of Christian Doctrine*, p. 38.

39. See esp. essays by Popper, Toulmin and Watkins in *Criticism and Growth of Knowledge*.

40. Newman, *Development of Christian Doctrine*, p. 186.

41. *Ibid.*, p. 20.

42. Kuhn, *Structure of Scientific Revolutions*, pp. 85, 89.

43. See, for example, *ibid.*, pp. 127, 148.

44. *Ibid.*, pp. 97-100.

45. *Ibid.*, p. 168.

46. Newman, *Development of Christian Doctrine*, p. 200 (emphasis added).

47. *Ibid.*, p. 177.

48. *Ibid.*, p. 173 (emphasis added).

49. *Ibid.*, p. 175.

50. Kuhn, *Structure of Scientific Revolutions*, p. 137.

51. *Ibid.*, pp. 38, 158.

52. *Ibid.*, p. 102.

53. *Ibid.*, p. 146.

54. Newman, *Development of Christian Doctrine*, pp. 42-43.

55. *Ibid.*, p. 39.

56. *Ibid.*, p. 39.

57. Kuhn, *Structure of Scientific Revolutions*, p. 92.

58. Albert Sorel, *Europe and the French Revolution*, trans. A. Cobban and J. W. Hunt (London, 1969).

59. See Richard Vernon, *Commitment and Change: Georges Sorel and the Idea of Revolution* (Toronto, 1978).

60. T. S. Kuhn, *The Copernican Revolution* (Cambridge, Mass., 1957), p. 183.

61. Kuhn, *Structure of Scientific Revolutions*, pp. viii, 6-7.

62. See Shlomo Avineri, *The Social and Political Thought of Karl Marx* (Cambridge, 1970).

63. See *Second Treatise*, secs. 225 and 230, and compare Toulmin's remark cited in note 37 above.

64. Kuhn, "Function of Dogma," p. 390.
65. Kuhn, *Structure of Scientific Revolutions*, p. 93.
66. *Second Treatise*, sec. 211.
67. Herbert Butterfield, *The Whig Interpretation of History* (London, 1931), p. 30. Butterfield himself has been accused of "falling into" it by E. H. Carr, *What Is History?* (Harmondsworth, England, 1964), p. 42.
68. Newman, *Development of Christian Doctrine*, p. 180.
69. *Ibid.*, p. 52 (emphasis added).

IV. HISTORY OF SCIENCE

SOME INTERTHEORETIC RELATIONS BETWEEN
PTOLEMEAN AND COPERNICAN ASTRONOMY[1]

MICHAEL HEIDELBERGER

Since the appearance of Thomas Kuhn's books on the *Copernican Revolution* and the *Structure of Scientific Revolutions*, the displacement of ancient astronomy by Copernican has gained renewed interest among philosophers of science.

For Kuhn the Copernican revolution is something like a "paradigm" of a scientific revolution. Hardly any other episode from the history of science is more frequently used by him to illustrate his major points. But it seems to be the case that the Copernican revolution itself cannot be very adequately accounted for by some of his general observations and conclusions.

For Kuhn the distinction between *context of discovery* and *context text of justification* ceases to make sense or is at best a questionable dichotomy. As a result, the status of the internal and external approach to the history of science changes to a considerable extent. Kuhn does not aim at a systematic and complete separation of these two aspects, but rather considers their amalgamation one of the most important goals of the historiography of science.[2]

As far as I can see, there are at least three alternatives to this point of view: for many historians, the conditions which make internal relations between scientific theories at all possible did not arise prior to the emergence of modern science.[3] For these historians, it is only natural then, that in general one cannot find a purely internal relation between Ptolemean and Copernican astronomy, which could be sufficient to justify the choice of the Copernican theory as rational.

The other points of view are well known: for some, the history of science can ultimately be explained only externally, for others, the history of science is also a rational process and is therefore internally reconstructible. For many, a rational reconstruction of history seems to be a futile and hopeless enterprise, while for others, it is the only one that really makes sense.

Without dwelling more on these different points of view, I would like to pose the question: what are the factors (if any) which could, in retrospect, show an internal superiority of the Copernican theory over the theory of Ptolemy?

With this, I come to my first thesis:

I

Copernicus' theory has two advantages over Ptolemy's: (i) 'distance' becomes a theoretical term for astronomy; (ii) the theory of Copernicus is 'structurally' simpler than Ptolemy's.

(i) The concept of astronomical distance as a first internal factor. In Ptolemy's theory, the distances of the planets are not generally measurable. One can observe a parallax for the sun and the moon, but not for the planets, as Ptolemy states disappointedly.[4] In order to arrive at a realistic picture of the universe, one must resort to qualitative speculations. But these speculations did not produce an unambiguous and satisfying result. Because of reasons both inherent in the then available technical means and in the structure of the theory itself, a truly "theoretical view," so to speak, of the structure of the universe was blocked. (This intrinsic property of Ptolemaic astronomy went well with the christian concept of humility in the middle ages: that of the position of man and his limited intellectual capacity.)

By means of the qualitative transposition of the order of the universe, Copernicus obtained a scientific method, by means of which the planetary distance became accessible in general. But this new method of measuring makes sense only for those who are willing to accept *a priori* the qualitative order of the universe, as it is induced by the theory.

Copernicus himself puts this in very clear and sharp terms. In *De Revolutionibus* he writes: "*Either*, we give up the geocentric model altogether, *or* we will *never* be able to obtain any certain idea about the order of the universe."[5]

It follows that one has to know something about the theory itself, before one is able to apply the term 'astronomical distance' to the planets, i.e. to measure it.[6] In contrast, to measure the longitudes and the latitudes does not presuppose any such knowledge at all. With this specific introduction of the concept of distance, the conditions for the possibility of a theory-founded realistic view of the universe were created. Planetary distance was for the first time empirically accessible, and the justification for the method that makes it possible is founded upon a specific theoretical world view.

(ii) The concept of the 'structural simplicity' as a second internal factor. With the following I do not intend to enter into the discussion on the simplicity of the Copernican theory after the fashion of most popular and other presentations. So let me first say what I do not mean by this term. I do not want to say that, with respect to the theoretical elements, the Copernican system is simpler than the Ptolemaic one. This view can be shown to be a myth.[7] On the contrary, Ptolemy and the Ptolemaic tradition make less use of epicycles than Copernicus in his *De Revolutionibus*.

Also, by 'structural simplicity' I do not mean that a theory is psychologically simpler to grasp or that the realistic picture of the world that normally accompanies the theory is simpler. On the contrary, the structural simplicity of the Copernican theory is to be found, roughly speaking, in the strong deductive interconnections in the basic vocabulary. Copernicus set up an interdependence of the terms longitude, latitude, and distance, so that a greater uniformity of the system was achieved.

Let us suppose that the same singular observational sentences follow from two theories. Then I would call one theory structurally simpler than the other one if the theory allowed us to see a greater number of regularities in these observational sentences than the other theory. For the less simple theory, there are facts that obtain only contingently, whereas for the simpler theory, these facts are necessary and are accounted for by sentences that express regularities.

Since this paper is meant to be limited mainly to history, I will not try to give a formal exposition of 'structural simplicity'. If suffices to know intuitively that structural simplicity has something to do with the extent to which a theory expresses regularities or its ability to systematize (its 'systematic power'). This will become clearer later, when I give some examples from Copernican theory.

Even though I find the term 'simplicity' not quite suitable when referring to the property in question, I will continue to use it as historians do when they deal with this property (which is very seldom the case).

But if I want to demonstrate the greater structural simplicity of the Copernican theory, I have to show that the Ptolemaic and Copernican theories are nearly equivalent with respect to the singular observational sentences that are deducible or explainable by means of the deductive-nomological model. And so I come to my second thesis:

II

A decision for or against the Copernican theory of 1543 could not be made on observational (empirical) grounds.

The theoretical transformation of the Ptolemaic theory by Copernicus does not lead to the Copernican theory gaining any empirical excess content with respect to singular observation sentences. If one looks at Copernicus' computation of longitudes and latitudes, one finds that Copernicus was guided by the techniques of the Ptolemean school. If one disregards secular changes, then the theories differ from each other by at the most 6' in the theory of longitudes, which is a very small amount compared to the contemporary observational exactitude of 10'.

This is similar in the case of the theory of latitudes. And even the relative variations in the distance of the planets are basically the same in both theories. Also, the Ptolemaic ratio of the epicyclic radius to the radius of the deferent has a counterpart in the Copernican theory. But here I will not explain these details at great length.

It is true that a thorough and complete computation of all Copernican values of planetary distances (which Copernicus does not offer) would have led to a discrepancy with the values at which the Ptolemean school arrives by metaphysical assumptions. But no Ptolemean would have seen this as being relevant to his theory. For him, a theory of distance was empirically relevant only with regard to the change of luminosity and diameter of the planets, the sun, and the moon. And, in principle, it would have been possible for a Ptolemean to give a phenomenological account of these variations without being forced to give up his qualitative view of the world. A reformulation of the "theory" of distances, which takes into account the actual variations in brightness and diameter was a *desideratum* of the Ptolemaic research program, at least since the criticism of the Neoplatonic Proclus (ca. 450 A.D.).[8]

It was well known to the direct successors of Copernicus that the (somewhat idealized) theories of Copernicus and Ptolemy were more or less equivalent with respect to their observational consequences. Tycho Brahe says, for example, that, regarding the computation of the actual appearances, he does not have any objections to Copernicus; as to the contrary, what he thinks absurd are the cosmological elements, the "physics" of Copernicus.[9]

Kepler made a similar claim: for him the theories of Ptolemy, Copernicus, and Brahe are in effect equivalent, if you consider their treatment of the visible phenomena.[10] And Galileo also thinks that the treatment of the appearances has found a perfectly satisfactory mathematical solution in the Ptolemaic mode of doing astronomy, on which the Copernican system did not improve.[11]

In order to show that the theory of Copernicus is structurally simpler we have still to illustrate that the Copernican theory encompasses more regularities than the Ptolemaic one, i.e. that the Copernican theory excludes models (in the model theoretic sense) which the Ptolemaic system does not, as a matter of fact.

I can only mention in passing this greater explanatory power of the Copernican theory (not, that 'explanation' is used here in the deductive-nomological sense): The limited elongation of the inner planets can be explained in the Copernican theory, not in the Ptolemaic; one also gets an explanation for the retrograde motions of the planets. (If the orbital period of outer planets is greater than a year the retrogradation must necessarily arise in the Copernican system, whereas in the Ptolemaic system motion without retrogradation is conceivable in this case.) One can also explain why the retrograde motion appears the greater, the closer the planet is to the earth, and why this is true for the outer planets only when they are in opposition and for the inner planets when they are in lower conjunction. In the Copernican system one can explain why the sun and the moon never move in a retrograde way, why exterior planets seem brightest in opposition, etc. All this cannot be explained by the Ptolemaic theory. But most important, in the Copernican system one can account for the peculiar way in which the sun governs the planets in the Ptolemaic system.[12]

But if Copernican theory is superior to Ptolemaic theory only with respect to the two internal factors mentioned, and if particularly the Ptolemaic theory throughout its history differs essentially from the Copernican one neither in the actually calculable values nor in the theoretical means it employs, then one important thesis of Thomas Kuhn must be questioned.

This leads me to my third thesis:

III

There was no crisis in Ptolemaic astronomy.

For Kuhn, the pre-Copernican system entered a crisis before the Copernican theory arose. The main evidence Kuhn offers in favor of this claim is the preface to *De Revolutionibus* which he calls "one of the classic descriptions of a crisis state."[13] In this passage, Copernicus writes that the tradition, like a sculptor, had moulded a theory. But instead of creating a proportionate sculpture, it created a monster by putting together different though wonderfully designed limbs which were mutually disproportionate. Kuhn interprets this metaphor to mean that the complexity of astronomy has increased so much over time, that it eventually became monstrous. To sustain this metaphor: gradually, the figure grew a hunchback, horns, tumors, etc. which are then (not directly by Kuhn but elsewhere) identified with the number of the supposedly accumulated epicycles. But Copernicus says expressly that all parts of the figure, taken by themselves, are perfectly in order: what eventually amounts to a monster is the attempted composition of mutually incompatible components. These obviously are the theories of longitude, of latitude, and of distance, which taken by themselves as devices for calculation satisfy any serious mathematician. But as soon as one tries to put together a uniform universe with these components, i.e. a three-dimensional picture of the universe, they do not fit together.

This is not the description of "a breakdown of the normal puzzle-solving activity" which remains "the core of the crisis."[14] Rather, Copernicus' account is a reflection on the internal coherence of the theory whose parts have not lost their ability to solve the traditional puzzles.

In the same passage, Copernicus mentions that up to his time the mathematicians were unable to determine the length of the year. Here, he is alluding to secular deviations, as for example the precession of the equinoxes, which was already discovered by Hipparchus before Ptolemy's time. According to Ptolemy, the vernal point moves by 36" a year, but in reality it amounts to 50". Since Ptolemy there was no essential change in the theory of precession so that a large though systematic deviation had accumulated in the course of time. This has not very much to do with a crisis state of a theory, but rather with insufficient observations in too short a time.

It is quite a different thing to say that these deviations functioned as a strong psychological motive for Copernicus to try out other ideas. To make a motive like that as the sole criterion of crisis is to illegitimately identify any private discontent of a scientist with his field with the objective state of a theory. Strongly felt discontent among members of a scientific community might be necessary for a crisis, but it is only sufficient when it is justified.

What will Kuhn's argument look like if no crisis preceded the most famous of all scientific revolutions? The absence of crisis is not an irrelevant matter since "crises are a necessary precondition for the emergence of novel theories"[15] and thus, the concept of crisis is essential to the inner consistency of Kuhn's argument. Besides the concept of paradigm it is mainly the concept of crisis which allows Kuhn (perhaps unaware) to oscillate between the internal and external aspects or to amalgamate them. The crisis state of a theory and the crisis-free state of the successor theory can function both as an internal rational justification and as an external explanation for the emergence and acceptance of a new theory. If there are no crises in Kuhn's sense, then no epiphenomenon has vanished but rather an important methodological instrument has become dulled.

If there was no crisis for Ptolemaic astronomy in what other way are we then to describe the emergence of Copernican astronomy?

IV

With the emergence of Copernicus' theory, no paradigm-shift occurs but rather a coalescing of two traditional paradigms.

Before I work out this thesis in detail, let me make a very important distinction. Kuhn's concept of a paradigm combines two components which I think have to be kept separate, especially in the case of the Copernican revolution. On the one hand, "paradigms are constitutive of science," and on the other hand "they are constitutive of nature as well."[16] Thus, a paradigm constitutes both a normal scientific tradition of continuous puzzle-solving and a world-view superimposed on the theory. Both aspects normally run parallel, but it is most important in the case of the Copernican theory to keep them apart. When I say that with the Copernican theory two paradigms merge into each other, by 'paradigms' I mean all the factors that constitute a scientific tradition, rather than a world-view.

Paradigm No. 1: the Ptolemaic tradition, in ancient times called astronomy or mathematical astronomy. Employing the maxim "to save the phenomena" it adopted the task of investigating the accidental aspects of the universe: the size, shape, and all the quantitative aspects of celestial bodies, although for Ptolemy himself the means which were allowed had to be justified qualitatively. The later tradition however increasingly liberalized this restriction and made room for any possible theoretical instrument as a fictional mathematical model, as long as it yielded the correct position of the planets. It is a mere accident if the structure acquired by the theory conforms to nature; this structure can be replaced by the structure of a different theory which supplies the same values. Because of its accidental nature the theory itself was no longer seen as contributing to the knowledge of the true structure of the universe. This question was left to theology and "physics."

Paradigm No. 2: the Aristotelian-Platonic one, called "physics" or physical astronomy. Its task was to lay open the nature of the universe, i.e. to find out all the causes of the heavenly phenomena; "cause" in the wide Aristotelian sense. Thus, physical astronomy deals with the substantial side of nature, and its theory has to agree with nature by necessity. There can only be one single correct theory, (and no one equivalent to it).

The saving of the phenomena was thought of as only a trivial and negligible step, which follows automatically, as soon as one has found the true causes. There even existed a theory which claimed to be successful in this respect: the theory of the concentric spheres of Eudoxus, Kallippus, and Aristotle himself. But since it never achieved the accuracy of the Ptolemaic theory in predicting celestial phenomena because of insufficient mathematical elaboration, it was never really seen as a serious rival to the Ptolemaic theory. Later on, Averroes, al-Bitruji and, shortly before Copernicus, Amico and Fracastoro also tried to construct a homocentric physical theory, but they did not succeed, either.

At the time of Copernicus, this situation had not changed in any essential respect. The "physicists" reproached the "astronomers" for having little or no concern for the true causes of celestial movements. But, they themselves were blamed by the astronomers for not having elaborated their theories to the extent of achieving any degree of exactitude in reproducing the actual celestial movements.

"It was the friction between these two schools," Duhem writes, "that fired the spark that set the genius of Copernicus aflame."[17] Consequently, there were two tasks Copernicus had to achieve: on the one hand he had to show that his system was as effective (if not better) in predicting planetary positions as the Ptolemaic one, in order to satisfy the Ptolemeans. But on the other hand, he had to find the causes, from which all appearances are shown to be necessary consequences, in order to satisfy the Aristotelians and Platonists.

According to Kuhn, a paradigm (disciplinary matrix) consists of at least four elements:[18] (i) symbolic generalizations, (ii) metaphysical or heuristic models, (iii) scientific values, (iv) exemplary solutions. In all four respects, Copernicus shows himself to be a true adherent of both the Ptolemean and the Aristotelian paradigms (in the sense of "paradigm constitutive of science"): He uses the same mathematical means, formulas, and tables as Ptolemy does; if he did not use Aristotelian ones it is because there were not any. He used the same models by applying the principle of uniform circular movement as postulated by both Plato and Ptolemy in an even more comprehensive way than Ptolemy himself. His way of practicing astronomy shows that he is fully satisfied by the degree of observational exactitude which Ptolemy had achieved and saw indispensable scientific value in it. And finally, the example of the *Almagest* was so binding for Copernicus that Kepler could say that Copernicus had set himself the goal of rendering and imitating Ptolemy instead of nature, to which nevertheless he came nearest of all.[19] But Aristotle and his tradition was also an exemplary model for Copernicus, as is seen in his great efforts to interpret his theory in the light of the Aristotelian program and to reinterpret certain proposed Aristotelian solutions in the light of his theory.[20]

If one looks at everything that constitutes the Copernican theory as such, one finds that Copernicus was not a revolutionary but rather a faithful adherent to the tradition. This connection with the tradition was also discernible in his own time and caused even Ptolemeans to adopt the Copernican theory. Without accepting heliocentrism some saw in it an improvement of the Ptolemaic research program and progress made by science. They looked upon the preface of *De Revolutionibus* and its book I, ch. 10, where Copernicus deals among other things with planetary distances and heliocentrism as a worldview, as philosophical blunders which were not to be taken seriously. (Similarly today, prefaces to books in physics are often viewed as speculative.) For them, Copernicus was progressive essentially because he used only circular motion which was uniform with regard to the center and not to the *punctum aequans*, a point slightly off-center, as in Ptolemaic theory.

Because of this, Erasmus Reinhold for example called the Copernican theory the completion and restoration of the tradition.[21] Many astronomers, especially from Wittenberg and the Jesuits, considered the Copernican theory practical and meaningful, but nevertheless refused to accept the Copernican world view. Copernicus proved himself to be a "Copernican" in his preface, yet his theory from 1543 is compatible with two different world-views.

With this, I come to my fifth thesis:

V

The Copernican theory is compatible with two adversary paradigms constitutive of nature.

Let me make some remarks on the concept of a paradigm constitutive of nature and experience. By such a paradigm I mean a set of any factors, material or ideal, which determine the ontology and epistemology of a theory in a certain way. And by an ontology of a theory I mean any opinion which says something about the things the theory furnishes the world with; that is to say, what the values of the variables are supposed to be. In an ontology one will mostly find something like correspondence rules or bridge-principles.

An epistemology of a scientific theory is then an opinion about the conditions that make it possible to gain knowledge about the things which are proposed by the ontology of a theory, whether these conditions are rooted in the perceiving subjects or in the scientific instruments used by them.

If this has not become sufficiently clear, then let me illustrate my definitions by giving some examples that are relevant for the Copernican revolution:

The Ptolemaic theory traditionally employed the doctrine of instrumentalism as its ontology. That is, the theoretical means, e.g. in the theory of longitudes, are not taken to represent real things and orbits in the universe. I.e. the curve, which the "planet" describes on the paper, if one constructs successive longitudes geometrically, is not in accordance with the orbit in reality. What does correspond to reality however is the longitude of a planet at a given time, which can be constructed as an angle of two lines on a piece of paper.

Copernican ontology on the other hand (but not necessarily the Copernican *theory* of 1543) is realistic: *all* aspects, which can be found in the theory's geometrical model on the piece of paper, have to correspond with nature. So if a (two-dimensional) model gives me, e.g. a correct longitude of a planet, it also has to show me the variation in distance.

But the theory of 1543 is also compatible with an instrumentalistic ontology. In this case, the terms 'epicyclic' and 'deferential radius' do not correspond to anything in reality, but are instead considered a mathematical fiction. Thus one can avoid the heliocentric view but still use the Copernican theory.

Two illustrations for an epistemology of a theory might suffice. For Ptolemy, the human capacity for correctly judging the changes of the celestial bodies' luminosity and diameter necessarily fails in astronomical distances. Thus he could defend the *prima facie* anomalies arising in his speculations on the planetary distances. There is a similar example in Copernicus' case: the immense distance of the fixed stars together with the relatively small orbit of the earth causes a parallax that is much too small to be perceived by the human eye.

280

Why then, one may ask, did the realist ontology emerge and super-sede the other paradigm (constitutive of nature) to such an extent that, by now, we connect it, perhaps even analytically, with the Copernican theory; and why did it determine for us the intended applications of the Copernican theory? Historically there were two principal factors; I am not completely certain whether they are internal or external. These factors are: "convention" and "theoretical curiosity."[22] By officially formulating an ontology for the theory of Copernicus and then condemning it, the church bears the main responsibility for the fact that realistic ontology and no other was adopted by convention. Theoretical curiosity, on the other hand, was the prevalent attitude in the Renaissance. It prompted scientists to say: let us interpret theories in a realistic way and see what will happen. This constituted a new trust in the independent capacity of the human mind. But I do not know whether these matters can be justified in a totally rational way. For a pronounced instrumentalist, these steps make no sense, while for a realist they are the best possible ones.

If these five theses are largely correct, we can draw several conclusions from them:

Kuhn's description and conceptual grasp of the Copernican revolution glosses over some factors that philosophers of science are very interested in. In the Copernican revolution, it is not just a matter of changing one paradigm in favour of another one. Although this is true in a sense, it is misleading unless it is specified more exactly. The Copernican revolution involves at least two processes: (i) the process of displacing Ptolemy's theory by the Copernican theory (in the narrow sense) and (ii) the transition from the Copernican theory to Copernicanism, i.e. from instrumentalism to the realistic paradigm constitutive of nature. Both these processes overlap and have varying effects on each other.

Concerning the first process: a "reduction relation,"[23] if it were a successful one, could very well provide a bridge by rationally justifying the transition from the Ptolemean to the Copernican theory. But then, we immediately become aware of the limits of this relation, because it cannot say anything about the second process. The transition from the instrumentalist interpretation of a theory to its realistic one cannot be rationally justified, or, at least, I do not know how such a justification could be achieved by means of a reduction relation. But it is in any case very clear that there is no "empragmatically accessible technique" by which one could operationally introduce planetary distances in the Copernican system without committing oneself beforehand to one specific realist world-view.

Does that mean that scientific progress is an irrational process? I would like to plead that we see in the progress of science not so much a growth of empirical content and accumulation of knowledge (Popper, Lakatos) or a continuous theoretical restructuring of knowledge (Sneed, Stegmüller), but also an increase in the maturity of knowledge. This maturity is caused by feedbacks taking place on a higher methodological level.

With this idea I am of course reintroducing teleological and organic elements, about which I can only speculate here. But, as every child has to learn how to see in perspective, perhaps in the same way our culture had to learn collectively the theoretical, three-dimensional view of celestial space. In this sense, scientific progress also consists in the growth of methodological insight. Thus a scientific revolution would among other things be the transition from one state of maturity to a higher one.

But these final remarks should be taken with a grain of salt.

NOTES

1. This paper is the summary of a part of an unpublished longer version. Preceding the talk, a short introduction to the general features of the Ptolemaic and Copernican system was given. The different treatment of planetary distances was especially stressed. Whereas in the Ptolemaic theory there is no general method of determining the planetary distances other than by metaphysical assumption, in the Copernican theory the dimensions of the planetary orbits can very easily be measured: for the inferior planets by finding the maximum elongation of the planet, for the exterior planets by comparing an opposition of the planet with the nearest case when sun and planet appear to form a rectangle as seen from the earth. For this, see Thomas S. Kuhn, *The Copernican Revolution*, Cambridge, Mass. 1957, p. 173. For details in the Ptolemaic theory cp. the excellent account of Karl Stumpff, *Himmelsmechanik*, Vol. I, Berlin 1959 and for the Copernican theory: Otto Neugebauer, "On the Planetary Theory of Copernicus," *Vistas in Astronomy*, Vol. 10, 1968, pp. 89-103.
2. Thomas S. Kuhn, "The History of Science," in D. L. Sills (ed.), *International Encyclopedia of the Social Sciences*, New York 1968, Vol. 14, p. 76.
3. e.g. Hans Blumenberg, *Die Kopernikanische Wende*, Frankfurt 1965, p. 8ff.
4. *Almagest* IX, 1.
5. "Oportebit igitur vel terram non esse centrum, ad quod ordo syderum orbiumque referatur, aut certe rationem ordinis non esse..." *De Revolutionibus*, I, 10.

6. 'Astronomical distance' thus becomes a T-theoretical term in the sense of Sneed's criterion of theoreticity. For this cp. Joseph D. Sneed, *The Logical Structure of Mathematical Physics*, Dordrecht 1971, p. 33f.

7. See for example Robert Palter, "An Approach to the History of Early Astronomy," *Studies in History and Philosophy of Science* 1, 1970, pp. 93-133.

8. Cp. Willy Hartner, "Mediaeval Views on Cosmic Dimensions," in W. Hartner (ed.), *Oriens-Occidens*, Hildesheim 1968, pp. 319-348.

9. J. L. E. Dreyer, *A History of Astronomy from Thales to Kepler*, 2nd ed. New York 1953, p. 360.

10. Johannes Kepler, "Astronomia Nova," in: Max Caspar (ed.), *Gesammelte Werke*, Vol. III, München 1937, p. 20: "...ut ipsae tres opiniones (quoad astronomiam, seu coelestes apparentias) in effectu ad unquem aequipollant et paria faciant."

11. Galileo Galilei, "Dialogo sopra i due massimi sistemi del mondo," in *Edizione Nazionale* Vol. VII, Firenze 1965, p. 369 (German ed. E. Strauss, Leipzig 1891, p. 356; English ed. S. Drake, Berkeley 1967, p. 341).

12. In the Ptolemaic system the direction in which the (mean) sun is viewed from the earth plays a peculiar role in the movement of the planets, frequently overlooked. This direction in fact is, in the case of the inferior planets, always parallel to the line connecting the *punctum aequans* and the center of the epicycle; in the case of the exterior planets, this direction is parallel to the line connecting the center of the epicycle (the mean planetary position) with the true planetary position.

13. Thomas S. Kuhn, *The Structure of Scientific Revolutions*, 2nd ed. 1970, p. 69.

14. *Ibid.*

15. *Ibid.*, p. 77.

16. *Ibid.*, p. 110.

17. Pierre Duhem, *To Save the Phenomena*, Chicago 1969 (first French ed. 1908), p. 62.

18. Kuhn, *op. cit.*, pp. 182-7.

19. Kepler, *op. cit.*, p. 141.

20. Op. Jürgen Mittelstrass, *Die Rettung der Phänomene*, Berlin 1962, pp. 201ff.

21. Dreyer, *op. cit.*, p. 316.

22. Hans Blumenberg, *Der Prozess de theoretischen Neugierde*, Frankfurt/Main 1973.

23. Cp. Sneed, *op. cit.*, p. 216ff and the article of Dieter Mayr, *Erkenntnis* 10 (1976), p. 275.

THE RECENT REVOLUTION
IN GEOLOGY AND KUHN'S THEORY
OF SCIENTIFIC CHANGE

RACHEL LAUDAN[1]

The 1960s witnessed a striking change in geology. Since at least the seventeenth century, one of the central problems of the subject had been the origin of the major irregularities of the surface of the globe—continents and oceans, mountain chains and ocean islands—irregularities that were not anticipated by most physical theories. Traditionally these features had usually been explained either as residual traces of events occurring during the very early history of the globe, or as the result of vertical movements of the earth's crust, caused, for example, by changes in the heat budget. The last two decades have seen an end to all this. The vast majority of geologists now believe that these irregularities largely result from the lateral movement of thin rigid plates covering the earth, a theory now know as "plate tectonics," but a theory which also has obvious parallels with the hypothesis of continental drift, in which it was postulated that continents can move laterally. The historical relations of these theories have been explored by a number of authors ([4], [9], [10], [12], [13], [19], [20], [23], [24], [29], and [30]). Turning to the history and philosophy of science for an account of scientific change that could encompass this development, geologists almost without exception dubbed it a "Kuhnian revolution." J. Tuzo Wilson [27], the Canadian geophysicist, was perhaps the first to argue for this analysis, and his conclusions were reiterated by three of the first four histories of the subject to appear. In 1973, Ursula Marvin claimed that "the story of continental drift as a geologic concept, with its slow, tentative beginnings and violent controversy, followed by the spectacular band-wagon effect which has swept up the majority of earth scientists, bears out in dramatic fashion a thesis developed by Thomas S. Kuhn" [19], p. 189). For her, the most important feature of Kuhn's analysis was his rejection of the notion that "science progresses in a linear manner by the steady increment of shared knowledge" ([19], p. 189). Allan Cox was equally impressed by the non-linear development of geology, as well as the incommensurability of pre- and post-plate tectonic research, and the heuristic value of plate tectonic theory in directing further investigation. The development of plate tectonics, he concluded, "fits the pattern of Kuhn's scientific revolutions surprisingly well" ([4], p. 5). Arthur Hallam, inturn, announced that, with respect to the earth sciences, "it is quite clear that plate tectonics is the currently held paradigm" ([13], p. 107). Although rather more critical of a Kuhnion analysis than the former authors, he nonetheless concluded that "the earth sciences do indeed appear to have undergone a revolution in the Kuhnian sense," ([13], p. 108) and he urged that "we should not be misled by the fact that, viewed in detail, the picture may appear somewhat blurred at the edges" ([13], p. 108).

The major attack on this interpretation has come from David Kitts, who has argued that by assuming that a Kuhnian revolution has occurred in geology "we may miss something significant about the history of geology and, more importantly, something fundamental about the very nature of geologic knowledge" ([17], p. 115). In Kitts' view, indeed, Kuhnian revolutions *cannot* occur in geology. In order to establish this point he makes the following claims. For the derivation of singular historical statements, which he takes to be the main aim of geology, geologists depend on a body of "fundamental and comprehensive scientific principles" ([17], p. 115). So strong is this dependence, Kitts adduces, that "the laws of physics are not questioned within the context of geologic inference. They are simply presupposed" ([17], p. 117). Kitts' reason for this strong claim is that without such reliance on comprehensive physical theories geologists would either be able to make any historical claims they wished, or alternatively, would be restricted to assuming that the past was exactly like the present ([17], p. 117). Kitts goes on to equate such general physical laws or theories with Kuhnian paradigms, and asserts that "geologists have had no role in the revolutions which have led to the overthrow of comprehensive theoretical paradigms" ([17], p. 119). Not only is this the case, but, Kitts continues, "it is clear that for Kuhn, paradigms exercise their pervasive influence by virtue of their being general knowledge systems. He recognizes different degrees of comprehension, but he does not consider any hypothesis which is concerned wholly with particular events" ([17], p. 119). Kitts concludes that since "the hypothesis of continental drift *is* concerned wholly with particular events" ([17], p. 119), the fact that it has been rapidly and widely accepted does not qualify it as a Kuhnian paradigm. Geologists are wrong in identifying it, or any other geological theory, as revolutionary, since, in Kitts' view, such theories are never general enough to satisfy what he takes to be the Kuhnian criteria for paradigms. Even where a geological theory appears to be of universal form, Kitts suggests that it acquires that generality by virtue of being incorporated into physical theory. Thus, although "there is in plate tectonics a crucial theoretical, and therefore general, general dimension which is not reducible to a description of events" ([17], p. 124), even plate tectonics cannot be regarded as a paradigm, for its "theoretical dimension is not provided by a geologic hypothesis formulated within the last decade but it comes from the familiar and inviolable 'super paradigm'" ([17], p. 124). Thus unlike the geologists and historians mentioned earlier, Kitts is unwilling to allow that geology in the 1960s and 1970s underwent a revolution in any sense related to the Kuhnian use of that term.

It is the purpose of this paper to criticise both the standard account of recent events in geology and also Kitts' attack on that account. I agree with Kitts that recent events in geology constitute a Kuhnian revolution only if that concept is understood in a very weak sense. I shall not spend much time arguing against the standard account, but devote the bulk of the paper to discussing Kitts' position. In brief, I have two chief quarrels with it. First, I believe that he is interpreting Kuhn too rigidly. Kuhn himself is willing to allow a Darwinian revolution in biology, or a Lyellian revolution in geology, neither of which involved an overthrow of fundamental physical and chemical principles. Provided a theory has a general form over and above being a description of specific events, as plate tectonics undoubtedly does, then I see no reason why, provided it satisfies other conditions that Kuhn lays down, it cannot be a paradigm. Second, and more serious, I am uneasy about Kitts' analysis of the nature of geology. This is a bold claim to make, since Kitts has thought about the philosophy of geology longer and more deeply than any other contemporary scholar. But just because this is the case, his ideas need careful consideration.

Kitts, it should be noted, claims that he is giving a purely descriptive account of the practice of geologists and refraining from any normative account of how they *should* behave ([17], p. 117). Yet I believe that it can be argued that even as a descriptive account, Kitts' analysis is too restrictive. Geologists frequently have been, and continue to be, concerned with more than simple historical description, and moreover they are prepared on occasion to challenge physical theory when it seems to them to conflict with the best available geology. As Stephen Brush has shown [3], the geologist

286

Thomas Chamberlin was prepared to develop a whole cosmology, and a rather successful one, in order to rescue his geology from conflict with the previously available cosmologies. True, it is rare for geologists to engage in such criticism of basic physical theory, but then as Kitts points out, many physicists and chemists never do so either ([17], p. 118). Nonetheless, the fact that this questioning is rare does not mean it never occurs. Such an occurrence is impossible in Kitts' view because he believes that the assumption of physical theory is necessary for the reconstruction of geological evidence. However, this is to overlook the fact that the whole of physical theory is not needed for each such reconstruction, and that physical theory itself is often not fully consistent. Thus I believe Kitts is overstating the case when he claims that geology can never experience a Kuhnian revolution because geologists always accept physical theory. In the case of the rejection and later acceptance of continental drift theory, I hope to show that the status of the theory with respect to basic physical principles was not the decisive factor.

In order to demonstrate this, some revision of the standard historical account of the career of drift theory is in order. This standard account suggests that drift was originally rejected because "no one had devised an adequate mechanism to move continents... through a static ocean floor" ([12], p. 163). Furthermore, so the story goes, continental drift (in the form of plate tectonics) was accepted once a suitable mechanism was found. Although the word 'mechanism' is used loosely in this connection, its usual meaning can be understood as physical cause. If the standard account is correct then, and the main reason for the rejection of drift was that it was inconsistent with the physics of the earth, then Kitts' point that geological science is always subservient to physics gains support. However, although I believe that the lack of a mechanism played a role in the rejection of drift, there are two reasons why I think that the standard account places too much stress on it as the primary factor. The first of these reasons is that certain geological theories have in fact been accepted even when there was no acceptable physical mechanism. The second is that drift (or plate tectonics) was accepted without the discovery of a mechanism for moving the continents (or plates). I shall examine these in turn.

Hallam addresses the former point when he points out that "gravity, geomagnetism, and electricity were all fully accepted long before they were adequately explained" ([13], p. 110). Even within the realm of geology "the existence of former ice ages, notably in the Pleistocene, is universally accepted but there is no general agreement about the underlying cause" ([13], p. 110). Hallam has put his finger on an important point here, although he does not go far enough as none of his examples are quite parallel to the case of continental drift in certain important respects. The problem with drift was not simply that there was no *known* mechanism or cause, but that any *conceivable* mechanism would conflict with physical theory. It is one thing to accept an hypothesis in the absence of a suitable cause if there is no competing theory that appears to rule out the very possibility of a cause, quite another if there is such a rival theory. In the case of drift, a rival did exist. Evidence drawn from a wide range of fields, including astronomy, cosmology, and experimental physics, but especially from seismology, suggested that the mantle of the earth, through which the continents were supposed to move on Wegener's theory, was solid. For example, not only were earthquake foci found to a depth of 700 kilometers, but the earth transmitted shear waves to a depth of several thousand kilometers, a phenomenon which could not occur in a liquid ([16]). Even one of the few supporters of drift in the northern hemisphere, Reginald Daly of Harvard University, was convinced that the evidence was overwhelmingly in favor of the solidity of the earth to a considerable depth ([5], ch. 3).

Even given this conflict with physical theories about the interior of the earth, however, it is still possible that drift might have been accepted, had the evidence for it been stronger. After all, as Wegener himself was quick to point out, the theory of isostasy (or vertical adjustments in the earth's crust) was widely accepted, even though such adjustments implied that flow had to occur in the mantle, that on rival physical theory was supposed to be solid. ([26], p. 43-46). The reason for this was that there was very good evidence that isostasy occurred. Both the relative rarity of gravity anomalies, and the undisputed rise of the land around the Baltic following the last Ice Age attested to this fact. Geologists were convinced that isostasy occurred, even if it conflicted with geophysical analysis of the structure of the earth's crust.

The situation was quite different with Wegener's theory. At the time when Wegener proposed his theory of continental drift, there was no geodetic means of testing directly whether or not the continents had moved relative to each other or to the poles. (Indeed, until well after the widespread acceptance of plate tectonics, there were no geodetic measurements that were sufficiently accurate to show the very slow rate of plate movement.) In the absence of such direct evidence, Wegener put forward three lines of indirect evidence in support of his theory of continental drift ([25], [26]). First, he claimed that the similarity of the coastlines of South America and Africa could best be explained by his hypothesis that at one time the two continents had been joined and that they had subsequently split apart. He made the further point that, in his belief, many of the rock formations on the one continent matched those on the other exactly, a claim that, if true, would obviously lend support to drift. Second, he advanced some paleoclimatic evidence. Working from the assumption that different types of climate have always formed approximately parallel bands between the equator and the pole, and that at least some of these climates at present are associated with characteristic rock formations (polar climates and glacial tills, for example), then the geologist might expect to find such deposits at similar latitudes in all periods of earth history. The fact that he does not do so was best explained, Wegener claimed, by the theory that the continents have moved. Third, most paleontologists were agreed that fossil fauna and flora found on continents now separated by hundreds of miles of ocean are very similar. Here, too, Wegener argued that the best explanation is that the continents have drifted apart. Now at first sight this is an impressive list of evidence for continental drift, drawn from a wide number of fields, particularly when expounded in full detail. ([12], p. 160-167 and [8]).

However, it is perhaps not sufficiently appreciated that Wegener's purported evidence was by no means beyond doubt. Take the question of the "fit" of the continents. Was the fit of South America and Africa merely an isolated coincidence or a major problem for geological science? Most geologists simply were not sure [21]. Even if it were significant, how could the continents have moved without crumpling? The additional evidence of matching formations was also questioned since geologists had been too badly burned in the previous century trying to trace Werner's "universal" formations to have much faith in matching formations, particularly non-fossiliferous ones, over long distances. If the evidence from the fit of the continents was dubious, so equally was the evidence from paleoclimates, since many geologists were not at all convinced that Wegener's alleged "tillites" were in fact tillites at all. Even the peculiar distribution of certain species lost much of its force as evidence when paleontologists pointed out that there were other cases of odd species distribution that could not conceivably be explained by continental drift ([19], p. 118) and that in any case, given the relative difficulties of moving continents on the one hand and providing and removing land bridges on the other, they would, quite reasonably, prefer the latter.

To conclude, I believe that *if* the evidence for continental drift had been stronger, then the absence of a mechanism would have counted against it much less than was in fact the case. Indeed, the amazing feature of the early reception of continental drift is that it was taken seriously at all. It is a measure of the desperation of geologists following the breakdown of Suess's synthesis of geological data, based on the contraction hypothesis, that they were willing to consider it ([5], [7], [15]). After all, it was only one of a number of rival theories that were put forward in the first part of this century to explain the origin and development of the surface features of the earth. In one of the few historical accounts to recognise the comparative nature of the evaluation, Greene has concluded that "in 1912 [Wegener's theory] was a legitimate but very tentative deduction from a great body of geological and geophysical evidence assembled in the last quarter of the nineteenth century, one of many different hypotheses created from the same materials. It had no particular claim to predominance" ([11], p. 477-8). This also leads to the conclusion that there was nothing corresponding to Kuhnian "normal" science in the fifty years before the acceptance of plate tectonics. There was no dominant paradigm in which all the geological community was working. There were conflicting theories, none of which had a hold on the majority of scientists. Nor was geology in a pre-paradigm stage, for there had been paradigms previous to this in the history of the subject. Of course, this half century could be the "period of crisis" prior to a revolution. Indeed, in view of the lapse of time Kuhn allows for the Copernican revolution, it is quite possible he would regard geology in the first half of the twentieth century in this light. But if so, and if we have to take such a long view, Kuhn's analysis is of little interest to the historian or philosopher trying to understand the cut and thrust of the scientific enterprise, for such periods, at least in geology, are more the exception than the rule.

It was during the 1950s that the situation changed dramatically. During the course of the decade two new lines of evidence—from paleomagnetism and from oceanography—became available, and although neither had to do with the question of mechanism, they raised again the question of whether or not the continents had moved relative to each other in the past. Despite the claim of certain historians that the "direct" evidence for continental drift, "that is, the data gathered from rocks exposed on our continents" [12], p 161), was just as good in Wegener's day as in the 1950s, in point of fact the first set of new evidence that drift had occurred was gathered from the sedimentary rocks of several continents. Methods had been developed for ascertaining the direction of the earth's magnetic field at various periods in the past by measuring the so-called remanent magnetism of rocks. To everyone's surprise the directions of magnetism at various stages of earth history turned out to be very different from the present orientation of the earth's magnetic field. Various hypotheses to explain this result were proposed and tested, prominent among them the possibility that the earth's magnetic poles had wandered, and even the possibility that the earth's field had not always been di-polar. Eventually, however, by the end of the 1950s a small but influential group of scientists had become convinced that the most plausible explanation for these results was that the continents had moved relative to each other ([2], [22]). They were convinced that drift was now a fact to be explained, and not just another hypotheses. This was *not* because they had discovered a cause of the movement; that remained as mysterious as before.

At almost the same time as the paleomagnetic results were coming in, the science of oceanography was also turning up surprising results. In Wegener's time, geologists had only explored the land surface of the planet, a mere third of the total surface. By the 1960s, by contrast, the results of two decades of exploration of the ocean floor were available to geologists. Various geophysical techniques for measuring heat flow and gravity anomalies, for example, as well as methods of collecting actual samples from the deep sea bed, had been developed and applied. Contrary to most scientists' intuitions, the ocean floors were strikingly dissimilar to the continents. They were marked by a world-wide system of "mid-ocean ridges" (actually enormous mountain chains) with peculiar physical characteristics, particularly a median rift valley marked by high heat flow. There seemed to be tensional features and the suggestion was made in 1960 and 1961 that the sea floors were "spreading" ([6], [14]). In 1963 Vine and Matthews predicted that the unusual patterns of magnetic anomalies that had been observed round the mid-ocean ridges were in fact the record of global magnetic reversals that had occurred while lava was welling up, solidifying and moving apart from the tensional cracks ([4], p. 232-237). Since global magnetic reversals had by this juncture been dated on the continents by radioactive methods, here was a potential test of the theory that the sea floor was moving apart and a measure of the rate at which this was occurring ([4], section 4). After some false starts, in 1965 parallel strips of magnetic anomalies were found and dated on both sides of one mid-ocean ridge system

([4], p. 265-264). By a couple of years later, most scientists were convinced that the sea floor was spreading. This did not automatically add support to continental drift theory. As in the case of the paleomagnetic results, a number of possibilities were considered, including the theory that these ridges were cracks resulting from the overall expansion of the earth. In order for sea floor spreading to be linked to continental drift, a theoretical innovation was required. Since the continents are different mineralogically from the sea floors, they had always been considered separate entities. Now the suggestion was put forward that the mineralogical differences were unimportant compared to the structural unity. Continents and oceans were welded together in rigid "plates" perhaps one hundred kilometers thick. It was postulated that the important entity that moved laterally was neither the continent nor the sea floor, but the plate. These plates were created along one edge at the mid-ocean ridges by the cooling of molten lava, moved slowly apart, accounting for sea floor spreading, and were destroyed at the other edge, either by sinking into earthquake zones or by being piled up into mountains. The theory of "plate tectonics" was ingenious and explained the major tectonic features of the earth very economically. However, it was still sadly lacking in independent evidence until two predictions, based on the theory, were made and shortly thereafter confirmed in a way that geologists found very impressive.

The first, proposed by J. Tuzo Wilson, was that if the earth really were covered by mobile rigid plates of material, there should be three kinds of junctions between the plates ([27]). Not only should there be the mid-ocean ridges and "subduction zones" already known, but there should also be a previously underscribed type of fault, which Wilson named a "transform fault" with a characteristic direction of movement, in the opposite direction to that expected on any other theory. By the late 1960s this prediction had been confirmed The second prediction resulted from the realisation that if the globe really were covered with mobile, rigid plates, then their movement would be rather closely constrained, and describable mathematically. When theoretical plate motions were compared to actual ones, the agreement in many cases was good to three significant figures. With the publication of these results, the acceptance of plate tectonics was essentially complete by the earlier 1970s.

Thus far I have mentioned nothing about the problem of mechanism, and the conflict between lateral movement of continents or plates and physical theory. It has sometimes been suggested that embedding the continents within the plates overcame this problem, since no longer were the continents required to plow through the ocean floor, but rather were carried along in it, like logs in an ice floe ([12], p. 165). But such a change in the theory by no means solved the problem of mechanism. There still remained the questions of how the deep-rooted continents, even embedded in the sea floors, could move through the solid mantle, and what force would be sufficient to propel them. The former question was rendered less urgent by a reinterpretation of seismic data. Analysis of seismic evidence had long indicated that there was a puzzling narrow low-velocity zone some one hundred kilometers below the surface of the earth, but no one had known quite what to make of it. During the 1950s, when drift was being revived, it was suggested that this was a plastic zone, deep enough in the earth that plates, including the roots of the continents, could slip on it. In this way the worst conflict with rival theory was avoided ([1]). However, the latter question of the nature of the force powerful enough to move the plates remained unresolved. As J. Tuzo Wilson concluded in 1976, "One very large question remains unanswered: What is the nature of the forces that move plates about?" ([30], p. 217). Here there is still as much tension with physical theory as ever there was, a conclusion that one of the participants, D. L. McKenzie, has argued for in a recent paper ([20], p. 97). Put another way, a *kinematics* of plate tectonics is essentially complete. Those historians and geologists who say that plate movement was accepted because a mechanism was found are thinking in terms of this kinematics. But the *causes* of plate movement are still a mystery. There is no lack of hypotheses, but no geophysicist would disagree with the claim that they are all tentative and fraught with difficulties. Those historians and geologists who say that plate tectonics was accepted in the absence of a mechanism are thinking of a *dynamics*.

Thus, in view of recent development in plate tectonics as well as the example of Chamberlin cited earlier, I believe that it can be shown that descriptively Kitts' account of geology, however accurate when applied to the day-to-day activities of the majority of working geologists, is inadequate as a general rule. Although Kitts' specifically disavows any intention of going further and making a normative claim, any attempt to extend his analysis and claim, as Duhem did earlier, that sciences other than physics must *always* take physical theory for granted, would be an unjustifiable prescription. But even in the more modest descriptive form, I find Kitts' reasons for his attack on a Kuhnian interpretation of geology untenable.

This leaves the issue of whether the more flexible interpretation of Kuhn espoused by geologists and historians is adequate. As I have already remarked, it seems to be too coarse-grained to do justice to the historical details. Furthermore, certain definitive features of Kuhn's account are lacking; there is, for example, no incommensurability between the pre- and post-tectonic geological theories; neither was plate tectonics proposed and advocated by a younger generation of geologists. Its proponents came from all stages of the career spectrum, including those who had earlier decisively rejected drift. If all Kuhn had meant by a revolution was a period of rapid theory change, then it would be appropriate to invoke his work. However, Kuhn surely had a great deal more in mind when he described scientific revolutions, almost none of which is exemplified in the construction and acceptance of plate tectonic theory.

As Frankel has argued in an interesting paper, Lakatos' methodology of scientific research programmes is perhaps more helpful in trying to understand the details of the changes ([9], [10]). Among the many new discoveries in geology in the 1960s, some, such as transform faults and the magnetic anomaly patterns around the mid-ocean ridges, were the result of testing the predictions made by the new theory. That is to say, the theory predicted novel facts in the full early Lakatos sense of being both unexpected on the basis of previous knowledge and temporally novel. These facts were clearly important in the acceptance of plate tectonics, and we do not even need to consider Lakatos' later (and weaker) senses of novelty in order to make this analysis. But it seems to me there is no reason to jump from this point to a full-blooded acceptance of Lakatos' analysis. In order for Lakatos' methodology of scientific research programmes to apply to this case, the predictions have to result from a series of auxiliary hypotheses added to the unchanging hard core of a research programme. But in this case it is by no means clear that there was a hard core. At *most* the hard core amounted to the statement that lateral movement was possible. But every other aspect, including the entities that were postulated (continents, sea floors, and plates) and the kinds of movement, changed drastically. If hard cores are no more specific than this, one wonders what force they have.

In conclusion, there seems to me no reason for terming the theory change in geology in the 1970s a Kuhnian revolution. To do so is to take any precision there might be out of this concept. Furthermore, there is no need to adopt Kitts' analysis of the nature of geology in order to reject the idea that the subject has undergone a

Kuhnian revolution. It now remains to be seen whether any of the other accounts of theory change developed in the last few years offer a better understanding of the introduction of plate tectonic theory in modern geology.

NOTES

1. I am indebted to David Hull for first raising with me the question of why drift was accepted in the continued absence of a mechanism. Richard Burian, Henry Frankel, Lorenz Krüger, Larry Laudan, Walter Pilant and Victor Schmidt all made helpful comments on an earlier draft of this paper.

REFERENCES

[1]   Anderson, D.L. "The plastic layer of the earth's mantle," *Scientific American* 207 (1962): 52-59. (As reprinted in [28]. Pages 28-35).

[2]   Blackett, P.M.S., Bullard, Edward, and Runcorn, S.K. (eds). *A Symposium on Continental Drift*. London: The Royal Society, 1965.

[3]   Brush, S. "A geologist among astronomers: the rise and fall of the Chamberlin-Moulton controversy," *Journal for the History of Astronomy* 9(1978): 1-41, 77-104.

[4]   Cox, A. (ed.). *Plate Tectonics and Geomagnetic Reversals*. San Francisco: Freeman, 1973.

[5]   Daly, R.A. *Our Mobile Earth*. New York and London: Scribner, 1926.

[6]   Dietz, R.S. "Continent and ocean basin evolution by spreading of the sea floor," *Nature* 190(1961): 854-857.

[7]   Du Toit, A.L. *Our Wandering Continents*. Edinburgh: Oliver and Boyd, 1937.

[8]   Frankel, H. "Alfred Wegener and the specialists," *Centaurus* 20(1976): 305-324.

[9]   _____. "The career of continental drift theory: an application of Imre Lakatos' analysis of scientific growth to the rise of drift theory," *Studies in History and Philosophy of Science* 10 (1979), 21-66.

[10] _____. "The reception and acceptance of continental drift theory as a rational episode in the history of science," *The Reception of Unconventional Science*. Edited by S.H. Mauskopf. Washington: AAAS.

[11] Greene, M.T. *Major developments in Geotectonic Theory between 1800 and 1912*. Unpublished Ph.D. Dissertation, University of Washington, 1978.

[12] Gould, S.J. "The validation of continental drift," *Ever Since Darwin: Reflections in Natural History*. New York: Norton, 1977.

[13] Hallam, A. *A Revolution in the Earth Sciences: From Continental Drift to Plate Tectonics*. Oxford: Clarendon Press, 1973.

[14] Hess, H.H. "History of ocean basins." *Petrologic Studies: A Volume to Honor A.J. Buddington*. New York: Geological Society of America, 1962: 599-620. (As reprinted in [4]. Pages 23-38.)

[15] Holmes, A. *Principles of Physical Geology*. London and Edinburgh: Nelson, 1945.

[16] Jeffreys, H. *The Earth: Its Origin, History, and Physical Constitution*. Cambridge: Cambridge University Press, 1st edition, 1924; 2nd edition, 1929; 3rd edition, 1952; 4th edition, 1959; 5th edition, 1970.

[17] Kitts, D. B. "Continental drift and scientific revolution." *Am. Ass. Petroleum Geol. Bull.* 58(1974): 2490-2496. (As reprinted in Kitts, D. B. *The Structure of Geology*. Dallas: Southern Methodist University Press, 1977, Pages 115-127.)

[18] Kuhn, T. *The Structure of Scientific Revolutions*. Chicago: University of Chicago Press, 1962.

[19] Marvin, U. B. *Continental Drift: The Evolution of a Concept*. Washington, D.C.: Smithsonian Institution Press, 1973.

[20] McKenzie, D. P. "Plate tectonics and its relationship to the evolution of ideas in the geological sciences." *Daedalus* 106(1977): 97-124.

[21] Pinkham, G. "Some doubts about scientific data." *Philosophy of Science* 42(1975): 260-269.

[22] Runcorn, S. K. (ed.) *Continental Drift*. New York and London: Academic Press, 1962.

[23] Takeuchi, H., Uyeda, S., and Kanamori, H. *Debate about the Earth: Approach to Geophysics through Analysis of Continental Drift*. San Francisco: Freeman, 1967.

[24] Uyeda, S. *The New View of the Earth: Moving Continents and Moving Oceans*. San Francisco: Freeman, 1978.

[25] Wegener, A. *Die Entstehung der Continente und Ozeane*. Braunschweig: Friedrich Vieweg und Sohns, 1915.

[26] _____. *The Origin of Continents and Oceans*. Trans. John Biram from the fourth (1924) German edition. New York: Dover, 1966.

[27] Wilson, J. T. "A new class of faults and their bearing on continental drift." *Nature* 207(1965): 343-347. (As reprinted in [4]. Pages 48-56.)

[28] _____. "Static or mobile earth—the current scientific revolution." *Am. Philos. Soc. Proc.* 112(1968): 309-320.

[29] Wilson, J. T. (ed.) *Continents Adrift*. San Francisco: Freeman, 1970.

[30] _____. (ed.) *Continents Adrift and Continents Aground*. San Francisco: Freeman, 1976.

THE KUHNIAN PARADIGM AND
THE DARWINIAN REVOLUTION
IN NATURAL HISTORY

JOHN C. GREENE

The publication of Thomas Kuhn's *The Structure of Scientific Revolutions* in 1962 was an important milestone in the development of the historiography of science. It was the first attempt to construct a generalized picture of the process by which a science is born and undergoes change and development. The main stages of development envisaged by Kuhn's model may be summarized as follows:

1. A pre-paradigm stage in which the natural phenomena that later form the subject matter of a mature science are studied and explained from widely differing points of view.

2. The emergence of a paradigm, embodied in the published works of one or more great scientists, defining and exemplifying the concepts and methods of research appropriate to the study of a certain class of natural phenomena, and serving as an inspiration to further research by its promise of success in explaining those phenomena.

3. A period of normal science conducted within a conceptual and methodological framework derived from the paradigmatic achievement, involving actualization of the promise of success, further articulation of the paradigm, exploration of the possibilities within the paradigm, use of existing theory to predict facts, solving of scientific puzzles, development of new applications of theory, and the like.

4. A crisis stage of varying duration precipitated by the discovery of natural phenomena that "violate the paradigm-induced expectations that govern normal science" and marked by the invention of new theories designed to take account of the anomalous facts.

5. A relatively abrupt transition to a new paradigm brought about by the achievements of a scientific genius who defines and exemplifies a new conceptual and methodological framework incommensurable with the old.

6. Continuation of normal science within the new paradigm.

Professor Kuhn's examples of the formation and transformation of paradigms are drawn entirely from the history of the physical sciences, but he gives us no reason to believe that his analysis is not applicable to the sciences generally. It may be worthwhile, therefore, to examine the developments leading up to the Darwinian revolution in natural history to see to what extent they fit the pattern of historical development described in Kuhn's book.

Perhaps the best way to begin the investigation is to ask: When did natural history first acquire a paradigm? When did it arrive at a state characterized by "research firmly based upon one or more past scientific achievements that some particular scientific community acknowledged for a time as supplying the foundation for its further practice"; achievements "sufficiently unprecedented to attract an enduring group of adherents away from competing modes of scientific activity," yet "sufficiently open-ended to leave all sorts of problems for the redefined group of practitioners to resolve?"

This is not an easy question to answer. On the whole, however, it seems that such a condition cannot be said to have prevailed in natural history until the emergence of systematic natural history in the late seventeenth century, its embodiment in the publications of John Ray and Joseph Pitton de Tournefort, and its apotheosis in the works of Carl Linnaeus.

Aristotle and Theophrastus had laid the foundations of scientific zoology and botany two thousand years earlier, but their achievements cannot be said to have given rise to a continuing tradition of research based on their precept and example. The herbalists cannot be said to have been continuing the Theophrastian tradition, nor can Pliny, Albertus Magnus, Gesner, and Aldrovandi be said to have been the continuators of Aristotle in the same sense that Brisson, Jussieu, Candolle, Cuvier, Lamarck, Hooker, and Agassiz were continuators of the tradition established by Tournefort, Ray, and Linnaeus. Doubtless the Aristotelian achievement was profounder, broader, and in some ways more fecund than that of the founders of systematic natural history, but it did not, like theirs, give rise to and dominate an enduring tradition of scientific research of the kind Kuhn has in mind when he speaks of normal science.

It may be objected, however, that systematic natural history as practiced by Ray, Tournefort, and Linnaeus, was not a science in Kuhn's terms because it did not explain anything, but only named, classified, and described natural objects. This objection raises the difficult problem whether science can be defined in absolute terms; that is, in such a way that the definition is valid for all sciences in all periods of history.

Kuhn himself seems to favor a loose, relativistic concept of science

298

that would allow for the fact that every great scientific revolution involves some redefinition of the nature and aim of science. He tells us that no man is a scientist unless he is "concerned to understand the world and to extend the precision and scope with which it has been ordered." On the other hand, he stresses the importance of respecting "the historical integrity of that [older] science in its own time." With respect to the acceptance and rejection of paradigms he asserts that "there is no standard higher than the assent of the relevant community," and he rejects flatly the view, which he attributes to Charles Gillispie, that "the history of science records a continuing increase in the maturity and refinement of man's conception of the nature of science."

It would seem, therefore, that whatever the ultimate truth about the nature of science may be, no objection to the scientific status of systematic natural history can be drawn from Kuhn's book. Systematic natural historians were concerned to understand the world and to extend the precision and scope with which it was ordered. They considered themselves scientists and were so considered by their contemporaries, including the physical scientists. True, they did not consider it their business as natural historians to explain the origin of species, but neither did Newton consider it his business as a natural philosopher to explain the origin of the solar system.

Like Newton, Ray and Linnaeus took for granted a static concept of nature that regarded all the structures of nature as created and wisely designed by an omnipotent God in the beginning. This assumption of the permanence and wise design of specific forms and of the basic structures of nature generally was an essential feature of the paradigm of systematic natural history, integrally related to the belief that the aim of natural history was to name, classify, and describe.

By every criterion laid down by Kuhn there was a paradigm of systematic natural history. Emerging from the scientific achievements of Ray, Tournefort, and Linnaeus, it involved commitments on all the levels—cosmological, epistemological, methodological, etc.— mentioned by Kuhn. Embodied in manuals and popularizations, articulated with increasing precision, communicated by precept and example, celebrated in prose and verse, it dominated the field of natural history for nearly two hundred years and helped to prepare the way for a far different, far more dynamic kind of natural history. To this extent, then, we can say that Kuhn's model of scientific development seems to fit fairly well with what is known concerning the emergence of systematic natural history as a science of nature.

Having established, at least to our own satisfaction, that natural history first acquired a paradigm in the Kuhnian sense through the work of Ray, Tournefort, and Linnaeus, we next inquire when this paradigm may be said to have been supplanted by a different one. Here it seems generally agreed that the publication of Charles Darwin's *Origin of Species* was the decisive event in the transition from a static, taxonomy-oriented natural history to a dynamic and causal evolutionary biology. Whatever the exact nature and causes of the Darwinian revolution, there can be little doubt that Darwin's work inaugurated a new era in the study of organic nature. Before discussing this revolution further, however, it will be well to inquire into its genesis in order to discover whether the development of natural history from Linnaeus to Darwin followed the pattern of normal science, anomaly, crisis, and paradigm invention described by Kuhn.

At the outset of this inquiry we are confronted with a phenomenon for which Kuhn's model makes no provision, namely, the appearance of a counter-paradigm coeval, or nearly so, with the establishment of the static paradigm of natural history.

In the same mid-eighteenth-century years when Linnaeus was rearing the edifice of systematic natural history on foundations laid by Ray and Tournefort, the Count de Buffon was publishing his splendid *Histoire Naturelle, Générale et Particulière*, based on a profoundly different concept of natural history from that which inspired Linnaeus and his forerunners. In Linnaeus' view, the function of the natural historian was to name, classify, and describe the productions of the earth and, above all, to search for a natural method of classification. In Buffon's opinion, classifications were arbitrary human devices that played a useful but subordinate role in the main business of natural history, which was to explain the observed uniformities in nature's productions as necessary results of the operations of the hidden system of laws, elements, and forces constituting primary, active, and causative nature. Where Linnaeus saw a world of plants and animals neatly ordered and perfectly adapted to their surroundings by the wise design of an omnipotent Creator, Buffon saw a confused array of living forms, some better adapted to their environment than others, all subject to modification through changes in climate, diet, and the general circumstances of life, all threatened in one degree or another by the activities of man and by the gradual cooling of the earth that had spawned these beings by its own powers. While Linnaeus described and catalogued species, genera, orders, and classes, searching for the natural method of classification (presumably one corresponding to a pattern in the mind of the Creator),

300

Buffon devoted his energies to studying the processes of generation, inheritance, and variation by which various kinds of animals had been produced and modified.

Like Darwin a century later, Buffon investigated the history of domesticated plants and animals and discovered the importance of artificial selection, both conscious and unconscious, in producing domestic races. He conducted experiments in animal hybridization. He compared the quadrupeds of the Old World with those of the New, and sought to understand their similarities and differences as effects of descent with modification. He collected and compared fossils from Europe, Asia, and America and attempted to envisage the epochs of earth history in the light of these discoveries. He canvassed the literature concerning human races, man-like apes, wild children, pigmies, and giants, and strove to portray the history of man as a part of the wider history of nature. Finally, like Darwin, he invented a theory of pangenesis to explain the apparent facts of heredity, growth, nutrition, and modification through environmental change.

In all of this there was much that was speculative, much that was tentative and incomplete. But the challenge to Linnaean precept and practice in natural history was clear and unmistakable. Buffon had promulgated and in a great degree exemplified a new kind of natural history—dynamic, causal, non-teleological, time-oriented, uniformitarian in principle if not always in practice, concerned with discovering the laws and mechanisms of organic change, aimed ultimately at control of nature through an understanding of her modes of operation. The difference in outlook between the new natural history and the old is apparent in the two following quotations:

Linnaeus: The study of natural history, simple, beautiful, and instructive, consists in the collection, arrangement, and exhibition of the various production of the earth.

Buffon: In general, kindred of species is one of those mysteries of Nature, which man can never unravel, without a long continued and difficult series of experiments. . . . Is the ass more allied to the horse than the zebra? Does the wolf approach nearer to the dog than the fox or jackal? At what distance from man shall we place the large apes, who resemble him so perfectly in conformation of body? Are all the species of animals the same now that they were originally? . . . Have not the feeble species been destroyed by the stronger, or by the tyranny of man. . . . Does not a race, like a mixed species, proceed from an

301

anomalous individual which forms the original stock? How many questions does this subject admit of; and how few of them are we in a condition to solve? How many facts must be discovered before we can even form probable conjectures?[1]

It appears, then, that natural history acquired *two* paradigms in rapid succession in the mid-eighteenth century, the Linnaean and the Buffonian, and that these paradigms were diametrically opposed in spirit, presuppositions, and concept of scientific method. The first, blending Aristotelian logic and teleology with a static form of the Christian doctrine of creation, identified natural history with taxonomy. The second, deriving from the Cartesian vision of nature as a self-contained system of matter in motion, sought to gain insight into this hidden system of nature by observing uniformities in the effects it produced and constructing models capable of explaining the observed effects as necessary consequences of the operations of the system.

The Buffonian paradigm was *not* a response to anomalies and contradictions within the Linnaean paradigm. Instead, it was a conscious attempt to introduce into natural history concepts derived from natural philosophy, from the seventeenth-century revolution in physics and cosmology. Buffon had had excellent training in mathematical physics and had played a significant role in the introduction of Newtonian ideas on the Continent. In his theory of generation he made an explicit analogy between his own organic molecules and the atoms of Newton, between his own internal molds and the force of gravitation.

But, despite these Newtonian analogies, Buffon was more Cartesian than Newtonian in his approach to nature. For him the uniformities observable in the motions of the planets were not, as Newton supposed, evidences of the Creator's wise design. Instead, they were a challenge to the natural philosopher to imagine a previous state of the system of matter in motion from which the solar system might have been formed by the operation of the Newtonian laws of motion. Likewise, the uniformities which comparative anatomy discerned in the organization of animals were not to be interpreted as evidences of design or manifestations of some transcendental idea, but rather as occasions for constructing a theory of generation that would display these uniformities as necessary products of the motions of organic molecules. Descartes and Leibniz, not Newton, were the sources of Buffon's paradigm of natural history.

How, then, are we to interpret the development of natural history from the death of Linnaeus (1778) and Buffon (1788) to the publication of Darwin's *Origin of Species?* Did the Linnaean paradigm predominate, develop internal contradictions and crises, and then give way to a new paradigm that had no history save the history of its development in the mind of Charles Darwin? Or did the Buffonian paradigm develop alongside the Linnaean paradigm, gradually claiming more converts until it found a decisive champion in Darwin? Or was there some interaction between the two paradigms, a thesis-antithesis relationship that eventually produced a Darwinian synthesis? Unfortunately, we know too little about the development of natural history in the nineteenth century to generalize with confidence on this subject, but it may help to consider various hypotheses in the light of what we do know.

When we examine the development of natural history in the period 1788-1859, we discover striking differences in theoretical approach to the data of natural history on both the individual and the national level. Kuhn gives us very little guidance in this kind of situation. In *The Structure of Scientific Revolutions* he treats the evolution of scientific thought and technique as if it were impervious to the influence of national cultural traditions. In another work, however, he argues that *Naturphilosophie* played a significant role in the genesis of the principle of the conservation of energy, and *Naturphilosophie* was a peculiarly German phenomenon.[2]

As will be seen, *Naturphilosophie* gave rise to something approaching a counter-paradigm in natural history in the early nineteenth century. Theories of natural selection seem to have been a purely British phenomenon in the same period. Apparently what is "normal" for the scientists of one country may be exotic from the point of view of another cultural tradition, and the cross-fertilization of ideas generated in different national contexts may play an important role in the development of scientific theory. For these reasons, as well as for the sake of convenience, we shall proceed country by country in our consideration of nineteenth-century developments in natural history.

We begin with France and the Museum of Natural History, the largest, best subsidized, best organized, best equipped establishment for the study of natural history in the world. Here, if anywhere, we should learn how a mature science develops. If we confine our attention to certain eminent figures at the Museum, notably A. L. de Jussieu and Georges Cuvier, we can make the Kuhnian model work without undue difficulty.

Building on the earlier work of Tournefort, Ray, Linnaeus, and his uncle Bernard de Jussieu, A. L. de Jussieu devised a system of botanical classification, the "natural system," that gradually gained acceptance in France, Switzerland, the Germanies, England, and America as the nineteenth century progressed. In zoology Cuvier revolutionized taxonomy by basing it squarely on comparative anatomy, Aristotelian functionalism, and Jussieu's principle of the subordination of characters. But this revolution, far from overthrowing the static paradigm of natural history, served only to strengthen and further articulate the taxonomic, teleological approach to natural history. Cuvier was proclaimed the Aristotle of the nineteenth century; his influence radiated throughout Western science.

At the same time, Cuvier dealt successfully with a major anomaly that emerged from his own researches, namely, the apparent fact that many species had become extinct. It is hard for us today to realize how anomalous this fact was for the naturalists of the eighteenth and early nineteenth centuries. In the static paradigm of natural history species had been defined as part of the stable framework of creation—"the Works created by God at first, and by him conserved to this Day in the same State and Condition in which they were first made."[3] It was inconceivable, therefore, that a species could become extinct. "For if one link in nature's chain might be lost," wrote Jefferson, "another and another might be lost, till this whole system of things should vanish piecemeal. . . ."[4]

Naturalists were extremely reluctant to envisage the possibility that species could perish, but by Cuvier's time the evidence to that effect had become overwhelming. Cuvier's work on the organic remains of the Paris basin removed the last vestige of doubt. The static paradigm of natural history was now confronted with a major anomaly demanding explanation.

It is a tribute to Cuvier's genius that he achieved a resolution of the crisis precipitated by his own researches. By extending the method and principles of comparative anatomy to the study of organic remains he simultaneously demonstrated the differences between living and fossil species and brought the latter within the domain of systematic natural history. At the same time, by adopting the geological catastrophism of Jean Deluc, he preserved the main features of the static paradigm. Species might become extinct as a result of dramatic geological upheavals of unknown origin, but in the intervals between these upheavals permanence and wise design reigned supreme, providing a stable framework for retrospective taxonomy.

By means of the doctrine of successive creations, which emerged from the researches of Cuvier, Parkinson, Buckland, and others, the static paradigm was given a new lease on life. This method of saving a paradigm by a compromise solution deserves fuller attention from Kuhn. Tycho Brahe's theory of the heavens is an earlier example of the same phenomenon.

On Kuhnian principles we should presumably look to further developments within the redefined static paradigm for the anomalies and crises that gave rise to Darwin's counter-paradigm. But the subsequent development of the "natural system" in botany and of Cuvierian ideas in zoology and paleontology failed to produce a crisis in systematic natural history. George Bentham's account of the development of botany in the first six decades of the nineteenth century is a tale of the progressive triumph of the "natural system," undisturbed by more than fleeting misgivings about the theoretical foundations of the system.[5] In zoology the chief successors of Cuvier were Owen and Agassiz, and, although both showed a tendency toward contamination by *Naturphilosophie*, neither ever doubted the essential soundness of the basic tenets of the static paradigm of natural history.

During the same half century, however, evolutionary concepts were slowly gathering momentum. From what source did they spring if not from difficulties encountered within the Linnaean-Cuvierian paradigm of *nommer, classer et décrire*? Strange to say (and this is a fact difficult to fit into the Kuhnian model), the chief source of evolutionary ideas in France during the period was the tradition of interpreting nature as a law-bound system of matter in motion, of which Buffon had been the chief exponent in the eighteenth century.

Although Cuvier established the static paradigm as the main tradition at the Museum of Natural History, the ghost of Buffon was never completely exorcised from the institution he had raised to greatness. In 1800, immediately after the death of the venerable Daubenton (to whom Buffon's ideas were anathema), Lacépède and Lamarck both published evolutionary speculations similar in outlook to those of their mentor Buffon. Twenty-five years later Étienne Geoffroy St. Hilaire, having already fallen afoul of Cuvier by his advocacy of transcendental anatomy, turned to evolutionary speculations of a distinctly Buffonian character. Indeed, one of his last publications contained an appreciation of Buffon.[6]

Concerning Lacépède's evolutionism little need be said, since Lacépède was soon drawn away from natural history into the Napoleonic administration, where, unlike Cuvier, he found little time for scientific research.[7]

305

Lamarck, on the contrary, was a major figure in the development of scientific natural history. Trained by Bernard de Jussieu, befriended by Buffon (whose son he tutored), Lamarck made a sufficient reputation as a botanist to be appointed to the chair of invertebrate zoology at the Museum of Natural History. There, less than ten years after his appointment, he sketched the outlines of a general "physics of the earth," embracing "all the primary considerations of the earth's atmosphere, of the characteristics and continual changes of the earth's external crust, and finally of the origin and development of living organisms." The first part of this science he called Meteorology, the second Hydrogeology, and the third Biology. Biology, he explained, was not to concern itself primarily with taxonomy, but rather with discovering the causes, laws, and direction of organic change.

How are we to regard Lamarck's effort to redefine the basic concepts and goals of natural history? From a Kuhnian point of view this was certainly an attempt at a scientific revolution affecting every level of natural history from the concept of a species to the definition of the ultimate goals of the naturalist. It had all the characteristics of a scientific revolution except success.

Unfortunately, Kuhn's analysis lays down no guidelines for dealing with unsuccessful revolutions in science. We cannot deny that Lamarck's ideas were revolutionary. In broad outline—geological uniformitarianism with its vast time scheme, descent with modification by natural causes, progressive development up to and including man, the search for the laws and causes of organic change—they were similar to the ideas Darwin was to champion half a century later. But the proposed mechanism of organic change was unconvincing, and the circumstantial evidence supporting the theory was scanty and sporadic.

Yet one feels entitled to ask why this revolution should have been attempted at this time. Was there an anomaly-generated crisis in natural history in the late eighteenth century that gave rise to Lamarck's counter-paradigm and the less fully articulated counter-paradigms of Erasmus Darwin, Lacépède, and others? It is hard to believe that any such crisis existed at that time. Evidence indicating widespread extinction of species did not become available until *after* Lamarck had arrived at the grand outlines of his theory, and, in any case, Lamarck did not believe that species became extinct. (So-called extinct species were for him simply the ancestors of living forms.) Likewise it seems unlikely that some anomaly or crisis in botanical or zoological taxonomy drove Lamarck to an evolutionary position, although Charles Lyell was later to ascribe Lamarck's evolutionism to the difficulties he encountered in distinguishing species from varieties.

On the whole, it seems more likely that Lamarck became convinced of the mutability of organic forms from his geological researches, and that he guessed the direction of organic change partly from the old idea of the scale of nature and partly from the researches of Jussieu and Cuvier on the anatomy of plants and animals.

Like Buffon, Lamarck started from the idea that nature was a law-bound system of matter in motion. But, whereas Buffon attributed the main features of the earth's surface to the action of tidal currents operating on the plastic surface of a cooling globe, Lamarck invoked the action of running water and the progressive displacement of ocean basins by the action of waves. As a result, he adopted a time scheme of millions of years for earth history in place of the tens of thousands envisaged by Buffon. Nature, he declared, had plenty of time and circumstances at her disposal, and everything conspired to prove that all of her works, even the largest and most imposing, were subject to slow change.

Thus, Lamarck drew from a thoroughgoing geological uniformitarianism the inevitable conclusion that organic forms were mutable. In the static paradigm of natural history inorganic, organic, and human history were assumed to be synchronous. The basic structures of inorganic nature were thought to have been perfectly contrived by the Creator to subserve the needs of the higher levels of existence, animate and rational. But if Lamarck and Hutton were right, if the inorganic environment had been undergoing constant slow change for millions and millions of years as a result of geological processes governed by the general laws of physics and chemistry, with no vestige of a beginning, no prospect of an end, then the organisms inhabiting the globe must have changed too, or they would have suffered extinction.

Thus, the first serious crisis in the static paradigm of natural history arose, not within the system of naming, classifying, and describing which constituted the heart and soul of the paradigm, but rather from a postulate affecting the wider framework of assumptions concerning the stability of the visible structures of nature and their hierarchical ordering with respect to each other. Being geologists rather than naturalists, Hutton and Playfair did not develop the implications of geological uniformitarianism for systematic natural history. But Lamarck could not escape them. Either he must accept the wholesale extinction of species as a logical consequence of his geological ideas, or he must conceive the organisms inhabiting the earth's surface as being endowed with a natural capacity to undergo the changes required for survival amid changing circumstances and seek to discover the means by which these changes had been effected.

Of these two alternatives Lamarck chose the latter, invoking use and disuse as the chief agencies of organic change. His next task was to explore the implications of his revolutionary hypothesis for taxonomy and the idea of a natural method of classification. Here Lamarck seems to have taken his clue from the old idea of the scale of nature. In any case, he devoted his energies chiefly to working out a classification that would reflect the path nature had followed in giving birth to progressively more complicated living forms.

It appears, then, that Lamarck's counter-paradigm sprang more from a predisposition toward a uniformitarian view of nature's operations than from a sense of difficulties to be resolved in the structure of systematic natural history. This is not to say that Lamarck did not find the evolutionary postulate useful in taxonomy, but only that taxonomic problems were probably not the main source of his belief in the mutability of species.[8]

However that may be, the question remains as to what role, if any, Lamarck's theory played in the eventual emergence of the Darwinian counter-paradigm. It is fashionable nowadays to deny Lamarck any status as a precursor of Darwin, but we had best postpone this question of the influence of Lamarck's *révolution manqué* on Darwin's *révolution véritable* until we deal with developments in Britain. Suffice it to say for the moment that Lamarck's ideas haunted natural history during the first half of the nineteenth century much as the spectre of communism haunted social theory in the second half. Darwin himself once referred to Lamarck as "the Hutton of geology," obviously intending to write "the Hutton of biology." That was a high compliment and a shrewd characterization. In extending the uniformitarian concept from geology to biology Lamarck foreshadowed the doom of the static paradigm of natural history.

Before turning to developments in Britain that proved decisive for the overthrow of the static paradigm, we must consider briefly another attempt at revolutionizing the conceptual framework of natural history, namely, the attempt associated with the rise of German *Naturphilosophie*. Although Goethe, Oken, Carus, and their followers did not break with the main tradition of systematic natural history as sharply as Lamarck did, their deviation from some of its basic tenets approached the dimensions of a genuine counter-paradigm and gave rise to a kind of evolutionism.

Naturphilosophie diverged from the Linnaean-Cuvierian tradition in natural history in several important respects.

1. It rejected the teleological functionalism of the dominant tradition in favor of a science of pure form, in which form was conceived as dictating function, not function form. The Cuvierian techniques in comparative anatomy were retained, but they were employed for a new purpose: the discovery of a uniform plan of organization pervading the organic world. Instead of the correlation of parts and their adaptation to each other and to the conditions of existence, the watchwords of transcendental anatomy were unity of plan and the correspondence of parts. Classification was still important, but it was subordinated to the search for archetypes.

2. Emphasis on development, on nature begetting, supplanted the traditional preoccupation with the description and classification of begotten forms. On the whole, the idea of development was restricted to embryological development, but embryological study led on to the idea of parallelisms between the levels of organization traversed in embryological development and the levels of organization revealed by comparative anatomy and (eventually) by the fossil record. By some writers these parallelisms were given an evolutionary interpretation.

3. Creationism was muted or abandoned outright in favor of pantheistic ideas of creative nature, spontaneous generation, and the like. Whereas in England most naturalists considered belief in spontaneous generation unscientific and atheistical, many German writers considered the doctrine of successive creations unscientific, preferring to resort to successive spontaneous generations to explain the changes in flora and fauna revealed in the fossil record.

How are we to regard these developments in the light of Kuhn's model? Was this another abortive revolution provoked by anomalous discoveries in systematic natural history? Such an interpretation would be hard to sustain. *Naturphilosophie* was an outgrowth of German idealistic philosophy. Perhaps it developed in reaction to certain aspects of the thought of the Enlightenment, as Charles Gillispie has suggested. But do we solve the problem of how science develops by casting whole scientific movements into the outer darkness with the label "subjective science" attached to them?

Naturphilosophie enlisted many able scientists under its banner. Its influence was felt throughout Europe, even in England, where Richard Owen became its leading exponent. In France, Étienne Geoffroy St. Hilaire elaborated a science of pure form independently of the German writers, and Geoffroy can scarcely be described as anti-Enlightenment. Shall we not rather say that the idea of an all-embracing unity of plan in the organic world was a natural and legitimate product of scientific imagination seeking ever wider generality in its ordering of nature?

But here again, as in the case of the very different visions of nature and natural science promulgated by Buffon and Lamarck, paradigm construction did not wait on the emergence of anomalies and crises in systematic natural history. On the contrary, it ran ahead of known facts, postulating a wider unity in nature than could be demonstrated in delving into the study of embryological development in search of confirmatory data.

In the end, the devotees of transcendental anatomy failed to establish their case. But their researches and many of their concepts, such as the ideas of homology, recapitulation, balancement, and even evolution, entered into the general fund of knowledge and speculation available to Darwin and his contemporaries.

We come now to Britain, where the main revolution in natural history was to take place, although from an unexpected quarter. Systematic natural history made slow progress in Britain after the brilliant work of John Ray in the late seventeenth century. Linnaean influence did not become entrenched there until the 1780s, when Sir James Edward Smith acquired a vested interest in Linnaean botany through his purchase of Linnaeus' herbarium, books, and letters and joined with the Reverend Samuel Goodenough and others in founding the Linnaean Society of London. In zoology, George Shaw adopted the Linnaean classification in preference to Thomas Pennant's system based on Ray.

As the nineteenth century wore on, British science responded to developments on the Continent and began to make solid contributions to the literature of natural history. In botany the so-called natural system of Jussieu and Candolle was gradually introduced by Robert Brown, John Lindley, George Bentham, and the Hookers, and Kew Gardens began to emerge as a center for the study of world botany. In zoology the dominant figure was Richard Owen, who combined Cuvier's techniques in comparative anatomy with the transcendental ideas of Oken, Goethe, and Geoffroy St. Hilaire in a way that would have dismayed Cuvier.

There was nothing very revolutionary in all this, nor does one sense a spirit of unrest or crisis among these naturalists. In Bentham's eyes the period before Darwin was characterized by the progressive triumph of the "natural system," leading many botanists to think that little was left for systematic botany but mopping up operations.

Joseph Dalton Hooker was privy to Darwin's subversive hypothesis from 1844 on, but Darwin's powerful ideas worked slowly on Hooker's imagination. Apart from his intercourse with Darwin, Hooker would never have broken out of the static paradigm of natural history. In zoology there was equally little evidence of a crisis psychology. The *Transactions* of the Zoological Society of London and the periodic progress reports of the British Association for the Advancement of Science gave little hint of the coming revolution. True, there was an extraordinary outcry against *The Vestiges of the Natural History of Creation*, but Chambers' book was a challenge from outside the natural history establishment, not from within.[9]

What, then, were the sources of the British revolution in natural history, if they are not to be found in the internal development of systematic botany and zoology? One might be tempted to find them in the eighteenth-century tradition of speculative philosophy of nature represented by Erasmus Darwin, but Erasmus Darwin's scientific impact, as distinguished from his popular influence, was negligible. Of far greater consequence for the evolution of natural history were certain developments in British geology and political economy in the years from 1775 to 1835.

Let us speak first of the progress of geology. The immediate impact of Hutton's uniformitarianism on systematic natural history was minimal, partly because his ideas were not widely accepted, but also because neither Hutton nor Playfair made more than passing reference to the organic remains embedded in the crust of the earth. Nevertheless, as we have seen in our discussion of Lamarck, geological uniformitarianism had momentous implications for the doctrine of the fixity of species. These implications were not lost on Playfair, as can be seen in the following passage from his *Illustrations of the Huttonian Theory of the Earth*, a passage used by Lyell as a motto for the second volume of his *Principles*:

> The inhabitants of the globe, then, like all the other parts of it, are subject to change: It is not only the individual that perishes, but whole *species*, and even perhaps *genera*, are extinguished.
> ... But besides this, a change in the animal kingdom seems to be a part of the order of nature, and is visible in instances to which human power cannot have extended.[10]

For the time being, however, British naturalists and paleontologists evaded the issues posed by geological uniformitarianism in the same way that Cuvier evaded them in France. They rejected uniformitarianism in favor of a theory of successive creations and extinctions and devoted themselves to naming, classifying, and describing the organic remains of former worlds and to discovering how to identify and correlate geological formations by means of them. In so doing they unwittingly set the stage for Charles Lyell's revolutionary extension of the uniformitarian doctrine to organic phenomena.

There is little evidence, however, that Lyell's great book was a response to a state of crisis in geological science. Instead, it seems to have been conceived as a reaffirmation of uniformitarian principles, and, what was crucial for the development of evolutionary ideas, an extension of them to the organic world, at least in regard to the extinction of species. Lyell's shift to a dynamic and causal view of organic nature is apparent in the opening paragraph of his *Principles*, where he says: "Geology is the science which investigates the successive changes that have taken place in the organic and inorganic kingdoms of nature; it inquires into the causes of these changes, and the influence which they have exerted in modifying the surface and external structure of our planet. By these researches . . . we acquire a more perfect knowledge of its present condition, and more comprehensive views concerning the laws now governing its animate and inanimate productions."[11] Lamarck himself could not have asked for a better statement of the aims and outlook of a comprehensive science of the earth and its productions.

But Lyell was not prepared to follow Lamarck down the uniformitarian path to a full-blown evolutionism. Like Lamarck, he drew from geological uniformitarianism the conclusion that plant and animal species must change with changing circumstances or perish. But, whereas Lamarck viewed organisms as endowed with an innate capacity to undergo the changes necessary for survival, Lyell, unconvinced that organisms possessed an unlimited capacity for variation, chose instead to envisage piecemeal extinction of species as the eventual consequence of their limited ability to adapt to changed conditions. Thus, whereas Lamarck's energies were directed toward imagining the processes by which organisms adapted to changing circumstances and toward tracing the path of their upward evolution, Lyell's were concentrated on studying the effects of environmental changes on the chances of survival of species possessing limited power of variation. Not evolution, but elimination in the struggle for survival, became the focus of his attention so far as species were concerned.

This was precisely the direction of thought that was to eventuate in the theory of natural selection. Moreover, it was a mode of thinking that came naturally to Englishmen, steeped as they were in the tradition of Adam Smith, Malthus, and Ricardo. Surely it is no mere coincidence that all of the men who arrived at some idea of natural selection in the first half of the nineteenth century—one thinks of William Wells, Patrick Matthew, Charles Lyell, Edward Blyth, Charles Darwin, A. R. Wallace, and Herbert Spencer—were British. Here, if anywhere in the history of science, we have a striking example of the influence of national habits of thought on the development of scientific theory, a phenomenon difficult to reconcile with Kuhn's internalist approach. For the cast of mind we have been describing affected not merely the timing of the revolution in natural history but its central concept, the idea of competition, survival of the fittest, and consequent progress.

Lyell himself stopped short of a theory of the origin of species, falling back on the traditional belief in special creation and wise design. But his uniformitarian explanation of the piecemeal extinction of species seemed to cry out for a correlative explanation of the origin of species by natural causes. The elements of a non-Lamarckian theory of evolution, stressing the struggle for existence and survival of the fittest, were present in his work cheek and jowl with his systematic exposition and discussion of the Lamarckian alternative to his own steady-state concept of earth history. Little wonder, then, that Lyell's *Principles* provided the impetus for evolutionary speculation in Britain from the time of its publication onward.

Chambers and Spencer, impressed more by Lyell's exposition of Lamarckian ideas than by his refutation of them, chose Lamarck's kind of evolutionism. Darwin and Wallace, aware of the inadequacy of Lamarck's theory of organic change but convinced of the essential truth of transmutationism, set out to discover the mechanism of change. Meanwhile, systematic natural history continued on its accustomed course, untroubled by any sense of crisis. A revolution was impending, but it was to come from outside, not from within, the establishment.

We come now to Darwin and the revolution in natural history associated with his name and achievements. From Kuhn's hypothesis we should expect this revolution to be non-cumulative in character and to involve the substitution of a new paradigm of natural history incommensurable with the static paradigm that had reigned before the revolution. The first question, then, is: Was the Darwinian revolution non-cumulative in character? That is, did it break sharply with the concepts, methods, and modes of thought that had prevailed before 1859?

313

From what has already been said it should be apparent that this question does not admit of a simple Yes or No answer. If we compare Darwin's ideas and methods with those that had prevailed in the main tradition of systematic natural history, namely, the tradition of Linnaeus, Jussieu, Candolle, Cuvier, Owen, and Agassiz, we discover a profound break with the past, though *not* one generated in response to internal difficulties in the tradition that was overthrown.

If, on the other hand, we compare Darwin's concepts and methods with those of Buffon, Erasmus Darwin, Lamarck, Étienne Geoffroy St. Hilaire, and Charles Lyell, we begin to have doubts about the non-cumulative character of the Darwinian revolution. We discover that some aspects of Darwin's thought and practice were more original than others.

Darwin himself made no claim to have invented the idea of organic evolution. He was too well acquainted with the writings of Lamarck, Geoffroy St. Hilaire, and his own grandfather, Erasmus Darwin, all of whom he had read or re-read on his return from the voyage of the *Beagle*, to make any such claim. He claimed only to have discovered "the means of modification and co-adaptation" in nature and thereby to have transformed a speculative idea of descent with modification into a workable theory of the origin of species. To this he might have added that he had done more than merely hit upon the idea of natural selection as the means of modification and co-adaptation. More important, he had deduced the consequences of his hypothesis and endeavored to show by observation and experiment that they actually obtained in nature. This combination of inductive and deductive methods had long prevailed in the physical sciences, but Darwin was the first to apply it systematically in natural history. His methods were as revolutionary as his theory.

Thus, one's judgment as to the cumulative or non-cumulative character of the Darwinian revolution depends largely on whether one stresses the general concept of descent with modification or the particular theory of natural selection as the means of organic modification in nature. The general concept had a history reaching back at least to Buffon. Indeed, Thomas Henry Huxley was inclined to credit Descartes with insight into what Huxley deemed "the fundamental proposition of Evolution," namely, that "the whole world, living and not living, is the result of the mutual interaction, according to definite laws, of the forces possessed by the molecules of which the primitive nebulosity of the universe was composed."[12] In one sense Huxley was right. Geological uniformitarianism and its corollary of indefinite mutability in the organic world were implied in the Cartesian program of deriving the present structures of nature from a simpler, more homogeneous state of the system of matter in motion by the operation of the laws of nature. The drawing out of this implication by Buffon, Lamarck, Lyell, and others sprang more from the appeal of this vision of nature and natural science to imaginative minds than it did from factual discoveries, which could always be interpreted differently by less imaginative observers.

Darwin himself conceded the importance of this dynamic and causal approach to nature when he wrote in 1863: "Whether the naturalist believes in the views given by Lamarck, by Geoffroy St. Hilaire, by the author of the 'Vestiges,' by Mr. Wallace or by myself, signifies extremely little in comparison with the admission that species have descended from other species, and have not been created immutable: for he who admits this as a great truth has a wide field opened to him for further inquiry."[13]

The difficulty was, however, that there could be no general acceptance of the idea that species have descended from species until someone could show convincingly *how* this could take place. The revolution in natural history had been prophesied for more than a century, but the fulfillment of the prophecy had to wait on the discovery and elaboration of a theory of natural selection. It was Darwin and Wallace who achieved this result, but, as we have seen, the way was cleared for them by Charles Lyell and by the British school of political economy. Patrick Mathew, Edward Blyth, and Herbert Spencer were products of the same climate of opinion.

Yet, curiously enough, although the theory of natural selection played an indispensable role in converting the scientific world to an evolutionary point of view, many who accepted transmutationism after Darwin rejected natural selection as the key to organic evolution. Neo-Lamarckian evolutionists, some of them distinguished scientists, were numerous in the late nineteenth century.

This fact brings us to the final question, whether Darwin's work effectively established a new paradigm incommensurable with the static paradigm of systematic natural history. If by establishing a new paradigm we mean simply establishing an evolutionary point of view in biology, Darwin certainly did that, and the new point of view can justly be described as incommensurable with the Linnaean paradigm, although no more incommensurable with it than the point of view of Buffon or Lamarck was. If, on the other hand, we mean that Darwin's work established the theory of natural selection and Darwin's general assumptions and methods as the norm of scientific thought and practice among biologists, this is a more dubious proposition.

As we have seen, many scientists accepted Darwin's evolutionism but not his emphasis on natural selection. Among systematists, moreover, although lip service was now paid to the Lamarckian and Darwinian idea that the natural method of classification was one that reflected phylogeny, taxonomic methods were slow to change. The anthropologists, far from following Darwin's lead in investigating the origin of human races, settled down to three-quarters of a century of hairsplitting racial taxonomy. As for Darwin's ideas on the subject of heredity and variation, they did give rise to a school of English geneticists led by Galton, Pearson, and Weldon. But, far from being generally accepted, these ideas were attacked strenuously by Weismann and others and were eventually overthrown by the rediscovery of Mendel's laws and the development of cytology. In fact, it could be argued that nothing approaching a "Darwinian" paradigm became established until the 1930s, and even that paradigm was Darwinian only in a very loose sense.

We conclude as follows:

1. Through the work of Ray, Tournefort, and Linnaeus natural history acquired a conceptual framework that dominated the study of natural history until Darwin published his *Origin of Species*, after which systematics was gradually reshaped and relocated within the broader framework of evolutionary biology.

2. Challenges to the dominance of the Linnaean framework in natural history arose both within and outside of that framework.

3. The challenges arising within the static view of nature and natural history failed to precipitate a search for new premises; they were either ignored or evaded by compromises such as the theory of successive creations.

4. Rival concepts, such as those propounded by Buffon, Lamarck, and the transcendental anatomists, arose from time to time, but not in response to anomalies or crises within the dominant view. These counter-concepts exerted a significant influence both on the static view of nature and on the developments that were to eventuate in its overthrow.

5. The evolutionary alternative to the static outlook developed chiefly outside the Linnaean framework in the form of a search for a science of nature that would derive the phenomena of nature from the operations of a law-bound system of matter in motion. The earliest and most powerful challenge to the static view of nature was the challenge implied in geological uniformitarianism. It was this postu-

late, rather than particular scientific discoveries, that drove Lamarck to an evolutionary position and led Lyell to envisage the piecemeal extinction of species through the struggle for existence.

6. The eventual emergence of the theory of natural selection in Britain seems to have owed a great deal to the influence of the competitive ethos that pervaded British political economy and British *mores* generally.

7. The Darwinian revolution displayed elements both of continuity and discontinuity with the past. It overthrew the static view of nature and natural history, but failed to establish a clear-cut paradigm in its place.

8. The Kuhnian paradigm of paradigms can be made to fit certain aspects of the development of natural history from Ray to Darwin, but its adequacy as a conceptual model for that development seems doubtful. The use of Kuhnian terminology in this essay should not be interpreted as implying belief in its general utility for the historiography of science. At the same time, it should be remembered that an inadequate hypothesis is better than none at all. Those who question the validity of Kuhn's model should feel themselves challenged to provide alternative interpretations of the genesis of revolutions in science. The present essay is intended less as a critique of Kuhn's stimulating book than as a tentative formulation of some general ideas about the rise and development of concepts of organic evolution.

NOTES

1. Carl Linnaeus, *A General System of Nature ... Translated from Gmelin's Last Edition ...*, William Turton, tr. and ed. (London, 1806), I, 2; Georges Louis Leclerc, Comte de Buffon, *A Natural History, General and Particular ...*, William Smellie, tr. (3rd ed., London, 1791), VIII, 33-34.

2. Thomas S. Kuhn, "Energy Conservation as an Example of Simultaneous Discovery," in Marshall Clagett, ed., *Critical Problems in the History of Science* (Madison, Wisconsin, 1959), 321-56.

3. John Ray, *The Wisdom of God Manifested in the Works of the Creation. . . .* (3rd ed., London, 1701), Preface (not paged).

4. Thomas Jefferson, "A Memoir on the Discovery of Certain Bones of a Quadruped of the Clawed Kind in the Western Parts of Virginia," *Trans. Amer. Philos. Soc.*, IV (1799), 255-56.

5. George Bentham, "On the Recent Progress and Present State of Systematic Botany," *Report of the 44th Meeting of the British Association*

JOHN C. GREENE

for the Advancement of Science in 1874 (London, 1875), 31ff.

6. Étienne Geoffroy St. Hilaire, *Fragments biographies précédés d'études sur la vie, les ouvrages et la doctrine de BUFFON* (Paris, 1838, 3-157. In this essay Geoffroy St. Hilaire exhibits in a striking manner the contrast between the Linnaean-Cuvierian concept of natural history and that of Buffon and presents Lamarck's evolutionary philosophy and his own belief in the mutability of species as a continution of Buffon's vision of nature as a system of *faits nécessaires*.

7. Bernard G. E. de la Ville sur Illon, Comte de Lacépède, *Histoire Naturelle des Poissons* (Paris, 1798-1804), II, 9-68.

8. The mental process by which Lamarck arrived at an evolutionary viewpoint in the last two or three years of the eighteenth century is difficult, if not impossible, to ascertain, but Lamarck's own statements lend considerable support to the interpretation I have advanced. In the opening sentences of the Appendix to his *Discours D'Ouverture de L'An X* he says:

I thought for a long time that there were constant species in nature, and that they were constituted of the individuals belonging to each of them.

Now I am convinced that I was in error in this regard, and that there are really only individuals in nature.

The origin of this error, which I shared with many naturalists who still hold to it, is found in the *long duration* with respect to us of the same state of things in each place which each living body inhabits; but that duration of the same state of things for each place has a limit, and with plenty of time it undergoes mutations at each point of the surface of the globe which change the circumstances for all the living bodies inhabiting it. . . . Elevated places are constantly degraded, and everything which is detached is carried toward the low places. The beds of rivers, of streams, of seas even are insensibly displaced, as well as climates; in a word, everything on the surface of the earth changes little by little in situation, in form, in nature and aspects. . . . [Here he cites his *Hydrogéologie*]

Thus, Lamarck argues that the mutability of species follows from the mutability of the earth's surface and that both types of mutability are hidden from man by the extreme slowness of the changes that take place. In his *Discours D'Ouveure de L'An Xi* (pp. 541-42) he makes it clear that organisms are *forced* to undergo change as a result of changes in their environments: ". . . we know . . . that a *forced and sustained change*, whether in the habits and manner of living of animals, or in the situation, the soil and the climate of plants, effects after a sufficient time a very remarkable mutation in the individuals exposed to it." (Italics mine.)

Finally, in his essay "Sur Les Fossiles" in his *Systéme Des Animaux Sans Vertèbres*, Lamarck reveals his awareness that, given the changes on the earth's surface postulated by geology, the alternative to transmutation of living forms is widespread extinction of species. Some naturalists, he says, have concluded from the lack of perfect resemblance between fossil and

318

living species "that this globe has undergone a universal *bouleversement*, a general catastrophe, and that as a result a multitude of species of animals and of plants have been absolutely lost or destroyed." But Lamarck will have nothing to do with such a universal catastrophe, "which by its very nature regularizes nothing, confounds and disperses everything, and constitutes a very convenient means for naturalists who wish to explain everything and who do not take the trouble to observe and study the process which nature follows in regard to her productions and in everything which constitutes her domain." Instead, he undertakes to show "that although many of the fossil shells are different from all known marine shells, this by no means proves that the species of shells have been obliterated, but only that these species have changed in the course of time." ["Sur Les Fossiles," *Système Des Animaux Sans Vertèbres*, (Paris, 1801), 408-409. Translation mine.]

Thus according to Lamarck, geology and paleontology present the naturalist with a choice: either (1) catastrophism and wholesale extinction of species, or (2) transmutationism on uniformitarian principles with little or no extinction of species. His own decision favors the second alternative, not only because of his uncompromising uniformitarianism in every branch of natural history but also because he finds in the transmutation hypothesis a neat solution to grave problems in taxonomy, an exhilarating sense of progress in nature, and a vindication of the wisdom of the Author of Nature, a wisdom which wholesale extinction of species would seem to impugn.

He seems never to have considered the possibility of combining uniformitarianism with acceptance of widespread extinction of species. It would take an Englishman to see the wise dispensation of the Creator in the competitive struggle for existence. [The passages from Lamarck's inaugural discourses are translated from the *Bulletin Scientifique de la France et de la Belgique*, XL (1906).]

9. This is not to say that there was no undermining of belief in the fixity of species among naturalists as the nineteenth century progressed. In botany Schleiden, Unger, and Rafinesque accepted transmutation by mid-century. But Darwin worked out his theory of natural selection in the thirties, largely in response to problems he had encountered on the voyage of the *Beagle*. Unfortunately, there has been too little research on the period 1830-1859 to warrant confident generalizations about the state of mind of naturalists in this period. My impression is that it would be difficult to prove the existence of a "crisis psychology" in the 1850s and impossible to do so for the 1830s.

10. John Playfair, *Illustrations of the Huttonian Theory of the Earth* (Edinburgh, 1802), 469-70. I have used the facsimile reprint of this work (Dover Publications, Inc., New York, 1964). Playfair envisages the modification as well as the extinction of species driven into new habitats by man: ". . . the more innocent species fled to a distance from man, and being forced to retire into the most inaccessible parts, where their food was scanty, and their migration checked, they may have degenerated from the size and strength of their ancestors, and some species may have been entirely extinguished."

319

11. Charles Lyell, *Principles of Geology* . . . (2nd ed., London, 1832), I, 1.

12. Thomas Henry Huxley, "Evolution in Biology," *Darwiniana: Essays* (New York, 1908), 206. This essay was originally published in 1878.

13. Letter from Charles Darwin to the *Athenaeum*, Down, England, May 5, 1863, quoted in Francis Darwin, ed., *The Life and Letters of Charles Darwin* . . . (New York, 1898), II, 207.

BIBLIOGRAPHY

WORKS BY THOMAS KUHN

Books:

The Copernican Revolution: Planetary Astronomy in the Development of Western Thought, Cambridge, Mass.: Harvard University Press, 1957. Revised editions: Modern Library (then Vintage) paperback, 1959; Harvard, 1966; Harvard paperback, 1971.

The Structure of Scientific Revolutions, Chicago: University of Chicago Press, 1962. Phoenix paperback edition, 1964. Second edition, enlarged, University of Chicago Press, 1970.

Sources for History of Quantum Physics: an Inventory and Report, Philadelphia: Memoirs of the American Philosophical Society, 1966, with John L. Heilbron, Paul L. Forman, and Lini Allen.

The Essential Tension: Selected Studies in Scientific Tradition and Change, Chicago: University of Chicago Press, 1977.

Black-Body Theory and the Quantum Discontinuity, 1894-1912, London: Oxford University Press, 1978.

Articles:

"Abstract" and "Comment" on General Education in a Free Society, Harvard Alumni Bulletin, (September 22, 1945), pp. 23-30 passim.

"A Simplified Method of Computing the Cohesive Energies of Monovalent Metals," Physical Review 79 (1950), 382-388, with J. H. Van Vleck.

"An Application of the W.K.B. Method to the Cohesive Energies of Monovalent Metals," Physical Review 79 (1950), 515-519.

"A Convenient General Solution of the Confluent Hypergeometric Equation, Analytic and Numerical Development," Quarterly of Applied Mathematics 9 (1951), 1-16.

"Newton's '31st Query' and the Degradation of Gold," Isis 42 (1951), 296-398.

"Robert Boyle and Structural Chemistry in the Seventeenth Century," Isis 43 (1952), 12-36.

"Newton and the Theory of Chemical Solution," Isis 43 (1952), 123-124.

"The Independence of Density and Pore-Size in Newton's Theory of Matter," *Isis* 43 (1952), 364-365.

"Carnot's Version of 'Carnot's Cycle'," *American Journal of Physics* 23 (1955), 91-95.

"La Mer's Version of 'Carnot's Cycle'," *American Journal of Physics* 23 (1955), 387-389.

"Newton's Optical Papers," in I.B. Cohen (ed.), *Isaac Newton's Papers and Letters on Natural Philosophy*, Cambridge, Mass.: Harvard University Press, 1958, pp. 27-45. Second edition, 1978.

"The Caloric Theory of Adiabatic Compression," *Isis* 49 (1958), 132-140.

"Energy Conservation as an Example of Simultaneous Discovery," in Marshall Clagett (ed.), *Critical Problems in the History of Science*, Madison: University of Wisconsin Press, 1959, pp. 321-356. Reprinted in Barber & Hirsch (eds.), *The Sociology of Science*, Glencoe, Il.: The Free Press, 1962.

"The Essential Tension: Tradition and Innovation in Scientific Research," in Calvin W. Taylor (ed.), *The Third (1959) University of Utah Research Conference on the Identification of Creative Scientific Talent*, Salt Lake City: University of Utah Press, 1959, pp. 162-177. Reprinted in Taylor and Barron (eds.), *Scientific Creativity: Its Recognition and Development*, New York: John Wiley & Sons, 1963, pp. 341-354.

"Committee Report on Environmental Conditions Affecting Creativity," *ibid.*, pp. 313-316.

"Engineering Precedent for the Work of Sadi Carnot," *Actes du IX Congrès International d'Histoire des Sciences* (Barcelona, 1961), 530-535. Reprinted in *Archives internationales d'histoire des sciences* 13 (1960), 151-155.

"Sadi Carnot and the Cagnard Engine," *Isis* 52 (1961), 367-374.

"The Function of Measurement in Modern Physical Science," *Isis* 52 (1961), 161-193. Reprinted in H. Woolf (ed.), *Quantification*, Indianapolis: Bobbs-Merrill, 1961.

Critique of papers by MacKinnon and Siegel, *The Rate and Direction of Inventive Activity: Economic and Social Factors*, Princeton: Princeton University Press, 1962, pp. 379-384, 456-457.

"Historical Structure of Scientific Discovery," *Science* 136 (1962), 760-764.

"The Function of Dogma in Scientific Research," in A. C. Crombie (ed.), *Scientific Change*, New York: Basic Books, 1963, pp. 347-369, 386-395.

"A Function for Thought Experiments," *Melanges Alexandre Koyré*, vol. I, Paris: Hermann, 1964, pp. 307-334.

"The Turn to Recent Science," *Isis* 58 (1967), 409-419.

"The History of Science," *International Encyclopedia of the Social Sciences*, New York: Macmillan, 1968, vol. 14, pp. 74-83.

"The Genesis of the Bohr Atom," *Historical Studies in the Physical Sciences* 1 (1969), 211-290.

"Comment [on the Relations of Science and Art]," *Comparative Studies in Society and History* 11 (1969), 403-412.

"Comment [on Technological vs. Scientific Acceleration]," *ibid.*, 426-430.

"Alexandre Koyré and the History of Science," *Encounter* 34 (1970), 67-79.

"Logic of Discovery or Psychology of Research?," in Imre Lakatos and Alan Musgrave (eds.), *Criticism and the Growth of Knowledge*, Cambridge: Cambridge University Press, 1970, pp. 1-23. Reprinted in P.A. Schilpp (ed.), *The Philosophy of Karl Popper*, The Library of Living Philosophers, vol. XIV, LaSalle, Il.: Open Court, 1974, pp. 798-819.

"Reflections on my Critics," *ibid.*, pp. 231-278.

"Comment [on Richard S. Westfall's 'Uneasily Fitful Reflections on Fits of Easy Transmission']," in Robert Palter (ed.), *The Annus Mirabilis of Sir Isaac Newton 1666-1966*, Cambridge, Mass.: The MIT Press, 1970, pp. 105-108.

"The Relations between History and History of Science," *Daedalus* (Spring, 1971), 271-304.

"Les notions de causalité dans le développement de la physique," in J. Piaget (ed.), *Les Théories de la causalité*, Paris: Presses Universitaires de France, 1971, pp. 7-18.

"Notes on Lakatos," *Boston Studies in the Philosophy of Science* 8 (1971), 137-146.

"Scientific Growth: Reflections on Ben-David's 'Scientific Role'," *Minerva* 10 (1971), 166-178.

"Second Thoughts on Paradigms," in Frederick Suppe (ed.), *The Structure of Scientific Theories*, Urbana: University of Illinois Press, 1974, pp. 459-482, and discussion, pp. 483-517 *passim*. Second edition, 1977.

"The Quantum Theory of Specific Heats: A Problem in Professional Recognition," *Proceedings of the XIVth International Congress of the History of Science* (Tokyō, 1975), vol. 1, pp. 170-182, vol. 4, p. 207.

"Tradition mathématique et tradition expérimentale dans le développement de la physique," *Annales* 30 (1975), 975-998.

"Mathematical vs. Experimental Traditions in the Development of Physical Science," *Journal of Interdisciplinary History* 3 (1976), 1-31.

"Theory-Change as Structure-Change: Comments on the Sneed Formalism," *Erkenntnis* 10 (1976), 179-199.

"Metaphor in Science," in Andrew Ortony (ed.), *Metaphor and Thought*, Cambridge: Cambridge University Press, 1979, pp. 409-419.

Foreword to the English translation of: Ludwik Fleck, *Genesis and Development of a Scientific Fact*, Chicago: The University of Chicago Press, 1979, pp. vii-xii.

"History of Science," in Peter D. Asquith, H. E. Kyburg (eds.), *Current Research in Philosophy of Science*, Philosophy of Science Association, 1979, pp. 121-128.

WORKS ABOUT THOMAS KUHN

I. *Philosophy of Science*

Agassi, J., [Review of SSR], *Journal of the History of Philosophy* 4(1966), 351-354.

————, "Tristam Shandy, Pierre Menard, and All That," *Inquiry* 14(1971), 152-164.

Amsterdamski, S., *Between Experience and Metaphysics: Philosophical Problems of the Evolution of Science*, Dordrecht: Reidel, 1975.

Ardley, G., [Review of SSR], *Philosophical Studies* 13(1964), 183-192.

Baillie, P. "Kuhn's Inductivism," *Australasian Journal of Philosophy* 53(1975), 54-57.

Beauchamp, E. W., *The Kuhn-Popper Debate*, University of Texas dissertation, 1975.

Bellone, E., "Thomas Kuhn e il libre della natura," *Scientia* 113(1978), 675-682.

Blanché, R. [Review of SSR], *Revue philosophique de la France et de l'étranger* 163(1973), 363-363.

Bloor, D., "Two Paradigms for Scientific Knowledge?," *Science Studies* 1(1971), 101-115.

Bohm, D. [review of SSR], *Philosophical Quarterly* 14(1964), 377-379.

Brown, H., *Perception, Theory, and Commitment: The New*

324

Philosophy of Science, Chicago: University of Chicago Press, 1977.

_____, "Reduction and Scientific Revolution," *Erkenntnis* 10(1976), 381-385.

Buchel, W., "Die Strucktur Wissenschaftlicher Revolutionen und das Uhren-'Paradoxen'," *Zeitschrift für Allgemeine Wissenschaftstheorie* 5(1974), 218-225.

Casini, P., "Theoria e stora delle revoluzioni scientifiche secondo Thomas Kuhn," *Revista filosofia* 61(1970), 213-218.

Cunningham, F., "Kuhn on Scientific Creativity: An Englesian Critique," *Dialectics and Humanism* 5(1978), 73-80.

Daniel, S. H., "On Understanding Kuhn's Clarification of the Paradigm Concept," *Dialogue* 19(1976), 1-7.

De Ruijter, A., "A contrecoeur contra Kuhn," *Algemeen Nederlands tijdschrift voor wijsbegeerte* 7(1979), 216-232.

Devitt, M., "Against Incommensurability," *Australasian Journal of Philosophy* 57(1979), 29-50.

Doppelt, G., "Kuhn's Epistemological Relativism: An Interpretation and Defense, *Inquiry* 21(1978), 33-86.

_____, "A Reply to Siegel on Kuhnian Relativism," *Inquiry* 23(1980), 117-124.

Draughton, W. E., *Kuhn, Feyerabend, and the Development of Scientific Knowledge*, New York University dissertation, 1971.

Dusberg, K. L., "Stegmüller über 'wissenschaftlichen Revolutionen'," *Zeitschrift für Allgemeine Wissenschaftstheorie* 8(1977), 331-341.

Fine, A., "How to Compare Theories: Reference and Change," *Nous* 9(1975), 17-32.

Flonta, M., "A 'Weak' and a 'Strong' Version of the Incommensurability Thesis," *Philosophie et logique* 20(1978), 395-406.

Gagnon, M., "Piaget et Kuhn sur l'évolution de la connaissance: une comparison," *Dialogue* 17(1978), 35-55.

Hammes, B. J., *The Views of Scientific Change and their Evaluation*, University of Notre Dame dissertation, 1978.

Hanson, N. R., "A Note on Kuhn'sMethod," *Dialogue* 4(1965), 371-375.

Hübner, K. [Review of SSR], *Philosophische Rundschau* 15 (1968), 185-195.

Jarvie, I. C., "Laudan's Problematic Progress and the Social Sciences," *Philosophy of Social Science* 9(1979), 484-497.

King, P., *Toleration*, London: Allen and Unwin, 1976, 144-153.

Kisiel, T. (with Galen Johnson), "New Philosophies of Science in the USA," *Zeitschrift für Allgemeine Wissenschaftstheorie* 5(1974), 138-191.

Kitcher, P., "Theories, Theorists, and Theoretical Change," *Philosophical Review* 8(1978), 519-547.

Kleiner, S., "Erotetic Logic and the Structure of Scientific Revolutions," *British Journal for the Philosophy of Science* 21(1970), 147-165.

Kocklmans, J. J., "On the Meaning of Scientific Revolutions," *Philosophical Forum* 11(1972), 243-264.

Kordig, C., *The Justification of Scientific Change*, Dordrecht: Reidel, 1971.

Kourany, J., *A Paradigm in Crisis: A Study of Thomas Kuhn's Philosophy of Science*, Columbia University dissertation, 1977.

Krüger, L., "Die Systematische Bedeutung Wissenschaftlicher Revolutionen, pro und contra Thomas Kuhn" in W. Diederich (ed.), *Theorien der Wissenschaftsgeschichte*, Frankfurt, 1974.

Lacharité, N., "Le Developpement des sciences est-il un proces norme?" *Dialogue* 17(1978), 616-633.

Lacoste, L. M., "Paradigmes et bon sens," *Dialogue* 16(1977), 629-652.

Ladrière, J., "Exposé de synthese," *Revue des questions scientifiques* 145(1974), 139-166.

Largeault, J. [Review of SSR], *Revue de synthèse* 97(1976), 290-293.

Lashchyk, E., *Scientific Revolutions: A Philosophical Critique of the Theories of Science of Thomas Kuhn and Paul Feyerabend*, University of Pennsylvania dissertation, 1969. (One of the first philosophers to argue that Kuhn does not present paradigm changes as irrational.)

————, "A Framework for the Solution to the Rationality Problem," *Proceedings of the 6th International Congress of Logic, Methodology, and Philosophy of Science, 1979.*

————, "A Rational Reconstruction of Kuhn's Model of Rationality in Science," *Proceedings of the 16th World Congress of Philosophy, 1978.*

Lakatos, I. and Musgrave, A. (eds.), *Criticism and the Growth of Knowledge*, Cambridge: Cambridge University Press, 1970. (Important papers by Kuhn, Popper, Feyerabend, Masterman, Watkins, and Pearce Williams).

Laudan, L., *Progress and its Problems*, Berkeley: University of California Press, 1977 (especially 133-151).

Lay, R. " 'Wissenschaftliche Revolutionen': Ein Beitrag Wolfgang Stegmüllers zu T. S. Kuhns Theorie Wissenschaftlicher Revolutionen," *Theologie und Philosophie* 50(1975), 231-241.

Lugg, A., "Kuhn and the Philosophy of Science" [Essay review of *The Essential Tension*], *British Journal for the*

Machan, T. R., "Kuhn's Impossibility Proof and the Moral Element in Scientific Explanation," *Theory and Decision* 5(1974), 355-374.

_____, "Kuhn, Paradigm Choice, and the Arbitrariness of Aesthetic Criteria in Science," *Theory and Decision* 8 (1977), 361-362.

Machemar, P. K., "Understanding Scientific Change," *Studies in History and Philosophy of Science* 5(1975), 373-381.

Malherbe, J.-F., [Review of SSR], *Revue philosphique de Louvain* 72(1974), 634-639.

McMullin, E., "Recent Work in Philosophy of Science," *New Scholasticism* 40(1966), esp. 502-505.

Meiland, J., "Kuhn, Scheffler, and Objectivity in Science," *Philosophy of Science* 41(1974), 179-187.

Meynell, H., "Science, the Truth, and Thomas Kuhn," *Mind* 84(1975), 79-93.

Miguelez, R., "Conflicto de paradigmas y analisis filosofice de las ciencias sociales," *Revista Latinoamericana de filosofia* 1(1975), 227-230.

Mosley, A., *Perspectives on the Kuhn-Popper Debate: New Directions in Epistemology*, University of Wisconsin dissertation, 1975.

Musgrave, A., "Kuhn's Second Thoughts," *British Journal for the Philosophy of Science* 22(1971), 287-297.
History of Science 12(1979), 289-295.

Nalimov, V. V., "The Receptivity of Hypotheses," *Diogenes* 100(1977), 179-197.

Novakovic, S., "Is the Transition from an Old Theory to a New One of a Sudden and Unexpected Character?" in R. S. Cohen and M. W. Wartofsky (eds.), *Methodological and Historical Essays in the Natural and Social Sciences* (Boston Studies XIV), Dordrecht: Reidel, 1974, 173-196. (Comment by W. Berkson, 197-210.)

Palmer, D. and Schagrin, M., "Moral Revolutions," *Philosophy and Phenomenological Research* 39(1978), 262-273. [Criticism of Parsons, below].

Parsons, K. P., "Nietzsche and Moral Change," *Feminist Studies* 2(1974), 57-76.

Paulos, J., "A Model-theoretic Explication of the Theses of Kuhn and Whorf," *Notre Dame Journal of Formal Logic* 21(1980), 155-165.

Purtill, R., "Kuhn on Scientific Revolutions," *Philosophy of Science* 24(1967), 53-58.

Putnam, H., "The 'Corroboration' of Scientific Theories" in P. A. Schillp (ed.), *The Philosophy of Karl Popper* (2 volumes), La Salle, Ill.: Open Court, 1974.

Quay, P., "Progress as a Demarcation Criterion for the Sciences," *Philosophy of Science* 41(1974), 154-170.

Radnitzky, G., *Contemporary Schools of Metascience*, 2nd edition, New York: Humanities, 1970.

Radnitzky, G. and Andersson, G. (eds.), *Progress and Rationality in Science*, Dordrecht: Reidel, 1978.

Rodnyi, N. I., "Das Problem der Wissenschaftlicher Revolutionen in der Kozeption der Wissenschaftsentwicklungen Th. S. Kuhns" in G. Domin (ed.), *Wissenschaftskonzeption: Eine Auswahl von Beitragen Sowjetischer Wissenschaftshistoriker zu Geschichte der Ideen über die Wissenschaft*, Berlin: Akademie-Verlag, 1978.

Rossi, A., "La Lotta fra 'paradigmi' nelle attuali scienze storico-sociali e l'opera di Thomas Kuhn sulle rivoluzioni scientifiche," *Giornale critico della filosophia Italiana* 52 (1971), 332-338.

Sarkar, H., *Methodology and Rationality: A Critique of Popper and Kuhn*, University of Minnesota dissertation, 1976.

Savary, C., "La Conception Kuhnienne de la science et le concept d'idéologie," *Dialogue* 17(1978), 266-285.

Schagrin, M. L., "On Being Unreasonable," *Philosophy of Science* 40(1973), 1-9.

Scheffler, I., *Science and Subjectivity*, Indianapolis: Bobbs-Merrill, 1967.

————, "Vision and Revolution: a Postscript On Kuhn," *Philosophy of Science* 39(1972), 366-374.

Schlegel, R., [Review of SSR], *Physics Today* 16(1963), 69.

Schuster, J. A., "Kuhn and Lakatos Revisited," *British Journal for the History of Science* 12(1979), 301-317.

Shapere, D., "The Structure of Scientific Revolutions," *Phi-*

losophical Review 73(1964), 383-394.

    _____, "Meaning and Scientific Change" in R. Colodny (ed.), *Mind and Cosmos*, Pittsburgh: University of Pittsburgh Press, 1966, 41-85.

    _____, "The Paradigm Concept," *Science* 172(1971), 706-709.

Shimony, A., "Comments on Two Epistemological Theses of Thomas Kuhn," in R. S. Cohen, P. K. Feyerabend, and M. W. Wartofsky (eds.), *Essays in Honor of Imre Lakatos*, Dordrecht: Reidel, 1976.

Shrader-Frechette, K., "Atomism in Crisis: An Analysis of the Current High Energy Paradigm," *Philosophy of Science* 44(1977), 409-440.

Siegel, H., "Meiland on Scheffler, Kuhn, and Objectivity in Science," *Philosophy of Science* 43(1976), 441-448.

    _____, "Epistemological Relativism in Its Latest Form," *Inquiry* 23(1980), 107-116.

Sneed, J., *The Logical Structure of Mathematical Physics*, Dordrecht: Reidel, 1971.

    _____, "Philosophical Problems in the Empirical Science of Science," *Erkenntnis* 10(1976), 115-146.

Stegmüller, W., "Structure and Dynamics of Theories: Some Reflections on J. D. Sneed and T. S. Kuhn," *Erkenntnis* 9(1975), 75-100.

    _____, *The Structure and Dynamics of Theories*, New York: Springer-Verlag, 1976.

    _____, "Accidental ('Non-substantial') Theory Change and Theory Dislodgement" in R. Butts and J. Hintikka (eds.), *Historical and Philosophical Dimensions of Logic, Methodology and Philosophy of Science*, Dordrecht: Reidel, 1977, 269-288. (Also in *Erkenntnis* 10(1976).)

Strasser, C., "Ciencia y paradigmas," *Revista Latinoamericana de filosofie* 2(1976), 74-78.

Suppe, F., "The Search for Philosophical Understanding of Scientific Theories" in F. Suppe (ed.), *The Structure of Scientific Theories*, Urbana: University of Illinois Press, 1974, 6-241 (esp. 135-151).

Stopes-Roe, H. V., [Review of SSR], *British Journal for the Philosophy of Science* 151(1964-5), 158-161.

Szumilewicz, I., "Incommensurability and the Rationality of the Development of Science," *British Journal for the Philosophy of Science* 28(1977), 345-350.

Tibbetts, P., "Hanson and Kuhn on Observation Reports and Knowledge Claims," *Dialectica* 29(1975), 145-155.

Toulmin, S., "Conceptual Revolutions in Science," *Synthese* 17(1967), 75-91. (Also in *Boston Studies in the Philosophy of Science, Volume III*, New York: Humanities Press, 1968; comment by L. Mink, 348-355.)

——, "New Directions in the Philosophy of Science," *Encounter* 36(1971), 53-64.

——, *Human Understanding*, I, Princeton, N.J., Princeton University Press, 1972.

Trigg, R., *Reason and Commitment*, Cambridge, Eng.: Cambridge University Press, 1973, esp. 99-118.

Watanabe, S., "Needed: A Historical-Dynamical View of Theory Change," *Synthèse* 32(1975), 113-134.

Wisdom, J. O., "The Nature of Normal Science" in P. A. Schillp (ed.) *The Philosophy of Karl Popper*, two volumes, La Salle, Ill., Open Court, 1974, 798-819.

——, "The Incommensurability Thesis," *Philosophical Studies* 25(1974), 299-301.

Zeitschrift für Allgemeine Wissenschaftstheorie 3(1972), articles by W. H. Austin, D. Böhler, J. Klüver, and P. T. Sagal.

II.   *History of Science*

Berry, C. J., "Kuhn and the History of Ideas" [Essay review of *The Essential Tension*], *British Journal for the History of Science* 12(1979), 295-298.

Blackmore, J., "Is Planck's 'Principle' True?" *British Journal for the Philosophy of Science* 29(1978), 347-349.

Buchdahl, G., "A Revolution in Historiography of Science," *History of Science* 4(1965), 55-69.

Cohen, I. B., "The Eighteenth-century Origins of the Concept of Scientific Revolution," *Journal of the History of Ideas* 37(1976), 257-288.

Crowe, M., "Ten 'Laws' Concerning Patterns of Change in the History of Mathematics," *Historia Mathematica* 2 (1975), 161-166.

Fang, J., "Is Mathematics an 'Anomaly' in the Theory of Scientific Revolutions?" *Philosophica Mathematica* 10 (1973), 92-101.

Finocchiaro, M., *A History of Science as Explanation*, Detroit: Wayne State University Press, 1973, esp. 188-198.

Gillispie, C. C., [Review of SSR], *Science* 138(1962), 1251-1253.

Greene, J. C., "The Kuhnian Paradigm and the Darwinian Revolution in Natural History" in D. Roller (ed), *Perspectives in the History of Science and Technology*, Norman: University of Oklahoma Press, 1971. (Followed by comments of W. Coleman and L. Wilson.)

Hall, M. D., [Review of SSR], *American Historical Review* 68(1963), 700-701.

Hall, R., "Kuhn and the Copernican Revolution," *British Journal for the Philosophy of Science* 21(1970), 196-197.

Heidelberger, M., "Some Intertheoretic Relations between Ptolemean and Copernican Astronomy," *Erkenntnis* 10 (1976), 323-336.

———, "Towards a Logical Reconstruction of Revolutionary Change: the Case of Ohm as an Example," *Studies in the History and Philosophy of Science*, 11(1980), 103-121.

Hesse, M., [Review of SSR], *Isis* 54(1963), 286-287.

Jørgensen, B. S., [Review of SSR], *Centaurus* 10(1964), 48-50.

Kitts, D. B., "Continental Drift and Scientific Revolutions," in his *The Structure of Geology*, Dallas: Southern Methodist University Press, 1977, pp. 115-127.

Klein, M., Shimony, A. and Pinch, T., "Paradigm Lost? A Review Symposium" [of *Black-Body Theory and the Quantum Discontinuity 1894-1912*], *Isis* 70(1979), 429-440.

Kourany, J., "The Nonhistorical Basis of Kuhn's Theory of Science," *Nature and System* 1 (1979), 46-59.

Laudan, R., "The Recent Revolution in Geology and Kuhn's Theory of Scientific Change" in I. Hacking and P. Asquith (eds.), *PSA 1978*, Philosophy of Science Association, 1980.

Mandelbaum, M., "A Note on Thomas S. Kuhn's *The Structure of Scientific Revolutions*," *The Monist* 60(1977), 445-452.

Mehrtens, H., "T. S. Kuhn's Theories and Mathematics: A Discussion Paper on the 'New Historiography' of Mathematics," *Historica Mathematica* 3(1976), 297-320.

Percival, W., "Applicability of Kuhn's Paradigms to the History of Linguistics," *Language* 52(1976), 285-294.

Ruse, M., "The Revolution in Biology," *Theoria* 36(1970), 1-22.

———, "Two Biological Revolutions," *Dialectica* 25(1971), 17-38.

Stengers, I., "La Description de l'activité scientifique par T. S. Kuhn," *Critique (Paris)* 30(1974), 753-781. (Mostly on Kuhn and biology.)

Trenn, T. J., "The Non-Rational Dimension of Natural Science," *Deutsche Vierteljahrsschrift für Literaturwissenschaft und Geistesgeschichte* 50(1976), 1-13.

Williams, L. P., [Review of SSR], *Archives internationales d'histoire des science* 16(1963), 182-184.

_____, "Michael Faraday: a Biography," *British Journal for the Philosophy of Science* 18(1967), 230-233. (Followed by a brief reply by Kuhn.)

_____, "The Essential Thomas Kuhn," *History of Science* 18(1980), 68-74.

Winston, M. E., "Did a (Kuhnian) Scientific Revolution Occur in Linguistics?" in F. Suppe and P. D. Asquith, *PSA 1976*, Volume I, Philosophy of Science Association, 1976, 25-33.

III. Sociology of Science

Barber, B., [Review of SSR], *American Sociological Review* 28(1963), 298-299.

Barnes, S. Barry, "Sociological Explanation and Natural Science: a Kuhnian Reappraisal," *Archives européennes de sociologie* 13(1972), 373-393.

_____, *Scientific Knowledge and Sociological Theory*, London: Routledge and Kegan Paul, 1974.

_____, *Interests and the Growth of Knowledge*, London: Routledge and Kegan Paul, 1977.

Barnes, S. Barry and Dolby, R. G. A., "The Scientific Ethos: a Deviant Viewpoint," *Archives européennes de sociologie* 11(1970), 3-25.

Ben-David, J., "Scientific Growth: a Sociological View," *Minerva* 2(1963-4), 455-476.

Bloor, D., *Knowledge and Social Imagery*, London: Routledge and Kegan Paul, 1976.

Böhme, G., "Die Soziale Bedeutung Kognitive Strukturen," *Soziale Welt* 25(1974), 188-208.

Crane, D., *Invisible Colleges*, Chicago: University of Chicago Press, 1972.

Dean, C., "Are Serendipitous Discoveries a Part of Normal Science?" *Sociological Review* 25(1977), 73-86.

Leibniz & Locke —

treaty to end war —
was that a form of contract (
which pt the conquered (
surrender rts to cong

creation of world — best that it coul
evil in the world. — connec
w/ free will).

Locke earth is property in common
Filmer- birthright. — Locke refu

Locke - rt to hold property is an a
to greater
born power — but equal amor
how acquired?

Locke- civil war is okay.
Bossuet would have fi

King, M. D., "Reason, Tradition, and the Progressiveness of Science," *History and Theory* 10(1971), 3-32.

Lammers, C., "Mono- and Poly-paradigmatic Developments in Natural and Social Science" in Whitley, R. D. (ed.), *Social Processes of Scientific Development*, London: Routledge and Kegan Paul, 1974, 123-147.

Law, J. and French, D., "Normative and Interpretive Sociologies of Science," *Sociological Review* 22(1974), 581-595.

Lodahl, J. B. and Gordon, G., "The Structure of Scientific Fields and the Functioning of University Graduate Departments," *American Sociological Review* 37(1972), 57-72.

McDonagh, E. L., "Attitude Changes and Paradigm Shifts: Social Psychological Foundations of the Kuhnian Thesis," *Social Studies in Science* 6(1976), 51-76.

Merton, R., "Sociology of Science: an Episodic Memoir" in R. Merton and J. Gaston (eds.), *The Sociology of Science in Europe*, Carbondale: Southern Illinois University Press, 1977, esp. 71-109.

Mulkay, M. J., "Three Models of Scientific Development," *Sociological Review* 23(1975), 509-526. (Comments by B. Barnes and J. Law in *Sociological Review* 24(1976), 115-124; reply by Mulkay, 125-133.)

_____, "Kuhn and the Sociology of Science" [Essay review of *The Essential Tension*], *British Journal for the History of Science* 12(1979), 298-301.

Urry J., "Thomas Kuhn as Sociologist of Knowledge," *British Journal of Sociology* 24(1973), 462-473.

Wade, N., "Thomas S. Kuhn: Revolutionary Theorist of Science," *Science* 197(1977), 143-145.

Weingart, P., "On a Sociological Theory of Scientific Change" in R. D. Whitley (ed.), *Social Processes of Scientific Development*, London: Routledge and Kegan Paul, 1974.

IV.   *Sociology*

Barnes, S. Barry, "Paradigms Scientific and Social," *Man* 4 (1969), 94-106.

Bottomore, T., "Competing Paradigms in Macrosociology" in A. Inkeles, J. Coleman, and N. Smelser (eds.), *Annual Review of Sociology*, Annual Reviews, 1975.

Bryant, C. G. A., "Kuhn, Paradigms, and Sociology," *British Journal of Sociology* 26(1975), 354-359.

Carroll, M. P., "Considerations on the Analysis of Variance Paradigm," *Pacific Sociological Review* 15(1972), 443-459.

Dawe, A., [Review of Friedrich's *A Sociology of Sociology*], *Sociological Review* 19(1971), 140-147.

Denisoff, R. S., Callahan, O. and Levine, M. H., *Theories and Paradigms in Contemporary Sociology*, Itasca, Ill.: F. E. Peacock, 1971.

Dixon, K., *Sociological Theory: Pretence and Possibility*, London: Routledge and Kegan Paul, 1973.

Friedrichs, *A Sociology of Sociology*, New York: The Free Press, 1970.

_____, "Dialectical Sociology: An Exemplar for the 1970s," *Social Forces* 50(1972), 447-455.

Galway, T. D. and Mahayni, R. G., "Planning Theory in Retrospect: the Process of Paradigm Change," *American Institute of Planners Journal* 43(1977), 62-71.

Heyl, J. D., "Paradigms in Social Science," *Society* 12(1975), 61-67.

Jones, K., "Some Epistemological Considerations of Paradigm Shifts," *Sociological Review* 25(1977), 253-271.

Kucklick, H. "A 'Scientific Revolution': Sociological Theory in the United States," *Sociological Inquiry* 43(1972), 2-22.

Lehman, T. and Young, R. T., "From Conflict Theory to Conflict Methodology: an Emerging Paradigm for Sociology," *Sociological Inquiry* 44(1974), 15-28.

Martins, H., "The Kuhnian 'Revolution' and Its Implications for Sociology" in T. J. Nossiter, A. H. Hanson, and S. Rokkan (eds.), *Imagination and Precision in the Social Sciences*, London: Faber and Faber, 1972.

Morris, M. B., "Creative Sociology: Conservative or Revolutionary?" *American Sociologist* 10(1975), 168-178.

Overington, M. A., "Doing What Comes Rationally," *American Sociologist* 14(1979), 2-12. (Comments, 12-31; rejoinder, 31-34.)

Perry, N., "A Comparative Analysis of 'Paradigm' Proliferation," *British Journal of Sociology* 28(1977), 38-50.

Phillips, D., *Wittgenstein and Scientific Knowledge: A Sociological Perspective*, Totona, N.J.: Rowman and Littlefield, 1977, esp. Chapters 3,5,7.

_____, "Paradigms, Falsification, and Sociology," *Acta Sociologica* 16(1973), 13-30.

_____, "Paradigms and Incommensurability," *Theory and Society* 2(1975), 37-61.

Raes, J., "Les Sciences sociales et le paradigme classique," *Revue des questions scientifiques* 144(1973), 560-579.

Ritzer, G., *Sociology: A Multiple Paradigm Science*, New York: Allyn and Bacon, 1975.

Schafer, L., "Theorie-Dynamische Nachlieferungen: Anmerkungen zu Kuhn-Sneed-Stegmüller," *Zeitschrift für Philosophische Forschung* 31(1977), 19-42.

Scholte, B., "Epistemic Paradigms: Some Problems in Cross-cultural Research in Social Anthropological History and Theory," *American Anthropologist* 68(1966), 1192-1201.

Smolicz, J. J., "Paradigms and Models: A Comparison of Intellectual Frameworks in Natural Science and Sociology," *Australian and New Zealand Journal of Sociology* 6(1970), 100-119.

Sherman, L. W., "Uses of the Masters," *American Sociologist* 9(1974), 176-181.

Westhues, K., "Class and Organization as Paradigms in Social Science," *American Sociologist* 11(1976), 38-48.

V.   *Political Science*

Almond, G., "Political Theory and Political Science," *American Political Science Review* 60(1968), 869-879.

Ball, T., "From Paradigms to Research Programs: Toward a Post-Kuhnian Political Science," *American Journal of Political Science* 20(1976), 151-177.

Bernstein, R. J., *The Restructuring of Social and Political Theory*, New York: Harcourt, Brace, Jovanovich, 1976, esp. 84-106.

Easton, D., "The New Revolution in Political Science," *American Political Science Review* 63(1969), 1051-1061.

Euben, J. P., "Political Science and Political Silence" in P. Green and S. Levenson (eds.), *Power and Community*, New York: Random House, 1970, 3-58.

Falter, J., "Die Behavioralismus-Kontroversie in der Amerikanishen Politikwissenschaft," *Kölner Zeitschrift für Soziologie und Sozialpsychologie* 31(1979), 1-24.

Holt, R. T. and Richardson, J. M., Jr., "Competing Paradigms in Comparative Politics" in Holt and Turner (eds.), *The Methodology of Comparative Research*, New York: Free Press, 1970, 21-72.

Landau, M., *Political Theory and Political Science*, New York: Macmillan, 1972.

————, "Sociology and the Study of Formal Organizations," *Papers in Comparative Public Administration*, Special Series, no. 8, 37-50.

Lijphart, A. "Structure of the Theoretical Revolution in International Studies," *International Studies Quarterly* 18(1974), 42-74.

Navarro, J., *Paradigms in Science and Political Science*, University of California (Santa Barbara) dissertation, 1978.

Pocock, J. G. A., *Politics, Language, and Time*, New York: Atheneum, 1971, 13-41.

Ricci, D., "Reading Thomas Kuhn in the Post-behavioral Era," *Western Political Quarterly* 30(1977), 7-34.

Smolicz, J. J., "The Amorphous Paradigms: a Critique of Sheldon Wolin's 'Paradigms and Political Theories'," *Politics* 6(1971), 178-187.

Stephens, J., "The Kuhnian Paradigm and Political Inquiry: An Appraisal," *American Journal of Political Science* 17 (1973), 467-488.

Thorson, T., *Biopolitics*, New York: Holt, Rinehart, and Winston, 1969.

Truman, D., "Disillusion and Regeneration: The Quest for a Discipline," *American Political Science Review* 60(1968), 869-879.

Wolin, S., "Paradigms and Political Theories" in King and Parekh (eds.), *Politics and Experience*, Cambridge: Cambridge University Press, 1968.

————, "Political Theory as Vocation," *American Political Science Review* 63(1969), 1062-1082.

VI. *Economics*

Baumberger, J., "No Kuhnian Revolution in Economics," *Journal of Economic Issues* 11(1977), 1-20.

Blaug, M., "Kuhn versus Lakatos, or Paradigms versus Research Programmes in the History of Economics," *History of Political Economy* 7(1975), 399-433.

Bronfenbenner, M., "The 'Structure of Revolutions' in Economic Thought," *History of Political Economy* 3(1971), 136-151.

Chase, R. X., "Why Economists Disagree," *American Journal of Economics and Sociology* 4(1977), 429-432.

Coates, A. W., "Is There a 'Structure of Scientific Revolutions' in Economics?," *Kyklos* 22(1969), 289-295.

Elias, N., "Theory of Science and History of Science," *Economy and Society* 1(1972), 117-133.

Gordon, D. F., "The Role of the History of Economic Thought in the Understanding of Modern Economic Theory," *American Economic Review* 55(1965), 119-127.

Kunin, L. and Weaver, F. S., "On the Structure of Scientific Revolutions in Economics," *History of Political Economy* 3(1971), 391-397.

Loasby, R. G., "Hypothesis and Paradigm in the Theory of the Firm," *Economic Journal* 81(1971).

Mehta, G., *Kuhn's Historiographical Framework and the Keynesian Revolution*, University of California (Berkeley) dissertation, 1971.

Peabody, G. E., "Scientific Paradigms and Economics: An Introduction," *Review of Radical Political Economy* 3 (July, 1971), 1-16. (Also papers in this volume by T. Behr, et al., M. Zweig, P. Sweezy, and J. Weeks.)

Stanfield, R., "Kuhnian Scientific Revolutions and the Keynesian Revolution," *Journal of Economic Issues* 8(1974), 97-109.

Stigler, G. J., "Does Economics Have a Useful Past?," *History of Political Economy* 1(1969), 217-230.

Tribe, K., "On the Production and Structuring of Economic Knowledge," *Economy and Society* 2(1973), 465-478.

Vroey, M. de., "La Structure des revolutions scientifiques et les sciences économiques," *Revue des questions scientifiques* 145(1974), 57-70.

Ward, B., *What's Wrong with Economics?*, New York: Basic Books, 1972.

Worland, S., "Radical Political Economy as a 'Scientific Revolution'," *Southern Economic Journal* 39(1972), 274-284.

VII. *Psychology*

Boring, E. G., [Review of SSR], *Contemporary Psychology* 1963, 180-182.

Buss, A., "The Structure of Psychological Revolutions," *Journal of the Behavioral Sciences* 14(1978), 57-64.

Hale, N., *Freud and the Americans*, London: Oxford University Press, 1971, 71-115.

Legrand, M., "Psychoanalyse et paradigme scientifique," *Revue des questions scientifiques* 144(1973, 506-512.

———, "Hypotheses pour une historie de la psychoanalyse," *Dialectica* 29(1975), 189-207.

Palermo, D. S., "Is a Scientific Revolution Taking Place in Psychology?" *Science Studies* 1(1971), 135-155.

Watson, R. I., [Review of SSR], *Journal of the History of the Behavioral Sciences*, 1966, 274-276.

———, "Psychology: a Prescriptive Science," *American Psychologist* 22(1967), 436-440.

VIII. *History*

Hollinger, D., "T. S. Kuhn's Theory of Science and Its Implications for History," *American Historical Review* 78 (1973), 370-393.

Kuklick, B., "History as a Way of Knowing," *American Quarterly* 22(1970), 609-628.

Kramick, I., "Reflections on Revolution: Definition and Explanation in Recent Scholarship," *History and Theory* 11 (1972), 26-63.

Starn, R., "Historians and 'Crisis'," *Past and Present*, 1971, No. 52, 3-22.

Stocking, G. W., *Race, Culture, and Evolution*, New York: 1968.

White, H. V., "The Tasks of Intellectual History," *Monist* 53 (1969), esp. 618-620.

Wise, G., *American Historical Explanations: A Strategy for Grounded Inquiry*, Homewood, Ill.: Dorsey Press, 1973.

IX. *Theology and Philosophy of Religion*

Barbour, I., *Myths, Models, and Paradigms*, New York: Harper and Row, 1974.

Gunnemann, J., *The Moral Meaning of Revolution*, New Haven: Yale University Press, 1979.

Malloy, E. K., "Theological Paradigms and the Question of Marriage in the Christian Tradition," *Revue des questions scientifiques* 144(1973), 554-559.

Mitchell, B., *The Justification of Religious Belief*, New York: Seabury, 1973.

Murphey, M., "On the Relation between Science and Religion," *American Quarterly* 20(1968), 275-295.

Quay, P., "A Distinction in Search of a Difference: The Psycho-social Distinction between Science and Theology," *Modern Schoolman* 5(1974), 345-359.

Vernon, R., "Politics as Metaphor: Cardinal Newman and Professor Kuhn," *Review of Politics* 41(1979), 513-535.

X.   Art and Literature

Ackerman, J. S., "The Demise of the Avante Garde: Notes on the Sociology of Recent American Art," *Comparative Studies in Society and History* 11(1969), 371-384.

Hafner, E. M., "The New Reality in Art and Science," *ibid.*, 385-397. (Cf. also comments on Ackerman and Hafner by R. Grew, 369-370; G. Kubler, 398-402; and T. Kuhn, 426-430).

Miall, D. S., "Metaphor as a Thought Process," *Journal of Aesthetics and Art Criticism* 38(1979), 21-238.

Ryan, S. T., "Importance of Thomas Kuhn's Scientific Paradigm Theory to Literary Criticism," *Midwest Quarterly* 19(1978), 151-159.

XI.   Education

Berry, J. M., Jr., "Great Men, Paradigms, and Scientific Revolutions," *American Biology Teacher* 33(1971), 345-347; 354.

Boldt, W. B., *Applications of T. S. Kuhn's View of Science to Science Teaching: An Exploratory Study*, University of Illinois dissertation, 1969.

Palter, R., "Philosophy of Science, History of Science, and Science Education" in R. S. Cohen, et al. (eds.), *PSA 1974*, Dordrecht: Reidel, 1976, 313-321.

Popp, J. J., "Paradigms in Educational Inquiry," *Educational Philosophy* 25(1975), 28-39.

Siegel, H. J., *Kuhn's Philosophy of Science and Science Education*, Harvard University dissertation, 1977.

_____, "Kuhn and Schwab on Science Texts and the Goals of Science Education," *Educational Theory* 28(1978), 302-309.

Smolicz, J. J., "Kuhn Revisited: Science, Education, and Values," *Organon*, 1974, 45-59.

Soltis, J. F., "Analysis and Anomalies in Philosophy of Education," *Philosophy of Education Society: Proceedings* 27 (1971), 28-46.